CLOSE UP:
THE CONTRACT DIRECTOR

General Editor: Jon Tuska

Associate Editor: Vicki Piekarski

Research Editor: Karl Thiede

The Scarecrow Press, Inc.
Metuchen, N.J.   1976

Library of Congress Cataloging in Publication Data

Main entry under title:

Close up.

    Includes index.
    1. Moving-picture producers and directors--United
States--Biography. I. Tuska, Jon. II. Piekarski, Vicki.
III. Thiede, Karl.
PN1998.A2C55   791.43'023'0922   76-41345
ISBN 0-8108-0961-3

TABLE OF CONTENTS

Film Checklists (by Karl Thiede and
Michael Terry) follow each article.

INTRODUCTION

I

This is the first book in my <u>Close-Up on the Cinema</u> series. Its subject is the contract director.

Long ago I despaired of ever being in a position to write intelligently on most aspects of motion pictures. Should the reader be familiar with my books on film history and personalities, I needn't complain again here of the appreciable amount of time required to screen films, and for traveling and interviewing; nor the care necessary to insure some degree of accuracy, no matter how prone to error the ultimate result may be.

So I decided to edit a series of books that would combine the talent and resources of a number of film historians, both established and novitiate, to provide the reader interested in the cinema with writing of an exceptional nature, factual, critical, and human. I am not a film critic, nor will I ever pretend to be. My concern has always been with human personality, with biography, with events and how they were shaped by men and how men and women became the product of circumstances. Precisely because of this limitation which I have imposed on myself, or which more properly has been imposed on me by my temperament, I have sought deliberately not to narrow the scope of the essays I have solicited for inclusion. They are rightly conceived from a number of perspectives and diverse points of view. Beyond this, I have striven for variety and thoroughness and sensitivity. In many cases in this book what has been written remains the most extensive coverage accorded these film directors to be found anywhere.

There are ten career studies in this book. I had best define what a career study is, and what it is not. It is not just an interview, on the one hand; nor is it an attempt at

full-scale biography, on the other. It lies between these ex-
tremities. Ideally, it is a portrait of an artist in terms of
his creations. It does not propose to present the whole man.
The field of vision is too circumscribed for that. But it
does make an effort to evoke his personality.

One of my own contributions to The Contract Director
is the career study on Lucky Humberstone. He is sufficiently
well-disposed toward me that I was able to surround the chron-
ology of his work in pictures and an appraisal of it with an
informal portrayal of him as a person. I will admit it is
very difficult to devise a structure so elastic that within its
boundaries can be compressed an objective outline of cinematic achievement and the subjective experience of a man's
personality, when the writer was in no sense a participant in
any of the biographical events he has chosen to narrate. I
am fond of this career study because it permitted me the opportunity to draw a character both objectively and subjectively.
The final result, however, can only be judged by the reader.

The men whose lives and films are recounted in these
essays shared one thing in common. They were all at one
time or another under contract to a motion picture studio.
Whatever the evils or advantages of the studio system, it
transformed filmmaking into a corporate endeavor and developed an assembly-line technique for film production. Players and directors alike might chafe, bitterly at times, at the
pictures they had to work on, but the system guaranteed
them a regular income just as the studio-affiliated theatre
chains guaranteed producing companies an outlet for their
films.

A contract director was usually required to direct a
given number of pictures every year. Only rarely did he
have choice of property; frequently he had to make the best
of what was handed him. That best, in view of the mediocrity of much of the material, the limitations of contract per-
sonnel, the often arduous production schedules, was finer indeed in many instances than anyone might have reasonably
expected.

The auteur theory of film direction which originated in
France rapidly gained adherence among American critics in
the 'sixties and 'seventies. In brief, the theory equates a
film director with a novelist, as the principal agent and
prime mover behind an artistic creation. The entire concept
strikes me as slightly fanciful and even a bit ungracious to

the efforts of so many others who combine to make a motion picture experience. Nor is the exact nature and function of a film director's job anywhere so evident as in the career of a contract director. In making a film, there were pressures from the sales department, the censors, the players, the writers. There was an associate producer to reckon with, and a studio manager, possibly a production manager, and, upon occasion, an executive producer. Even with latitude in casting, a studio may have needed another picture from a contract star, and so the star was arbitrarily assigned to the film. In some cases, the studio boss might have been in love with a female player and it was the contract director's responsibility to elicit a stunning performance from her.

The director's personality is important to me because it cannot but influence the character of his work. Even more, no matter what a gloomy prospect the human condition may present, nor how disappointing may be our fellow men, for me a man still is the measure of all the things in his life. As I write this, I recall a visit with Sam Peckinpah when he screened dailies for me.

"The only important thing in my life is up there," he said, pointing to the editing screen. I cannot imagine a more significant statement the man could have made about his personal life.

"Pictures used to be such a pleasure to make," Les Selander commented. "We had so much fun on the set. The fun relaxed everyone. I think we got better pictures when the pace was more leisurely."

John Ford once told me that the one thing that stood out in his memory about his films was the time he spent thinking up pranks to play on Ward Bond.

A lot of fun has left the business. Production schedules are tighter. It is almost too serious today. The spontaneity and affirmation of life true of older pictures is something you scarcely find on a modern set. The fun belongs very much to the era depicted in this book, despite the fact that several of these directors are currently working.

How does a director go about achieving his effects? The question has always intrigued me because I am so little a film buff. I want to go behind the scenes. I found it quite amusing to see how Joe Kane got a performance out of Duke

Wayne in a picture with Vera Hruba Ralston which Duke
swore he would never make, or how Lucky Humberstone
managed to work easily with Sonja Henie and actually turned
out such a successful picture that the studio had to renew her
contract.

I was fortunate enough to see ROOSTER COGBURN
(Universal, 1975) long before its release. It is certainly one
of Wayne's best pictures. I could not help marveling at how
its producer, Hal B. Wallis, who replaced Darryl Zanuck at
Warner's in the early 'thirties, has been able to produce
popular films for four decades no matter what the alterations
in public taste and values. The secret may well not be a
matter of changing techniques or modern story lines alone.
It has, I believe, mostly to do with concentrating on the
drama and comedy of human emotions. Wallis, as a producer, has not been an auteur, primarily concerned with
presenting repeatedly his own personal point of view; he has
striven to tell a story about real people and has generally
been able to so cast a picture as to assure the audience's
involvement. Most of the success enjoyed by the directors
in this book is due to that same penchant for getting caught
up in a story and its characters, rather than being obsessed
with some private, nearly inarticulate inner vision. As in-
congruous as this group of directors may appear on the surface, among them, in one way or another, almost every kind
of motion picture and almost every aspect of film direction
has been encountered.

II

A short biographical sketch has been provided for each
of the contributors to The Contract Director. There have
been exceptions. I had best deal with them here, in the Introduction, because even the basic notion for the book I owe
to Rosemary Ingham. Rosemary was for some time my
managing editor at Views & Reviews Magazine. It was she
who first suggested that the subject of contract directing
would be an interesting one and one hitherto neglected.

Her immense enthusiasm is a sustaining delight. She
wears wire-frame glasses that make her look like Leon
Trotsky and has a sufficiency of liberal political and social
views to fit the part. She assisted me when I was writing
The Filming of the West (Doubleday, 1976) and regularly

spent Saturdays with me screening Westerns. Her background
was not film but theatre, and she brought to bear a sharply
divergent perspective.

"You really ought to write something on Yakima
Canutt," she said, after seeing myriad Westerns he had
worked on. When Yak offered me his cooperation, I accepted
Rosemary's advice.

An avid nutritionist, we wiled away the time on the
train from New York to Metuchen discussing the virtues of
a milk and soy bean diet. At lunch with Eric Moon and Albert Daub of the Scarecrow Press, I remarked on how Rosemary felt I was subverting her, what with getting her to
smoke cigarettes again and sitting around in hotel rooms
sipping Jameson's Irish whiskey. Mr. Moon approved of the
brand of whiskey, but Mr. Daub was curious about the details of the diet. I had complained about momentary depres-
sions in the morning. I outlined Rosemary's nutritional solution.

"Strictly anti-depressant," I told Mr. Daub.

Mr. Daub shook his head in negation.

"Such a diet," he said, "would drive a man to whiskey,
not away from it."

It was hot and muggy in Washington, D.C., in June of
1974 when Karl Thiede, research editor for the Close-Up
series, joined me on a visit to David L. Parker at the Library of Congress. Karl has a massive research library,
copies of all the trade papers, complete files of reviews,
cost and budget sheets on thousands of films, exhaustive records of production schedules. His knowledge is so singularly
extensive that, early in our association, I took to calling him
"Doctor" Thiede, despite the fact that he was a hasty casual-
ty to boredom with a university education. He is tall and
physically huge.

We were walking back to our hotel in Washington along
the wooden planks covering the metro system under construction. It was the end of day. We stopped at a store so he
could purchase two large bags of provisions for a snack before we went to dinner. The doctor is an extremely slow
walker, constantly nagging at you, wondering where the fire
is or why you insist on racing. As we neared the hotel, his

pace became more and more retarded.   A flight of steps led
down from the elevated street to the sidewalk and another
flight led up to the side door of the hotel.   As we were going
down the flight leading to the sidewalk, the doctor suddenly
stopped altogether.   He stood there in the heat, his arms
clutching the bags, his eyes tightly closed.   Perspiration
ran down his face.   When I reached the bottom, I realized
he was no longer beside me.   I turned back and asked him
if anything was wrong.

"I've run out of gas," he sighed.

"Are you just going to stand there?   Can't I help with
the groceries?"

"No," he said.   "Go on without me."   His eyes were
still closed.

I hesitated.   Then, grudgingly, I began up the steps to
the hotel, looking back at him every other moment.   There
was no movement from him until I was nearly at the top.
Then, in a flash, he charged down the steps, took the sidewalk in a few strides, and shot past me toward the revolving
door.

"Wait a minute," I called after him.   "Where's the
fire?"

"Don't talk to me," he said over his shoulder, holding onto the bags.   "I want to make the room before I lose
my second wind."

He can sit among a group of film historians and amaze
them with his encyclopedic knowledge of release dates, of
running times, of casts and credits.   I have rarely seen him
screen any film without a stop-watch and a cast sheet clipped
to a board.   He wants cinema books to be of lasting referen-
tial value and to be, above all, accurate.   I know he has
made this an infinitely better book than it could ever have
been without him.

Vicki Piekarski has acted as my editorial assistant on
The Contract Director.   She has watched all the films with
me; she has traveled everywhere with me; she has asked the
doctor's questions of those directors still living whose career
studies appear in these pages; she has sat for hours in interviews and transcribed notes and recorded anecdotes and sorted
out tangled memories; she worked with the contributors; she
checked all the facts and dates; she did all the typing.   She

has such an engaging smile and gay personality that people
have invariably opened up to me and told me things I am sure
otherwise I should never have learned.   And if that were not
enough, like Rosemary who trained her she takes her whiskey
straight, but her dietary inclinations culminate in a preference
for Chinese-American restaurants.   When we met Lesley
Selander at the Cafe Universal at the Sheraton-Universal, for
a breakfast conference, Les asked me what nationality I was.

"Bohemian," I said.

"I thought your name was Polish," he said, and smiled.

"Vicki's is."

Les raised his eyebrows.

"Ms. Piekarski," I introduced her.

"Ms. what?" Les asked.

"It actually has only nine letters," Vic said.   "P-I-E,
car with a K, and a SKI."

We were shown to our table.

"You really should change that name," Les chided her.
"Why don't you get married?"

"Never!" Vic retorted.   "I've always had a slash in
my title.   I was first an underwriter/assistant.   Then, when
I went to work for Jon, I was a clerk/typist, next a recep-
tionist/proof-reader; now I'm Jon's secretary/companion.
If I married, I'd lose my slash.   I wouldn't like that."

The doctor has long been fixated on costs, budgets,
and grosses.   Where possible, this information has been included.   The pictures made by these directors almost invariably made money; why they did, and how much, is a
vital ingredient to assessing their respective accomplishments.
Those whom I have met are fine gentlemen.   It may well be
this particular attribute of personality which has had the most
to do with the special and lasting quality of their work.   They
sought only to entertain.   I hope the reader will find the story
of how their films were made as entertaining as surely their
films have been.

New York City
November, 1975

KEY TO FILM CHECKLISTS

P	Production Company
D	Director
C	Cast
NC	Negative Cost
DG	Domestic Gross
FG	Foreign Gross
WWG	World-wide Gross
ft. /m.	footage /running time

Walter Lang. Photo courtesy of the Museum of Modern Art.

Chapter 1

WALTER LANG*

by Joel Greenberg

When Walter Lang died on 7 February 1972 at the age
of seventy-three the obituaries were few and brief.   One or
two did mention titles like CAN-CAN (20th-Fox, 1960) or
THE KING AND I (20th-Fox, 1956), but none paid adequate
tribute to a man whose forty-year motion picture career
yielded over a dozen silent feature titles and about fifty
sound ones, including among the latter some of the most delectable entertainments ever to come out of Twentieth Century-
Fox, the studio to which Lang was contracted for over twenty
years.

There he made elegant romantic comedies and elaborate Shirley Temple vehicles in the 'thirties, women's pictures, farces and brilliant musicals in the 'forties, and high-
powered song-and-dance blockbusters in the 'fifties.   Before
that, he had been associated with movie entrepreneurs like
Dorothy Davenport Reid, William Randolph Hearst, and Harry
Cohn, and with filmmakers like James Cruze.   He brought to
his films a painter's trained pictorial eye, skillful but unobtrusive camera technique, and a fine feeling for family senti-
ment and civilized comedy.

Though not as great as either's, his talents resembled
those of George Cukor and Mitchell Leisen, similarly deft and
light and sensitive, concealing considerable artistic cunning
behind seeming simplicity.   But whereas Cukor and Leisen
were lucky enough to be critically "discovered" during their
lifetimes, their films analyzed and studied and re-run at
retrospectives, no such good fortune befell Lang, whom serious critics--even in France--constantly ignored.

Yet if they had taken the trouble to examine his oeuvre
they would have been richly rewarded; charitably one assumes
that many titles had been long unseen, particularly in Britain
and Europe.   Certainly his 'forties color musicals, buoyant
and handsome and superlatively crafted, are totally unknown
quantities to most people today.   So are the majority of his
'thirties works, including such exquisite satirical comedies
as THE BARONESS AND THE BUTLER (20th-Fox, 1938), a
piece not unworthy of Lubitsch, and I'LL GIVE A MILLION
(20th-Fox, 1938), a delicious fable based on a story by
Cesare Zavattini.   And the fact that Lang contributed ma-
terially to the careers of Alice Faye, Betty Grable and Clifton Webb, and directed stars like John Barrymore, Carole
Lombard and Tyrone Power is all but forgotten.

Of course, he was a lightweight, a craftsman devoid
of intellectual pretensions, a quintessential "studio" man.
Like Cukor, Leisen, Jean Negulesco and many others of
Hollywood's heyday, even Michael Curtiz, he functioned best
within a large corporate set-up, content to merge his individuality with the studio's.   Luckily for him--and for us--
Twentieth Century-Fox under the dynamic and creative des-
potism of Darryl F. Zanuck was perhaps the most technically
well-endowed lot in Hollywood, its pictures unmistakable for
their crisp, razor-sharp images, their incomparable art direction, their stunningly recorded soundtracks and their general air of high polish.   Indeed, it is not too much to say
that without Twentieth Century-Fox there would have been no
Walter Lang, for without the studio's great resources, without its gifted writers and expert technicians, its unique roster
of stars and strongly individualized small-part players, his
talent could never have fully flourished.

That it did flourish was immediately obvious to Zanuck
after the director's smoothly professional handling of his initial assignments, the romantic comedies WIFE, DOCTOR AND
NURSE (20th-Fox, 1937) and SECOND HONEYMOON (20th-Fox,
1937), both starring Loretta Young.   Even today they still be-
guile, but it was Lang's third Twentieth Century-Fox feature,
THE BARONESS AND THE BUTLER, that displayed his special qualities at their best: Lubitsch would not have been
ashamed to sign it, nor those responsible for MIDNIGHT
(Paramount, 1939).

Based on a play by Ladislas Bus-Fekete, this stylish
political satire about a conservative Hungarian prime minister's butler elected to parliament on the anti-conservative

Social Progressive ticket offered some delightful variations
on the theme of class differences, a favorite late-'thirties
movie preoccupation.   From its opening scene, in which--
before we have been told his household status--we see William
Powell being served breakfast in bed by a pert maid (Lynn
Bari), the film's wit rarely falters.   Any illusions that he
might be the master of the household are dispelled when we
see him in the capacious kitchen reviewing the assembled
domestic staff ("There was a butterfly in the dictionary yesterday").   Despite the fact that he strongly opposes his master's policies not only over the radio but also from the floor
of parliament, Powell, in a role not dissimilar to his part
in MY MAN GODFREY (Universal, 1936), continues as a
loyal, faithful, and efficient domestic servant, even respect-
fully pointing out in the Chamber of Deputies that the PM's
sock suspenders have slipped ("Look to your supporters!").
Eventually, of course, he winds up marrying his master's
once haughty daughter (Annabella), and we fade out as Annabella in maid's uniform serves Powell, her former underling,
breakfast in bed, their roles reversed.

        The film's situations are piquant, and exquisitely
realized.   Similar virtues distinguished the same year's
I'LL GIVE A MILLION: here Warner Baxter played a millionaire disguised as a tramp who has the population of a
French Mediterranean port believing that he'll give away a
million francs to anyone who is nice to him in his hobo guise.
The town immediately becomes a tramps' paradise, as trains
disgorge them by the score and the bourgeoisie invite them in
off the street to give them the best of everything.   The
Marxist moral even has Brechtian possibilities, and the fa-
natically detailed art direction with its spot-on Pagnol atmosphere is a marvel.   The rich collection of supporting
players boasts Peter Lorre as a benign tramp, Sig Rumann
as a circus owner, and Fritz Feld as his nitwit son.

        It was a measure of Zanuck's confidence in Lang that
he next assigned him the two most lavish and lovingly mounted
of all Shirley Temple pictures, for she had been throughout
the 'thirties the studio's top moneymaking star and was now
entering an awkward stage of her career.   THE LITTLE
PRINCESS (20th-Fox, 1939) was her first color vehicle, and
it remains one of her finest.   In this late Victorian Cinderella
fable Shirley played an inmate of an exclusive girls' seminary
who is reduced to the status of domestic slavey when her
daddy (Ian Hunter) is mistakenly believed killed at Mafeking.
The formidable Mary Nash was her chief tormentor, and as
well as impressively staged scenes of mass rejoicing at the

relief of Mafeking--which recalled CAVALCADE (Fox, 1933)
--there was a delicious fantasy sequence especially designed
by Richard Day, all done in rhyming couplets and music.

If THE LITTLE PRINCESS was expensive but never
vulgar, THE BLUE BIRD (20th-Fox, 1940), Lang's second
picture with Temple, was both, the vulgarity due mainly to
Ernest Pascal's script, which played havoc with the Maeterlinck original.   But the film did have some very beautiful
designs and a remarkable performance by Gale Sondergaard
as Tylette the Cat; her feline gestures, the voluptuous arch-
ing of her black-clad body, the white-gloved hands drooping
like paws, and of course that silky, cunning, smooth purring
voice were all memorably deployed.   Her death in a brilliantly special effects-managed forest fire was perhaps the
film's highlight, but scenes in the Kingdom of the Future of
unborn children--all white Caucasians--awaiting translation
earthwards were all too reminiscent of the Ziegfeld Follies
in their meringue-white decor: little wonder that THE BLUE
BIRD effectively finished Temple's reign as the screen's
leading juvenile star.

It was Lang's ill luck the same year to direct another declining major personality when he made THE GREAT
PROFILE (20th-Fox, 1940), in which a plainly sick and dying John Barrymore parodied himself as he had in TWENTI-
ETH CENTURY (Columbia, 1934), but with distinctly less
happy results.   For all its superficial energy and drive the
film was a melancholy exercise.   STAR DUST (20th-Fox,
1940), however, also done in 1940, was something else, a
charming if minor addition to Hollywood's gallery of films
about itself, directly in the tradition of A STAR IS BORN
(United Artists, 1937).   It introduced the appealing Linda
Darnell as a soda-jerking discovery of touring talent scout
Roland Young, and despite its essentially marshmallow center its scenes of drama coach Charlotte Greenwood unsuc-
cessfully attempting to have Darnell perform a simple action
for her screen test, or of studio executive Donald Meek trying to "kill" the test to discredit his rival Young, gave plain
hints of Screenland's unattractive underside.

Lang's fourth 1940 film, TIN PAN ALLEY, the first
of his many marvelous musicals and of his six pictures with
Betty Grable, remains irresistible in its sparkle, joie de
vivre and superb production gloss.   Beginning with an elec-
trifying pre-credits montage of New York song-publishing
offices circa 1915, it offers John Payne and Jack Oakie as a

songwriting pair who hire sisters Alice Faye and Grable to
plug their tunes. Betty, vivacious and cute, and Alice,
warm and honey-voiced, made an unforgettable team, and
Faye's rendition of "On Moonlight Bay"--Leon Shamroy's
camera maneuvering around a resplendent New York nightclub set--and particularly "America I Love You" with the
Brian Sisters and a male chorus are among her most affecting.

While TIN PAN ALLEY was in monochrome, all
Lang's subsequent 'forties musicals were in some of the
lushest and most glowing Technicolor of the period. And
none was more exciting than MOON OVER MIAMI (20th-Fox,
1941), with its exhilarating introductory montage of Miami's
scenic highlights, its thrillingly performed and recorded original songs, its sense of stylistic freedom and adventure,
its kaleidoscope of dazzling images credited to three cameramen. Nothing Lang subsequently did in this genre quite
matched it, although CONEY ISLAND (20th-Fox, 1943),
bursting with energy and pep and stunningly mounted in every
technical department, ran it close. WEEKEND IN HAVANA
(20th-Fox, 1941), SONG OF THE ISLANDS (20th-Fox, 1942),
and GREENWICH VILLAGE (20th-Fox, 1944) were altogether
slighter, less immediately striking, while STATE FAIR (20th-
Fox, 1945) had some fine tunes but little else.

Besides musicals, the prolific Lang also specialized
in farces and weepies during this period. He was an un-
ashamed sentimentalist, with a deep and genuine feeling for
family life, and a gift for rendering it convincingly on the
screen. That is what characterizes MOTHER WORE TIGHTS
(20th-Fox, 1947), a movie devoted to demonstrating that show
folk are Nice People, and CHEAPER BY THE DOZEN (20th-
Fox, 1950), both written by Lamar Trotti. The latter picture had Clifton Webb in the unlikely role of paterfamilias;
as Lynn Belvedere in Lang's SITTING PRETTY (20th-Fox,
1947) he had descended on a suburban household observed
with all Lang's sympathy for domesticity, although today--
especially with Robert Young's presence--it looks rather like
a rehearsal for "Father Knows Best." Similar comments
apply to the mid-Western couple portrayed by James Stewart
and Barbara Hale in THE JACKPOT (20th-Fox, 1950), a
satirical comedy in the same mold as the sub-Capraesque
MAGNIFICENT DOPE (20th-Fox, 1942).

However, his finest film of this type, often transcend-
ing its novelettish ingredients, is CLAUDIA AND DAVID

(20th-Fox, 1946), the sequel to Edmund Goulding's CLAUDIA
(20th-Fox, 1943).   Not exactly "sitcom" or marital drama or
tearjerker but something of each, it has that understated,
minor-key excellence traditionally associated with the better
English product.   Its seventy-eight minutes boast Lang's
most refined and tightly controlled direction, while the dis-
creet playing of the principals (especially Mary Astor and
Rose Hobart), Joseph La Shelle's lovely images and an ex-
quisitely recorded sound track combine to form what may
well be the director's best non-musical film.

        The remainder of Lang's career reflects the declining
fortunes of Hollywood and Fox as faithfully as the 'forties
had reflected their apogee.   Superficially his 'fifties musicals
became grander, more inflated, richer, but in fact their
length and size only served to emphasize a loss of creative
energy, a drying up of the verve and gaiety that had marked
their predecessors.   Certainly WITH A SONG IN MY HEART
(20th-Fox, 1952) had flashes of the old fire, notably in Leon
Shamroy's often striking color images, but not even that fine
cameraman's artistry could redeem the stodginess of CALL
ME MADAM (20th-Fox, 1953), the strident vulgarity of
THERE'S NO BUSINESS LIKE SHOW BUSINESS (20th-Fox,
1954), or the longueurs of THE KING AND I (20th-Fox, 1956).

        By the time he made SNOW WHITE AND THE THREE
STOOGES in 1961, Lang was thoroughly dispirited by the
state of the industry, by the sudden predominance of actors
and money men over creators, by the failure of motion pictures adequately to meet the challenge of television, and
above all by the disappearance--as he significantly remarks
in the interview--of the sense of fun which had heretofore
accompanied filmmaking, at any rate for him.   That was
when he decided to retire, and despite offers from Zanuck
to direct THE SOUND OF MUSIC (20th-Fox, 1965) he spent
the remaining decade of his life happily painting pictures.

        I remember him as a genial, suntanned figure, plump
and relaxed in his handsome Palm Springs hilltop home, a
fund of stories about people like William Randolph Hearst
and Marilyn Monroe at his fingertips.   Lang had been an
assistant director in Hearst's motion picture company in the
early 'twenties, and he recalled that, while making a picture
about Washington crossing the Delaware during a blizzard,
Hearst had expressed dissatisfaction with the miniature mock-
ups devised by the director and staff and insisted on restag-
ing it for real.   Accordingly he called up a high-ranking

Army connection to request the use of 5,000 men for the
picture. The request granted, W. R. commandeered a train
to take five-hundred seamstresses--exactly twice the Western
Costume Co.'s normal maximum complement--to the location
site, where they would toil and spin, running up the men's
costumes while artificial ice was laid on a nearby river.
When the sequence was shot at a cost of something like
$100,000, the tycoon was appalled because the figure of
Washington was barely discernible on the screen, obscured
behind lashings of snow. So he had the scene re-done as
originally conceived. Four men died during that fiasco.

In George Seaton's THE SHOCKING MISS PILGRIM
(20th-Fox, 1946) Marilyn Monroe had a bit part as a switch-
board operator. Visiting the set one day, Lang heard a
woman's voice repeating the word "hullo" over and over in
various inflections. It was Marilyn, aided by her voice
coach, practicing for her big moment. But when it came
she'd completely forgotten what to say.

Other anecdotes, some unprintable, involved Charles
Laughton, Richard Barthelmess, Louella Parsons, and Lionel
Barrymore. But there was no malice in anything Lang said;
to the end--he died little more than three months after our
meeting--he retained the kindliness and warmth that informed
his best pictures, illuminating such moments as Clifton
Webb's "toddle" dance with Jeanne Crain in CHEAPER BY
THE DOZEN, Shirley Temple and Arthur Treacher's "Walking Down the Old Kent Road" duet in THE LITTLE PRINCESS,
or Rose Hobart's confrontation with Dorothy McGuire in
CLAUDIA AND DAVID with an incandescent Langian glow.

The following interview at Mr. Lang's residence in
Palm Springs, California, on 28 October 1971, is the last--
perhaps the only comprehensive one--he ever gave.

LANG: I was born in Memphis, Tennessee [10 August 1898],
and mostly wanted to be an artist. I started drawing pictures and painting in little ways, and one account I had was
to draw Sunday illustrations for men's fashions, for which I
was paid $25--or given credit for that amount. At the age
of seventeen I found myself with over $100 a month to spend
on clothes, so I became one of the best-dressed young men
in Memphis; $100 in those days could buy an awful lot of
clothes. Then at one time I turned actor with a woman
named Emma Bunting who was playing stock in Memphis. I

was given the role of a minister in her play, and when she
came to have her illegitimate baby baptized she handed me
the "baby"--which was a small log wrapped in a shawl--and
I dropped the log out of the shawl, whereupon it rolled into
the footlights and caused quite a sensation that night.   That
almost ended my acting career at that time.

Q: From here, what were the steps by which you eventually
came into motion pictures?

A: Well, the war came along in 1917.   I was under age
and couldn't enlist because of the draft law until I was eighteen, so I went off to a government project in Alabama, a
nitrate plant, and became secretary to the construction manager and superintendent.   When I turned eighteen and was
drafted, I left for the war--went off and spent almost a year
there.   Because I could read and write, I was immediately
made a corporal and put in charge of the rookies from that
part of the country at the camp.   A man named Calvin C.
York who came from Arkansas would lean on the back of
the railroad car and as he called it, "chunk rocks" all the
way....   When I came back from the war I realized who he
was, because by then he had become the greatest hero of
World War One.   When I got back home, the superintendent
of the nitrate plant was having trouble holding workmen on
the job because of the war being over, so he asked me to
come back and build a little theatre and the clubhouse and
be the director of entertainment at that plant, to try to hold
the men there.   I put on plays, and also the government
wanted someone to write a history of that job--the first men
on it and all the difficulties they had gone through.   I finished that, and when the nitrate plant was finished too, I
took my report to New York and turned it over to the government.   I then stayed in New York, tried being an artist
again, found out that I was starving to death that way, and
got a job in the business office of a picture company.   That
led more or less to meeting fellows who were putting on
pictures, and I started from that.   I became connected with
a man named Daniel Carson Gutman who was making pictures
at that time.   He was married to Alma Rubens.   I was assistant director on one of their pictures, and I stayed with
his company for about two-and-a-half years, when Mr.
Hearst, hearing about his great achievements at low cost,
hired Dr. Gutman to come over to Cosmopolitan Productions,
of which Marion Davies was the principal star, and make
pictures with him.   I accompanied Dr. Gutman and stayed
with him in New York for about two years.   We came out to

California to do two weeks' location work on a picture called
ZANDER THE GREAT [M-G-M, 1925]. We were put up at
the Hollywood Hotel, and stayed there almost a year before
we turned a camera, during which time Hearst went to his
ranch--which we knew nothing about--and liked it so much he
decided to stay out here; and that's how he started making
pictures here throughout the rest of Marion Davies' career.
When that film was over, I became connected with a woman
named Mrs. Wallace Reid who--her husband having died of
addiction to narcotics--entered upon a crusade of anti-drug
pictures. She hired me as an assistant director to do her
second picture, and while we were preparing the picture she
decided she didn't want to try directing this one but wanted
me to do it. That's the first picture I directed, in 1926
[RED KIMONO]. After that I made another picture with her
called THE EARTH WOMAN [Associated Exhibitors, 1926],
and then I think she gave up her career as a producer.

Q: What were your duties as an assistant director up to
this time?

A: I prepared the schedule, found the locations, prepared
all the cost sheets on it, and helped write the story. It had
already been written in its original form, but we improved
it a great deal before we started shooting ... these were
my principal duties.

Q: Did you find that the transition from this to direction
came easily to you?

A: Fairly easily, because I was so familiar with the material which we'd mostly written. Also, she was a lovely
person to work with, and we enjoyed the whole thing im-
mensely.

Q: Were you familiar by this time with camera technique
and related matters?

A: Oh yes, I had known that from being in pictures so long
as an assistant director and from being around the company.

Q: You made several silent films starring people like
William Boyd, Richard Arlen, and Ricardo Cortez: were
these made for independent companies or large firms?

A: They were mostly made for independent companies like
Chadwick and James Cruze and people like that--people who

just made smaller pictures.

Q: About this time, too, sound entered the movies: how
did this affect you?

A: Everything was kind of upset in those days, and when
Cruze wanted to make a sound picture he hired me to do one
called HELLO SISTER [Sono Art/World Wide, 1930]. But
before I talk about that I want to tell you an interesting
thing: he had an idea connected with sound, of playing the
whole of a two-reel picture on a record, then taking the record out on the set and having the actors mouth with the record. Well, that turned out to be quite a disaster, as you
can imagine. After I completed my first all-talking picture
I saw it in its finished form and was so depressed I decided
to forget the whole picture business and went to Paris to go
back to my first love of being an artist. I had very little
luck with that--I had a lot of fun but no money--and finally
decided that I wanted more than I could make as an artist
and came back to this country to do pictures again.

Q: Then you went back to Columbia, resuming an association with Harry Cohn which had begun back in 1927: what
are your memories of Harry Cohn about this period?

A: I thought he was a very smart fellow. He was very
shrewd, very brusque, and not always expressing himself in
the best of taste, but a very smart businessman.

Q: He made pictures rather cheaply and well at the same
time?

A: Yes, he did quite a few notable independent pictures in
those days, but no big ones that you'd remember now. The
first big one he made was called SUBMARINE [Columbia,
1928].

Q: You made several pictures for James Cruze...

A: James Cruze was at one time the highest priced director
in the world. From the time he made THE COVERED
WAGON [Famous Players-Lasky, 1923] he was paid $1,000
a day, including Sundays, until the time he left Paramount to
form his own company. He was a wonderful, sort of simple
but learned man in pictures. He'd been an actor with his
wife, Marguerite Snow, and as a director he was certainly
the tops of his day. He did pictures in a very short time--

in half the time most other directors took--so the salary they paid him was well spent.

Q: Among the pictures you made for him, which would you single out as being the most notable?

A: I think a picture I made with Leo Carrillo called HELL BOUND [Tiffany, 1931]. That was memorable because it was the first picture--at least among the independents Cruze made--ever to crash the Music Hall in New York. From that booking it got big bookings all over the country and made quite a lot of money for him. It was about the life of Joe Colosimo, a New York gangster, and his love affair with a girl who had come in to kill him on a "contract," as they now call it. She fell in love with him and he with her; it was quite exciting for a gangster picture in those days.

Q: One doesn't normally associate Leo Carrillo with gangster parts of this kind?

A: No, it was a complete departure from the type of thing he had done on the stage, but being a fine actor he gave a fine performance.

Q: Then you made a picture for Jesse Lasky called WARRIORS' HUSBANDS [Fox, 1933]...

A: Yes, that was the film version of a New York play in which Katharine Hepburn starred. It was mostly about the reversal of the sexes--that is, the women having the principal role in life and the men being the little weaklings at home. It was set back in the mythical days of Greece; most of the characters were mythical.

Q: It sounds a bit like AMPHYTRION.

A: Yes, but this was completely farce comedy.

Q: MEET THE BARON [M-G-M, 1933] at Metro?

A: That was a picture with Jack Pearl, and he was a big sensation on radio at that time with a catch-phrase of "Vos you dere, Charlie?" Metro was then signing up a lot of radio stars like Ed Wynn and Jack Pearl and those people; and they made one or two pictures and then got out.

Q: What can you remember of your experience of working

at Metro? In what way did it differ from the other places
you'd been in?

A: I enjoyed it. I had a lot of personal friends there.
The only thing that worried me is that when I went to work
we had no script; the writers were still writing it. And,
the actors being under contract, the producer wanted me to
start work with what he called a "kicking mule" sequence.
That was all--he gave me Jack Pearl and a bucking mule
and sent us out to work. So we did what we could for three
or four days, at the end of which time the script was still
not finished. Then he told me to do one of Pearl's radio
broadcasts, so we did that for a couple of days. By then
some of the script was finished, and we started on the
picture.

Q: Then you went back to Columbia to do WHOM THE
GODS DESTROY [Columbia, 1934]?

A: Yes. That was a picture with Walter Connolly and
Doris Kenyon--I think it was based on an actual case involving the "Titanic"--in which he, to escape a sinking ship,
wore women's clothes and got into one of the lifeboats and
was saved. After that he always lived under the cloud of
possibly being found out, and he was found out. It was
quite an interesting picture.

Q: It does sound interesting. Was it an elaborate production?

A: No, it was a medium Columbia picture of those days--
no comparison with now--but it included several people like
Walter Brennan and Akim Tamiroff playing all these people
who were on the "Titanic" when it sank at that time. It
was notable for that reason if for no other.

Q: At Columbia, did you use more or less the same technicians such as cameramen on each picture, or did you have
different ones all the time?

A: Well, you had to take the cameraman not working at
that time. Sometimes--usually--you'd worked with him before. They only had about four or five directors, so you
occasionally duplicated.

Q: Did you find anyone among the cameramen who was in
rapport with you perhaps more than another?

Sally Eilers, Walter Lang, Dickie Walters and Lee Tracy
behind the scenes on the set of CARNIVAL (Columbia, 1935).
Photo courtesy of the Museum of Modern Art.

A: Yes, I think one such man was Joe Walker, who worked with Capra almost exclusively after that, and another was Peverell Marley, with whom I worked later at Fox.

Q: What was it about their styles that you found sympathetic?

A: Well, there was no such thing as their "styles" exactly, except that they were great cameramen. But mostly it was in the rapport you had with them, the closeness with which you worked--in other words, you set out to do a certain amount of work each day, and they were apprised of that and talked it over with you. And it was the speed with which they worked that achieved their great results.

Q: Did their contributions to the pictures ever go beyond mere camerawork? Did they suggest set-ups and compositions?

A: Sometimes, but only seldom; the director usually picked out the angles himself. The cameraman didn't usually object to it, although he might have sometimes said, "Don't you think it would be a little better this way?" And you'd look at it, and maybe it would be, so you'd change it. But there were no arguments or anything like that--not at all-- only cooperation.

Q: Can you remember much about NO MORE ORCHIDS [Columbia, 1932]?

A: Yes I can, because it was my first picture with Carole Lombard, one of my closest friends and the godmother of my son. We had so much fun, and the picture turned out so well, that the friendship grew from there till her death. I think I actually made only one other picture with her called LOVE BEFORE BREAKFAST [1936], out at Universal. Perhaps we were so very close because my wife had been associated with her as her secretary-manager since her beginnings at Sennett's, where my wife was a comic actress and Carole was in the Bathing Beauties; and it went from there right on till the time Carole died. They were together all that time, until we married in 1938.

Q: She was a stunning comedienne...

A: And a lovely person, a great person.

Q: Then you did your first picture for Fox, THE MIGHTY BARNUM [United Artists, 1934]: how did this come about?

A: I don't know, except that my agent arranged for me to go and see Zanuck, and I did. We got along fine. We made that picture before Twentieth Century merged with Fox, at the Goldwyn Studio. It came out well. When I finished the picture he talked to me, saying he had some ideas and would I like to work for them when they made the merger with Fox? I told him I would. This was when I made BARNUM, and that's how it started.

Q: Did the picture attempt to cover Barnum's entire career, or did it just concentrate on a section of it?

A: It covered his entire career after he became well known. It was mostly a character study of the man himself. Incidentally, it showed Tom Thumb and all of the things that he had in his museum. It was very funny, and I had a lot of fun working on it.

Q: LOVE BEFORE BREAKFAST was a typical mid-'thirties romantic comedy, very light, very charming...

A: Oh yes. Carole was not quite at the top, but she showed all the talent which took her there. She was wonderful to work with. She would stay behind till any hour of the night, and if something bothered us we'd get together at night and go over it and get it solved. She was always on time and knew her lines, and was a great, great artist.

Q: Were you altogether happy with Preston Foster's performance in this film?

A: His was rather a stiff-necked role, and I think it worked well against her.

Q: I enjoyed the storm at sea, and the scenes aboard the yacht: were these all done in the studio?

A: Yes, it was done on the back lot. Carole worked all day; she'd never get out of that water or out of her wet clothes. She'd want to keep on working, till we insisted she get out and have something hot to drink and get into dry clothes--at least to rehearse in until the next plunge. But she was into everything, very much like Katharine Hepburn later on. She had the same interest in the story and the

people and the casting and the camera and everything that
Hepburn had--and still has.

Q: The way she was lit and photographed reminded me a
great deal of the way Dietrich was lit and photographed about
the same time.

A: There was a very good reason for that. There was a
man named Ted Tetzlaff, who was a cameraman. He was
at Columbia when we--Carole and I--made our first picture,
and Carole loved the way he'd photographed her. Meantime
he went to Paramount and worked on different pictures with
Dietrich, and when Carole was going to make LOVE BE-
FORE BREAKFAST she went out to see if she could get him,
and did get him. So that was the reason for that.

Q: She went deliberately after the Dietrich look?

A: That's right.

Q: I remember a rather funny scene in which they fool
somebody at a ball into believing that they're deaf.

A: That was funny, but I have since many times regretted
it because it was poking fun at deaf people. I didn't mean
anything by it, you know; they were just having fun. But a
lot of people took umbrage at that.

Q: Then you went over to Twentieth Century-Fox, where
you stayed for the rest of your career with one or two exceptions: what was it about the studio that you found so
congenial?

A: Firstly, I got along well with Darryl Zanuck. Also, I
liked the producers who were working there, and I liked the
crews. It was about the only studio I know that had kind of
a "family" feeling to it, which certainly wasn't at Metro or
any other studio. The same people stayed there all the
time, and you began to find out what you could depend upon
them for, and they on you: that made for mutual respect
among all the people you worked with, which I think made
it great. Then there was no backbiting that I can remem-
ber--nobody trying to take someone else's job. It was, as
I say, just a family feeling that made it enjoyable.

Q: Certainly the "look" of the films of this period suggests
that enormous care was taken even with small pictures to

get their art direction to look just right...

A: Well, we had some of the best art directors in the business right there. We were also very careful with costumes; we had very good designers for them.

Q: Did you, with your background in painting, contribute much towards the costume and sets?

A: I think I contributed greatly in that, having been connected with art quite a lot, I felt I had some knowledge of composition which certainly became very important to me. I used it all the time in costumes, lighting, and the grouping of people.

Q: You seem to have specialized largely in comedies and musicals.

A: I think they were my favorites, and I had the greatest luck with those. If you made one musical, you know, and it turned out to be a success, of course you'd do a second-- which happened until the musical cycle ran out.

Q: Your first picture there was WIFE, DOCTOR AND NURSE [20th-Fox, 1937], with Warner Baxter, Loretta Young and Virginia Bruce: what was this about?

A: It was about a doctor, his wife, and a head nurse. The wife was Loretta Young, and she became somewhat jealous of his nurse, Virginia Bruce, because he spent so many hours in the office. One thing led to another until she accused him of being in love with his nurse, which had not occurred to him, nor to his nurse, until the wife suggested it. It went on from there into what they thought was love, but it turned out all right and Baxter went back to Loretta. The whole idea was that they didn't fall in love until someone had planted the seeds.

Q: I have seen SECOND HONEYMOON [20th-Fox, 1937], which is very charming. This is the one with Tyrone Power, Loretta Young, and Binnie Barnes, very much in the style of WIFE, DOCTOR AND NURSE, a very light romantic comedy about a married couple. Tyrone Power's career had just shot off the ground, hadn't it?

A: He was "in" because his first (big) picture, LLOYD'S OF LONDON [20th-Fox, 1936], had made a star out of him.

He was a great personal friend of mine. I knew him when
he was sixteen years old, when he left here to go to New
York to his mother with a voice coach. As the son of the
famous actor Tyrone Power he wanted to be an actor too.
He couldn't get a job in New York, so finally he was hired
as an understudy in a Katharine Cornell play, THE BAR-
RETTS OF WIMPOLE STREET. One night the actor whom
he was understudying fell sick and he stepped in; it was
quite a sensational moment for him, and he went on from
there.

Q: THE BARONESS AND THE BUTLER [20th-Fox, 1938] is
one of your finest comedies, comparable in my opinion with
those of Lubitsch. Can you tell me how you came to be
associated with this project?

A: It was assigned to me at the studio because of its come-
dic content as well as emotional climate. It contained a
great cast: William Powell, who'd been one of my closest
friends since I'd started in California, and a great girl
called Annabella, who'd made a big success in Europe. It
was a charming story, a political fable laid in Hungary. It
was a joy to work on from beginning to end, but we had
some trouble with Annabella's accent...

Q: Not Hungarian but French?

A: We had trouble with the audience's understanding of it;
we didn't want to dub in another voice so we left it that way,
but it hurt the picture quite a bit.

Q: Did you consciously go after a Lubitsch style here?

A: No--I had been a great admirer of Lubitsch's for years,
but I certainly didn't try to copy him.

Q: That enormous set of the Hungarian parliament...?

A: That was built on the lot, an exact replica of the parliament in Budapest. It was built for this particular picture
and cost quite a bit because it had a lot of filigree and stuff
in it. But we sent an art director over to see it, take
pictures and get all the details.

Q: What can you remember about that fine actress Helen
Westley?

A: She was a great character woman. I first saw her in
CAROUSEL--not the musical but the original play in which
she played a circus owner. She was a fine character actress, sharp at everything and just great.

Q: And Joseph Schildkraut?

A: Well, I'd known Joe, and of course he was a fine actor,
as his father was before him. He played the "menace" in
the thing--a very good actor.

Q: Was this picture a commercial success?

A: I think so, but not a big money-maker. I think it got
out of the red, but it didn't make a lot--not enough to carry
its weight.

Q: I'LL GIVE A MILLION [20th-Fox, 1938] had a very original idea, about a millionaire who conceals his identity.

A: I remember that he met this girl who was in a circus.
His relatives were waiting for him to die. They found out
about his disappearance and heard that he had amnesia, and
they tried to find him. They also heard that he'd taken on
the identity of a tramp, so they advertised and offered a
million dollars for any tramp who turned up and could identify himself as the millionaire. That led to a lot of compli-
cations like hundreds of tramps arriving in town and the
fanciful stories they put forward in order to try to identify
themselves. But he fell in love with this girl from the circus and did not reveal himself.

Q: Peter Lorre was one of the performers in this picture:
can you remember anything about him?

A: He was a wonderful actor. He had worked with a distant uncle of mine, Fritz Lang, in a picture called M [Nero-
film, 1931] in Germany. It was a sensational success, and
he was brought to this country for pictures. He was very
gentle, very nice--most enjoyable to work with. Unfortunately he was limited in his choice of parts by his accent
and appearance.

Q: This picture was laid in Marseilles and was very notable for its pronounced French atmosphere: did you contribute to this feeling of authenticity?

A: When I could.   I had been to Marseilles although I had
never seen a circus there, but I put what I generally remembered of it into the picture.

Q: From these relatively inexpensive movies you then went
on to make two very expensive ones with Shirley Temple.
How did this happen?

A: It happened because I love working with children a great
deal, and had proven that I could handle emotional things
fairly well--or so Zanuck thought.   And when this one came
along he talked to me, and I was very anxious to do it.
Shirley was one of the phenomena of that era.   She had
great charm.   Her mother and father were wonderful people.
They didn't intrude on the set.   They were there, but they
left everything entirely to the director, and that child could
do almost anything--from music to tears, and all sincerely.
I think she was the one great child star we ever had in this
business.   Even now she's quite a woman.

Q: At this stage of her career, though, she was not quite
a child and yet not quite an adult.

A: She was just at the time of change; in fact, the change
happened while we were on that picture [THE LITTLE
PRINCESS].   Her mother took it in her stride, and so did
she.   We worked right on after that.   They were delightful
people.

Q: THE LITTLE PRINCESS had a beautiful and brilliant
musical color fantasy sequence in which Mary Nash, who
played Shirley's evil guardian, was featured as a wicked
witch.   What can you tell me about Mary Nash?

A: She was a great New York actress and a delightful woman.   She had a fine part in this picture.   Shirley was
crazy about her, and she about Shirley.   Shirley was not the
kind of precocious child that "got in your hair," so to speak.
She came to the set, she knew what she was supposed to do:
she knew not only her lines but all the other people's lines.
If you happened to go "off" at a certain moment she'd give
them a little cue.   She was invaluable as a property and
was, I think, the top money-making star at that time.

Q: You had a marvelous cast in this picture: Cesar Romero, Miles Mander, Ian Hunter...

A: I thought that was a very sad scene between Shirley and her father in the hospital. He had amnesia and she brought back his memory, and it was all capped with the visit of Queen Victoria to the hospital. I've always remembered that--it was a great scene. Cesar Romero, who's still our close friend, gave me a big window one Christmas that's still in my house. It came about this way: Shirley could only work a certain amount of hours each day, which were usually up by four o'clock. After that time we did all the scenes in which she did not appear, usually including a scene where Cesar--whom we called "Butch"--was looking out of his window across the way from her house. So we had at least ten of those shots in the picture, all done around six o'clock or thereafter. It became such a joke that it provided the reason for his gift of the window.

Q: Do you remember the sequence in which Shirley and Arthur Treacher sang "Strolling Down the Old Kent Road?"

A: Yes. He was a great foil for Shirley. We had a lot of fun, and many times we broke up in a scene with him because he affected Shirley so that she couldn't control her laughter. We allowed him to do that because she loved it. He's still working in New York. There was also a little English girl in that who played the slavey. Her name was Sybil Jason. She played in many pictures here, then she went back and I understand is married now and has children of her own.

Q: Your next picture after that was an enormously expensive version of Maurice Maeterlinck's THE BLUE BIRD [20th-Fox, 1940].

A: It was a beautiful picture. I think it was ahead of its time. It was not a commercial success. It was a success on the stage and could have been, I guess, on the screen, but it was too difficult for the audience to follow the connections in it.

Q: You mean the transitions from the framing story to the fantasy story?

A: Yes. It kind of "got lost" in there. It turned out according to Maeterlinck's conception but it was not quite the kind of thing audiences went for in that day.

Q: Nevertheless, there had recently been pictures like

THE WIZARD OF OZ [M-G-M, 1939] and SNOW WHITE
[RKO, 1937], which seem to suggest that this was the kind
of thing people did want.

A: Well, those were based on fairy stories whereas this
tended to make "animals" of people and things of that kind;
it was a little deep, I thought for the audience of that time.

Q: Still it had many beautiful things in it, particularly the
scenes in "heaven" when the children are waiting to be born.

A: That's right. They were interesting, I thought, but
overall ... maybe it was my fault, maybe I shouldn't have
done it, but to me it just didn't come off somehow.

Q: I can't entirely agree, because I think the film does
succeed, on the whole, in what it sets out to do--to provide
a fantasy for children which also contains a moral lesson.

A: Yes, but I wonder if children got that point though.

Q: Well, I saw it as a child and I remember thoroughly
enjoying it. Seeing it again, I was tremendously impressed
by the performance of--among others--Gale Sondergaard as
Tylette the Cat. She was brilliant in her "feline" movements and speech. Can you remember much about how this
role was conceived with her? Did you consult with her
closely in her interpretation?

A: She read it, we talked it over, and she seemed to like
it very much. She was a fine actress, and this role particularly suited her fanciful ways of doing things; she was
quite unusual.

Q: The most startling sequence in the picture was the
forest fire: can you remember how this was achieved?

A: We had a special effects department at the studio; quite
a lot was done in miniature and quite a lot in reality--with
doubles, of course. That's the way it was achieved: quite
a big job for the special effects department.

Q: Color films of the late 'thirties had a beauty that has
seldom been achieved since.

A: In those days they had color people out on the set to
see that everybody's nails were the right color, and lips

were the right color, and that all of the costumes blended
together--those things which now they don't pay any attention to at all. It was quite a big thing. Another thing was
that we couldn't see our rushes for four or five days; you
never knew how yesterday's work came out for four or five
days, and we'd probably finished on that particular set by
then, so if anything had to be redone it was quite expensive
to have to go back and light that set and do all that work
again.

Q: I remember also in THE BLUE BIRD the performances
of Nigel Bruce and Laura Hope Crews as Mr. and Mrs.
Luxury, and Jessie Ralph as the Fairy. To what extent did
you participate in the casting of this picture and pictures
like it?

A: When you put out your cast list, you gave it to the casting department and they would suggest names. You knew
them all, and you would choose from among their suggestions. But on the main roles, such as those of Mary Nash
and Arthur Treacher, you would also consult with Zanuck
and the head office. On all the other roles they would offer
suggestions--Jessie Ralph, for instance. They could get her
from Metro at the time. They suggested Gale Sondergaard
also. If you liked the idea you saw the people, who came
in for interviews; it was done that way.

Q: Did you test any?

A: Sometimes. You wouldn't have to test a woman like
Jessie Ralph because you knew her work, you were familiar
with what she did. You might however test the costumes to
see how they looked. I think we tested all of Gale Sondergaard's costumes because they were quite fanciful.

Q: How soon after you finished a picture would Zanuck look
at it?

A: We had a cutter on the picture all the time, and as we
went along I would talk to the cutter about how I felt. Usually he could tell how to cut it from the way I shot, so he
would try to keep up with it as much as he could. When
we had finished the picture and he had a couple of days to
cut the last part, I would look at it and get it straightened
out by making any suggestions I had. I would then show the
first cut to Zanuck. From that time on, it was all done
with Zanuck and the director and the cutter.

Q: Did what he say prevail, or did he accept suggestions
from you and the cutter?

A: Many times he'd have a suggestion. He might think one
part too slow, for instance, and you agreed with him or you
didn't. He was not the type to say: "You don't know what
you're talking about." He'd say: "Maybe you're right.
Let's try it this way." Then, after we'd got the picture in
shape and all agreed on it, we took it out and had a preview.
That showed us how we'd done. We would take a tape recorder to the preview and record the laughs as they came
along and how the audience was taking everything, and come
back and let that guide us. Many times we'd take big sequences out of pictures...

Q: Can you remember any such sequences?

A: We had one sequence in SITTING PRETTY [20th-Fox,
1948] which we took out in its entirety. It wasn't too long,
but it did nothing, it got no great reaction. It didn't help
the story, so it obviously didn't belong there and we took it
out, and thereby made it a much better picture.

Q: Can you recall any occasions when you and Zanuck
might not have seen eye to eye on the inclusion of a sequence?

A: No, I don't think so. We had an ending on SITTING
PRETTY which I didn't like and he did. We shot it and ran
it at the preview but it didn't turn out well, so we came
back and shot the one that I had suggested. That happened
to be good, so we kept it in. Zanuck was adamant about
some things but not about suggestions like that. He wasn't
dictatorial, he wouldn't make you do things his way.

Q: How closely, if at all, did you participate or consult
with the composer when he came to score the picture?

A: On a picture like TIN PAN ALLEY [20th-Fox, 1940],
Mack came up with two or three songs he liked after having
had the project on his schedule for several weeks or months.
We played them for Zanuck on his office piano, and if he
liked them they were in, and if he didn't they were out.
And many times he would take a score like Rodgers' and
Hammerstein's for THE KING AND I [20th-Fox, 1956] and
wouldn't tinker with it that much; it had proved itself. I
remember that on CALL ME MADAM [20th-Fox, 1953], for

which Irving Berlin had written all the music, it was stipu-
lated in his contract that he must write all the film music
for it, of any kind. So, except for using different songs in
certain scenes, we needed one thing, a march down to meet
the Grand Duke and Duchess of Lichtenburg. We needed
some kind of march, and our music director was Alfred Newman, a great friend of Dick Rodgers. We put in "Pomp and
Circumstance." It worked well for the walk down to the
Duke, but because Irving hadn't written it we couldn't use it,
and we had to find a new one for that purpose.

Q: What I had in mind, really, was not so much the use of
music that was already familiar from some stage production
but original incidental music written for the picture individu-
ally by, say, Alfred Newman himself or one of the other
people under contract: how closely did you participate here?

A: Very closely. I was always there with them on the recording, when the music was scored into the picture. But
it was usually so good because he was quite a master at it,
and it's no criticism of Newman's work to say that it was
much better than he thought it was.

Q: Of course, Twentieth Century-Fox's sound department
was superb.

A: It was beautiful, and I think it was the best music recording outfit we had here.

Q: I think so too, having seen all the musical films of this
era. After THE BLUE BIRD you then made a picture called
STAR DUST [20th-Fox, 1940] which I happen to like very
much, set in Hollywood...

A: Yes--it had a little sixteen-year-old girl in it, Linda
Darnell. They'd signed up a boy named John Payne from
New York; I don't know what he'd done. But they put all
of these newcomers, these young kids, in the picture, and
then pepped it up with Jack Oakie, Charlotte Greenwood and
people like that. It was a conventional kind of thing, the
showbiz trials of young kids coming to Hollywood and trying
to get into pictures--what they went through, etc.

Q: I liked Roland Young's performance in it enormously:
it seemed to have a depth to it that perhaps one or two of
the other performances didn't have.

A: Well, that was because Roland Young had that depth in
himself, you see. He was a fine, fine actor, and he made
almost everything he did authentic. It was a part of the
plot to contrast him with the kids' inexperience. It was a
cute little picture.

Q: The cameraman Peverell Marley did a fine job...

A: Yes. He later married Linda Darnell.

Q: How did you feel about directing John Barrymore in
THE GREAT PROFILE [20th-Fox, 1940]?

A: He had begun to disintegrate, more or less; he did this
picture in New York as a play. We had great fun in it,
and it introduced a girl named Anne Baxter. It was her
first picture. She was about seventeen. I found Jack to be
one of the greatest people I've ever known. He was not
only a wonderful actor but a great intellect too, and a hard
worker. But by that time he had been drinking so much
that he didn't care about anything so long as he made enough
money to pay off some of the suits that were being taken
out against him. It was remarkable to see this man who
couldn't remember lines at all. They had cards with different lines on them, and he had about four people with him
who all stood at different points. He could look supposedly
at a man but really over his shoulder reading his next line;
and when he'd finished that he'd look somewhere else and
catch the next board. He was a great master at that, very
funny. But it kind of always hurt me a little bit to be doing that picture because I remembered when he played HAM-
LET in New York and I just got mad. He played in THE
JUST with his brother and in other pictures, and I thought
he was almost the greatest thing I'd ever seen; and to see
him doing this clowning and making fun of himself kind of
hurt me a little bit. But it was fun to do and he enjoyed it.

Q: I very much enjoyed the scene in which Anne Baxter
descended on John Barrymore with her play manuscript just
as he's about to retire wearing a nightgown and chinstrap.

A: He loved all those scenes too. But many things that
happened during the picture caused me a little trouble, like
his being able to get a drink during the day while he was
working. It always mystified me how it was done.

Q: Towards the end of the picture there was a scene in a

theatre where we had Lionel Atwill on stage, practically reduced to a foil for Barrymore: was his part at all bigger
originally?

A: No, I don't think so. He had done the stage original,
and he wanted to do it in the film.

Q: Now we come to your wonderful series of musicals beginning with TIN PAN ALLEY. Do you have any observa-
tions to make in general on Fox musicals of the 'forties?

A: I think they were, overall, the best made of that time,
and certainly the biggest money-makers. TIN PAN ALLEY
was fun, because Alice Faye had been on the lot and made
several pictures before it, but she had a mannerism involving her mouth that we tried to get rid of. And then I
worked with John Payne again, and Jack Oakie. It was,
however, the first time I worked with Betty Grable. She
and Alice worked perfectly together and had a lot of fun.
We also had a man named Billy Gilbert in a number called
"The Sheik of Araby." I remember mostly the war coming
on, and Alice seeing off her soldier sweetheart on a cold
night, and crying. I always liked that picture very much.

Q: The opening scenes had a splendid vitality about them,
set in the songwriting area of New York before World War
One.

A: It also made mention of a woman who was a great friend
of mine, Nora Bayes; she was played not by herself but by
another person.

Q: The one to whom the song "America I Love You" was
given?

A: Yes, and it was very interesting from that standpoint, I
think. It was very authentic, all that brownstone era of
songwriters.

Q: It gave the impression of having been very carefully re-
searched.

A: It was; they made a good job of it.

Q: I particularly liked the sequence in which the Brian
Sisters get together and sing "America I Love You" unac-
companied. That was beautiful.

A: That was a medley of songs all strung together.

Q: I also remember with great pleasure a scene in which Grable and Faye do a duet, each of them dressed in a sarong.

A: That song was used as a running gag throughout the picture: "Beautiful Katie." It was given in different versions, variations on the same melody to coincide with Katie's various destinations, but with different words. They tried it out in Hawaiian, in Negro music, in fast jazz; they tried it out every way until it finally became that song.

Q: To what extent did you participate in the creation of musical sequences like this?

A: We always had a choreographer, and he would have big ideas about how to put it on. I would participate in shooting it, watching rehearsals and okaying the thing as a whole. If there was something we didn't like we'd change it, and that's the way it was done.

Q: Of course, all the numbers were pre-recorded?

A: Yes, they were pre-recorded, and the chorus people were out on the set rehearsing the whole number with stand-ins for the principals whom we were using in the other scenes. So that was covered by our schedule, and until the number was scheduled we didn't shoot it.

Q: So you had shooting and rehearsals simultaneously?

A: That's right. We'd get it all ready and just step in. The principals had rehearsed their numbers when they were recording them.

Q: Were there any signs of rivalry between Miss Faye and Miss Grable at this time?

A: There might have been, but it was kept subdued as much as possible. They appeared to love each other very much, but I heard little wafflings which I don't think were important because they were friends right up until the time Alice left.

Q: If anybody were to nominate your best musical of this period, there'd be a very good case to be made out in sup-

port of MOON OVER MIAMI [20th-Fox, 1941], which I think
is a dazzling, wonderful piece of work.

A: Yes, I think so, but I like pictures with music, comedy,
and emotional quality; and therefore I'd pick out TIN PAN
ALLEY for that reason. Of course, I'm not talking about
the days of THE KING AND I, which was a compromise, but
I like the emotional side to a musical too, otherwise it becomes just froth. And MOON OVER MIAMI was a good musical, I think. It had wonderful music and entertainment in
it, but it to me lacked the depth that some of the others
had...

Q: Such as MOTHER WORE TIGHTS [20th-Fox, 1947]?

A: That's right. I loved MOTHER WORE TIGHTS for that
reason, and particularly loved WHEN MY BABY SMILES AT
ME [20th-Fox, 1948], which was based on the old play
BURLESQUE, because that had great emotional content; and
I think that Dan Dailey hit his peak in that particular one.
But all of Betty's pictures were good, they were just dif-
ferent. I felt MOON OVER MIAMI was a delightful musical,
and Pev Marley was also the cameraman on that.

Q: How was the opening montage conceived, with its exhilarating aerial shots of the swimming pool and the racehorses
and so on? Did you just go out on location, or what?

A: No, a second unit went to Miami and shot all of those
scenes. We had wanted that over the titles.

Q: Was this planned in detail on paper?

A: Not each scene, but we more or less said, "All of
these things--aerial shots of racetracks, pools, things of
that sort--will give the atmosphere of Miami." So they
were to be put back of the titles. Then the second unit
would go out with their director and get things to cover that
material for the titles while we proceeded with shooting.
As they sent their film in, we would look at it in the projection room, select the scenes we wanted and put them
under the titles. They were just the length we needed.

Q: Was Carole Landis your first choice as the second female lead in this picture?

A: I don't know. It wasn't talked about because she was

under contract, and Betty was under contract, and they were
already assigned to the picture when it was given to me.
The boys were Cummings and Ameche, and Cummings was
the only one not under contract at that time. I thought he
was good; I liked him very much. Charlotte Greenwood and
Jack Haley were in it; she performed her famous high kick.

Q: They had a wonderful number together, "Is That Good?"
In fact the whole score was brilliant, full of memorable original tunes and lyrics, superbly performed by the Fox orchestra.

A: Now that picture was an adaptation of one made earlier
called THREE BLIND MICE, and it's been done twice since
then under other names, including HOW TO MARRY A MIL-
LIONAIRE [20th-Fox, 1953]: that was quite a stock play we
had there! Every time we ran out of material we used that!
But it also had one thing that I remember: I had a letter
from England saying that during the war their rationing allowed them very few eggs, and I put a thing in this picture
where Bob invited the girls home to meet his millionaire
father. It was late at night, two or three o'clock in the
morning when they got there, and the father went in the
kitchen and made what he called "ranch-house eggs." It had
another name but we couldn't use that. They're made by
taking a piece of bread with a hole in the middle, breaking
an egg in the hole and frying it in butter: you break the
yellow in there, browning it on one side of the bread then
turning it over and browning it on the other. It's a great
late supper idea, and because of the shortage of eggs in
England at that time it played in one theatre seven or eight
weeks; they just came to look at that!

Q: After MOON OVER MIAMI you went on to WEEKEND IN
HAVANA [20th-Fox, 1941], which was your first association
with Carmen Miranda, wasn't it?

A: Yes. She had made a picture at the studio before that.
She was a very funny, very sweet little woman, and worked
hard. But her so-called dialect was her own, and we had
many laughs out of that; she didn't put it on, you know.
She was a genuine malaprop. Of course, she had her own
group of musicians behind her, and she sang those songs
like nobody in the world has ever done them.

Q: Did she virtually take charge of her own numbers?

A: She'd have a number, and then we'd have a choreographer because we usually worked in a crew of people behind
her who had to be integrated with her, you see. So she
would rehearse the number with the chorus, and they were
finally recorded as we did them. She also had single numbers but we didn't have to worry about them because she
would record them on the sound stage and come out and re-
do them; so it all depended on her, and she was an expert
at synchronizing.

Q: Even in those terribly fast and complicated Portuguese
songs?

A: Yes, because only she knew them, you see!

Q: Here again you had Alice Faye and John Payne and Cesar Romero...

A: The "stock company," as we called it.

Q: Can you remember anything special about this picture
that set it apart from any of the others? Was it all studio-
made?

A: Oh yes. A song Alice Faye sang out on the balcony of
one of the hotels comes to my mind; it seemed to be a hit
song of that time but I can't remember the name. It was
very beautiful. Alice had a quality, a feminine warmth that
none of the other girls seemed to have at that time, not
Betty or any of them; and for that reason I think she was a
star. There was a certain warmth to her, a simplicity that
made her very valuable, I think. But when the rah-rah age
came in, she kind of went out.

Q: Alice projected a more mature image than her "succes-
sor," Grable--still beautiful, but mature.

A: That's right.

Q: SONG OF THE ISLANDS [20th-Fox, 1942] was an amusing picture.

A: Yes, that had Victor Mature in it. I remember countless days when Betty and Vic had to do a little "sailing
trip" on a hot set; it was quite an ordeal getting that to look
right. I liked the picture because it had a woman named
Hilo Hattie in it, and Tom Mitchell. All the luaus and those

things were interesting because I'd been to Hawaii and knew
them, and our research involved building them up a little
bit and fancifying them.

Q: It had some good comedy: there was a very funny scene
in a hut, with Billy Gilbert as a potentially cannibal chief
mistaken for a native girl by a sleeping Jack Oakie.

A: He thinks they're cannibals, and she takes him to dinner
with her father who's dressed in dragons' teeth and things
like that. They were eating poi, and Oakie was always
afraid they would eat him too.

Q: I haven't seen THE MAGNIFICENT DOPE [20th-Fox,
1942]: can you tell me a little bit about it?

A: It was first called THE MAGNIFICENT JERK. The
censors leaped upon that and we had to give it another
name. It was the story of a country boy (Henry Fonda)
coming to the city on one of those "learn to be a salesman
in five days" things, or "learn to be" some kind of genius.
This company and its secretary were exploiting the country
boy, making a fool out of him to their advantage. Lynn
Bari as the secretary stepped in and fought that concept.
Henry got on to it, it came out well, and he turned out to
be a wonderful success.

Q: It sounds very much like Capra material, doesn't it?

A: Yes. I remember one time during the filming of it,
before we were to do a love scene in a park involving Henry
and Lynn. Henry lived close to my house, and one Sunday
he suddenly called me up saying, "You've got to get up here
right away." So I went up. He had a tractor of some kind,
and on the immediately preceding Saturday he'd gone up to
his ranch and had been working this tractor. He'd run over
his hand somehow and broken some fingers, and a doctor
had encased his hand in kind of a wire harp arrangement.
So we had to shoot the scene and hide his hand, and we devised a scheme whereby he put his arm around her so that
his hand with the big wire arrangement on it was out of
camera range, and stuck a false hand on the other shoulder!
And that's the way they played that love scene. That happened at about the end of the picture, so we were lucky in
that respect.

Q: Then you did a couple more musicals, one of which,

CONEY ISLAND [20th-Fox, 1943], had exceptional vitality--
a vitality that sort of hit you off the screen.

A: It was a vital period and a vital subject, and all the
people in it were ambitious. That had a boy in it whom I'd
used in STAR DUST named George Montgomery. He played
one of the leading parts in it and was very good, and also
my old friend Cesar Romero. It included Phil Silvers too,
and a man I used in STATE FAIR [20th-Fox, 1945] named
Charlie Winninger, who was a great favorite of mine. So it
was altogether kind of a wild "fun" picture. I remember
one song that Betty was singing, and Montgomery was trying
to make a star out of her: she got all dressed up for her
number and came out on the stage with a lot of big roses,
and egrets in her hair, and things around her waist and
bracelets; and he tore them all off and made her rather
tastefully dressed. She sang the song tied to a tree.

Q: Were sequences like this in the script or did you ever
think of them yourself?

A: No, they were all planned before we started. Now it
might have been my idea to tear these things off her, but
that would have come up during the writing of the story with
the writer, if I thought of it. Maybe he thought of it, I
don't remember now. But that's the way we went about it.
You didn't do things on the set.

Q: You never believed in improvisation?

A: Not too much, because you needed things with which to
shoot these scenes--props and different things of that kind--
and they couldn't always be just available. Little pieces of
business might occur to you on the set--to the actor, to the
director, to anybody. They might happen that way, but
there was no big improvisation on the set because it would
have thrown everybody into confusion, and these were expensive pictures.

Q: GREENWICH VILLAGE [20th-Fox, 1944] was again a
superbly made entertainment...

A: Now let me tell you about that. I had lived in Greenwich Village and knew it, so I had fun personally with the
picture. But during that picture Carmen Miranda's fiancé
died in Rio, I think, and she went all to pieces--went into
shock and couldn't work. So we put her into the hospital

for several days with doctors in constant attendance, and
when she came back she remembered her lines but she
couldn't hear what other people were saying. So we had to
shoot the rest of that picture cutting her off above the hips,
and when it came time for her to speak--she had read it,
she knew what was going on but she couldn't hear--we would
have to poke her with a stick out of range of the camera to
give her the cue to speak her lines. About two or three
months after that, her hearing returned. But it was very
difficult, and we were very tender with her because we
loved her. She tried everything, you know, but she just hit
a snag when that happened. I've never seen a person disintegrate as she did over that.

Q: I myself vividly remember Don Ameche composing the
"Whispering" Concerto in this picture.

A: Newman had written that, and we teased him along into
making that arrangement. Newman, as usual, composed
"big" in every musical we did; so much depended on him.
He had his regular musical meetings with all the departments in the studio before we started a picture. They
heard the music, and the choreographer would tell them
what he needed to stage it, how many days it would usually
take to do it, and when he could schedule the recording of
it. And that recording was done precisely, with all the
chorus people in the numbers--not the same people, because
we'd have singers do the singing that the chorus did. Then
it would have to be rehearsed with the dancers we'd hired
for the number.

Q: So they had to hire two sets of people--a set of singers
and a set of dancers?

A: That's right--and doubles always for the principals.
Then the principals would come in, and it would usually
take them a day to get into it. We would rehearse some
numbers before the picture started, to get them out of the
way; and they had to be finished in perfect order before we
could record them.

Q: Music, words and movements all perfectly synchronized?

A: That's right. Then the choreographer and the dancers
would brush up on it again with the finished soundtrack.
There was no direct recording of the songs, ever.

Q: Wasn't Hermes Pan involved on many of these?

A: Yes, many. He was one of Betty's favorites. There
was also a little New York choreographer whose name I've
forgotten. He did TIN PAN ALLEY, but I think Hermes did
almost all of the rest of the films with me.

Q: Although it's many years since I saw it, I seem to recall that GREENWICH VILLAGE had more elaborate and
costly and spectacular musical numbers than perhaps some
of your other pictures, involving great trickery with lights.
Is that correct?

A: It seems to me that one of Betty's pictures had the
most costly number we did, which was all taken in one
scene; we only cut when the film ran out. Its length was
amazing, and all the different scene changes occurred right
in front of you: in other words, it would go from a field
of daisies to a plantation in the South, and the columns
would all come up out of the floor. They'd lower the plantation house behind it, and all the bushes would move in
with wires; the scenes would transfer right in front of your
eyes. That was the most costly of our sequences. I think
maybe the reason you think of GREENWICH VILLAGE like
that is because of the lighting with its bizarre background,
but I don't believe it was as costly as some of the others.

Q: Vivian Blaine came from New York, didn't she?

A: Yes. I took a test of her before this picture, but this
was the first big part she had. In those days she was rather heavier than she became later. It's interesting that
when she finished the picture she didn't like herself in it,
so she started dieting and completely dehydrated herself.
She was never able to regain that weight.

Q: Then you did STATE FAIR which, although a wonderful
picture, to my way of thinking rather suffered from too
much studio work.

A: Yes, that's true. I hated that part too, but we couldn't
find a farm where we could work and light people properly
and do all these musical things we had to do. So we had
to kind of "build" it, but I thought that the scenes overrode
that; I hope they did.

Q: I think the material certainly survived. I liked Dick

Haymes in it very much.

A: Yes, I did too. He was one of my favorites--still is.
He's a fine singer, not sufficiently appreciated, one of our
best.

Q: Fay Bainter, Charles Winninger, and Jeanne Crain all
had wonderful scenes...

A: Yes, they did. They were great, I thought, especially
Charlie Winninger in the scenes where he has his hog judged.
The whole thing was, I thought, the best musical version,
because the last time they did it Alice Faye, funnily enough,
played the mother. I can't remember who played the father
now, but he wasn't my idea of a father on a farm. It just
didn't seem to come off. Of course, our version of STATE
FAIR had the advantage of a Rodgers and Hammerstein script.
They wrote the music, and added "It Might As Well Be
Spring," which was sung in the picture by Dick Haymes and
Jeanne Crain. A funny thing happened: our contract stipu-
lated that when we finished certain of the big numbers in
the picture we had to send them to Rodgers and Hammerstein to see how they liked them. When we finished "It
Might As Well Be Spring"--which I did with the girl sitting
by a window and the camera almost imperceptibly creeping
up on her till it came to a big close-up; we did it simply
because I thought it was a mood song; and so did Al New-
man--we sent it to Hammerstein and Rodgers for their opinion. We got back a letter saying they were very disappointed.
They thought it should have had a big production behind it because it was one of the big numbers in the score. So we
put a big production behind it costing about $100,000 and
sent it to them to see if it fitted in with the way they'd suggested it be done. They sent it back saying, "Put it in the
way you had it first. That's the way it should be, and that's
what we want."

Q: What happened to the $100,000 sequence?

A: It went out the window. Things like that happen in
pictures.

Q: These were the days, of course, when you could afford
to have that happen because nearly every picture made
money.

A: That's right. Up until THE SOUND OF MUSIC [20th-

Fox, 1965], that picture was one of the eight biggest gross-
ers in the industry, so they could afford to spend a bit on
it.

Q: Who were the producers you mostly worked with during
this period? What was the nature of their contribution?
Was it purely administrative or did it ever go beyond that?

A: Zanuck would assign a producer like Bill Perlberg certain pictures to make during the year. He would then get
the scriptwriters to start a script. When the script was
finished he would then call in the director, and if the director liked the script he'd be assigned, and if the producer
agreed to any changes the director might like to make he
was still assigned. When STATE FAIR was assigned to Bill
Perlberg he procured Hammerstein and Rodgers to write the
script and the score. Then I was assigned to it. The whole
idea seemed good to me, and that's the way it went from
there. Now the producer watches it as it goes through to
see that it doesn't go too much over budget or over time
and things of that nature. But he works with the director,
he doesn't sit out on the stage like they do on TV; he's the
executive back in the office.

Q: He didn't have any artistic influence, wanting you to
shoot a scene in a certain way perhaps?

A: No, never that. He might have an artistic influence in
the conception of a scene, making suggestions in the office
before you went out and did it. But he wouldn't come out
on the set. He would call you on the phone and say, "The
rushes were great," or "I don't like this particular thing--
did you notice that?"

Q: Did you ever do any uncredited work at this time, when
a director maybe fell sick or had to go on leave for some
reason or other?

A: Yes, I stepped in without credit on two or three pictures, I think, including George Seaton's APARTMENT FOR
PEGGY [20th-Fox, 1948]. I stepped in on that for a week
while George was away recuperating. There were others
but I don't remember the names.

Q: SENTIMENTAL JOURNEY [20th-Fox, 1946] was a woman's picture, as its name suggests, but there's nothing
necessarily wrong with that.

A: That was voted by Harvard the worst picture of all time.
It was a weepie, and I loved weepies.   I'd cry right with the
actors.

Q: You'd get terribly involved?

A: Oh, sure.   If I don't cry, it's no good.

Q: Well, there was an awful lot of crying going on in this
one.

A: It didn't make much money.   It had John Payne as a
dramatist and Maureen O'Hara as his actress wife.   I can't
remember the name of the little girl in it.   She was under
contract to the studio.   I thought she was very good [Connie
Marshall].

Q: CLAUDIA AND DAVID [20th-Fox, 1946], which you made
the same year, was of course a sequel to Edmund Goulding's
CLAUDIA [20th-Fox, 1943].

A: I liked that very much.   It marked the beginning of my
association with Bob Young.   Dorothy McGuire's a great
actress: she played in the stage original and in the movie
they made here.   Rose Franken, who had written them all,
was a very great friend of mine.   We enjoyed it very much.

Q: MOTHER WORE TIGHTS [20th-Fox, 1947] and WHEN
MY BABY SMILES AT ME [20th-Fox, 1948] each featured
Grable and Dailey, and they sort of go together, don't they?

A: Well, I think that when a particular man and woman
work together a certain rapport happens, a "chemical" mixture that happens when they have a great and sincere respect
for each other's talent; and, liking each other so much,
this might have something to do with what comes off the
screen.   They'd both had somewhat similar experiences to
those of the characters in MOTHER WORE TIGHTS, and I
think that had something to do with it.

Q: They played a showbiz couple, didn't they?

A: Yes.   The film had an emotional side to it which I
liked, as did the one I liked best of theirs, WHEN MY
BABY SMILES AT ME.

Q: I remember especially in MOTHER WORE TIGHTS a

a scene of a lavish holiday resort where the Mona Freeman
character was rather ashamed of her parents...

A: That's right. It culminates in a school graduation cere-
mony in which she pays tribute to her father. It was a lot
of fun, because I knew vaudevillians of that type, and how
they struggled in the theatre.

Q: It certainly had a feeling of great authenticity. Of
course, a lot of the virtue of these things must have lain in
the writing.

A: Yes, in getting the conception ... I remember being impressed in that particular picture with a scene of Christmas
night when the kids came home from school, and they sang
"Silent Night" around the piano: that kind of clutched me
at the time. It was about a family that loved each other,
and as the people did like each other it helped a great deal.
The subject-matter of WHEN MY BABY SMILES AT ME was
the old play BURLESQUE, which Barbara Stanwyck had
played in New York. They had made a movie of the original [THE DANCE OF LIFE (Paramount, 1929)] and this was
the musical version of it. It was mostly about a man ad-
dicted to drink, and Betty as his wife trying to keep him
straight--the different things they went through. It had June
Havoc and Jack Oakie with them. It was a bit of a weepie:
Dan has the DT's and goes to the hospital and has quite a
thing with Jimmy Gleason, I remember. It was set in a
vaudevillian environment.

Q: SITTING PRETTY [20th-Fox, 1948] was a film that had
practically no imitators.

A: That was kind of made out of whole cloth. A man
named Herbert had written it. I had been married a few
years when I made it, and I put everything I knew into that
picture--like coming home at night and having to get out of
your car to take a bicycle off the driveway. We used those
things all the way through, and of course it represented the
"blossoming out" of Clifton Webb. He was so precise and
funny: it was his own character, practically, that he played.
The situations in it were very funny, such as the bowl on
the kid's head...

Q: Was this a screen original?

A: Mr. Belvedere was a character written by some woman,

I don't remember who. It came from her book, but greatly
improved and with many things added. Many people said to
me, "How could you dare slap that bowl of mush over the
little kid's head like that?" "I didn't," I said. I planned it
first so that the brothers were slinging this mush across
the table at each other, and then the baby, watching it,
picked up a spoon and slammed it. When I'd established
that the baby did that too, I took the scene where the baby
picked up the spoon and threw it and cut right to Clifton
Webb's head. Clifton Webb said, "Now, little boy, if you
do that again I'm going to put that bowl of mush over your
head!" Later on, when they started slinging the mush
around again and Clifton tried to stop it, I cut to the father
and mother out in the garage. They heard the baby yelling,
so when they ran to the window and looked in, the baby already had the mush on his head. We put that mush on the
baby's head so that it streamed down his face, and the baby
loved it; he was licking all the mush, and would put the
mush bowl on his own head--having a ball! We finally had
to wire the bowl on to the kid's head and get the kid to cry.
Now there was no way to get the kid to cry because he was
having so much fun, so we had to sit there with the camera
running and tell the baby that its mother and father were
going home. We had to slam doors to make it think they'd
gone home--everything in the world until it finally began to
cry. That's how that scene was made.

Q: What was the position of the Clifton Webb character in
the household?

A: He was brought in as a babysitter, to take care of these
three children while their mother and father were working,
and it all grew out of that situation. Because they saw his
ad in the paper, which read "Lynn Belvedere," they expected
a woman to appear. So they were quite shocked when he appeared and immediately took over; there was no way of getting rid of him or doing anything about it. He knew everything, was an expert on everything. Then they became very
fond of him. He really loved the kids but he was so austere
with them...

Q: YOU'RE MY EVERYTHING [20th-Fox, 1949] reunited
you with Anne Baxter, whose first film you'd directed, and
with Dan Dailey. She was very exuberant in this picture,
wasn't she?

A: Yes--they were show people too, I think, and they had

a daughter whose name I've forgotten. She was quite good,
and they were trying to get her into pictures because Shirley
Temple was such a success. I remember one scene where
Dan took his daughter to Zanuck's office. We used a replica
of Zanuck's office, and he rolled back the rug and put on a
number right in the office for Zanuck.

Q: Did the audience see or hear Zanuck in the picture?

A: No, another man of similar type, but we used all of his
mannerisms--for instance, a little riding crop he used to
carry with him all the time. However, we did use Mack
Gordon, who had written the number we were doing: he
played the piano.

Q: I seem to remember stills of Anne Baxter doing a
Charleston on a tabletop.

A: That's right. She wasn't much of a dancer but she got
away with it.

Q: This takes us up to 1950, when you did CHEAPER BY
THE DOZEN, a film which seems to mean a lot to you personally.

A: That was because it had so many children in it. SIT-
TING PRETTY had come out so well that I was teamed up
with Clifton again. They had Myrna Loy as the mother, and
it was based on the life of an engineer [Frank Gilbreth] who
did have twelve children because he thought it was cheaper
to raise twelve than one. He was a time and motion expert.
Jeanne Crain was in it too. It was a very interesting picture, based on a real-life man. I went up to Westport,
where they had a house at Nantucket out on the beach, and
we copied that house exactly.

Q: This was a color production, unlike SITTING PRETTY,
and I think it's rather a shame that you didn't do the sequel
to CHEAPER BY THE DOZEN--BELLES ON THEIR TOES
[20th-Fox, 1952].

A: I'll tell you: they all failed, more or less, after the
initial film because that contained the shock of introducing
the Clifton Webb character. After they had seen it, they
came to expect all the things that he did; there was no more
surprise, you see.

Q: THE JACKPOT [20th-Fox, 1950]... ?

A: That was done with a pal of mine, Jimmy Stewart, and
Barbara Hale. It was based on a real thing; they had those
contests on the air during that time. One aspect of it was
that when these prizes were delivered they also had government men in attendance; no one ever thought of the tax they
would have to pay on these things. They were taxable, and
if people won $100,000 worth of prizes they were liable to
be taxed on that amount. Well, you don't find amounts like
that in most middle-class families, so they had to go out
and sell their stuff to raise money for the taxes! That was
something they overlooked in all the excitement of winning
the contest.

Q: ON THE RIVIERA [20th-Fox, 1951] was a remake of
FOLIES BERGERE [United Artists, 1935] which had starred
Maurice Chevalier and Merle Oberon.

A: I wasn't conscious of that. I read the story, and I enjoyed it. They had Danny Kaye signed up, and he was a
great artist. It also had Gene Tierney in it, and was a joy
from beginning to end. It was a farce of the in-and-out-of-
door type, involving a great deal of trick photography to accommodate Kaye's double role.

Q: Was this particularly difficult to do in color?

A: No more than in black-and-white. That introduced a
girl named Gwen Verdon; she went from that to New York,
and turned out to be what you know her to be now. She
was a dancer in it, and did some specialty work.

Q: Was it all made in Hollywood, or did you go abroad on
location?

A: It was all made in Hollywood. Gene Tierney was terribly photogenic. She had her problems, but she was a nice
girl and is still a beautiful woman.

Q: Then came WITH A SONG IN MY HEART [20th-Fox,
1952], the life story of Jane Froman starring Susan Hayward...

A: That, to me, was remarkable for Susan, because I had
known her for a long time. Jane Froman was out here
with us; she made the soundtracks, and Susan was with her

when she recorded them.   She watched her and worked with
her, and I think of all the people I've worked with in musicals, Susan was the best on synchronizing.   Maybe it's because she went through the recording sessions with the person who did it, but she was remarkable.   I loved that picture, and it was all based on fact, every bit of it.   And
there again Al Newman came to the fore in its finale, because he put together a ten-minute medley of songs to finish
the picture.   I enjoyed it very much, and that little character woman, Thelma Ritter, was a joy too.

Q: You probably had nothing to do with the trailer, but I
remember it as being especially striking: it opened with
Susan Hayward's silhouetted figure against a red background...

A: That was in the film.   The reason Jane Froman didn't
do the picture was rather funny: it was because she stammers greatly.   But she only stammers when she talks; when
she sings, none of that comes out at all--it's the only thing
she can do without stammering, and that's the reason she
couldn't make the picture.

Q: Now we come to the 'fifties and CALL ME MADAM
[20th-Fox, 1953], which of course had been a huge personal
success for Ethel Merman on the stage...

A: Yes, it had.   I'd gone to New York and watched her do
it.   We tried to get into it everything they had in the play,
and I think we did.   Working with Ethel was a joy.   We all
felt very big about it; Sol Siegel was the producer.   But
audiences somehow didn't respond.   Ethel, as you know,
has a kind of brassy delivery of songs.   You have to see
her--the records wouldn't mean anything to you, they'd just
annoy you.   The picture didn't make the money we thought
it would; it made some, but not as much as it should have.

Q: Did she just reproduce her stage performance, or did
you try to make her vary it?

A: She's a good actress.   We kept some of the stage performance, like the song hits that Donald O'Connor did with
her; they were the same, and one of these particular songs
stopped the show.   But George Sanders was the one who
surprised us because he could sing very well.   He was very
good in that, I thought.   It was a good picture to make.
We had the great designer Irene Sharaff come out and do
Ethel's clothes.   She hadn't done them for the original play,

but she did them for this. She was great. I used her all
the time after that--on THE KING AND I, for instance,
which she did in New York.

Q: Shortly after you finished CALL ME MADAM, the studio
took up CinemaScope in a big way...

A: That was because attendance was falling off in the
theatres, and everybody was looking for something to combat that at this time. Skouras had known the people working on these different inventions, and he's the one who
brought in CinemaScope, which in fact did prove a shot in
the arm to the industry for a while. But there was no way
to stop the attendance decline, and it kept declining from
then on.

Q: It might have provided a shot in the arm to the industry,
but it certainly provided a headache to cameramen and directors.

A: On THE KING AND I [20th-Fox, 1956], we had these big
boxes over the cameras. That was a terrific problem, but
the biggest trouble we had with CinemaScope was that there
were two pieces of film going through the camera at all
times, thicker film than usual; and the sides of the aperture
occasionally scraped a little of the emulsion off that film,
which caused a curlicue of hair to form on the lens and
dance about in front of your action all the time, and that's
all you could look at. So after each take we'd have to stop
and inspect the camera to see if that hair was in the lens.
Many times you couldn't see it, and it turned out to have
been there a day later or two days later. So you'd have to
re-do that scene on whatever sets you could find. Many
times we'd find a hair and we'd have to take that scene
again, sometimes as many as ten or fifteen times. In THE
KING AND I the problem was almost insurmountable because
I had little children doing dramatic things, and they would
wear out in that length of time. For some of the big dances
and production numbers it would sometimes take an hour to
set up a scene; and if you had to re-do all that it was very
costly.

Q: On THERE'S NO BUSINESS LIKE SHOW BUSINESS [20th-
Fox, 1954], your first CinemaScope picture, did you find
composing for the new dimensions presented any problems?

A: Only inasmuch as that if you paint any picture you not

only try to make your immediate subject interesting, but all
parts of the painting. So in a wider field you have to fill it
up with more interesting things than you would in a narrow-
er field.

Q: Did you deliberately go for a more vivid color palette?

A: I don't think there was any notable change in that; I'm
not conscious of any. It was about the same, but the eye
had a bigger field to play with, so you began to learn how
to compose your people for that.

Q: How about recording on more than one track for stereo-
phonic sound?

A: When we started, we had to have about ten or fifteen
mikes all around; it was almost like when sound came in.
But as we went along that was simplified until multitrack recording became a regular feature. As well, we had to have
more glass to provide a bigger cover over the camera to
keep its sound out of the way of the microphones; we had to
find a way to cover the camera without putting another sheet
of glass over the lens. So that had to be rectified.

Q: Who was the cameraman?

A: Leon Shamroy. He was my favorite cameraman of all
time. We did STATE FAIR and many others together and,
as I say, at night when we'd finished work the cameraman
and I, the assistant director and the producer would get together in his office and have a midnight drink and talk about
what we were going to do the next day. So there were no
surprises: the cameraman knew what we expected to cover
although sometimes we didn't always make it. But we knew
what we were planning to do; the assistant director had
everything arranged for that, so it turned out to be a great
benefit.

Q: Did you preplan a lot of shots and set-ups on paper?

A: Mostly it wasn't done that way, but if we said, "Tomorrow we'll do Donald's dance number and get it all lighted
up," the cameraman had the choreographer put it on for him
to look at. He looked at it and saw where it went and what
he had to cover, so when he got there the night before, he
and the gaffer--the head electrician--could arrange where
they would put the lights; and in the morning when I'd get

there at about a quarter to nine it would pretty well be
lighted, requiring only minor corrections, so it was a valuable way to work.

Q: You certainly had a high-powered cast--Ethel Merman,
Donald O'Connor, Mitzi Gaynor, Dan Dailey, Marilyn Monroe: how did they blend in production?

A: As perfect as anything in the world with the exception
of Marilyn.

Q: What was her trouble?

A: She didn't seem to fit in with that group. She was
worried about herself all the time. It just didn't work out
as far as we were concerned. I guess her limited ability
worried her for one thing, because these were all professionals, and also good. She felt she was green, and felt a
little self-conscious about it. She never seemed to be able
to work by the clock: if you wanted her at nine o'clock you
might get her at ten-thirty, no matter what the set-up. She
did that without any regard for the cost. It never occurred
to her that those people had to wait and that it was costing
a lot of money, but she just couldn't make it; and it became
worse and worse until she finally didn't make it at all.
Apart from that the picture was a great joy, and because it
was a show business story the studio just wanted to load it
with names--because, as I said, Ethel Merman wasn't the
star they expected her to be; she didn't make enough money.
So even with all those other people in it, that didn't seem
to be enough without having Monroe's name in it too. She
was the hottest thing in the business then, so they put her
in it. She fitted the part all right, and did several good
numbers in it but just didn't seem to be able to work with
the rest of us.

Q: She did her own singing?

A: Most of it. It was very difficult to get that soundtrack.
She ended up doing most of it herself, but only little bits
at a time.

Q: Your next assignment at the studio was its biggest production of the year, THE KING AND I, based on Rodgers'
and Hammerstein's famous musical play...

A: I saw the show many times, and talked to Hammerstein

about it.   I had always wanted Deborah [Kerr] in that part
after Gertie Lawrence died.

Q: What made you see her in the part?

A: I had known her so long, and knew she had dignity and
great ability.

Q: She didn't sing, though, did she?

A: Another girl sang it, Marni Nixon.   Deborah was available when she recorded it, and she studied Deborah's accent
so ultimately you couldn't tell the difference.   The great
trouble with that picture was this, and I don't know whether
you noticed it or not: but when we got through with the
picture, something had happened to the processing of the
sound, and we had to throw the complete soundtrack out and
dub the whole thing from beginning to end--mostly dialogue,
because the recording of the music was all right, they had
that on other film.   The only thing we kept from the original
soundtrack was an emotional sequence with a Chinese girl
in it; they kept that with all its imperfections, and worked
and worked to get them out.   Aside from that, we had to go
through and re-do the whole thing.   Of course, luckily the
music was safe because, as I say, they had that on other
film.

Q: Wasn't this shot in a larger process than conventional
35mm., and with different equipment?

A: That's right.

Q: Then came DESK SET [20th-Fox, 1957], with Katharine
Hepburn and Spencer Tracy...

A: That came about because of these two people.   It was
written by Henry and Phoebe Ephron.   We all enjoyed it.
Katie was a wonderful gal.   She's a strange person but I've
always admired her greatly, and Spence, of course, was
the best.   He felt he was too old for the part, and he was;
but Katie wanted him and I wanted him.   We all wanted him,
so he did it.   She was the kind who would come in and look
at sets and say, "I've got just the thing at home for this,"
and bring it in next day.   She was also in on the casting,
went to New York with Spence and the casting director and
picked out two girls, one of whom was the daughter of a
friend of hers.   So she was in on everything, and Spence

would kid the life out of her saying, "Shut your mouth--go
back where you belong in vaudeville and keep out of here.
I thought that scene was lousy, it was terrible." And she'd
say, "You don't know what you're talking about--the director
knows what he's doing." That kind of thing made them a
great joy to work with. It was all in all a fun kind of film.

Q: Although it did show its stage origins very plainly,
didn't it? It never left the set.

A: That's right.

Q: The following year you did BUT NOT FOR ME [Para-
mount, 1959] on loan-out to Paramount...

A: That was because Clark Gable and I had been friends
for so many years, and he wanted me to do it. But first I
had to go to the hospital with ulcers and peritonitis, and
things kept happening all the time after that so I couldn't do
it, and they postponed making it still further till I got out.
We made it during a time when I wasn't getting too many
assignments from my own studio, Fox, because I'd turned
down THE GREATEST STORY EVER TOLD. My refusal
took place after I'd done THE KING AND I. Skouras wanted
me to do GREATEST STORY EVER TOLD, and I refused.
That made him mad, and he wouldn't give me any more pictures to do; and during the long period of my struggle with
Fox I made BUT NOT FOR ME with Clark Gable and Carroll
Baker at Paramount, the only loan-out I ever had from 1937
till 1961. It was based on ACCENT ON YOUTH [Paramount,
1935], an old Paramount picture about a young girl falling
in love with an older man. He was always lying about his
age, and several things happened before he finally told her
how old he was--not fifty-six as she thought, but fifty-eight.
It was quite a nice comedy.

Q: Almost the last film you did at Fox was the large and
lavish musical, CAN-CAN [20th-Fox, 1960].

A: That was the era when things were kind of like a mad-
house because the actors were taking over. I'd known
Frank [Sinatra] for quite a while but there were certain
things about him I didn't know. There was a man making
pictures then called Buddy Adler; he was in charge of the
studio at that time. And I didn't know that he had made a
deal with Frank whereby Frank got fifty-one per cent of the
profits or owned fifty-one per cent of the company. So when

I found that out. I knew then that Frank had the last say on
everything, and if he wanted to come in at eleven o'clock in
the morning and work till five, that was it.   I shot everything I could outside of those hours, but it was difficult because the electricians had to go to lunch at three o'clock in
the afternoon; it threw everything out of kilter.   And while
we didn't have any real trouble on the picture, actors were
then taking over, telling you what they'd do and what they
wouldn't do.   That's when the fun went out of directing for
me, when I gave up and wanted to get out.

Q: Of course, this was the beginning of the end for the old
studio system too.

A: That had been gradually happening for the previous five
or six years.   Everybody knew it, and they were trying to
cut all the corners, to make just as big pictures as before
for less money.   And they couldn't do it because all the
unions had come in and raised salaries, so it cost infinitely
more than it had cost to make a picture of the same size,
and they wanted to make them constantly bigger.   So the
handwriting was on the wall, with the stars believing they
could rule the whole thing.   That came in and died out
pretty fast too, you know, because no person is complete
unto himself on a big achievement like that; everything is a
result of the combined effort of the people who work on it.
And any man who thinks that he is the one person in the
world who can do this--and better than anybody else--is
wrong.

Q: This has been proven over and over again, at a cost of
millions.

A: That's right.   It's too bad because, as I told you, I
saw almost the beginning of feature pictures from 1920 till
1961-62--saw the heyday of it when almost anything you did
made a lot of money.   You made entertainment, that's all.
Then it got to a point where only a big lavish production
could get its head above water.   So those films failed: it
didn't matter how much they spent on them, the audience
didn't want it.   It reached a point where you almost had to
have a specialty or a road show or something to make a
picture: you just can't operate that way.   Since then the
era of dirty pictures has come in, which I think will die of
its own weight in short order.   Nobody wants to make pictures and get into them any more.

Q: The whole spirit has gone out of it.

A: That's right. Then when the money men came in, that
had a big influence too. They weren't creative at all--they
couldn't create, didn't understand it and didn't want it.
They thought it was unnecessary, and that had a big effect.

Q: Can you tell me something about your last movie, MAR-
RIAGE-GO-ROUND [20th-Fox, 1960]?

A: That had been done on the stage with Claudette Colbert
and Charles Boyer. It was a pretty good property but there
again it was just wrangling on a false basis, I think.

Q: You left the industry voluntarily?

A: Yes.

Q: You decided you couldn't continue in it as it was?

A: That's one of the reasons. The other was that I wanted
to get back to painting. When Zanuck bought THE SOUND
OF MUSIC he offered it to me and wanted me to make it.
The studio was in decline at that time, and he wanted me to
go off salary and wait a year before I made it. I told him
that I couldn't afford to do that as I was having physical
troubles and when I got rid of them I'd come back and talk
to him. Well, I was in retirement when he made it so I
never made a picture again. I decided I'd had enough, and
by that stage there was practically no more Twentieth Century-Fox. In desperation, trying to make money to keep
the overhead going, they would give anybody almost any deal
they wanted just to keep the studio running. For instance,
Marlon Brando made a picture at Paramount which brought
in no profit at all to the studio, but they took the deal because it kept the studio open; it paid the overhead. That
way it got to be a very desperate situation, and now they're
selling props...

Walter Lang, thank you very much.

WALTER LANG

A Film Checklist by Michael Terry

1. ZANDER THE GREAT (4 May 1925). P: Metro-
    Goldwyn-Mayer. C: Marion Davies, Holbrook Blinn,
    Harrison Ford. 8 reels.

2. RED KIMONO (14 February 1926). P: Vital Ex-
    changes. C: Priscilla Bonner, Theodore von Eltz,
    Tyrone Power. 7 reels.

3. THE EARTH WOMAN (4 April 1926). P: Associated
    Exhibitors. C: Mary Alden, Priscilla Bonner, Rus-
    sell Simpson. 6 reels.

4. THE GOLDEN WEB (1 September 1926). P: Lumas
    Film Corporation. C: Lillian Rich, Huntly Gordon,
    Jay Hunt. 6 reels.

5. MONEY TO BURN (6 December 1926). P: Lumas
    Film Corporation. C: Dorothy Devore, Malcolm
    McGregor, Eric Mayne. 6 reels.

6. THE LADYBIRD (N.Y. première, 1 July 1927; general
    release, 15 July 1927). P: First Division Pictures.
    C: Betty Compson, Malcolm McGregor, Sheldon
    Lewis. 7 reels.

7. THE SATIN WOMAN (1 August 1927). P: Lumas Film
    Corporation. C: Mrs. Wallace Reid, Rockliffe
    Fellowes, Alice White. 7 reels.

8. SALLY IN OUR ALLEY (3 September 1927). P: Co-
    lumbia. C: Shirley Mason, Richard Arlen, Alec B.
    Francis. 6 reels.

9. BY WHOSE HAND? (15 September 1927). P: Colum-
    bia. C: Ricardo Cortez, Eugenia Gilbert, J. Thorn-
    ton Baston. 6 reels.

10. THE COLLEGE HERO (9 October 1927). P: Columbia.
    C: Bobby Agnew, Pauline Garon, Ben Turpin. 6
    reels.

11. THE NIGHT FLYER (5 February 1928). P: Pathé.

C: William Boyd, Jobyna Ralston, Philo McCullough.
7 reels.

12. THE DESERT BRIDE (26 March 1928). P: Columbia.
C: Betty Compson, Allan Forrest, Edward Martindel.
6 reels.

13. THE SPIRIT OF YOUTH (15 February 1929). P:
Tiffany/Stahl. C: Dorothy Sebastian, Larry Kent,
Betty Francisco. 7 reels.

14. HELLO SISTER (15 February 1930). P: Sono Art/
World Wide. C: Olive Borden, Lloyd Hughes,
George Fawcett. 80m.

15. COCK O' THE WALK (N.Y. première, 11 April 1930;
general release, 15 May 1930). P: Sono Art/
World Wide. C: Joseph Schildkraut, Myrna Loy,
Philip Sleeman. 74m.

16. THE BIG FIGHT (1 September 1930). P: Sono Art/
World Wide. C: Guinn Williams, Lola Lane, Stepin
Fetchit. 69m.

17. THE COSTELLO CASE (15 October 1930). P: Sono
Art/World Wide. C: Tom Moore, Lola Lane, Ros-
coe Karns. 76m.

18. BROTHERS (15 November 1930). P: Columbia. C:
Bert Lytell, Dorothy Sebastian, William Morris.
78m.

19. COMMAND PERFORMANCE (19 January 1931). P:
Tiffany. C: Neil Hamilton, Una Merkel, Helen
Ware. 80m.

20. HELL BOUND (1 May 1931). P: Tiffany. C: Leo
Carrillo, Lola Lane, Lloyd Hughes. 81m.

21. WOMEN GO ON FOREVER (15 August 1931). P:
Tiffany. C: Clara Kimball Young, Marion Nixon,
Paul Page. 67m.

22. NO MORE ORCHIDS (25 November 1932). P: Columbia. C: Carole Lombard, Walter Connolly, Louise
Closser Hale. 74m.

23. THE WARRIOR'S HUSBAND (28 April 1933). P: Fox
    Film Corporation. C: Elissa Landi, Marjorie Ram-
    beau, Ernest Truex. 72m.

24. MEET THE BARON (20 October 1933). P: Metro-
    Goldwyn-Mayer. C: Jimmy Durante, Jack Pearl,
    Zasu Pitts. 67m.

25. THE PARTY'S OVER (30 August 1934). P: Columbia.
    C: Stuart Erwin, Ann Sothern, Arline Judge. 65m.

26. WHOM THE GODS DESTROY (July 1934). P: Colum-
    bia. C: Walter Connolly, Robert Young, Doris Ken-
    yon. 69m.

27. THE MIGHTY BARNUM (25 December 1934). P:
    United Artists. C: Wallace Beery, Adolph Menjou,
    Virginia Bruce. 87m.

28. CARNIVAL (10 February 1935). P: Columbia. C:
    Lee Tracy, Sally Eilers, Jimmy Durante. 76m.

29. HOORAY FOR LOVE (14 June 1935). P: RKO Radio
    Pictures. C: Ann Sothern, Gene Raymond, Bill
    Robinson. 72m.

30. LOVE BEFORE BREAKFAST (9 March 1936). P:
    Universal. C: Carole Lombard, Preston Foster,
    Janet Beecher. 70m.

31. WIFE, DOCTOR AND NURSE (17 September 1937). P:
    Twentieth Century-Fox. C: Loretta Young, Warner
    Baxter, Virginia Bruce. 88m.

32. SECOND HONEYMOON (19 November 1937). P:
    Twentieth Century-Fox. C: Loretta Young, Tyrone
    Power, Lyle Talbot. 82m.

33. THE BARONESS AND THE BUTLER (18 February 1938).
    P: Twentieth Century-Fox. C: William Powell,
    Annabella, Helen Westley. 82m.

34. I'LL GIVE A MILLION (22 July 1938). P: Twentieth
    Century-Fox. C: Warner Baxter, Marjorie Weaver,
    Peter Lorre. 78m.

35. THE LITTLE PRINCESS (17 March 1939). P: Twenti-

eth Century-Fox.   C: Shirley Temple, Richard
Greene, Anita Louise.   Technicolor.   93m.

36.   THE BLUE BIRD (22 March 1940).   P: Twentieth
Century-Fox.   C: Shirley Temple, Spring Byington,
Nigel Bruce.   Technicolor.   83m.

37.   STAR DUST (5 April 1940).   P: Twentieth Century-
Fox.   C: Linda Darnell, John Payne, Roland Young.
85m.

38.   THE GREAT PROFILE (25 October 1940).   P: Twentieth Century-Fox.   C: John Barrymore, Mary Beth
Hughes, Anne Baxter.   72m.

39.   TIN PAN ALLEY (29 November 1940).   P: Twentieth
Century-Fox.   C: Alice Faye, Betty Grable, Jack
Oakie.   94m.

40.   MOON OVER MIAMI (4 July 1941).   P: Twentieth
Century-Fox.   C: Don Ameche, Betty Grable,
Robert Cummings.   Technicolor.   92m.

41.   WEEKEND IN HAVANA (17 October 1941).   P: Twentieth Century-Fox.   C: Alice Faye, John Payne, Carmen Miranda.   Technicolor.   81m.

42.   SONG OF THE ISLANDS (13 March 1942).   P: Twentieth Century-Fox.   C: Betty Grable, Thomas Mitchell,
Victor Mature.   Technicolor.   75m.

43.   THE MAGNIFICENT DOPE (12 June 1942).   P:
Twentieth Century-Fox.   C: Henry Fonda, Lynn
Bari, Don Ameche.   85m.

44.   CONEY ISLAND (18 June 1943).   P: Twentieth Century-
Fox.   C: Betty Grable, George Montgomery, Cesar
Romero.   Technicolor.   96m.

45.   GREENWICH VILLAGE (September 1944).   P: Twentieth Century-Fox.   C: Carmen Miranda, Don Ameche,
William Bendix.   Technicolor.   85m.

46.   STATE FAIR (October 1945).   P: Twentieth Century-
Fox.   C: Jeanne Crain, Dana Andrews, Dick
Haymes.   Technicolor.   101m.

47. SENTIMENTAL JOURNEY (March 1946). P: Twentieth
     Century-Fox. C: John Payne, Maureen O'Hara,
     William Bendix. 97m.

48. CLAUDIA AND DAVID (May 1946). P: Twentieth Cen-
     tury-Fox. C: Dorothy McGuire, Robert Young,
     Mary Astor. 78m.

49. MOTHER WORE TIGHTS (September 1947). P: Twenti-
     eth Century-Fox. C: Betty Grable, Dan Dailey,
     Mona Freeman. Technicolor. 110m.

50. SITTING PRETTY (April 1948). P: Twentieth Century-
     Fox. C: Robert Young, Maureen O'Hara, Clifton
     Webb. 85m.

51. APARTMENT FOR PEGGY (October 1948). P: Twenti-
     eth Century-Fox. D: George Seaton, Walter Lang,
     uncredited. C: William Holden, Jeanne Crain, Ed-
     mund Gwenn. Technicolor. 96m.

52. WHEN MY BABY SMILES AT ME (November 1948).
     P: Twentieth Century-Fox. C: Betty Grable, Dan
     Dailey, Jack Oakie. Technicolor. 100m.

53. YOU'RE MY EVERYTHING (August 1949). P: Twenti-
     eth Century-Fox. C: Dan Dailey, Anne Baxter, Ann
     Revere. Technicolor. 94m.

54. CHEAPER BY THE DOZEN (April 1950). P: Twenti-
     eth Century-Fox. C: Clifton Webb, Myrna Loy,
     Jeanne Crain. Technicolor. 85m.

55. THE JACKPOT (November 1950). P: Twentieth Cen-
     tury-Fox. C: James Stewart, Barbara Hale, James
     Gleason. 87m.

56. ON THE RIVIERA (May 1951). P: Twentieth Century-
     Fox. C: Danny Kaye, Gene Tierney, Corinne Cal-
     vet. Technicolor. 89m.

57. WITH A SONG IN MY HEART (April 1952). P:
     Twentieth Century-Fox. C: Susan Hayward, Rory
     Calhoun, David Wayne. Technicolor. 120m.

58. CALL ME MADAM (April 1953). P: Twentieth Cen-
     tury-Fox. C: Ethel Merman, Donald O'Connor,

Vera-Ellen. Technicolor. 117m.

59. THERE'S NO BUSINESS LIKE SHOW BUSINESS (December 1954). P: Twentieth Century-Fox. C: Ethel Merman, Donald O'Connor, Marilyn Monroe. Cinemascope. DeLuxe Color. 117m.

60. THE KING AND I (July 1956). P: Twentieth Century-Fox. C: Deborah Kerr, Yul Brynner, Rita Moreno. Cinemascope. DeLuxe Color. 133m.

61. DESK SET (May 1957). P: Twentieth Century-Fox. C: Spencer Tracy, Katharine Hepburn, Gig Young. Cinemascope. Eastmancolor. 103m.

62. BUT NOT FOR ME (August 1959). P: Paramount. C: Clark Gable, Carroll Baker, Lilli Palmer. 105m.

63. CAN-CAN (January 1961). P: Twentieth Century-Fox. C: Frank Sinatra, Shirley MacLaine, Maurice Chevalier. DeLuxe Color. 131m.

64. THE MARRIAGE-GO-ROUND (January 1961). P: Twentieth Century-Fox. C: Susan Hayward, James Mason, Julie Newmar. Technicolor. DeLuxe Color. 98m.

65. SNOW WHITE AND THE THREE STOOGES (June 1961). P: Twentieth Century-Fox. C: Carol Heiss, Moe Howard, Larry Fine, Joe de Rita. Cinemascope. DeLuxe Color. 107m.

Chapter 2

H. BRUCE HUMBERSTONE

by Jon Tuska

I

It was in a screening room on the Warner Brothers
Burbank lot that we had agreed to meet. I had arranged to
have projected THE DRAGON MURDER CASE (First National,
1934) and CHARLIE CHAN AT THE OPERA (20th-Fox, 1937),
both of which Lucky Humberstone had directed. Keye Luke,
who had played Number One son to Warner Oland's Chan,
was working on sound stage seven in a movie for television
called KUNG FU. He had promised to look in on us if he
got a break. It was February, 1971.

Lucky threw down a package of American filter cigarettes.

"You've got me back on these things, thanks to this
damned interview. "

It was, as I recall, the first remark he ever made
to me.

As the pictures were screened, Lucky would make
comments here and there as his memory was jarred. He
had forgotten how the DRAGON MURDER CASE came out, so
he cautioned me not to reveal the murderer's identity. But
he did remember that when Darryl Zanuck had seen the
dailies from CHARLIE CHAN AT THE OPERA, he had insisted it was really a musical. Zanuck was right. Many of
Lucky's best films for Fox would be musicals.

We adjourned to a restaurant across the street from
the lot and continued talking. Lucky arranged for the interview to be concluded at his Beverly Hills apartment. We

57

Lucky Humberstone in his salad days. Photo from The
Memory Shop.

went there.   His daughter Robyn was home ill.   He had
raised her alone since she was six.   Lucky had taken over
the lease to the apartment from his close friend, Edmund
Goulding, after Goulding died.   We sat in the living room
and I produced a small tape recorder, placing it on the floor
between us.

"What's that?" Lucky asked.

"It's a tape recorder," I said, extending the micro-
phone arm to within a few inches of his face.

"Don't turn it on."

"Lucky, how can I record what you're saying if I
don't turn it on?"

"But I don't want you to record what I'm saying."

"You're just afraid of being recorded."

It was the first time in all my years of interviewing
that I had attempted to tape a conversation, and it was the
last.   We went on arguing about it.   My wife Ruth had accompanied me.   She urged him, too.   Lucky remained adamant.

"But Ruth doesn't take shorthand," I explained.

"I don't care," Lucky said.

So we talked, and I remembered and wrote it down
afterwards.

When it came that I wanted to do a career study on
Lucky in the Summer of 1975, I went to him fully prepared.
Lucky had changed his apartment.   Robyn had married Spike
Jones, Jr.   Lucky still looked the same, medium height,
graying hair, bright eyes, and he had not lost his energetic
manner.

"I'm ready for you this time," I said, as we sat
down to drinks in his comfortable living room.

"See," said Vicki, my secretary, holding up two
shorthand notebooks.

"I've had quite a life, honey," Lucky said, grinning. "I hope it'll be enough."

I told Lucky we had been out to the Metro lot to visit Sam Peckinpah.

"How did it go?"

"Fine," I said. "I'm in the process of a divorce, as Sam knows. Sam leaned forward and held up a hand with his fingers and thumb outstretched. 'You've bought yourself a divorce, Jon,' he told me. 'I've bought myself five of them.' "

"What did you say to that?" Lucky asked.

"I said, 'Give me another twenty years.' "

"I've had only two," Lucky responded. "That was two more than I needed."

Vicki reached for a little horn on the cocktail table in front of her. She squeezed the rubber ball at the end; it made a honking sound. (At Lucky's, guests are to honk when they want another drink.) Lucky got up to make her a drink.

"She's afraid, Lucky, that you and I are going to sit around here all night commiserating with each other, and never get down to the interview."

Vicki said, "After spending hours together, Jon and Sam could only come up with one sentence that was usable."

"And what was that, honey?" Lucky asked, setting down her drink.

"Sam said, 'I wonder why the fuck I make movies. Then I watch television, and I know why.' " Vicki cocked her head at a sharp angle, and smiled.

"Let's start at the beginning," I suggested.

"All right," Lucky said, bumming a cigarette from Vicki's pack. "I haven't had one of these for four months. And then this guy comes to visit me again, and I'm back on them." He lit the cigarette. "Take down what I say.

That's okay. But stop writing when I tell you."

I shook my head, no.

"What's wrong with you?" Lucky asked, settling himself in a rocker. He had refilled my drink at the same time
as he had made Vicki another one.

"I'm trying to write film history," I returned, "but
almost everything everybody tells me is off the record."

"I can't imagine why," Lucky said, chuckling.

We began.

II

H. Bruce Humberstone was born at Buffalo, New
York on 18 November 1903. As a youth, he attended public
schools in Cleveland and was sent to the Miami Ohio Military Academy. When he was in his teens, the Humber-
stones relocated to Los Angeles. Lucky found work as a
prop boy and assistant cameraman at Universal Pictures
when he was nineteen. "Uncle" Carl Laemmle was in
charge of the studio.

Humberstone's first assignment was on a Hoot Gibson
Western directed by John Ford for which the unit went on
location north of Hollywood to the Vasquez rocks. Ford,
the Hooter, and the rest of the company had mounts. Humberstone didn't. He carried the raw film stock in cans under his left arm, the camera under his right, and the tri-
pod on his back. Reaching the crest of a high plateau, the
troupe paused and waited for Lucky to catch up to them.
Puffing, exhausted, he made it. Ford snapped his first
words at him.

"Humberstone! What do you think of this location?"

"I think," Humberstone said, wanting to impress
Ford with his perspicacity, "that the top of that plateau
over there would be better."

"Okay!" Ford shouted. "You heard the kid. Everybody over to the other plateau."

Once he had lugged his gear the great distance while
the riders watched him, grinning and joking among themselves, Humberstone had come upon a first principle when
working on a Ford picture. If the director asks you a rhe-
torical question, keep your mouth shut.

Lucky got a part as a juvenile in a Laura LaPlante
picture. He was promoted to a second assistant director.

I asked Lucky how he got his nickname. The version he related to me differed somewhat from the one I gave
in my book The Filming of the West (Doubleday, 1976).

"This is how it really happened," Lucky assured me.
"After work at night I used to eat at John's Cafe right
across Hollywood Boulevard from Musso and Frank's.
Breezy Eason and Hoot Gibson occasionally ate at John's.
One night as I walked up the Boulevard, I saw an ambulance
parked outside John's. Two attendants came out carrying
Tom Mix on a stretcher. I went inside. Hoot and Breezy,
who was directing Gibson's pictures, were sitting at a table.
Mix and Gibson had had a fight. Both of them were drunk.
Breezy wanted to get a quart of bootleg Scotch, although
neither he nor Hoot needed any more.

"I felt Breezy was too loaded to drive. He asked
me to drive his Stutz for him. He knew a bootlegger. We
set out but we never got there. Breezy decided he wanted
to go to a party instead. We drove up into the Hollywood
hills. The lights were out in the house when we got there
and everyone, men and women, were naked. They had the
hooch in huge tubs. I got loaded. I was just a kid.
Breezy got loaded all over again. When we left, Breezy
drove. We hit a culvert and the car rolled over three
times. Breezy and I were thrown clear. When I reported
for work the next day, everyone on the lot kept calling me
Lucky, having heard the whole story from Breezy. The
name stuck."

In 1925, Lucky was promoted to first assistant director. He made a two-reeler titled UNIVERSAL IN 1925
as an exploitation vehicle for the Universal sales force. It
was so good that Universal released it theatrically. As a
result, Lucky was slated to make a series of two-reelers,
but Ernst Laemmle wanted to make them and he had the
advantage of being a relative. Lucky lost out. When Bill
Koenig, Universal's production manager, refused to let

Lucky assist on THE PHANTOM OF THE OPERA (Universal, 1925), Lucky quit.

Metro-Goldwyn-Mayer had gone into production on BEN-HUR. Fred Niblo was the director. Lucky went out to the Culver City lot where the crowd scenes were being filmed. He applied for an assistant directorship. Breezy Eason was charged with the chariot race. William Wyler, who directed the remake in the sound era, was also among those assisting on the picture. Lucky was put on to help handle 3,500 extras. He wore a bright red sweater. Niblo sat on a platform high above the bustle. He was favorably impressed by the young man in the red sweater. By the time production concluded, Niblo placed Lucky under a personal contract as his assistant, increasing his salary from $85 to $175 a week.

THE TEMPTRESS (M-G-M, 1926) with Greta Garbo and Antonio Moreno came next. It was then that Edmund Goulding requested that Lucky be permitted to assist him on the filming of PARIS (M-G-M, 1926) which starred Joan Crawford and Charles Ray. Goulding and Lucky became friends. At the end of the shooting schedule, Goulding offered Lucky a contract at $400 a week to work for him as his first assistant. When Niblo heard of Goulding's offer, he countered it by raising Lucky to $500 a week. Niblo had signed with First National, which was still independent of Warner Brothers, and was set to direct CAMILLE (First National, 1927), with Norma Talmadge and Gilbert Roland. Lucky told Niblo that he would accept his offer but he had to assist Dimitri Buchowetzki first on the film VALENCIA (M-G-M, 1926), which starred Mae Murray. Niblo agreed to hold up production on CAMILLE until Lucky could join him.

Following CAMILLE, Lucky went to work at United Artists in the capacity of a first assistant director to directors in general who were signed to direct pictures for United Artists' release. His initial undertaking was TOPSY AND EVA (United Artists, 1927), directed by Del Lord. Location shooting was to be done at Lake Tahoe. Lucky went there with the cast, which included Rosetta and Vivian Duncan (the drunken sisters, as they were called), and Nils Asther. Nils was in love with Imogene Wilson. When the troupe was safely checked in at a resort during the off-season awaiting Del Lord's arrival, their solitude was interrupted by Harry D'Abbadie D'Arrast who was directing a

picture for Paramount. His company showed up and reserved rooms at the same resort. Lucky's group was composed mostly of blacks. D'Arrast's included mostly women.
The groups began pairing off at night. Myron Selznick,
later a powerful talent agent, was production supervisor on
TOPSY AND EVA. He had a case of Scotch delivered to
his room every day, never stuck his head out, and courted
various women from both companies. Lucky did not complain and Myron always had the warmest respect for Lucky's
discretion. When Lucky's troupe returned to Hollywood,
D. W. Griffith was assigned to do the retakes.

MY BEST GIRL (United Artists, 1927) was directed
by Sam Taylor. Lucky assisted. Mary Pickford was the
star, Buddy Rogers her co-star. Mary and Buddy fell in
love.

"Writers are still after me to tell what I know about
it, " Lucky reflected. "I figure it's nobody's business. "

He looked crossly at Vicki's empty glass.

"I was going to honk, " Vicki responded to the un-
asked question, "but I didn't want to break your train of
thought. "

"No trouble at all, " Lucky said, jumping up to make
another round.

"Vicki's just getting accustomed to film research, " I
told Lucky. "If we have an interview in the morning, she
has two or three sociable drinks. Then, if there is another
in the afternoon, she may have four or five sociable drinks. "

"Which, " Vicki chimed in, "only gets me tuned up
for the all-night interviews. "

Lucky laughed as he handed her a refill.

THE DEVIL DANCER (United Artists, 1927) was directed by Fred Niblo. Originally, Sam Goldwyn had engaged
Alfred Raboch to direct it with Lynn Shores as his assistant.
Then Shores was made the director with Raboch as his assistant. When Niblo took over, he received sole screen
credit. During THE DEVIL DANCER and Niblo's next picture for Sam Goldwyn, TWO LOVERS (United Artists, 1928),

starring Ronald Colman and Vilma Banky, Douglas Fair-
banks developed a positive rapport with Lucky. Henry
King, with whom Lucky would eventually clash at
Twentieth Century-Fox a decade later, was taken off
THE WOMAN DISPUTED (United Artists, 1928) starring
Norma Talmadge. Lucky assisted his replacement.
King had already left before Lucky began.

Fairbanks requested Lucky to assist Allan Dwan on
his next swashbuckler, THE IRON MASK (United Artists,
1929). Dwan wasn't too pleased with Fairbanks' choice but
he went along with it. The first project he gave Lucky was
to compute costs and design sets. Lucky went to Palm
Springs and worked out an elaborate series of plans. When
he reported back to Dwan, the director threw the sheaf of
papers aside.

"There are two things a good assistant director of
mine always keeps in mind," Dwan said. "He knows I never
read papers and he never asks questions."

Once the picture started, Dwan became increasingly
appreciative of Lucky's acumen. When the unit manager ir-
ritated Dwan with his excessive questions, Dwan fired him
and offered the job to Lucky. Lucky was willing to assume
the additional responsibilities if Dwan would still allow him
an assistant director's credit and give him a raise of $100
a week. Dwan acquiesced.

COQUETTE (United Artists, 1929) teamed Mary Pickford with football hero Johnny Mack Brown. Sam Taylor directed with Lucky assisting. Taylor had shared directorial
duties with Henry King on THE WOMAN DISPUTED. By
now, he was a great favorite of Mary Pickford's. There
was no question in Mary's mind, when next she was cast
opposite Doug for THE TAMING OF THE SHREW (United
Artists, 1929), that Sam Taylor must be the director.
Doug insisted on Lucky as Taylor's assistant.

It was a remarkable situation, worse even than
TOPSY AND EVA. Mary was openly in love with Buddy
Rogers. Doug was in love with Lupe Velez. Mary was not
talking to Doug and Doug was not talking to Mary. Hollywood's most glamorous marriage was a bust. Sam Taylor
directed Mary. Lucky was in the middle. If Mary was

displeased with anything, she would tell Lucky to tell Doug; Doug would only communicate through Lucky to either Mary or Taylor. Sam made his bid for immortal fame when he credited the story to "William Shakespeare, with additional dialogue by Sam Taylor." It wasn't merely a posture. Taylor happened once to overhear Lucky talking to another production assistant. He called Lucky over afterwards and reprimanded him.

"There's too much familiarity around here," he said. "I am not Sam to you. I am Mr. Taylor."

Mary happened to pass by. She thought Taylor was becoming hopelessly pompous and told him so.

Wesley Ruggles was the director on CONDEMNED (United Artists, 1929). Ronald Colman was the star. Sam Goldwyn told Lucky that, although only ten days in production, the picture was already behind six. Lucky talked over the matter with Ruggles. Wes was having an affair which required long lunch hours and all-night sessions. Goldwyn, when he learned the cause, pulled Ruggles off the picture. Lucky went to Sam and declared that he did not want to direct it; Wes should be put on again. Goldwyn gave in. Wes returned and the film was completed in ten days.

Sam's next problem was with George Fitzmaurice. He was signed for RAFFLES (United Artists, 1930). Ronald Colman again had the lead. Harry D'Abbadie D'Arrast took it over. Lucky assisted both of them. Sam tried Fitzmaurice once more on ONE HEAVENLY NIGHT (United Artists, 1930). Lucky found the director more bewildering the more he worked with him. Fitzmaurice might have a grand piano in a scene for three days' shooting and, on the spur of the moment, decide to do the rest of the scene without it. Yet, should a book of matches on a coffee table be moved so much as a fraction of an inch, Fitzmaurice would throw a fit. John Boles was the star of ONE HEAVENLY NIGHT. There was a dessert scene coming up and Fitzmaurice told Lucky he wanted very unusual desserts. Lucky knew better than to try anything conventional. He arranged for the best chefs, from the Ambassador, from Maxine's, from the Pig and Whistle, from The Elite, to prepare all manner of exotic desserts. He brought them to the studio to practice their art. Fitzmaurice rejected one dessert after another. It wasn't until Goldwyn stepped in that production resumed. Fitzmaurice was still dour, though; the desserts just weren't right.

Sam became co-producer with Florenz Ziegfeld on
WHOOPEE (United Artists, 1930), using the entire New York
cast with Eddie Cantor in the lead.   Lucky assisted director
Thornton Freeland.   Alfred Newman did the songs, Busby
Berkeley the choreography.   Lucky worked closely with
Berkeley in organizing the dance numbers for the camera.
As part of the preparations, Lucky ran a newspaper adver-
tisement for girls.   He interviewed five hundred who re-
sponded.   Among those Lucky picked were Betty Grable,
Lucille Ball, Virginia Bruce, Barbara Weeks, and Paulette
Goddard.   Sam approved Lucky's selections.

King Vidor was signed to direct STREET SCENE
(United Artists, 1931).   Sylvia Sidney was the female lead.
Much of the film took place on a New York city street.   It
had to be shot outdoors.   A set was designed.   Exteriors
could only be filmed during the morning hours.   Lucky went
to Sam with an idea.   Why not build the identical set facing
the other direction?   In the afternoon, the camera could
turn.   Shooting would be done from the other side, thus
maximizing the sunlight.   Sam was excited.   The additional
set was erected.   The picture was completed in twenty-two
days.   Lucky was given a $6,000 bonus.

After STREET SCENE, Goldwyn summoned Lucky to
his office.   He informed him that John Ford had been contracted to direct ARROWSMITH (United Artists, 1931) and
that he wanted Lucky to assist.   Ford was on loan-out from
Fox Film Corporation.   Lucky was to oversee the entire
production.   If anything went wrong, he was to report it to
Sam even if Sam was sitting on the toilet.

Ronald Colman was the star.   Ford told Lucky that
he expected his assistant directors to rehearse all the day's
scenes before he arrived in the morning.   Lucky nodded.

Near the end of shooting, there was a scene in a
hotel lobby in which Ronald Colman was to exit from an
elevator.   Lucky designed the set and hired several extras
to give the scene verisimilitude to a busy hotel.   When
Ford came in, he studied Lucky as sardonically as he had
when, years before, he had watched him lug film cans
among the Vasquez rocks.

"Run through the scene," Ford demanded.

Lucky had the scene played with people milling about,

Colman leaving the elevator and making his way through the
crowd.

"Is that your conception of it?" Ford asked, when it
was over.

Lucky said it was.

Ford became dyspeptic. He demanded that everyone
get off the set. Colman was to come out of the elevator
and walk through an empty lobby. That was his conception
of the scene. And it was filmed that way.

When Lucky saw the rushes, he went to Goldwyn's
office. Sam had just fired Sam Taylor. Taylor's comment
to Lucky was laconic: "There isn't room enough for two
Sams on this lot." Goldwyn was testy. He had a reputation
for interference with his directors and especially for firing
them. Lucky told Sam that he felt Ford was mishandling
the scene. Sam had the rushes screened. He seconded
Lucky's opinion.

Goldwyn went onto the ARROWSMITH set and spoke
to Ford about the advisability of reshooting the lobby scene.
Ford listened in icy silence. When Sam finished, Ford got
up and walked off the picture. Sam, somewhat perplexed
by Ford's irascibility, suggested to Lucky that he should
phone Mary Ford and attempt to smooth it over. This got
Lucky nowhere. Mary told Lucky that Ford was in one of
those black moods where he would close himself in his library and not come out for days. She would only open the
sliding doors as long as it took to shove in a case of Scotch
and leave him alone.

Suddenly Ford vanished. Not even Mary, apparently,
had any idea where he had gone.

Lucky was asked to finish the picture. There was
very little left to do. Lucky did it under Sam's supervision.

Lowell Sherman was engaged to direct THE GREEKS
HAD A WORD FOR THEM (United Artists, 1932). Lucky
assisted. After two weeks of shooting, Sam was dissatisfied with the rushes. He confined Sherman to directing dialogue and put Lucky in charge of photography. Sherman
had been a stage director. Sam thought him too inexperienced in terms of creative use of the camera.

King Vidor had been sufficiently struck by Lucky's
work during their association on STREET SCENE to request
him as his assitant for BIRD OF PARADISE (RKO, 1932).
David O. Selznick now headed up production at RKO. BIRD
received his personal attention. After making the necessary
arrangements with Goldwyn to borrow Lucky, Vidor gave
Lucky a copy of the synopsis to read. A conference with
Selznick was set up. It started off poorly when Selznick insisted that Lucky use an RKO crew. Lucky stated that he
had his own crew and that they worked well for him on all
Sam's pictures. Selznick compromised to the extent that
Lucky could bring his own crew along provided RKO also
supplied him with a second crew, even if the latter group
did nothing on the picture. Lucky shrugged his shoulders.

Early in his association with Edmund Goulding, Lucky
had met Joseph P. Kennedy when Kennedy was producing
THE TRESPASSER (United Artists, 1929) and Goulding was
directing it. Kennedy was quite taken with Gloria Swanson,
the film's star. During his thirty-two months in Hollywood,
Kennedy managed to earn five million dollars. Little of it
came from his backing Swanson pictures or his promotion
of Fred Thomson and other Western players at Film Booking
Office; rather it was a consequence of a merger he negotiated between Film Booking Office, Pathé Pictures, the Keith-
Orpheum theatre circuit, and General Sarnoff's RCA Photo-
phone company. The new firm was called RKO Radio Pictures. Selznick was put on to create unforgettable and prestigious pictures.

He asked Lucky about suitable locations. Lucky proposed Mazatlan, or Tahiti, or, the biggest gamble, Honolulu.

"You're working with me," Selznick responded, "not
Goldwyn. Don't worry about the cost. We're going to Honolulu."

The troupe embarked for the islands. Vidor had already been there for some time. When he met Lucky, he
complained bitterly. He had hoped to find a location with
a quiet surf, white sand, and hundred-foot palm trees. For
weeks Vidor had searched the islands without success.

Lucky found a quiet beach with white sand. He contacted the chamber of commerce and received permission
to cut down fifty palm trees and transport them to the location. The trees, replanted, were held in place by wires.

Lucky phoned Vidor to tell him he had found a location.
Vidor should come and inspect it.

The wires excaped Vidor's notice. He was astonished.

"Let's shoot," Lucky said.

"There's still no script," Vidor said.

Selznick had several writers working on it, of course.
As it now stood, there was only one short scene to be
filmed. Vidor went into production on it. With the camera
close enough to mark no more than eight square feet of sand,
Dolores Del Rio and a young Joel McCrea, the stars of the
picture, were brought in. Dolores was to lie on her back
on the sand, which she did. McCrea came into camera
range, fell on top of her, and Vidor yelled "Cut!"

Then it began to rain. For fifty-five days it rained.
Lucky kept calling Selznick back on the coast. Selznick kept
telling Lucky to stay put. The same fifty-five days and no
script. Finally, Selznick gave in and recommended that the
troupe return to the mainland until such a time as a script
was actually completed. Everyone packed up.

The day before he was to depart, Lucky received a
cable from Sam Bischoff, head of production at a small independent producing company called Tiffany. The cable indicated that Bischoff wanted Lucky to direct a picture for him.
He offered Lucky $1,500 to do it and assured him of the
fact that, upon arrival on the mainland, he could secure his
release. Lucky showed the cable to King Vidor.

"Why don't you do it?" Vidor asked.

"Because I'm making $25,000 a year as an assistant,"
Lucky returned. "Why should I quit to make $1,500 flat?"

"Do it anyway," Vidor said. "It's a chance to direct
your own picture."

Lucky thought it over. He cabled Bischoff.

"If script meets my approval," he wired, "I can get
immediate release."

I started closing reference books.

"What are you doing?" Lucky asked.

"It's late," I said.   "We've been at it nearly eight hours. "

"Eight hours," Lucky echoed me, "and you haven't even got me past my assistant director days. "

"I call a time out," Vicki said, honking softly.

"A good idea," Lucky agreed.   Soon he was mixing drinks.   "You know who I met on the boat on the way back from Honolulu?   I was walking along the deck at night and I ran into Mary Ford.   'Mary,' I said, 'what are you doing here?'   'I had to go to the Orient to get Jack,' she said. He hadn't been in Hollywood since he walked off ARROW-SMITH. "

Lucky laughed.

"And it wasn't a picture he was coming back for. Roosevelt was threatening to take us off the gold standard if he was elected.   Mary told me Jack had a million dollars in gold in safe deposit boxes.   She could only get him to come back out of fear of what Roosevelt might do. "

We chatted pleasantly for another half hour.   I mentioned to Lucky that we were off next day to visit with Howard Hawks in Palm Springs.

"He's one of the three best we've ever had out here," Lucky said.   "Howard Hawks, Jack Ford, and Henry King. "

Almost a week intervened before again we saw Lucky. Much had happened in the interim and he was curious to learn about all of it.

"Should we finish tonight," Lucky said, "I want you people to come back, just to visit. "

"We will," Vicki said.

Lucky put the small horn in front of her.   "Where were we?" he asked.

"Aboard ship," Vicki answered.

"Okay," Lucky said, "find your place, then. Aboard
ship. Yes, well, I decided to take Vidor's advice. I
wanted to direct. But I was intent on its being the right
picture with which to start on what amounted to a new career."

III

When Lucky's boat docked, Sam Bischoff was waiting
for him with a copy of the script. The screenplay was
based on Tiffany Thayer's story, "Strangers of the Evening."
Bischoff wanted to film it in a style similar to that of
FRANKENSTEIN (Universal, 1931). Lucky took the script
home with him.

The next time they met, Lucky told Sam he would do
the picture if he could treat it as a comedy.

"You maybe don't remember it," Bischoff said, "but
I worked with you when you were an assistant on BEN-HUR.
I promised myself then that if I was ever a producer, I
wanted you to direct for me."

Bischoff offered Lucky a contract. Lucky got Sam to
agree that should Bischoff sell the contract to anyone else,
Lucky was to receive 50% of whatever it was sold for. Zasu
Pitts was given top billing even though she did not appear
until midway through the film and had a relatively small
part. Eugene Pallette, who had been portraying Sergeant
Heath in Paramount's popular Philo Vance photoplay series,
was cast as the police sergeant.

It was an offbeat picture, later reissued under the
title THE HIDDEN CORPSE. Some of the humor is obviously intentional, but some of it not. The production schedule
was limited to nine days. It was a short film. But most
scenes consisted of only master shots with no intercuts,
making it seem longish today, however consistent this may
have been with the prevailing techniques of the time. Lucky
devised the hand pantomime for Zasu Pitts' routines. She
retained it as part of her screen personality. Pallette was
given an opportunity for genuine comedy, not always at his
own expense as it was in the Philo Vance films.

Joe Brandt, impressed with Zasu's performance,

signed her for another picture to be called THE CROOKED
CIRCLE (WorldWide, 1932).

Sam Bischoff had become Harry Cohn's production
supervisor at Columbia in 1928.   Tiffany Productions, which
emerged in 1929, became part of E. W. Hammons' Educational Pictures conglomerate.   Bischoff directed several
short comedies for Hammons before Hammons appointed him
production manager for the Tiffany subsidiary in 1931.
Shortly after STRANGERS OF THE EVENING was released,
Bischoff decided to set up his own production company.   He
went into a partnership with Burt Kelly and William Saal and
the three called the company KBS Productions after their ini-
tials.   The films of the new outfit were still physically distributed through the Educational exchanges.

Joe Brandt had started in the industry as a secretary
to Carl Laemmle at Universal.   In 1921, he joined Harry
and Jack Cohn in founding CBC Productions, which soon became Columbia Pictures.   Disgusted by the perpetual fighting
between the Cohn brothers, Brandt finally sold out to Harry
Cohn in February 1932.   By May 1932 Joe took his money
and invested it in E. W. Hammons' floundering conglomerate.
He was given the title of president of WorldWide Pictures
and the added title of vice president of Educational Pictures.
In November 1932 Brandt resigned.   THE CROOKED CIRCLE
was made during his rather brief tenure.

Zasu Pitts asked for Lucky as her director on THE
CROOKED CIRCLE.   It was supposed to be a mystery-
comedy with Ben Lyon, C. Henry Gordon, and James Gleason as a motorcycle cop.   But Gleason injected so much
comedy that the haunted house theme receded into the background.   C. Henry Gordon played a swami who was actually
a secret serviceman in disguise.   The dialogue was poor.
The picture took fourteen days to shoot.

E. W. Hammons, in a desperate move, sold off his
exchange network to Ray Johnston and Trem Carr.   Trem
Carr had been producing extremely cheap Westerns for
Tiffany-WorldWide release.   Carr and Johnston now founded
Monogram Pictures.   They devised a new Western series
starring young John Wayne and hired Yakima Canutt to stunt
and handle all the action.   Hammons signed an agreement
with the Fox Film Corporation in 1933 for them to distribute
Educational product through the Fox exchanges.   Sam Bischoff, discouraged by all of Hammons' manipulations, chucked
KBS and joined Warner Brothers as a production supervisor.

For the moment, Lucky was out of a job. Tiffany
Thayer was among the contributors to an unusual production
at Paramount titled IF I HAD A MILLION (Paramount, 1932).
The picture was to consist of several episodes, each directed by an important director from Paramount's roster,
detailing what happens to a number of persons who at random have been selected to inherit a million dollars by an
eccentric millionaire on his death bed.   The story eventually
became the basis for a successful television series.   Paramount signed Lucky to a short-term contract.   Emmanuel
Cohen was currently in charge of the studio.   It was suggested that perhaps Lucky's first assignment should be Mae
West's SHE DONE HIM WRONG (Paramount, 1933).   Mae
specifically wanted Lowell Sherman to direct it.   Lucky had,
of course, once assisted Sherman.   After Mae's small part
in NIGHT AFTER NIGHT (Paramount, 1932) made the picture
a hit, she got her way.   Lucky was handed the George Raft
episode for IF I HAD A MILLION.

Paramount wanted to promote Raft.   His physical re-
semblance to Valentino had been emphasized in NIGHT AFTER
NIGHT.   He played a check forger in IF I HAD A MILLION.
Lucky felt a sense of challenge in that Ernst Lubitsch and
Josef von Sternberg had both contributed episodes and his
work would be judged along with theirs.   Upon release,
Lucky was praised.   Cohen felt Lucky ready for a big picture
and so he gave him KING OF THE JUNGLE (Paramount,
1933).

Originally, Paramount had wanted Cecil B. DeMille
to direct it.   DeMille wasn't interested.   Frightened by the
magnitude of the undertaking, Lucky nonetheless consented.
Buster Crabbe was the star.   The story had a circus setting.
Arrangements were made to use the Barnum and Bailey Circus.   This required erecting sound stages near the river
bottom where the circus was camped.   Much shooting had to
be done at night.   The picture ran way over schedule and
far exceeded its budget.

Cohen, upon occasion, would summon Lucky to his
office to explain the delays.

"Lions aren't actors," Lucky said.   "Sometimes you
have to run through a scene a dozen times before it's right."

Paramount was teetering on financial ruin.   Lucky's
option, after KING OF THE JUNGLE, was not renewed.

The night the picture opened, Los Angeles was hit by a de-
vastating earthquake. Lucky made a pact with himself that
he wouldn't attempt to direct any picture again which he
didn't feel was right for him.

RKO Radio did at last finish BIRD OF PARADISE,
but by then Selznick had returned to Metro-Goldwyn-Mayer.
In eary 1933, Lucky joined RKO briefly as a contract director. He was given the script to THE LOST PATROL
(RKO, 1934), but declined. He thought only Bill Wellman or
John Ford could do justice to the picture. Lucky did make
GOODBYE LOVE (RKO, 1933) with Charles Ruggles, Verree
Teasdale, and Sidney Blackmer, a semi-comedy about female golddiggers. He was unhappy with it. RKO kept
throwing scripts at him. Lucky kept rejecting them. Warner Brothers then approached him with a proposed two-
picture contract with them. Lucky accepted. The trades
termed Lucky's departure from RKO a "walk-out."

The first picture Lucky directed was MERRY WIVES
OF RENO (Warner's, 1934), on which Bob Lord was the production supervisor. It featured Margaret Lindsay, Donald
Woods, and Guy Kibbee. The comic plotline sought to dem-
onstrate that divorce could be amusing.

Hal B. Wallis, in charge of production at Warner
Brothers, was impressed with the film. He summoned
Lucky to his office and handed him a screenplay titled THE
DRAGON MURDER CASE. It was a Philo Vance story the
studio had purchased when William Powell was under contract. Powell had now signed with M-G-M. He had played
Philo Vance in all but one of the American photoplays based
on S. S. Van Dine's novels. Now a new Philo Vance would
have to be found.

"This is going to be your next picture," Wallis informed Humberstone.

Lucky took the script home and read it. He showed
up the next day and told Wallis, no. He knew that Michael
Curtiz, Archie Mayo, Mervyn LeRoy, and Alfred Green had
all turned the picture down; and more, he knew why. It
was a terrible story. Lucky disappeared from the studio and
went out of town. While resting in a hotel, Wallis called
him. He said that the writers had gone to work on THE
DRAGON MURDER CASE and had really improved it. He
should return to the lot at once. Lucky did.

When he walked into Wallis' office, he was handed the same yellow-covered script he had been given before.

"I won't do it," he protested.

Wallis made an appointment for Lucky to see Jack L. Warner personally. Ushered into Warner's office, Warner studied the new director.

"How much are you making?" he asked.

"Seven hundred and fifty dollars a week," Lucky replied.

"How old are you?" Warner asked.

"Twenty-nine," Lucky said.

"Do you know how much I was making when I was your age?" Warner asked. "Twenty-five bucks a week, selling meat." He paused for emphasis. "So, why don't you want to make this picture?"

"Because it's a lousy story," Lucky responded.

"Listen," said Warner, "I don't care if it is a lousy story. You're going to make this picture. Do you think it matters that it's lousy? That picture, with my theatre chain, is going to make me fifty thousand dollars, good story or not. So you're going to make it for me. Or," he paused again for emphasis, "or you're never going to direct another picture in this town. "

Lucky agreed to direct the picture.

I have written elsewhere that THE DRAGON MURDER CASE (First National, 1934) is my own preference among the Philo Vance films. Lucky's creative use of tropical fish in the aquarium rooms spurred a national interest in collecting them and, for a time, Lucky himself became an enthusiast. Warren William was cast as Vance, Eugene Pallette returning as Sergeant Heath. Margaret Lindsay and Lyle Talbot provided the love interest. The picture was budgeted at $320,000 and became one of the top releases that year for First National, by now a Warner's subsidiary.

For the première, Lucky had his agent invite most

of the noteworthy producers then in Hollywood to attend.
The picture was extremely well-received. Jack Warner col-
lared him afterwards, saying, "Humberstone, don't sign with
any of these guys. We want you. " But a few days later the
trades carried a story about how H. Bruce Humberstone had
"walked out" of Warner Brothers. Lucky was once more
without a job.

Months went past and nothing turned up. It was
more than half a year since THE DRAGON MURDER CASE
when Lucky's agent told him to report for an interview with
Sol Wurtzel, head of production at Fox Film Corporation.
Wurtzel said he knew all about Lucky's stubborn streak and
the problems he had had at RKO and then Warner's. But
he was willing to give him a chance on a detective story
slated for immediate production. Lucky would be working
for Fox on a per picture basis.

LADIES LOVE DANGER (Fox, 1935) starred Gilbert
Roland as a playwright and amateur sleuth, with Mona Barrie and Donald Cook in support. Robert Ellis and Helen
Logan, subsequently associated on so many of Lucky's pictures in the years ahead, did the screen adaptation. Variety,
in its review, praised Lucky: "More than ordinary credit
should go to H. B. Humberstone for his direction which
never overlooks a point in developing suspense. "

Wurtzel at once gave Lucky a script for SILK HAT
KID (Fox, 1935). It had a complicated plot with Lew Ayres
as a bodyguard for cafe owner Paul Kelly. On the whole it
was a pedestrian affair.

Lucky then went to Metro to make THREE LIVE
GHOSTS (M-G-M, 1936), with Richard Arlen and Beryl Mercer as Arlen's greedy, gin-drinking mother who turns in
Arlen's best friend for the reward money. Lucky had depicted a somewhat lunatic mother in THE DRAGON MURDER
CASE, but Beryl Mercer was the epitome of an unsentimental,
if not wholly unsympathetic, characterization. Variety lauded
Humberstone for his direction, though another trade paper
complained that it was unsavory to see a mother figure so
dependent on alcohol to get on in life.

"But that was nothing, " Lucky commented, "compared to working with Warner Oland, who was only good as
Charlie Chan if he was stoned. "

Vicki sat forward and honked.

"The lady needs a break," I said.

"I can't get over the fact that you people are whiskey drinkers," Lucky said, standing in front of his built-in bar. "Everyone out here is a Vodka drinker. The women started it, in pictures. Vodka doesn't give you a liquor breath."

"With all the drinking I've been doing on these interviews," Vicki said, "it's not my breath I'm worrying about."

Lucky set down our glasses and fixed himself another tumbler of Vodka martinis. He bummed a cigarette from Vicki and we resumed.

Twentieth Century Pictures was formed early in 1933. Joseph Schenck, brother to Nicholas Schenck, president of M-G-M, set up the producing company and recruited Darryl F. Zanuck from Warner Brothers to be head of production. Louis B. Mayer's money was behind the venture. At lunch at the Brown Derby on 18 April 1933, Joe Schenck closed the deal by giving Zanuck a check for $100,000, signed by Mayer. Mayer wanted his son-in-law William Goetz to become involved in his own production company. Goetz' official position was that of being Zanuck's assistant.

Joe Schenck was president of United Artists. Since the original founders of the company--principally Charlie Chaplin, Mary Pickford, and Douglas Fairbanks--had cut back on new production, or ceased altogether, it was up to Sam Goldwyn and now Darryl Zanuck to provide the bulk of the pictures for the United Artists' releasing schedule. Zanuck's films, with a single exception, were extraordinarily successful. Schenck, restless at United Artists, approached Sidney R. Kent, president of the failing Fox Film Corporation. Fox had one of the finest distribution networks in the country. The two companies merged, becoming Twentieth Century-Fox. Zanuck was in charge of "A" picture production. Sol Wurtzel, who had been with Fox in various capacities since 1915, supervised the "B" unit.

The Charlie Chan films with Warner Oland were one of Fox's most successful series. Sol Wurtzel engaged Lucky to direct CHARLIE CHAN AT THE RACE TRACK (20th-Fox, 1936). Robert Ellis and Helen Logan worked on the screenplay; John Stone was the associate producer. Oland had long

been a heavy drinker. During the racing sequence, shot on
location at the Santa Anita race track, Warner disappeared
and the entire crew set out to find him. He was in a dead
sleep in the track restaurant. Lucky wanted an intercut
shot of Warner supposedly watching the horse race, but
Warner kept dozing off. Yet, for all that, Lucky encouraged
Oland to keep slightly inebriated throughout his scenes.
Watching rushes, Warner had to agree that alcohol improved
his characterization. A sterling actor, when sober he re-
cited his lines too quickly; alcohol fogged his memory and it
seemed, on screen at least, as if the Oriental detective was
grappling with a difficult, alien language when he was only
groping for a line. Lucky started casting Jimmy Flavin
regularly in character roles in his films, regarding Jimmy
as sort of a good luck charm. RACE TRACK did business
and was well-received. Wurtzel used Lucky again for
CHARLIE CHAN AT THE OPERA (20th-Fox, 1937).

It was Lucky's idea to cast Boris Karloff as an am-
nesiac opera singer in the film. Initially, Wurtzel resisted
the notion because of the added expense, but Lucky won out
and the picture was a hit. In its production, Lucky utilized
several of the elaborate sets Zanuck had had built for E. H.
Griffith's CAFE METROPOLE (20th-Fox, 1937). Griffith had
shot most of his scenes in extreme close-up. When Zanuck
saw the production value the sets brought to OPERA, he remarked to both Wurtzel and Bill Dover, Darryl's right-hand
man: "This son-of-a-bitch, Humberstone, is making my
'A' directors look sick turning out a 'B' that looks like this.
Put him under contract." Wurtzel did.

CHARLIE CHAN AT THE OLYMPICS (20th-Fox, 1937)
was Lucky's first picture under his contract. Once more it
was an excellent entry, with varying locales and an expert
use of stock footage of everything from a Zepplin to the
Olympic games of 1936 in Germany. C. Henry Gordon was
prominently cast as a murder suspect.

CHECKERS (20th-Fox, 1938) came next. John Stone
was the associate producer. Lynn Root and Frank Fenton,
who would later work on the Falcon series at RKO in the
'forties, did the screenplay. The story had a horse-racing
background. The trades praised both Lucky and John Stone
for saving the picture from banality.

At three o'clock one morning Bill Dover called Lucky
at his home to congratulate him. Dover told him that Darryl

had decided Lucky was to make no more "B" pictures and
he wanted to see him at his office at ten the next day.
When Lucky showed up, Zanuck explained through clouds of
cigar smoke that Henry King was presently reading the script
for a major production entitled IN OLD CHICAGO.   Zanuck
had just purchased screen rights for HEIDI.   He now wanted
to give King HEIDI and put Lucky on IN OLD CHICAGO.
Lucky was optimistic.   IN OLD CHICAGO was budgeted at
nearly two million dollars.   Since Irving Thalberg had died,
Darryl Zanuck was generally considered the most consistent
production chief in the industry.   Both Hal B. Wallis and
David O. Selznick were brilliant makers of individual films,
but Zanuck alone, it would appear in retrospect, could make
fine films in quantity.   Zanuck was responsible for producing
one picture every twelve days.   Three of every four of
Zanuck's "A" productions made an impressive profit.   Lucky
was happy at the prospect of joining Zanuck's inner circle.

     Henry King balked.   He told Zanuck that unless he
was permitted to make IN OLD CHICAGO, he would walk out
on his contract.   Zanuck argued and negotiated.   He finally
worked a compromise.   King would direct the film until the
cow kicks over the lantern; from that point on, Lucky was
to direct the fire sequences and all the special effects.
King agreed.   Most of the reviews singled out the special
effects for high praise.   Lucky's next assignment was
RASCALS (20th-Fox, 1938) with Jane Withers and Robert
Wilcox.

     Both The Hollywood Reporter and Variety customarily
extracted a substantial portion of their income through ad-
vertisements sold to people in the industry.   The pressure
was tremendous for one seeking his livelihood in the picture
business to buy space; even reviews might improve.   Lucky
allotted $2,000 a year for each of them.   He was coerced
into running an ad credit for himself for directing the fire
in IN OLD CHICAGO (20th-Fox, 1938).

     At the Academy Awards, IN OLD CHICAGO was nom-
inated for Best Picture.   Alice Brady was nominated for
Best Supporting Actress for the picture.   Niven Busch was
nominated for the Best Original Story.   E. H. Hanson won
an Oscar for Best Sound Recording.   And Robert Webb won
an Oscar as assistant director on the film.

     In those days, the Academy was unable to nominate
for Best Director two or more directors who had worked on

a single picture. Although Henry King was credited as the
director of IN OLD CHICAGO, he felt Lucky's ads in the
trades had been the reason for his losing the nomination.
Angry and hurt, perhaps somewhat understandably he tried
to get Zanuck to force Lucky to print a retraction of his ad-
vertisements. This Lucky refused to do. Zanuck pointed
out to King that, after all, Lucky had directed the special
effects. One night, King followed Lucky all the way out of
the studio lot, heaping abuse on him for his obstinacy. Next
day, King confronted Darryl, telling him flatly that either
Humberstone was to leave or he would.

       "I've no choice," Zanuck explained to Lucky.   "Henry
King is the best director I have working for me."

       Lucky apparently was out of a contract and out of a
job.

       The production schedule had called originally for
Lucky to start shooting PASSPORT HUSBAND for Sol Wurtzel
on 21 March 1938. His "suspension" postponed production
until 9 May 1938, with James Tinling directing.

       It was in May that Lucky telephoned Bill Goetz and
asked him if it was safe for him to return. Goetz expressed
his disapproval of what happened and assured Lucky he would
fix it with Zanuck.

       Lucky came back, but he was again a "B" unit di-
rector. His first assignment was the pilot picture for a
new detective series, TIME OUT FOR MURDER (20th-Fox,
1938). Irving Rice, who subsequently worked on the Falcon
films, did the original story. Michael Whalen played a roving reporter, with Chick Chandler for comic support, June
Gale and Jean Rogers, the latter a graduate of FLASH GOR-
DON (Universal, 1936), and Cliff Clark as a dumb cop.
The picture proved a success and was rapidly followed by a
second entry, WHILE NEW YORK SLEEPS (20th-Fox, 1939).
This time Jean Rogers and June Gale switched roles, with
Jean in the female lead. Chick Chandler was cast in the
same part. Lynn Root and Frank Fenton did the original
screenplay, creating the comically stupid police team of
Cliff Clark and Edward Gargan that eventually became a fixture when they were scripting the Falcon series. The
trades singled out Lucky's direction as accounting "for an
easy fluidity of narrative."

Warner Oland, on a visit to his home town in Sweden, fell ill with pneumonia and died in his mother's bed. His passing came as a great shock to everyone, nowhere more so than at Fox. The current Charlie Chan picture was three days into production, awaiting his return. It was changed into a Mr. Moto film with Peter Lorre.

A search was mounted to find a new screen Chan. Without Warner, Keye Luke no longer wanted to continue and asked that his contract not be renewed. After much testing, character actor Sidney Toler was given the role of Charlie, while Victor Sen Young was cast as his Number Two son, Jimmy Chan. Sol Wurtzel asked Lucky to direct the first Toler entry, CHARLIE CHAN IN HONOLULU (20th-Fox, 1939). Lucky was dissatisfied with Sidney's performance and suggested Toler try the part after a few stiff jolts. Sidney was also a heavy drinker. Alcohol had almost as beneficial an influence on his interpretation as it had had on Warner's. HONOLULU may have been, in the final analysis, the finest Chan film that Sidney Toler made. Much of it was set on a ship and a lion figured prominently in the action.

PARDON OUR NERVE (20th-Fox, 1939) was third in Fox's "Big Town Girl" series, praised by the trades as the best so far in laughs and suspense due to Lucky's direction. Robert Ellis and Helen Logan did the screenplay. Michael Whalen appeared in a featured role with Lynn Bari and June Gale as the female leads.

Lynn Bari was back for PACK UP YOUR TROUBLES (20th-Fox, 1939), which starred Jane Withers and the Ritz Brothers. Critics claimed that the film was the most hilarious farce on the Great War since TWO ARABIAN NIGHTS (United Artists, 1927) from the silent era, directed for Howard Hughes by Lewis Milestone.

"I've got something special for you, Humberstone," Sol Wurtzel told Lucky after completion of PACK UP YOUR TROUBLES. "You're going to make a Cisco Kid picture for me. I'm even going to name it after you."

"That would be LUCKY CISCO KID (20th-Fox, 1940)," I said, consulting one of several reference books piled around my chair.

"You've got the title right," Lucky said, "but it can't

be that year.   I think it was 1938. "

        "Nope, " I said.   "The picture was released on 28
June 1940. "

        "Then that book is wrong, " Lucky insisted.

        "Cesar Romero was Cisco, " I said.   "It has to be
1940. "

        "Well, it can't be, " Lucky retorted.

        Lucky got up and walked over to the coffee table in
front of Vicki and picked up her package of cigarettes.

        "Don't worry, " she said.   "I have more in my
purse. "

        Lucky lit a cigarette.   He studied her empty glass.
"Why didn't you honk?" he asked her.

        "I was wondering which to do first, " Vicki said,
smiling.   "Honk, or ask to go to the bathroom. "

        After some discussion, it was determined that Vicki
should go to the bathroom, Lucky would make another round,
and I was to find another volume among all the reference
books that gave a 1938 release year for LUCKY CISCO KID.
Ten minutes later, we all had refills.   Vicki sat poised with
her pen and notebook.

        "I dislike having to let everyone down, " I said, "but
I'm afraid 1940 is the year. "

        "That can't be, " Lucky returned.   "Then all those
books are wrong. "

        "Let's just hope, " said Vicki, lifting her drink and
sipping from it, "that I'm within ten years of the release
date when I come to transcribe my notes. "

        Lucky's next assignment was THE QUARTERBACK
(Paramount, 1940), on loan-out.   The picture was a comedy
in which Wayne Morris played twins and Virginia Dale was
the girl.

        When he returned to Fox this time, Lucky was allowed

to join Darryl Zanuck's "A" unit. Sol Wurtzel had become
embroiled in personal problems which led to his termination
from the company. The friction with Henry King was forgotten. Lucky was given TALL, DARK AND HANDSOME
(20th-Fox, 1941) to make. It starred Cesar Romero, Virginia Gilmore, Milton Berle, and Sheldon Leonard. In it,
Romero played a soft-hearted gangster, with Berle as his
chief assistant and Leonard as the head of a rival gang. It
is one of the films of which Lucky is quite proud. He perfected a camera technique for it that he had first used in
CHARLIE CHAN AT THE RACE TRACK. The camera would
whip from right to left or left to right at the end of one
scene and into the next scene. It gave the picture an ac-
celerated tempo. Zanuck was so impressed by the effect
that he invited all of his directors to a private screening to
witness the results.

     Darryl and Virginia Zanuck went on vacation at Sun
Valley. Lucky was invited along as Darryl's guest. While
there, Zanuck came to think the location ideal for a skating
picture with Sonja Henie, one of the novelties then under
contract. Darryl left Lucky in the Valley and sent up two
writers to join him to devise a story. Robert Ellis and
Helen Logan were the writers. Lucky felt it an apt opportunity to make use of Glenn Miller and his Orchestra, then
the foremost performing band in the country.

     SUN VALLEY SERENADE (20th-Fox, 1941), in addi-
tion to Miller (it was his second and last picture) and Henie
(it was supposed to be her last picture), featured John Payne,
Milton Berle, and the Nicholas Brothers. The film had
seven hit songs of which "Chatanooga Choo-Choo" with a
dance routine by the Nicholas Brothers was far and away
the show stopper. Some of the plot ingredients for Sonja
Henie were developed by story department head Julian Johnson and associate producer Harry Joe Brown together with
S. S. Van Dine, work which was terminated by the detective
story writer's death in 1939; the most important of them
was Henie's ballet on black ice. The picture opened to a
heartening box-office. It set the tone for a whole series of
excellent Fox musicals. And it acted as such a catalyst
for Sonja Henie's slumping career that Darryl, who hoped
he would be rid of her, was compelled finally to send Joe
Schenck to New York to negotiate a new three-picture deal
with the skater.

     Lucky read the story I Wake up Screaming by Steve

Fisher which Zanuck had scheduled for production. Lucky
wanted to direct it.   Zanuck demurred on the grounds that
Lucky was best at musicals and this was to be a psychological murder mystery.   Lucky persisted.   At last, Darryl
gave in.   Betty Grable and Victor Mature were to be the
stars.   In the novel, Fisher had based his character of the
psychopathic cop Cornell on Cornell Woolrich.   Lucky cast
rotund Laird Cregar in the role.

Lucky Humberstone with his head next to the camera, third
from left, directing a scene from I WAKE UP SCREAMING
(20th-Fox, 1941), with Victor Mature and Betty Grable.
Photo courtesy of the Museum of Modern Art.

There was no ending to the picture when it was
screened one night for the executives, including Zanuck,
Virginia, Otto Preminger, Harry Joe Brown, and Humberstone.   Zanuck took Virginia out to her car and returned to
the screening room afterwards.   He had had an idea.

"Humberstone," he said, "there are only two things
wrong with this picture, as it stands.   One: it is a Betty
Grable picture in black and white.   That's bad enough.   But,
second: the exhibitors will never sit still for a Grable picture where she doesn't sing one song!"

"But, Darryl," Humberstone objected, "you yourself said this was a psychological murder mystery. She can't sing. It wouldn't be consistent with the whole thrust of the picture."

"Listen," Zanuck said, sweeping all that aside with a wave of his cigar, "I've got the perfect ending. The camera, in the last scene, pans into the basement of a busy department store, with dozens of extras running around, buying things, and so on. It tracks in to a close shot of Grable, sitting at a piano, singing a number. She works there, see, and this is the happy ending: her singing a song for the customers."

Lucky went out and shot the scene as Zanuck wanted it. It was spliced into the work print and screened again for the executives. Once more Zanuck took Virginia out to her car, when it was over, and returned, gloomily shaking his head.

"Humberstone, Virginia agrees with me," he said gravely. "You've got to be crazy to have Grable singing at the end of a picture like this. It's a psychological picture. It doesn't fit. Get a new ending."

Lucky didn't bother with remonstrance. He went home and thought and thought about how to end the picture. Near dawn, he fell asleep. And he had a dream. The next morning he rushed into Zanuck's office.

"I've got the ending," he said confidently.

"What is it?" Zanuck asked.

Lucky began, "Laird Cregar is a screwy cop. He has photos and ads of Carole Landis, the murdered girl, all over his apartment. Vic Mature goes there, to the apartment, at the end of the picture, and he sees this. He meets Cregar, who's coming home with some flowers to put beneath his shrine to Landis. Mature tells him that they've caught Elisha Cook and that he's confessed everything, including how Laird had him cover up. Cregar takes poison and dies. That's how the picture ends, with Laird dying, a suicide, surrounded by all the pictures of Landis. He was in love with her, but afraid to say anything once she became a celebrity."

"That's great!" Zanuck exclaimed. "Why didn't you

think of it before this? You've held up production almost two weeks on this picture. "

"Because I just dreamed it," Lucky said.

"You dreamed it!" Zanuck said sarcastically.

But that's how the picture ended. When Lucky first told me about it, I asked him if he knew that Laird Cregar had committed suicide in 1945 by taking an overdose of seconal. He didn't. He was astonished. But it had happened. Maybe he had foreseen it. Raymond Burr, who admired Laird and sought to emulate his screen work, got his chance to appear in the non-official remake of I WAKE UP SCREAMING (20th-Fox, 1941)--PITFALL (United Artists, 1948), which starred Dick Powell and Lizabeth Scott.

Darryl Zanuck bought screen rights to WILD GEESE CALLING for $400,000. He wanted Lucky to direct it. Lucky read the script and told Darryl it was a lousy story. Zanuck grew arched. He insisted that Lucky do the picture. At seven o'clock one morning on the way to the studio, driving through Coldwater Canyon, a landslide came down on Lucky's car. He skidded. His head went through the windsheild. In the process, his nose came off and had to be grafted back onto his face. Lucky was hospitalized.

Zanuck said, "That son-of-a-bitch Humberstone will do anything to get out of a picture. "

Months later, Zanuck, after talking to New York, told Lucky what a poor showing the picture had at the box office.

"I did it," Zanuck commented, "just to meet my quota. "

The property Lucky wanted was TO THE SHORES OF TRIPOLI (20th-Fox, 1942). He asked Zanuck to buy it, once he was back to work.

"But you don't know anything about the Marines," Zanuck protested.

"By the time we finish the picture," Lucky said, "we'll be at war. "

Zanuck, who was a personal friend of Franklin D.
Roosevelt, scoffed at the idea.

"Okay, Humberstone," he said.   "I'm going to teach
you a lesson.   You start shooting in ten weeks."

The conference was interrupted by Lew Schreiber,
Fox casting director, who wished to remind Darryl that
Randolph Scott's contract was up.   Zanuck was all for letting
Scott go.   Lucky said he wanted him for TRIPOLI.   Darryl
renewed Scott's contract.

Shooting began at Camp Pendleton.   The troupe returned to the studio for a number of interiors and then went
back to Camp Pendleton to do the equivalent of a West Point
graduation.   Lucky was given only a six-minute notice to
clear out one day because the camp had to be evacuated.
Shooting was resumed at the studio for two days when Milton
Sperling, the nominal producer on the picture, told Lucky to
wrap up the company.   Sperling, viewing the rushes of men
marching this way and that, was convinced that the picture
Lucky was making was a bomb.   Lucky walked off the set.
Zanuck summoned Humberstone back to the studio for a
screening of the assembled rushes.   Darryl loved it.   In
three more days, TRIPOLI was completed.   Sperling was
taken off the picture and Zanuck became the producer.   The
last day of production was 7 December 1941.   Seven months
after release, Bill Goetz presented Lucky with a check for
$25,000.

"It was decided some time ago by the board of directors," he said, "that the first Twentieth Century-Fox
film to net a million dollars would earn its director a
$25,000 bonus.   TRIPOLI was the first."

William LeBaron, Mae West's producer at Paramount
in the 'thirties, was Lucky's producer for his next picture,
ICELAND (20th-Fox, 1942).   It starred Sonja Henie and was
scripted along the lines of SUN VALLEY SERENADE, this
time featuring Sammy Kaye and his Orchestra.   John Payne
was again the male lead with Jack Oakie and Jimmy Flavin
among the supporting players.

HELLO FRISCO, HELLO (20th-Fox, 1943) started out
to be a remake of IN OLD CHICAGO, but ended up a much
lighter type of musical comedy.   Alice Faye was the star,
supported by John Payne, Lynn Bari, Jack Oakie, and Laird

Cregar. It was old home week for Lucky. Milton Sperling was credited as the producer, although he was already enlisted in the service.

Like HELLO FRISCO, HELLO, Lucky's next picture, PIN-UP GIRL (20th-Fox, 1944), was in Technicolor. If it wasn't Betty Grable's best picture, it was nonetheless responsible for a large measure of her war-time fame as a result of the cheese-cake still of her, in a white sharkskin bathing suit with her curvaceous backside turned enticingly toward the camera, released as publicity for the film. American servicemen all over the world took to patting her bottom for luck before every dangerous mission, or merely for the fun of it. John Harvey, Martha Raye, and Eugene Pallette were featured in the cast. William LeBaron was the producer.

Darryl was in the military, but off and on he was running the studio, although technically Bill Goetz had replaced him. Zanuck offered Lucky a chance to do SOMETHING FOR THE BOYS, Mike Todd's Broadway hit. Lucky refused to do it. Darryl told Lucky that if he could find an outside picture of comparable stature, he'd let him off the hook. Lucky landed WONDER MAN (RKO Radio, 1945) for Sam Goldwyn, starring Danny Kaye, Virginia Mayo, and featuring Vera-Ellen in some exceptional tap dance routines. The film proved a hit and Lucky was singled out for his directorial contribution.

Darryl was getting fed up with Lucky's pickiness, especially as his contract was up for renewal. Zanuck had offered Lucky THUNDER BIRDS (20th-Fox, 1942). Lucky had refused it. Zanuck got William Wellman to make it, provided he also gave Wellman THE OX-BOW INCIDENT (20th-Fox, 1943), a picture Wellman really wanted to make. Humberstone persisted in being highly selective about what pictures he would or would not direct. Darryl demoted Lucky to the "B" unit until his contract ran out. He had his choice of scripts. Lucky chose WITHIN THESE WALLS (20th-Fox, 1945). Production was begun with Thomas Mitchell and Mary Anderson in the lead roles. Lucky decided to use Mark Stevens from the roster of Fox contract players as the romantic lead. The role established Stevens as a comer. Zanuck was affected by the reports he received that Humberstone, no matter what the budget, was simply incapable of making a "B" picture that looked like a "B" picture. Zanuck gave in with a sigh of resignation. Lucky's option was renewed for three years at $3,000 a week.

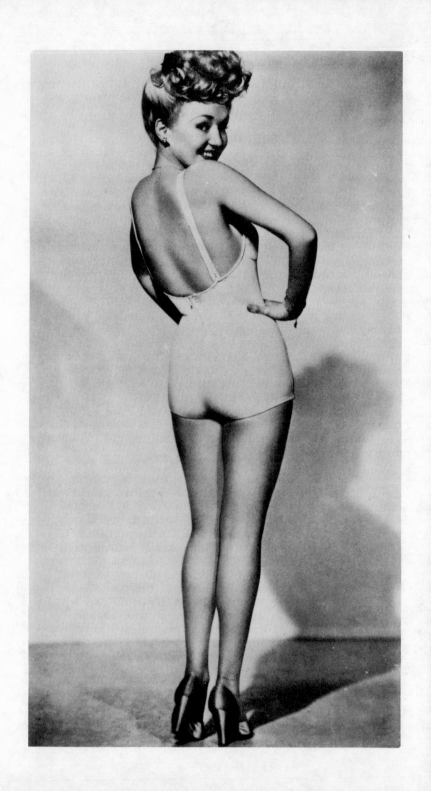

After a ten-week stint on loan-out to Columbia to do preliminary work on THE JOLSON STORY (Columbia, 1946), the first film Lucky was to make under his new Fox contract was THE HOMESTRETCH. Fate intervened. Zanuck asked Lucky to join him in screening rushes from THREE LITTLE GIRLS IN BLUE (20th-Fox, 1946), by then some forty days in production. Lucky told Darryl that he thought the problem not with the director but with the casting. He recommended the picture be started over with wholly different leading men. Zanuck agreed, provided Lucky direct it with a cast of his own choosing. Vivian Blaine, Vera-Ellen, and June Haver made up the trio of women who set out to find millionaire husbands. Celeste Holm made her debut in the picture. Robert Ellis and Helen Logan worked on the screenplay. Mack Gordon was the producer. The story later served as the basis for HOW TO MARRY A MILLIONAIRE (20th-Fox, 1953), directed by Jean Negulesco, with Betty Grable, Marilyn Monroe and Lauren Bacall.

HOMESTRETCH followed in production back to back. The picture had a horse-racing setting and several famous tracks were used as locations. The action was set in 1938. The conflict was between the principals, Cornel Wilde and Maureen O'Hara, but Jimmy Gleason in the comic role of a trainer nearly stole the picture.

Darryl had promised Lucky a vacation if he would get both pictures out consecutively without a break. Lucky went to Palm Springs. Almost four months went past before George Jessel, now working as a producer for Zanuck, called Lucky. He asked Lucky to read the script for I WONDER WHO'S KISSING HER NOW. Lucky responded that he was on vacation. Jessel said he was calling at Darryl's behest. Zanuck wanted an answer. Jessel sent Lucky the script and kept after him until he read it. When finally Lucky did read it, he told Jessel he didn't like it. He was waiting for Zanuck to prepare a screenplay for THE GUS KAHN STORY. He wasn't aware at the time that Zanuck had scrapped that project.

Whatever his genius as a filmmaker, Darryl's resentments ran very deeply. After the success of THE RAZOR'S EDGE (20th-Fox, 1946), Darryl signed its director

---

Opposite: The shot of Betty Grable's posterior which became more famous than her picture, PIN-UP GIRL (20th-Fox, 1944). Photo courtesy of Movie Star News.

Lucky sitting between Danny Kaye and Rosanne Murray, kissing while filming WONDER MAN (RKO, 1945). Photo courtesy of Movie Star News.

Edmund Goulding to a generous contract which required
Goulding to make only four pictures during the next five
years, for which he would be paid a million dollars at the
rate of $200,000 a year. NIGHTMARE ALLEY (20th-Fox,
1947) was the first. Zanuck then had an altercation with
Goulding. He later heard that Goulding had mimicked the
things he said to him to a number of people at the Palm
Springs Racquet Club. As a punishment, Zanuck assigned
Goulding to a very small office next to the elevators. Although he kept paying him, he offered Goulding only an occasional script of inferior quality. It was Goulding's pride
Zanuck wanted to humble. In these terms, a man's talent
as a director was of no consequence.

Zanuck kept Lucky unemployed for a year. Lloyd
Bacon, whom Zanuck had assigned for a brief period to
THREE LITTLE GIRLS IN BLUE when Lucky was ill, offered Lucky what he felt to be sage advice on how to survive in
the studio system. Most screenplays were bad. Like a
lot of directors, Lucky's tendency was to change things
around until they played well. It wasn't so for Bacon. He
would always shoot a script as written. This way the associate producer on the picture would scurry in alarm to
Zanuck, seemingly save the picture, and come out looking
good. Because Bacon's producers invariably looked so
good, his services were much in demand. Lucky jeered.
Making a favorable impression on Zanuck and keeping his
job wasn't as important to him as making pictures he felt to
be fine and which he thought within the range of his capabili-
ties.

"Humberstone," Zanuck said to him as they sat together in a screening room, "I don't like these dailies, but
I don't know why."

The scene was a troop of cavalry riding along a
dusty trail.

"They're not grimy enough," Lucky observed.

"You're right," Zanuck agreed. "I want you to go to
location in Arizona and take over the picture."

Shooting was being done in and around the old Tucson
town set which Wesley Ruggles had erected for his epic
ARIZONA (Columbia, 1940). Lucky packed his bag and left
for location. It was a Western titled FURY AT FURNACE

CREEK (20th-Fox, 1948), set in 1880 and starring Victor
Mature and Coleen Gray. Albert Dekker was the villain.
Although the plot was conventional, with Indians attacking a
fort and a wagon train, Lucky handled the action sequences
commendably and the shoot-out at the end was properly suspenseful.

It was some time after the picture was released that
Zanuck imparted the bad news to Lucky. Since FURY AT
FURNACE CREEK was the only production Lucky had worked
on for a year, his entire salary had to be charged to its
budget. This so increased the negative cost of the film that
it made breaking even prohibitive. To satisfy the board of
directors, Darryl was forced not to renew Lucky's contract.
The board felt it had paid far more than it received back in
creative contribution. The severance from Twentieth Century-
Fox this time was final. Lucky informed his agent Lew
Wasserman at Music Corporation of America of the situation
and commenced to freelance.

Whatever the advantages of being independent, security was scarcely one of them. Lucky's first picture was for
Universal-International. Bill Goetz, when he left Fox, with
the help of Louis B. Mayer and others set up International
Pictures with Leo Spitz. In 1946, International merged with
Universal, Spitz and Goetz becoming production managers
for the combined facilities. When Lucky was engaged to
direct SOUTH SEA SINNER (Universal-International, 1950),
the company was only a year away from its takeover by
MCA. SINNER had a complex plot, featuring Macdonald
Carey and Shelley Winters, the latter doing a wan imitation
of Mae West. Jimmy Flavin was given a character role, but
even his reassuring presence couldn't save the picture from
mediocrity.

HAPPY GO LOVELY (RKO-British, 1951) proved a
life saver. It was produced by Associated British in collaboration with N. Peter Rathvon, an American financing company. American money paid for the director and the leading stars, David Niven, Vera-Ellen, Cesar Romero; Associated British paid for the rest, including production costs
for shooting the picture in England. It was a Technicolor
musical comedy that all the trades declared played like a
house of fire. Lucky received 15% of the picture in addition to his salary. It supported him for years. Niven,
whose career had ebbed, was rediscovered. RKO bought
domestic distribution rights.

Lucky's career went on the upswing. Warner Brothers contracted him to direct two musicals for them, SHE'S
WORKING HER WAY THROUGH COLLEGE (Warner's, 1952)
and THE DESERT SONG (Warner's, 1953). SHE'S WORKING
HER WAY THROUGH COLLEGE was a bright musical with
Virginia Mayo, Ronald Reagan, and Don Defore. Gene Nelson did the song and dance numbers. THE DESERT SONG
was described by one trade reviewer as "tuneful hijinks in
the sandy Sahara." It was actually Warner Brothers' third
make of the property, succeeding the 1929 and 1943 versions.
Katherine Grayson and Gordon MacRae starred.

Although they were met with good attendance, it was
nearly two years after the Warner Brothers films that Lucky
worked again. He was hired by Harry Joe Brown, whom he
had known when they both worked at Fox, to direct an entry
in Randolph Scott's continuing series of color Westerns for
Columbia release. Scott and Brown were co-owners of the
producing company. TEN WANTED MEN (Columbia, 1955)
was a cut above many entries in the series, but for one reason or another Lucky was unable to achieve the effects with
Scott, despite having directed him previously at Fox, that
Budd Boetticher managed in his splendid entries in the
series during the late 'fifties. But then, Lucky's strong
suits were musicals and detective stories, not Westerns.

Back at Universal, Lucky next directed PURPLE
MASK (Universal-International, 1955). It was a swashbuckler set in the Napoleonic era, starring Tony Curtis and featuring Coleen Miller and Gene Barry.

Lucky changed agents. Work was not forthcoming.
On Christmas 1956 Lucky's new agent called him with an
assignment in London. TARZAN AND THE LOST SAFARI
(M-G-M, 1957) had been in production for six months with
four different directors. At first, Lucky objected. But he
must keep his hand in the game, his agent argued. Lucky
consented. He went to London and shot the whole picture
on three sound stages with only one exterior of the tree
house and stock footage. The British production crew
thought him insane when he staged a forest fire indoors at
the conclusion of the film. His experience on the fire sequences for IN OLD CHICAGO served him well. He carried it off without a mishap.

Sol Lesser, who was the executive producer for the
Tarzan series, was elated. He contracted Lucky to direct

the next picture in the series, TARZAN'S FIGHT FOR LIFE
(M-G-M, 1958).   Gordon Scott played Tarzan in both films.
In all probability what Lesser liked most of all was how
competently Lucky could shoot outdoor pictures on sound
stages without shattering the illusion of the African jungle.

MADISON AVENUE (20th-Fox, 1962) was the last film
Lucky directed.   He was also credited as its producer.
Starring Dana Andrews, Eleanor Parker, Jeanne Crain, and
Eddie Albert, it was a moderately budgeted comedy about
the advertising industry in which milkman Eddie Albert was
transformed into a successful tycoon.

"How about a night cap?" Lucky proposed, rising
from his rocker.

Vicki reached for the horn and honked weakly.

"Come on," Lucky said.   "Where's your energy?
The night is still young!"

Vicki gave him a pale smile and honked twice more,
as weakly.

"The lady is exhausted," I said.

"You know," said Lucky, "I believe you're right."

Everyone was quiet for a moment, recovering from
the pain and intensity it somehow always takes to remember.

IV

The third and last visit with Lucky occurred the night
before we had to continue on our travels.   Lucky met us at
the door to his apartment with a whiskey over ice in each
hand.   He gave Vicki one and the other to me.

"That's all you wanted anyway," he said playfully and
began closing the door to his apartment.

"Just a minute," Vicki said.   "We came for a slightly longer visit than this."

"Oh," said Lucky, opening the door wide.   "In that
case, why don't you come on in?"

Once we were seated, Lucky eyed Vicki suspiciously. She was dressed in a black body shirt with a beige skirt and a turquoise scarf tied in a knot around her neck. Her blond hair was fluffed, her bluish-green eyes sparkling.

"Did you bring all your notebooks?" he asked. "We can go over them and check the facts."

"I think I did," Vicki said, searching her leather shoulder bag. "If I didn't leave them in the car."

"In the car!" Lucky exclaimed in mock disgust. "Some secretary!" He turned to me. "How is she in the hay?"

I was in the process of lighting a cigarette.

"Here they are," Vicki said, pulling out the note-books. "And," she added, raising an eyebrow, "tell him, if he's so interested, that you have no idea how I am in the hay, but that I'm fantastic in bed."

Lucky chuckled.

"Have you a cigarette, honey?"

"Sure," Vicki said, grinning. "A really good secretary always carries an extra pack."

Lucky and Vicki lit up off the same match.

"If you get bored," Lucky addressed me, "you can always go out and get a sandwich or something while Vicki and I go over this stuff."

"It's an idea," I conceded.

"What he doesn't know won't hurt him, honey."

"He'd probably find out," Vicki returned, "and in-clude it somewhere in the course of your career study."

"Hey," said Lucky, "I want to read this thing before you publish it."

"You will," Vicki promised. "I type all Jon's manu-scripts and I'll be certain to smuggle you a copy as soon as he finishes it."

"She's a pretty girl," Lucky said, toasting his martini glass at her, but winking at me.

"And I can type, too, right?" Vicki responded.

There was laughter.

"Not only is she liberated," I told Lucky, "but she doesn't want to work in pictures."

"Sam Peckinpah offered me a job any time I cared to try it," Vicki said. "Provided he had a part for a female with small breasts."

"What did you say to that?" Lucky asked.

"Nothing. He chewed on my arm." She stretched out her right arm. "See." Then she smiled. "But I still love him."

Lucky became serious.

"Vicki said over the telephone that you had gone to ONCE IS NOT ENOUGH [Paramount, 1975]."

I nodded.

"Well, maybe you should think of some way to bring that picture in at the end of what you write about me. The last fifteen years have been for me much as they were for Kirk Douglas in the picture. I have spent them raising Robyn by myself."

"I don't suppose it has been easy," I said.

"Never that," Lucky said. "I could measure the days by how much she grew and what she was learning or doing. I didn't want to remarry and I didn't want any women around constantly. But she turned out fine."

"And beautiful," Vicki said, sipping her drink.

"Everywhere I went, she came along," Lucky went on. "If I went out socially, Robyn was always invited. We were companions. Now she's married to a traveling musician. It's difficult getting accustomed to being alone."

I leaned forward and honked.

"Where are you two off to next?" Lucky asked, as he mixed another round.

"Arizona," Vicki said.

"Nogales," I clarified.   "I want to visit again with Tim McCoy."

"The movie cowboy?" Lucky asked, setting down my drink.   "I thought he was dead."

"No," I said.   "He's very much alive at eighty-five."

The image of Tim sitting in the enclosed patio of his hacienda at dusk came to mind.   Surrounded by his books and mementos, now in retirement, it is his wont to sit listening to the fountain and sip Scotch and let a sense of quiet well-being gently preoccupy him.

Lucky, Vicki, and I talked far into the night.   When we rose to depart, amid plans to visit soon again, Vicki put her arm around Lucky and kissed him on the mouth.

"Take care, you two," he said from the doorway.

"Better yet," Vicki said, "I'll see to it that Jon writes to you, and I will, and I'll send you the typescript as soon as it's ready.   You have my word on it."

Jacaranda trees lined the street outside Lucky's apartment house.   They were in bloom and the night was alive with their rich fragrance.   I had hoped to get a photograph of Vicki standing beneath one of them.   But now it was too late and too dark.   Vicki pressed my hand reassuringly as we walked in silence to the car.

H. BRUCE HUMBERSTONE

A Film Checklist by Karl Thiede

Assistant Director

1. BEN-HUR (N.Y. première, 30 December 1925; general release, 8 October 1927). P: Metro-Goldwyn-Mayer. D: Fred Niblo. C: Ramon Novarro, Francis X. Bushman, May McAvoy. NC: $3,967,000. 11,693ft. /130m.

2. PARIS (24 May 1926). P: Metro-Goldwyn-Mayer. D: Edmund Goulding. C: Charles Ray, Joan Crawford, Doublas Gilmore. 5,580ft. /62m.

3. THE TEMPTRESS (3 October 1926). P: Metro-Goldwyn-Mayer. D: Fred Niblo. C: Greta Garbo, Antonio Moreno, Roy D'Arcy. NC: $669,000. 8,221ft. /91m.

4. VALENCIA (18 December 1926). P: Metro-Goldwyn-Mayer. D: Dimitri Buchowetzki. C: Mae Murray, Lloyd Hughes, Roy D'Arcy. NC: $277,000. 5,680ft. /63m.

5. CAMILLE (N.Y. première, 21 April 1927; general release, 4 September 1927). P: First National. D: Fred Niblo. C: Norma Talmadge, Gilbert Roland, Lilyan Tashman. 8,700ft. /97m.

6. TOPSY AND EVA (24 July 1927). P: United Artists. D: Del Lord. C: Rosetta & Vivian Duncan, Gibson Gowland. NC: $341,309.99. DG: $353,348.31. 7,456ft. /83m.

7. MY BEST GIRL (31 October 1927). P: United Artists. D: Sam Taylor. C: Mary Pickford, Charles Rogers, Sunshine Hart. NC: $483,103.57. DG: $1,037,174.63. 7,460ft. /83m.

8. THE DEVIL DANCER (19 November 1927). P: Goldwyn-United Artists. D: Fred Niblo. C: Gilda

Gray, Clive Brook, Anna May Wong. NC: $457,850.06.
DG: $535,384.01. 7,600ft. /84 1/2m.

9. [No entry.]

10. TWO LOVERS (12 August 1928). P: Goldwyn-United
     Artists. D: Fred Niblo. C: Ronald Colman, Vilma
     Banky, Noah Beery, Sr. NC: $720,356.58. DG:
     $797,722.75. 8,817ft. /98m.

11. THE WOMAN DISPUTED (21 October 1928). P: United
     Artists. D: Henry King. C: Norma Talmadge,
     Gilbert Roland, Arnold Kent. Production started:
     21 March 1928. NC: $660,740.09. DG: $807,764.29.
     8,129ft. /90m.

12. THE IRON MASK (9 March 1929). P: United Artists.
     D: Allan Dwan. C: Douglas Fairbanks, Sr., Belle
     Bennett, Marguerite De La Motte. Production started:
     29 August 1928. NC: $1,495,603.02. DG:
     $1,540,136.99. Part talkie. 8,855ft. /98m.

13. COQUETTE (12 April 1929). P: United Artists. D:
     Sam Taylor. C: Mary Pickford, John Mack Brown,
     Matt Moore. Production started: 17 December 1928.
     NC: $813,108.10.. DG: $1,408,562.15. 6,993ft. /
     78m.

14. BIG NEWS (7 September 1929). P: Pathé. D: Greg-
     ory La Cava. C: Carole Lombard, Robert Arm-
     strong, Tom Kennedy. Working title: FOR TWO
     CENTS. Production started: 13 May 1929. 6,028ft. /
     67m.

15. THE TAMING OF THE SHREW (26 October 1929). P:
     United Artists. D: Sam Taylor. C: Mary Pick-
     ford, Douglas Fairbanks, Sr., Edwin Maxwell. Pro-
     duction started: 1 July 1929. NC: $649,319.49.
     DG: $1,147,740.11. 6,116ft. /68m.

16. CONDEMNED (7 December 1929). P: Goldwyn-United
     Artists. D: Wesley Ruggles. C: Ronald Colman,
     Ann Harding, Dudley Digges. Production started: 1
     August 1929. NC: $608,449.64. DG: $947,153.99.
     7,448ft. /83m.

17. RAFFLES (26 July 1930). P: Goldwyn-United Artists.

D: George Fitzmaurice, Harry D'Abbadie D'Arrast.
C: Ronald Colman, Kay Francis, Bramwell Fletcher.
Production started: 15 February 1930. NC:
$685,468.66. DG: $876,926.07. 6,509ft. /72m.

18. WHOOPEE! (27 September 1930). P: Goldwyn-United
     Artists. D: Thornton Freeland. C: Eddie Cantor,
     Eleanor Hunt, Paul Gregory. Production started: 7
     April 1930. NC: $1,023,971.78. DG: $1,756,632.18.
     Two-color Technicolor. 8,393ft. /93m.

19. ONE HEAVENLY NIGHT (10 January 1931). P: Gold-
     wyn-United Artists. D: George Fitzmaurice. C:
     Evelyn Laye, John Boles, Leon Errol. NC:
     $810,165.28. DG: $546,647.80. 7,342ft. /81 1/2m.

20. STREET SCENE (5 September 1931). P: Goldwyn-
     United Artists. D: King Vidor. C: Sylvia Sydney,
     William Collier, Jr. , Max Montor. Production com-
     pleted: July 1931. NC: $532,016.84. DG:
     $836,968.25. 80m.

21. ARROWSMITH (27 February 1932). P: Goldwyn-
     United Artists. D: John Ford. C: Ronald Colman,
     Helen Hayes, A. E. Anson. Production completed:
     September 1931. NC: $692,889.56. DG:
     $796,980.08. 110m.

22. THE GREEKS HAD A WORD FOR THEM (13 February
     1932). P: Goldwyn-United Artists. D: Lowell
     Sherman. C: Ina Claire, Joan Blondell, Madge
     Evans. Production completed: October 1931. NC:
     $555,063.91. DG: $397,866.60. 80m.

23. BIRD OF PARADISE (12 August 1932). P: RKO Radio
     Pictures. D: King Vidor. C: Dolores Del Rio,
     Joel McCrea, John Halliday. Production completed:
     March 1932. NC: $850,000. 80m.

Director

24. STRANGERS OF THE EVENING (15 May 1932). P:
     Tiffany Productions. C: Zasu Pitts, Eugene Pallette,
     Lucien Littlefield. Production completed: March
     1932. 80m.

25. THE CROOKED CIRCLE (25 September 1932). P:
     World Wide. C: Ben Lyon, Zasu Pitts, James Glea-
     son. 70m.

26. IF I HAD A MILLION (November 1932). P: Paramount.
     D: Ernst Lubitsch - Rasberry sequence; Norman
     Taurog - Prologue, Epilogue; Stephen Roberts - Vio-
     let, Grandma sequences; Norman McLeod - Road Hog,
     China Shop sequences; James Cruze - Death Cell se-
     quence; William A. Seiter - The Three Marines se-
     quence; H. Bruce Humberstone - Forger sequence.
     C: Gary Cooper, Wynne Gibson, George Raft. 95m.

27. KING OF THE JUNGLE (10 March 1933). P: Para-
     mount. C: Buster Crabbe, Ronnie Cosbey, Frances
     Dee. 74m.

28. GOOD-BYE LOVE (10 November 1933). P: RKO
     Radio Pictures. C: Charlie Ruggles, Verree Teas-
     dale, Mayo Methot. 66m.

29. MERRY WIVES OF RENO (12 May 1934). P: Warner
     Brothers. C: Margaret Lindsay, Donald Woods,
     Guy Kibbee. 64m.

30. DRAGON MURDER CASE (25 August 1934). P: First
     National. C: Warren William, Margaret Lindsay,
     Lyle Talbot. 67m.

31. LADIES LOVE DANGER (3 May 1935). P: Fox Film
     Corporation. C: Mona Barrie, Gilbert Roland, Don-
     ald Cook. Working title: SECRET LIVES. 69m.

32. SILK HAT KID (19 July 1935). P: Fox Film Corpora-
     tion. C: Lew Ayres, Mae Clarke, Paul Kelly.
     6,250ft. /69 1/2m.

33. THREE LIVE GHOSTS (10 January 1936). P: Metro-
     Goldwyn-Mayer. C: Richard Arlen, Beryl Mercer,
     Dudley Digges. 5,576ft. /62m.

34. CHARLIE CHAN AT THE RACE TRACK (7 August
     1936). P: Twentieth Century-Fox. C: Warner
     Oland, Keye Luke, Helen Wood. 6,300ft. /70m.

35. CHARLIE CHAN AT THE OPERA (8 January 1937).
     P: Twentieth Century-Fox. C: Warner Oland,

Boris Karloff, Keye Luke. Production started: 16
September 1936. 6,175ft. /68 1/2m.

36. BREEZING HOME (31 January 1937). P: Universal.
D: Milton Carruth. C: William Gargan, Binnie
Barnes, Wendy Barrie. Working title: I HATE
HORSES. Production started: 27 November 1936.
64m. H. Bruce Humberstone doesn't remember work-
ing on this picture, or for Universal or for Edmund
Grainger, its producer. At least two prime sources
list him as director at the start of production.

37. CHARLIE CHAN AT THE OLYMPICS (21 May 1937).
P: Twentieth Century-Fox. C: Warner Oland,
Katherine De Mille, Pauline Moore. Production
started: 19 January 1937. 6,400ft. /71m.

38. IN OLD CHICAGO (15 April 1938). P: Twentieth
Century-Fox. D: Henry King, H. Bruce Humberstone - Fire sequence. C: Tyrone Power, Alice
Faye, Don Ameche. Production started: 14 June
1937. DG: $1,500,000. 10,002ft/111m.

39. CHECKERS (2 October 1938). P: Twentieth Century-
Fox. C: Jane Withers, Una Merkel, Stuart Erwin.
Production started: 15 October 1937. 7,050ft. /
78m.

40. RASCALS (20 May 1938). P: Twentieth Century-Fox.
C: Jane Withers, Rochelle Hudson, Robert Wilcox.
Working title: GYPSY. Production started: 17 De-
cember 1937. 6,900ft. /77m.

41. TIME OUT FOR MURDER (23 September 1938). P:
Twentieth Century-Fox. C: Gloria Stuart, Michael
Whalen, Douglas Fowley. Working title: MERIDIAN
7-1212. Production started: 16 May 1938.
5,367ft. /59 1/2m.

42. WHILE NEW YORK SLEEPS (6 January 1939). P:
Twentieth Century-Fox. C: Michael Whalen, Jean
Rogers, Chick Chandler. Production started: 7
July 1938. 61m.

43. CHARLIE CHAN IN HONOLULU (13 January 1939). P:
    Twentieth Century-Fox. C: Sidney Toler, Phyllis
    Brooks, Sen Young. 6,074ft. /67 1/2m.

44. PARDON OUR NERVE (24 February 1939). P: Twenti-
    eth Century-Fox. C: Lynn Bari, June Gale, Guinn
    Williams. 68m.

45. PACK UP YOUR TROUBLES (20 October 1939). P:
    Twentieth Century-Fox. C: Jane Withers, Ritz
    Brothers, Lynn Bari. 6,850ft. /76m.

46. LUCKY CISCO KID (28 June 1940). P: Twentieth
    Century-Fox. C: Cesar Romero, Mary Beth Hughes,
    Dana Andrews. 6,089ft. /68m.

47. THE QUARTERBACK (4 October 1940). P: Para-
    mount. C: Wayne Morris, Virginia Dale, Lillian
    Cornell. 69m.

48. TALL, DARK AND HANDSOME (24 January 1941). P:
    Twentieth Century-Fox. C: Cesar Romero, Virginia
    Gilmore, Charlotte Greenwood. 7,100ft. /79m.

49. SUN VALLEY SERENADE (29 August 1941). P:
    Twentieth Century-Fox. C: Sonja Henie, John Payne,
    Glenn Miller. NC: $1,300,000. 7,732ft. /86m.

50. I WAKE UP SCREAMING (14 November 1941). P:
    Twentieth Century-Fox. C: Betty Grable, Victor
    Mature, Carole Landis. Working title and trade
    shown under the title HOT SPOT. 7,372ft. /82m.

51. TO THE SHORES OF TRIPOLI (10 April 1942). P:
    Twentieth Century-Fox. C: John Payne, Maureen
    O'Hara, Randolph Scott. DG: $2,300,000.
    7,800ft. /87m.

52. ICELAND (2 October 1942). P: Twentieth Century-
    Fox. C: Sonja Henie, John Payne, Jack Oakie.
    DG: $1,700,000. 7,119ft. /79m.

53. HELLO, FRISCO, HELLO (26 March 1943). P:
    Twentieth Century-Fox. C: Alice Faye, John Payne,

Jack Oakie.   DG: $3,400,000.   Technicolor.
8,939ft. /98m.

54.   PIN-UP GIRL (May 1944).   P: Twentieth Century-Fox.
      C: Betty Grable, John Harvey, Martha Raye.   Tech-
      nicolor.   7,450ft. /83m.

55.   WONDERMAN (© 8 June 1945).   P: Goldwyn-RKO
      Radio Pictures.   C: Danny Kaye, Virginia Mayo,
      Vera-Ellen.   Technicolor.   98m.

56.   WITHIN THESE WALLS (July 1945).   P: Twentieth
      Century-Fox.   C: Thomas Mitchell, Mary Anderson,
      Edward Ryan.   6,406ft. /71m.

57.   THREE LITTLE GIRLS IN BLUE (October 1946).   P:
      Twentieth Century-Fox.   C: June Haver, George
      Montgomery, Vivian Blaine.   DG: $3,000,000.
      Technicolor.   90m.

58.   THE HOMESTRETCH (May, 1947).   P: Twentieth
      Century-Fox.   C: Cornel Wilde, Maureen O'Hara,
      Glenn Langan.   DG: $2,350,000.   Technicolor.
      96m.

59.   FURY AT FURNACE CREEK (May 1948).   P: Twenti-
      eth Century-Fox.   C: Victor Mature, Coleen Gray,
      Glenn Langan.   88m.

60.   SOUTH SEA SINNER (January, 1950).   P: Universal-
      International.   C: Shelley Winters, Macdonald Carey,
      Helena Carter.   88m.

61.   HAPPY GO LOVELY (18 July 1951).   P: RKO Radio
      Pictures.   C: David Niven, Vera-Ellen, Cesar Ro-
      mero.   Technicolor.   88m.

62.   SHE'S WORKING HER WAY THROUGH COLLEGE (12
      July 1952).   P: Warner Brothers.   C: Virginia
      Mayo, Ronald Reagan, Gene Nelson.   DG:
      $2,400,000.   Color.   101m.

63.   THE DESERT SONG (30 May 1953).   P: Warner
      Brothers.   C: Kathryn Grayson, Gordon MacRae,
      Steve Cochran.   DG: $2,000,000.   Technicolor.
      110m.

64. TEN WANTED MEN (February 1955). P: Columbia.
C: Randolph Scott, Jocelyn Brando, Richard Boone.
Technicolor. 80m.

65. THE PURPLE MASK (July 1955). P: Universal-International. C: Tony Curtis, Colleen Miller, Gene
Barry. Color. 82m.

66. TARZAN AND THE LOST SAFARI (3 May 1957). P:
Metro-Goldwyn-Mayer. C: Gordon Scott, Robert
Beatty, Yolande Donlan. Technicolor. 7,237ft./80m.

67. TARZAN'S FIGHT FOR LIFE (11 July 1958). P:
Metro-Goldwyn-Mayer. C: Gordon Scott, Eve Brent,
Carl Benton Reid. Color. 7,766ft./87m.

68. MADISON AVENUE (January 1962). P: Twentieth
Century-Fox. C: Dana Andrews, Eleanor Parker,
Jeanne Crain. Scope. 94m.

Olga Belaieff and William Dieterle in costume from the period when Dieterle was an actor. Photo courtesy of the Museum of Modern Art.

Chapter 3

WILLIAM DIETERLE

I: Interview with Tom Flinn

William Dieterle exhibited none of the reticence so often displayed by his Hollywood contemporaries. He was eager to talk about his career and especially about his years at Warner Brothers. When I wrote to him and told him I was interested in his impressions of Warner's, he replied that in his opinion Warner Brothers was the most important American studio during the years from 1930 to 1950, and when I arrived in Munich in July 1972, he quickly agreed to an interview in spite of a lingering cold. As we sat in the library of his modest home and talked, I became aware of the disappointment that fed his eagerness to discuss his films. With a rueful grin he showed me an invitation to the opening of Henri Langlois' Musée du Cinéma, which due to some Gallic inefficiency arrived the day after the opening was to take place.

But the disappointment Dieterle felt did not stem solely from a lack of critical recognition, for it was obvious that he was still bitter about the way his American career ended. Dieterle was the quintessential "liberal" director of the 'thirties, his films championed the liberal, democratic, enlightenment tradition, and if some of them such as THE LIFE OF EMILE ZOLA seem pretty tame today, it is well to remember the conditions in which they were created and the restraints under which they were made. Viewed against the outrageous concessions movie moguls like L. B. Mayer made to Hitler and the reluctance of the big studios to deal with any facet of the Jewish experience more controversial than that portrayed in THE JAZZ SINGER, ZOLA becomes an important document in the American cinema. Dieterle's uncompromising anti-Nazi stand in the 'thirties was not limited to films like ZOLA or BLOCKADE (United Artists, 1938). Dieterle and his wife, Charlotte, helped many German refugees, including Bertolt Brecht, and, as a result, the Dieterles were labeled "premature anti-fascists" during the McCarthy era. Although he was never formally on any blacklist, Dieterle found it impossible to get work after the State Department held up production on ELEPHANT WALK (Paramount, 1954) by withholding his passport for three months pending "investigation."

William Dieterle died in December 1972. As far as I know, this was his last interview. I only wish that he had lived to see it in print. While editing and transcribing the tape (which runs over three hours) I couldn't help but recall my feeling that Dieterle's spirit somehow still matched his films, and I marveled that the opinions and aspirations that had informed those works and remained unchanged in spite of the years and disappointments that followed. I also remember how Dieterle's commanding presence was reflected in the modest splendor of his study, with its sturdy renaissance desk and wood-paneled protestant simplicity, broken only by shelves of books and a single picture--a framed photograph of Max Reinhardt.

Part I: Germany in the 'Twenties

Q: You, like many other German cineastes, got your start with Max Reinhardt. Was he an important influence on your subsequent work?

A: Of course. Reinhardt was the architect of the "new" theatre which succeeded the realism of Braun. When you come into such an atmosphere, and you work with him, you can't help but adopt something. My first appearance with Reinhardt was as Brutus in JULIUS CAESAR. It was a grand production at the Grosses Schauspielhaus with Werner Kraus, Emil Jannings, and Moise. That was in 1921; I had just come from Zurich. Then Reinhardt opened Salzburg with EVERYMAN. Moise played Everyman; I played the friend. This was in the summer of '21, I think. From then on--well, when you belong to a great ensemble, as this was, you play constantly. This was repertory theatre, playing different roles every night. By the end of 1922, I had started in films as well.

Q: Why did you go into films?

A: At first I had no intention of going into film, because I was sold on the stage. I was not very enthusiastic at first. But soon I was working a lot in films--more than I wanted really, because I realized you cannot serve two masters at the same time. But this was during the inflation, and you had to work like the devil to make your living. Sometimes I was paid four times a day. When you got the money you often couldn't even afford to ride home in the streetcar (it cost five billion marks). You just can't understand it unless you've gone through that miserable time. So I had to work. Since the stage didn't pay enough, I was forced into film work. The pay was a little better, and sometimes you even got dollars, which was paradise.

Q: What was Reinhardt's orientation towards expressionism? Were any of the plays you appeared in staged in the expressionist manner?

A: No. Reinhardt was not an expressionist. Expressionism came in, I believe, with Karl Heinz Martin, who directed DIE WANDLUNG by Ernst Toller. I myself acted in only two films, HINTERTREPPE (BACKSTAIRS, 1921) and DAS WACHSFIGURENKABINETT (WAXWORKS, 1924), in the expressionist style. On the stage expressionism didn't last because it was driven further by the work of Leopold Jessner at the Staatstheater. He staged WILHELM TELL and RICHARD III on steps only--no sets except steps. It was, in a way, expressionist, but different in that it was first conceived with cross-eyed stage--everything upside down-- surrealistic, I would say, more than expressionistic. This all happened while Reinhardt was still working--to his great chagrin, let's say. He was heartbroken really, because he was the uncrowned king of the Berlin theatre world until Jessner came along. Jessner had to come after the war; Reinhardt's theatre, with all his romanticism, was passé. His was a baroque theatre really, because he was actually such a baroque nature himself, like the Viennese he was until his very end.

Q: Didn't Jessner direct HINTERTREPPE? What part did Paul Leni play in that production?

A: Leni was only the art director. Later, Leni was both art director and director of DAS WACHSFIGURENKABINETT. He designed the sets and gave the directions, but that picture had bad luck because some Russians financed it and, as usual, they ran out of money. So the last sequence was

hardly touched, a sort of compromise so they could sell it.
This was a great pity, because if they had had a few more
weeks or a few thousand marks, it would have been a much
better picture.

Q: Was DAS WACHSFIGURENKABINETT a success?

A: Yes, it was a great success here. But I think then it
was the last of its kind.   The majority of people didn't care
about expressionism; they just wanted a good story.   In Germany we had a series of Heimat films, a sort of folkloristic
thing about the mountains and flowers, a kitschy, schmaltzy,
saccharine thing at its worst, but these films were popular,
and they took the wind out of the sails of the modern style.
Expressionism was a wonderful artistic revolution; it didn't
last but it served well, because much of the old stuff was
burned out.

Q: Marlene Dietrich was in the first film you directed,
wasn't she?

A: Yes, it was one of her first films.

Q: What made you want to direct?

A: I always wanted to create things in their completeness.
I was very dissatisfied with what was being shown. I picked
one of those wonderful folktales by Tolstoy, and we got together, Volker, Marlene, myself and a few others. We had
no money. We were just four or five very young, enthusiastic, and revolutionary people who wanted to do something
different.   We brought it out; it didn't make any money,
but was shown, and it was a very interesting experiment.

Q: You also acted in many of the films you directed. Did
that cause problems?

A: Well, most of the time I had to save money. It didn't
bother me. I did it a lot. That's how the business of the
gloves got started. I wore gloves while directing because
I was always changing scenery, moving props, or building
things.   When that was done I could just throw away the
gloves and I was ready to act. It saved time. But the
Hollywood press agents really loused that up. They said it
was because I had to have clean hands for the ladies, that
I was an aristocrat, and so forth. Once, and this will show
the lengths those press people would go for publicity, I came

home and found two doctors and my insurance agent.   They
told me to take my clothes off.   I thought they were crazy
until I found out that one of the pressmen had written that I
wore gloves because I was a bleeder.   Can you imagine
that?   So naturally the insurance company thought I was
cheating them.

Q: Did you like working with Murnau on FAUST?

A: Very much, because I loved him, and I think he was the
finest German director--in spite of all the rest.

Q: Did he spend much time on the visuals?

A: Yes, very much.   He was very particular about this
and he made, without demands from upstairs as in Hollywood, retakes when he thought, artistically, they were
needed.   He was a great poet, a wonderful man first, and
a great artist.   He was very serious.   The films he did
were all exquisite material.   You could not buy him for
anything.   If he didn't like a project there was no go.   He
would have starved rather than do anything he didn't like.

Q: What was your biggest success as a director in Germany?

A: There was a novel called Die Heilige und ihr Narr (The
Saint and Her Fool), a great schmaltzy success.   I hadn't
read it, but when my wife called and asked if I wanted to
star in it and direct, I jumped at the chance.   I found out
later that I got the film because the original director's wife
was not suitable for the lead role.   So rather than fight
with her, he gave it to me, and it was a great success (it
has been remade three times).   It was a crazy romantic
story, no better, no worse than many others, but it helped
my career quite a bit.

Part II: Warner Brothers in the 'Thirties

Q: How and why did you come to Hollywood?

A: Well, I had worked for First National in Germany, but
I really didn't expect to be called to Hollywood.   In Berlin
it was a running joke if the phone rang at a restaurant;
they said, "It must be Hollywood."   Well, one night my
wife and I were out dining and it really happened.   I couldn't

believe it, but next morning I went to the Friedrichstrasse
(the 42nd Street of German cinema) and talked to the American representative of First National. I was hired to make
synchronizations. Sound had just come in, and Hollywood
was afraid of losing foreign markets. So they hired German, French, and Spanish units to make foreign versions of
important features. I got four scripts and was able to hire
about five actors (just for the leads). We got passports and
off we went.

The four films we were to make had already been
completed. All the sets were still standing and dressed--we
used the same costumes and everything. The big difference
was that we had just ten days to make each picture.
The supervisor of all this was Henry Blanke, a nice
guy, and very talented. He was supposed to direct but the
closer we got to shooting the more nervous he got. So,
finally, he said, "Would you like to direct? I've got so
much to do."
It was difficult. Ten days is not much time. For
one picture, MOBY DICK (1930), I think we had fourteen
days, but we still had to work fast. Of course in those
days everyone worked until 8 P.M., and Saturdays we
worked until sundown (God, how they hated that). These
long hours were not changed for about five years after I
came to Hollywood.

Q: Didn't you play Captain Ahab?

A: Yes, MOBY DICK was the only story I did that I had
known since childhood. I loved it. It was great fun. It
had never been done in Germany. They didn't have the
means, the big sailing ship, the whale. It was a sensation.

Q: Did you have any difficulties adjusting to the Hollywood
studio system?

A: I was shooting different than they were. It was at the
beginning of sound, remember, and for a scene like the
three of us sitting here, they would have four cameras, one
on each of the principals and a master shot. I said this
was crazy and wasteful. But they said it must be shot this
way. So finally, I said, "We'll shoot it your way first and
then my way with one camera." They said that they'd never
be able to cut it, but I told them to just go ahead and try.
The next day when the rushes came back everyone was
amazed. Three days later the boss, Hal Wallis, came down

and asked if I wanted to stay. I accepted.

Q: What made you want to stay in Hollywood?

A: Well, there was Hitler, of course, but I admired the
magnificent organization which you just didn't have in Europe.
Here there are so many fly-by-night producers who would
go to cafés, get a little money together, and start a film.
It was hard work, and many times I didn't get paid.

In Hollywood, I was fascinated by the organization,
the technique, and the studio morale (which you don't have
today anywhere). People were always there on time, and
you could start shooting at nine o'clock. They were enthusiastic, and when you started a picture you were on it to
the end. In Europe, actors were often making three or four
pictures at the same time, which naturally led to all kinds
of confusion.

Q: Did you have trouble making the camera mobile during
the early days of sound?

A: They were shocked by the revolution of sound, it was
so gigantic. But it wasn't the camera so much--they didn't
know how to cut film. The sound at Warner's was not on
tape, but on enormous records. To get this synched with
the film was an enormous job for the cutter. So they were
scared stiff.

Q: Was THE LAST FLIGHT (1931) your first English-
language American film?

A: Yeah. Now we come to the problem the Warner Brothers had with me: what do we give the guy? He has shown
us he can direct. He's done four pictures and completed
them on time (and that impressed them much more than any
artistic qualities they might have had). So I read many
stories until finally I found one that I liked, "The Lady in
the Red Shoes," which was in the Saturday Evening Post.
It was by John Monk Saunders, a disciple of Hemingway, a
wonderful chap--later he killed himself. "The Lady in the
Red Shoes" was an autobiographic tale, the story of four
American flyers in Europe after the war. My English still
wasn't that good so I had Blanke read the story to me. We
went over it and translated it. The more I worked on it
the more enthusiastic I got. I thought it was great, but
Blanke said, "Nobody else wants to do it, you'd better not
risk it." I said, "This is what I want to do." It was a

brilliant story.   It starts in a hospital as the war ends,
"Boys, La guerre est fini.   Now what?"   "Get tight. "
"Then what?"   "Stay tight. "   That's the motto of the book
and that's exactly how we opened the picture.   The flyers
refuse to return home and be heroes.   They each have a
little tic, each one has been wounded physically or psychologically by the war.   They want to live life as they find it
from day to day, train station to train station.   Somebody
says, "What's happening in Spain?"   And someone says,
"Well, let's go and see what's happening. "

The cast was magnificent.   Barthelmess was in it,
and Helen Chandler, who never really made it as a star;
she was great.   We made the picture in a very short time,
and it was a big success.   Would you believe that it was
shown two years ago in New York and London and hailed as
a "forgotten masterpiece?"   I saw it last year at a local
museum--it's still a brilliant picture.

Q: What about JEWEL ROBBERY (1932); were you interested in that picture?

A: Not very much.   It was a Viennese story and kind of
slight.   I was only interested in it because of William
Powell.   With him you could steal horses.   He has such a
light touch.   It was a charming story, but without much substance.

The most important thing to be over there--which became the theme of my career in America--was how to get a
good story, because a director is only as good as his story.
To be a big success you must first have the ingredients for
success, and in the picture business this means a good
story.   Now comes the problem.   At Warner's there were
ten directors ahead of me--two top directors, LeRoy and
Curtiz.   They were very well connected.   LeRoy had married a daughter of Warner's, and Curtiz was the friend and
polo-playing companion of Zanuck.   A further problem I
had was that I knew nothing about cards, and if you don't
play poker in Hollywood, well, poor fellow, because that's
where the pictures are cast and the deals made.

It was a constant struggle to get ahead.   They had
ten directors, and they had to make about sixty pictures a
year in those days.   All could not be top stories, that's
obvious.   There must be "B" pictures.   So naturally the
newcomer gets the "B" pictures.   But I didn't want to direct "B" pictures.   And I was getting paid as a top director,
but I wasn't doing it for the money.   I could have gone to
France or England; I didn't want to go back to Mr. Hitler.

But I wanted to make good pictures, that was the problem.
        It was very, very hard.   There were so many other
directors.   Not that I was discriminated against as a foreign-
er--this didn't matter at all.   I think Warner's was the most
democratic studio in Hollywood.   There is no question about
this.   They had Lubitsch before me; Curtiz was Hungarian.

Q: What about SCARLET DAWN (1932)?

A: That picture might have helped me a lot, but why didn't
it?   It was so terribly underwritten, so recklessly put together.   That was something that only happened to me under
Zanuck, never with Wallis.   You know we had to start that
picture with only ten pages of script.   A film should have a
unified over-all conception.   If I don't know the ending, how
can I motivate the beginning?   What does it mean?   Where
does it lead to?   Oh, the fights we had sometimes.   So
much of the stuff was so careless; there's a better word in
English, "superficial."   The motivations were so cheap.
The bacchanal scene (in SCARLET DAWN) was good, but I
did it just to get something on the screen.   It all should
have been good.   It could have been a good picture, but we
got no help from upstairs.   It was the system.   We had to
shoot four-five pages of script a day and those poor fellows,
the writers, had to produce so many pages a day from nine
to five, whether they had an idea or not.   They had to deliver or lose their job.
        If a director wasn't fast enough, or gave them too
much trouble, they replaced him, usually with Mike [Cur-
tiz].   Mike did everything.   He could finish a picture at 11
and at 1 P.M. start a new picture.   He was extraordinarily
talented.   He didn't always know what he was doing, but he
had such an instinct for film, he could do it.   I couldn't.
If I didn't have my script, I was helpless.
        Once I had a big clash with Zanuck.   He said, "Bill,
I don't know where you're going."   I said, "I've only got
two pages for tomorrow.   Do you know where we're going?"
"How dare you ask me where we're going?"   Sometimes the
conditions under Zanuck were just terrible.

Q: MADAME DU BARRY (1934) is an interesting picture.
Was that a success?

A: In Europe it was just torn to bits.   They had no fun
with it.   They thought that because Madame Du Barry was
decapitated, it had to be all serious.   But her life was such
a farce.   Other directors got away with historical farces,

William Dieterle directing Dolores Del Rio on the set of
MADAME DU BARRY (Warner's, 1934). Note the white
gloves. Photo courtesy of the Museum of Modern Art.

Korda with THE PRIVATE LIFE OF HENRY VIII and Lubitsch, of course, he invented the genre.   I don't think my
DU BARRY can be compared with Lubitsch's DU BARRY;
mine was not meant to be a big epic but a nice historical
farce.   I thought Dolores [Del Rio] played it just right.

Q: Do you prefer doing historical, period pictures?

A: No, but if I can't get a good modern story, I'll do one
gladly.   The story is more important to me than the historical details of time and place.

Q: Tell me about the genesis of A MIDSUMMER NIGHT'S
DREAM (1936)?

A: Well, Reinhardt was in Hollywood, staging the play at
the Hollywood Bowl.   That version of the play cannot be
compared with his earlier Shakespearian adaptations.   It
was a better "show" perhaps, but Shakespeare died somewhere along the way.   Do you know the Bowl?   With 20,000
seats, it's not a theatre, not even a hall, it's a "place."
It was a "show" and not a play, and Reinhardt knew it.   He
was a man who was suddenly lost.   All his theatres in
Europe were taken away by Hitler.   He was a "guest," but
there are all kinds of guests, and though he was treated
like a visiting celebrity, he never forgot he was a refugee.
He was very conscious that he could never go back.
        So that was the situation when I suggested he make a
film of the production.   I wanted to give him something to
think of, because Reinhardt, if he wasn't planning something
new, was a lost man.   He answered, "Why not?"
        I used several approaches to sell Warner Brothers.
First of all, they were interested in Olivia de Havilland.
They liked Olivia, and they hired her, and they were impressed with the show.   I said, "Let's do it because here
we have something that will raise Warner Brothers from a
second-rate studio right into the ranks of the aristocrats."
They worried about Reinhardt's English, so I told them I
would help with the technical side of the production and the
language problem, but I would let Reinhardt direct the play
since it was very much his show.
        It was a nice, sweet marriage--we worked well to-
gether.   We did have a hard time getting started because of
the script.   Reinhardt wanted to be absolutely faithful to
Shakespeare's dialogue, but he kept adding elaborate pantomime sequences.   He had brilliant ideas, but we had to remind him that the film as he conceived it with all Shakes-

peare's scenes plus Reinhardt's embellishments would be too
long.

The technique of picture-making was new to him.   He
was very shy about it.   He would rehearse the actors.
When he thought it was right, he would sit down and I would
arrange it for the cameras.   It went very well, and we finished on time--but not without a scare.   About one week
after we started filming, the unit manager called me up and
said, 'Bill, you've got to stop production.   Mickey [Rooney,
who played Puck] has broken his leg. "   I told him not to
stop it.   I called the casting office and asked them to round
up all the kids that looked like Mickey.   We chose a double
from about two hundred kids.   We used the double for all
the longshots.   Rooney was still in a cast, but for the close-
ups we had to have him in a sling, carried about by labor-
ers, because Puck moves all the time.

I had the good fortune to work with Hal Mohr on the
photography.   At first Ernie Haller was the cameraman,
but he was too much a ladies' photographer.   He couldn't
get the right mood, and we were lucky enough to find an
outside man, Hal Mohr, who did a great job.

Q: What happened after that?

A: Well, I thought I was in for a real good assignment.
Then they gave me a story, and it was really terrible.   I
said, "No," and they gave me a two-week vacation.   I was
having a great time when I got a wire which said, "Come
back immediately.   We have a wonderful story. "   Well, it
was the same script, DR. SOCRATES, only sweetened up--
it had been rewritten for Paul Muni.

Now, I could refuse to do it.   All Warner's directors
could refuse three scripts.   But here is how it worked: you
get a story you don't like--out it goes; you get one you like
even less--so there's your second refusal; then you get one
that's even worse, and you begin to think that first one isn't
so bad.   That's how it worked.   They were so clever at
Warner's.   They knew there were many ways to skin a cat.

I talked to Muni.   I told him they had an outline for
a picture on Louis Pasteur.   So we went to Warner's and
he said, "I'll make this lousy picture if you give us Louis
Pasteur. "   They were so glad to get Muni to do DR. SOC-
RATES (he was very difficult) that they agreed to give us
Louis Pasteur.

So, we finished DR. SOCRATES (1935) as quickly as
possible and got into PASTEUR.   It was paradise.   It was
also the beginning of the second phase of my career in

Hollywood.   Later they called me the "Plutarch of Hollywood," because I loved to do biographies.   What's the difference if I do a great man's story or the story of Dr. Socrates?   To me, DR. SOCRATES was just a little picture,
but there was magnificent material in the story of Pasteur.
I thought the drama of Pasteur's struggle against the old
professors who were against any change or progress would
appeal to students and young people around the world.

Q: Were you involved in writing the script for THE STORY
OF LOUIS PASTEUR (1936)?

A: Well, I had both written and directed before, but never
at Warner's, and I wouldn't do it again.   I believe it needs
a fresh mind.   Before I start my preparation I would rather
not know the story and all the details of the script, but approach it fresh and bring my talents as a director to it.   I
know there are many others who write and direct, but that's
not for me.   I would rather work on a new story.   When I
have created a story then I have given myself; it's all there
on paper.   But when I read a new story, it speaks to me,
gives me ideas.

Q: Whose idea was the opening sequence?

A: Mine, completely mine.   It's a very funny story, typical of Hollywood and typical of Warner's.   When the PAS-
TEUR script was done, it was sent to all the departments
and also to Jack Warner for final approval.   He said,
"Pasteur, who's he, the milkman?"   The story got around
and everyone had a big laugh, but I said to Blanke, "Don't
laugh, he's right in a way.   I've got to figure it out.   We
don't have to start right away; give me a few days to come
up with something."   So I went on a camping trip to the
Grand Canyon.   Suddenly at two in the morning, I woke my
wife and said, "Charlotte, I know exactly what I'll do."   So,
I start the picture in France, a man finds a leaflet, reads
it, and says, "Who's Pasteur?"   Next the question goes to
a police station, "Who's Pasteur?"   Then it goes to the
doctors, the ministers, and finally to the Emperor himself.
The audience is not only intrigued with the question, but re-
assured that Pasteur wasn't much better known in the nine-
teenth century than he is today.

Q: After the success of PASTEUR did you have any more
problems doing the kind of films you wanted to do at Warner's?

A: Well, PASTEUR won an Oscar and raised the prestige
of Warner's considerably, but at Warner's the moment you
had a success they gave you something terrible to keep you
from getting a swelled head.   They would force you to do a
lousy story as a routine method of keeping you in line.

They gave me SATAN MET A LADY (1936) with Bette
Davis.   The story, The Maltese Falcon by Dashiell Hammett,
had been filmed, and they wrote such a lousy script for me.
John Huston later made a great picture out of it, but he
stuck to the story.   This was the picture Bette Davis walked
out on.   She hated that script, everyone did, and the film
was badly cast as well.

Q: What about THE WHITE ANGEL, with Kay Francis as
Florence Nightingale?

A: That was a beautiful story but it was, shall I say,
written by the wrong people--they wanted to be so correct
with the English.   We had so much trouble with the English
censor; in the end it almost killed the story.   It had to end
with Florence getting some kind of recognition by the Queen
but we were not allowed to show the Queen.   It seems that
even if she is long dead you were not supposed to show an
English Queen.   Figure out that nonsense.   I mean it was
easy to shoot around her, but with that kind of finicky censorship writers cannot write well, and THE WHITE ANGEL
(1936) was not as well written as ZOLA or PASTEUR.

The human element of that story was wonderful: a
girl goes out, leaves her home, turns her back on society,
and says, "I'll do what I want to do," and what she wants
to do is to help those poor devils in that crazy, lousy war.
But the script was written with kid gloves on.   The film
itself could have been a lot better, but one of the things
that we had to face at Warner's, a mark, a shadow upon us,
was that we hardly ever made a retake after a preview.
You probably know all about M-G-M, how they would preview a picture and find out what good material they had and
then build it up.   Sometimes they practically remade the
entire picture.   At Warner's the attitude was, "Just let it
go, it will sell."   We never really took care.   Once Wallis
liked it, it was okay.

Q: You mean Hal Wallis?

A: Yes, in many, many ways I like him very much, and
I know what a wonderful producer he was and still is, but
the fact is that he made hundreds of pictures for Warner's--

all conforming to his mind--all are Wallis pictures in a way, and that is not good.   He should have at least had a brain trust, people who would feed him new ideas.   He couldn't stand criticism at all--"This is the way I like it."   Even if he realizes he's wrong, it goes out and he saves on time and cost.   This was in direct contrast to M-G-M, Fox, and Paramount where you could shoot numerous retakes.

Q: Do you blame the producers or the writers for the bad scripts you got?

A: It's the system.   I don't say anything against the writers, because they had, if anything, a rougher time than the directors.   From nine to five they had to write whether they had an idea or not.   There was one fellow, a novelist, who fooled them.   At that time every writer was supposed to put out five pages a day.   This guy had no trouble, he just wrote long descriptions of the sets he wanted, which is a lot easier than writing five pages of good dialogue.   Some directors did very similar things, just changing the camera angle slightly and calling it a new take.   But these tricks just point up the false economy of so many of the rules and regulations they had.   The only thing that matters is the story, and every penny and hour spent on that comes right back.

Q: Did you enjoy THE GREAT O'MALLEY or ANOTHER DAWN?

A: THE GREAT O'MALLEY (1937) was a different story, a police story.   My only interest in that was in Bogart.   This was the first time I worked with him.   When I like people, I can do something with them.   But outside of Bogart, I wasn't very interested in THE GREAT O'MALLEY.   It wasn't my cup of tea.
    ANOTHER DAWN (1937) could have been something. It was from a Laird Doyle story, and Flynn of course....

Q: Was he difficult to direct?

A: Outside of Gable I think he was the most wonderful personality Hollywood ever had.   It's hard to believe you don't see him any more--his radiance, his personality.   He was not a great actor by any means, but he was not just a shallow charmer either.   It was just the way he walked, the way he talked, the way he behaved.   He was a modern Apollo.   He was such a wonderful chap, and I liked him

because he was different. He didn't care if he had money
or if he didn't. He just wanted to live life. He was the
lone adventurer, the last modern adventurer.

  If you knew and liked him, it was the same as with
Bill Powell. He would come in all hungover and plead,
"Just one hour, Bill. " So I would say okay, and he goes
and gets a shower, sauna and massage, while I shoot around
him for a while. When he came back, he gave me more in
a few hours than the others did all day.

  Film is still a matter of personality. You think
Marilyn Monroe was a genius at acting? Definitely not.
But she fascinated the world. Whether you or I liked her
made no difference. It was the same with Flynn; he was
the darling of the entire world.

Q: I take it THE LIFE OF EMILE ZOLA (1937) was your
favorite biopic?

A: Yes, in a way, though we had the same problems with
that as with all the others. We could only use the word
"Jew" three times (and I think two of them were cut out).
And the French banned that picture. Can you believe such
hypocrisy?

Q: What about JUAREZ (1939)?

A: I can't understand why that's not shown now. It should
be the biggest kind of picture right now--a big modern army
worn down by guerrilla fighters. The parallel with Vietnam
is so obvious.

  It was a very difficult picture to make. We were
shooting in Mexico, so we had to be very careful with the
whole political question, and, of course, the French were
offended.

Q: Did you have trouble controlling so many volatile per-
formers--Muni, Bette Davis, Brian Aherne, Garfield? ...

A: Ah, Garfield, what a shame, so young to die, what a
natural actor. But to answer your question, no. Muni I
had known so long I knew all his tricks and could deal with
him.

Q: Why did you leave Warner's?

A: Well, by the time I left for good, I had some outside
experience. I had done BLOCKADE (United Artists, 1938)

for Walter Wanger and THE HUNCHBACK OF NOTRE DAME
(RKO, 1939) at RKO for Pandro Berman. My agent had
some good deals lined up--I was supposed to go to Paramount, I was supposed to go to M-G-M--but I said to my
agent, "I want to make my own pictures." I think RKO was
the right choice at the time; it certainly offered the most
freedom.

Q: What was your favorite film at RKO?

A: I think ALL THAT MONEY CAN BUY (RKO, 1941),
which is the title they gave to "The Devil and Daniel Webster." I read the story and wanted to do it. I worked with
Stephen Vincent Benét on the script. With his patched, ill-
fitting clothes he looked like a nineteenth-century poet who
just stepped out of his garret. He was delightful to work
with, as was Walter Huston who played Mr. Scratch (the
devil).

Q: I noticed a very Germanic sequence, the dance of death.
How did you get that unearthly effect?

A: Well, I have to give the credit to Joe August, who was,
perhaps, the best cameraman I ever worked with. He had
been in pictures since the beginning, and had photographed
everything--documentaries, Westerns, everything. For that
scene he took out a brush and painted a circle of vaseline
around the lens. He did it with such assurance and delicacy
and the results were terrific. He was a true artist.

Q: Tell me about SYNCOPATION (RKO, 1942). I've never
seen that.

A: SYNCOPATION was another picture I enjoyed. It was
the story of jazz. It began with slaves being brought over
from Africa and traced the development of jazz from folk
art into the sophisticated musical form it was already in
the 'forties. Just as in "The Devil and Daniel Webster" it
was the folkloristic elements that attracted me.

Q: After RKO you went to M-G-M; how did you like that?

A: Not at all. Mayer was such a dictator. I'll never forget an interview I had with him where he told me, "I'm the
boss. You Europeans think you know, but I'm here and I
know."

Q: Did he interfere with your films?

A: Yes, in very stupid ways. In TENNESSEE JOHNSON
(M-G-M, 1943) we had the leading radical Republican con-
gressman dressed as history tells us he was. He was so
totally wrapped up in his cause and didn't care about his appearance. So we dressed him as our research told us.
Well, everything was fine until L. B. saw the rushes. "Who
is that guy?" he asked, "Is he a Republican or a Democrat?"
I told him he was a Republican and Mayer had a tantrum,
"Listen here, I'm a Republican and Republicans don't look
like that. " So we had to reshoot all those scenes and we
lost a lot of character detail.

Q: It's been said that M-G-M had the best technical facilities. Did you find it so?

A: In a way, but I think M-G-M was overrated. I showed
[Cedric] Gibbons, the head architect, small period water-
colors and got huge overlit monstrosities for sets.

Q: What about your work with Selznick? You worked on
DUEL IN THE SUN (Selznick, 1947), didn't you?

A: Yes, and I got no credit for it, though I shot at least
forty-nine days. I would say that at least twenty per cent
of the film is mine. I reshot the beginning and the end.
Selznick, like the people at M-G-M, was never satisfied,
always making retakes.

Q: PORTRAIT OF JENNIE (Selznick, 1949), which you directed for Selznick, is one of my favorites.

A: Yes, I liked it too, but that picture is as much, or
more, Selznick's as mine. He was always trying to top
GONE WITH THE WIND (M-G-M, 1939). I read the treatment of PORTRAIT OF JENNIE and convinced him to do it
because it was something different, a small, intimate, romantic picture. Well, as we were shooting he added miles
of extra dialogue and then inflated a thunderstorm into a
typhoon with the aid of people from the Walt Disney studio.

Q: Why did you go to Paramount?

A: Selznick got in financial difficulties and sold my contract to Wallis at Paramount. I was not very happy with
Wallis at Paramount. I felt he used me to try to make

something out of very second-rate material.   He forced me
to use a certain actress he was involved with and she was
very difficult to work with.

Q: Why did you leave Hollywood?

A: That's simple, I just couldn't get work.   My last American picture, ELEPHANT WALK (Paramount, 1954), was
held up for four months while the State Department decided
to give me a passport so I could go to Ceylon and do the
picture.   You see, I was branded a "premature anti-fascist"
because my wife and I had worked throughout the 'thirties to
get people out of Germany, and we helped Bert Brecht and
many other members of the Hollywood refugee colony.
Though I was never to my knowledge on any blacklist, I
must have been on some kind of a gray list because I
couldn't get any work.

II: Biographical Sketch

by Nancy K. Hart

First, to explain Dieterle's "gray listing," as he
calls it, is to explain the careers of many Hollywood enthusiasts during the 'thirties and 'forties.

It would require a long article and much research to
tell the stories of the pressures exerted on a number of
people because of the film BLOCKADE (United Artists, 1938)
which Dieterle directed.   It may have been the beginning of
the drive against meaningful content in motion pictures
which culminated in the House Committee on UnAmerican
Activities.

The screenwriter of BLOCKADE, John Howard Lawson, one of the imprisoned Hollywood Ten, explained the
film and the controversy surrounding it: "The battle over
BLOCKADE began even before the film opened.   It was
scheduled to have a gala preview at Grauman's Chinese
Theatre in Hollywood on 19 May 1938.   An elaborate souvenir program was prepared, but the preview was called off
at the last minute.   Walter Wanger published an apology in
the trade papers, admitting that he was 'unable to show the
picture at this time.'

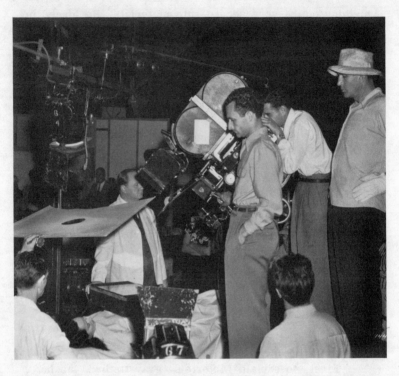

Dieterle in his white gloves directing THIS LOVE OF OURS
(Universal, 1945).   Photo courtesy of Movie Star News.

"A delayed preview took place in a more modest location (the Village Theatre in Westwood) on 3 June.   The
souvenir program contained a message from Wanger in
which he paid tribute to William Dieterle, saying, 'I am
proud to have had him associated with me in opening a
field of current events as dramatic screen-fare.' Wanger
also thanked me for a splendid script.

"I have no wish to defend my work on BLOCKADE.
The script has weaknesses, and in many ways William
Dieterle's skill and imagination as the director compensated
for my limitations in handling the difficult and challenging
material.

"But the importance of BLOCKADE lies in its being
the only film made in Hollywood during the Spanish Civil

War which dealt with the essential issues--the blockade imposed by the allegedly 'neutral' powers, the strangling of the
legal government of Spain by cutting off its food and supplies,
the attack on civilian populations, the danger of world war
and the use of Spain by Hitler and Mussolini as a rehearsal
for World War II (as in the bombing of Guernica)."

Unlike many Hollywood directors of this period, however, Dieterle did not deal only in controversial subjects.
In the one hundred-plus pictures with which Dieterle has
been connected, he runs the gamut of film types from the
"sublime to the ridiculous."

Dieterle said, "I believe the story is more important
than technological gimmicks, and that a story should have a
message. You may be sure that the studio that makes
films for the so-called advanced audiences will be the studio of tomorrow."

Dieterle did feel that the director could best tell the
story and had this as his life-long ambition. It was not by
any means that Dieterle left acting because he was frus-
trated in that profession.

Dieterle was, in fact, a successful actor at a very
early age. From the age of thirteen, after being trained in
carpentry, Dieterle expressed a desire to be on stage. At
sixteen, he became an apprentice with a group of traveling
players.

Dieterle got a chance at acting on the stage of the
Mannheim Theatre, just across the river from Ludwigshaven,
Rhenpfalz, Germany, where he was born on 15 July 1893.

It was with the touring acting group that Dieterle
learned the art of "staging." Dieterle shifted scenery and
was a general handyman as well as an actor.

During a production of WILHELM TELL on stage in
Zurich, Dieterle was what Hollywood language would term
"discovered." His best chance came from Max Reinhardt,
the most distinguished theatrical producer of post-war Germany. He gave Dieterle a contract to appear on the Berlin
stage. Dieterle soon played parts such as Danton or Brutus, opposite a number of prominent actors. From 1919
until his departure for the U.S. Dieterle played a number
of varying roles for Reinhardt.

Dieterle's first actual appearance in a film came in 1911, FIESCO, while he was on tour in Heidelberg. His second motion picture role did not come until early in 1921, opposite Henny Porten, "the sweetheart of Germany's silent movies." The film, GEIERWALLY, was shot on location in the Bavarian Alps. Altogether, Dieterle appeared in five films in 1921.

In 1922, Dieterle played in eight pictures, but still had the desire to direct. In a Sight and Sound interview with Dieterle, Francis Koval, the author, commented on Dieterle's early predicaments.

"On the screen, Dieterle was seen mostly in parts of country yokels and simpletons, which he played with great gusto and to the public's enormous delight. It sounds almost paradoxical, but it was just his popularity that prevented him from putting into practice his dream of directing. No producer wanted to listen to his suggestions. After all, Dieterle's name printed in big letters on top of the bill spelled box-office attraction, but the same name placed in small print under the heading 'directed by' wouldn't be worth even the printing ink--so the producers argued."

Nevertheless, in 1923, Dieterle first tried writing and directing movies. His first effort was MENSCHEN AM WEGE (MEN AT THE CROSSROADS). Dieterle himself played the romantic lead. The film also starred the nineteen-year-old Marlene Dietrich in her first film. Dieterle appeared in a few more films that year.

In 1924, Dieterle opened his "Das Dramatische Theater." This did not stop his acting career, however, and that year he starred in MUTTER UND KIND (MOTHER AND CHILD). The next year he starred in even more films than any previous year--eleven! In the succeeding years, Dieterle continued to pursue his career as an actor, with minor chances at directing squeezed in where possible.

Dieterle not only directed and starred in but also wrote DAS GEHEIMNIS DES ABBE X (SECRET OF ABBE X) next. It was the story of a priest and his inner conflicts which lead to disaster.

DIE HEILIGE UND IHR NARR (THE SAINT AND HER FOOL) was probably one of the last films in which Dieterle achieved great success in 1928. This was just before the arrival of the talkie, which caused new problems for all directors and actors, and just before Dieterle's own departure from Germany. In this film, Dieterle's comparatively short, but successful, acting career in Europe culminated in the moving part he played of the deeply human fool.

In 1928 Dieterle did do a number of other small films for his own production company. It was Zelnik, then head of Deutsche First National, a subsidiary of the Hollywood firm, who suggested that Dieterle organize his own production unit.

In 1929 Dieterle again switched companies. This time he was employed by Deutsche-Universal, a German subsidiary of the U.S. Universal, where he directed and starred in two homely tales: FRUEHLINGSRAUSCHEN (MURMURS OF SPRING) and DAS SCHWEIGEN IM WALDE (THE SILENCE OF THE FOREST).

Already in 1929, Dieterle was directing biographical films which would one day make him famous. His last silent film was about the tragic life of King Ludwig II of Bavaria who commits suicide. As with many of his films, Dieterle had the difficult task of both directing and acting in the film.

In 1930, Dieterle left Germany for Hollywood, attracted by the prospect of directing a German version of an American film. A good number of French and German filmmakers were being imported for the foreign versions of all major productions being put together during the first years of sound.

The European directors brought with them a knowledge that was important to American filmmaking. Both the artistic and technical levels of the German directors were such that they could aid the American cinema in Hollywood.

At the onset of Dieterle's career, one author said, "Dieterle's calm and efficient manner, coupled with his youthful enthusiasm, impressed the American producers. When Warner Brothers suggested a long term contract, he eagerly accepted, forsaking without regret his commitments in Berlin."

Soon Hollywood would see the talents of many German artists as Nazi oppression increased.

The film company that imported Dieterle was First
National. He started his career by directing THE DANCE
GOES ON (First National, 1930), which again found Dieterle
not only directing but also in an acting role.

As with many new directors, the first films assigned
Dieterle were "B" pictures. Probably the first eight or ten
are not familiar or well-remembered, but during this time
Dieterle was experimenting with new assignments--English-
speaking pictures, for example. In directing these films,
Dieterle gained needed experience in American filmmaking
and established a reputation of being "extremely scrupulous,
not fussy at all on the floor, and always dead on time within
the schedule." Dieterle's first English-speaking picture was
THE LAST FLIGHT (First National, 1931). Then he showed
his versatility even further and his second English-speaking
picture was a musical, HER MAJESTY, LOVE (First National, 1931). It starred Ben Lyon, W. C. Fields, and Marilyn
Miller.

For a while after these pictures, during which the
U.S. suffered in the throes of depression, Dieterle did a
number of programmers, but at least it kept him working.

By 1934, it was time for Dieterle to welcome his
former benefactor, Max Reinhardt, to Hollywood. He was to
assist Reinhardt in the screen version of A MIDSUMMER
NIGHT'S DREAM (Warner's, 1936). Unfortunately, many obstacles had to be overcome. It was Reinhardt's first and
last film venture. For a while the picture's problems
seemed endless. Color was absent from a picture that des-
perately needed it. Reinhardt knew practically nothing about
technical aspects of the American set-up and Dieterle was
left with the bulk of camera set-up and staging.

Dieterle and his wife, German actress Charlotte Ha-
genbruch, were always willing to help refugees from Nazi
Germany. They became American citizens. A magazine
article at the time said this of Dieterle: "His personal ha-
bits and way of life were not affected in the least by his
change of nationality. He always ridiculed the 'swell guys'
who after a few years in America put on airs of Yankees
born and bred, and always insisted on speaking German to
those whose mother-tongue it was."

Dieterle is probably best remembered for his biographies. He once said, "The lives of important people can

carry a message to the screen." He convinced Warner's of that fact and THE STORY OF LOUIS PASTEUR (First National, 1936) was made on a budget of only $300,000. It made much more money than that and brought an Oscar to Paul Muni. Muni and Dieterle had worked together the previous year on DR. SOCRATES (Warner's, 1935).

Again a list of good but not memorable films found their way onto Dieterle's credit list. In 1938 Dieterle was slowed down by an automobile accident that left him laid up for five months.

Dieterle's career with Warner's began to slow when, in 1939, he did HUNCHBACK OF NOTRE DAME for RKO. A few more bio pictures, and Dieterle decided to form his own company. He then produced and directed two films, ALL THAT MONEY CAN BUY (RKO, 1941) and SYNCOPATION (RKO, 1942), but neither proved a real commercial success.

So Dieterle went to M-G-M to do TENNESSEE JOHNSON (M-G-M, 1943) and KISMET (M-G-M, 1944), this time with Marlene Dietrich. A number of other films with important actors and actresses followed until 1946 when Dieterle returned to Europe to direct and did one of his best films, PORTRAIT OF JENNIE (Selznick, 1949).

The versatility of Dieterle was seen once more in the picture VOLCANO (United Artists, 1953), which was shot on location in Italy. It starred Anna Magnani, but Dieterle said, "The picture did not do well ... because Magnani was not so well publicized in 1949 as now."

Dieterle commented further on the picture in an early Sight and Sound interview:

"The life and work on our tiny island was really great fun. I certainly could have made much more money in Hollywood during that time, but I could hardly have had such fun. When I first received the ten-page synopsis of the subject sent to me by the scriptwriter and co-producer Renzo Avanzo, I had the feeling that this was a challenge to make a worthwhile film without all the technical resources of a Hollywood studio. That is why I accepted. After all, technique is so much over-estimated nowadays, and I want to make pictures which should stimulate the eyes and the minds of people. Tackling one subject after another on the

studio floor can become a routine job--one develops the
mental attitude of 'sitting back. '

"The life on Vulcano--that's the name of our island--
was certainly different. We had to rough it for three months
or so, and we all thoroughly enjoyed it. I had about twenty-
five people with me and we had to bring from the mainland
everything we needed: not only the cameras and the usual
paraphernalia, but even our own generators to provide the
current, and all the food for the unit. We even had to build
our own pier to land all the heavy equipment.

"A number of people warned me against all these difficulties, convinced that I would give up sooner or later.
But against all expectations, everything went off smoothly,
and in forty-five days we finished our shooting, strictly within schedule. This includes twelve days of underwater shooting which was done without diver suits and with the help of a
tiny special camera built by Italian technicians in Palermo.
They and the other members of my unit--all Italians--proved
such an excellent team that I didn't know whether to admire
more their skill or their daring. These shots of sponge-
fishing on the rocky sea-bed were pretty tricky, and the sequences involving rock-fall and the eruption of a volcano
were really fraught with dangers.

"In the mass-scenes and many minor episodes the
whole population of the island took part. In some cases we
even brought over the fisherfolk from the neighboring islands.
The strange life of these extremely poor people fascinated
me, and it forms a very colorful background to our story.
The little villages are practically run by women whose husbands and fathers have emigrated to America or New Zea-
land. Emigrated is, of course, a wrong word. They have
gone abroad in order to provide money for the family and
to come back with some savings. They always return,
sometimes after five or ten years, sometimes after twenty-
five, and sometimes in their coffins. One such tragic return occurred during our stay on the island, and it figures
in our picture. "

Dieterle was asked to compare his film with STROM-
BOLI (RKO, 1949), shot on another island with somewhat the
same story and starring Ingrid Bergman.

"The fact that both films are based on a similar
story doesn't mean a thing. There isn't an original subject

under the sun any more, and everything depends on the treatment. If Rossellini's film turns out better than mine, well--may the better man win. But our two stories will be as different from each other as my personality is from Rossellini's and Anna Magnani's acting from Ingrid Bergman's."

Dieterle's personality did fit into many of his films. After VOLCANO he did another on-location film, SEPTEMBER AFFAIR (Paramount, 1951), and went back to Hollywood.

ELEPHANT WALK (Paramount, 1954), for Dieterle, is a memorable film from the production aspect. It was done on-location in Ceylon. Halfway through, Vivien Leigh had a nervous breakdown and was forced to quit, which left Elizabeth Taylor in the role. Quite a favorable editing and matching job was done in the cutting room.

Dieterle kept up an active directing career until the time of his death. He will be remembered not only for his contribution to the art of the cinema expressed in his films, but also for the many pictures he aptly directed, sometimes produced, and often acted in that have survived him.

WILLIAM DIETERLE

A Film Checklist by Karl Thiede

Director

1. MENSCHEN AM WEGE (1923). P: Osmania. C: William Dieterle, Heinrich George, Alexander Granach.

2. DAS GEHEIMNIS DES ABBE X (1927). P: Charha. C: William Dieterle, Marcella Albani, Alfred Gerasch.

3. DIE HEILIGE UND IHR NARR (1928). P: Defu. C: William Dieterle, Lien Deyers, Felix de Pomes, Gina Manes.

4. GESCHLECHT IN FESSELN (1928). P: Essem. C:

William Dieterle, Gunnar Tolnaes, Hans Heinz von Twardowski.

5. ICH LEBE FUER DICH (1929). P: Deutsche Universal. C: William Dieterle, Lien Deyers, Olaf Foeness.

6. FRUEHLINGSRAUSCHEN (1929). P: Deutsche Universal. C: William Dieterle, Lien Deyers, Julius Brandt.

7. DAS SCHWEIGEN IM WALDE (1929). P: Deutsche Universal. C: William Dieterle, Rina Marsa, Julius Brandt.

8. LUDWIG DER ZWEITE, KOENIG VON BAYERN (1929). P. Deutsche Universal. C: William Dieterle, Eugen Burg, Hubert von Meyerinck.

9. EINE STUNDE GLUECK (1930). P: Cicero. C: William Dieterle, Evelyn Holt, Harald Paulsen.

William (Wilhelm) Dieterle arrived in New York from Germany on Saturday, 26 July 1930. William Dieterle went to Hollywood on 27 July 1930.

10. DER TANZ GEHT WEITER (THE DANCE GOES ON) (November 1930, Berlin). P: First National. C: Lissi Arna, Carla Bertheel, William Dieterle. In production: September 1930. 72m.

11. DIE MASKE FAELLT (1930). P: First National. C: Lissi Arna, Anton Pointner, Karl Etlinger. In production: October 1930.

12. KISMET (1930). P: First National. C: Gustav Froehlich, Dita Parlo, Vladimir Sokoloff. Production started: 24 November 1930. German version.

13. THE LAST FLIGHT (29 August 1931). P: First National. C: Richard Barthelmess, Helen Chandler, John Mack Brown. 77m.

14. HER MAJESTY LOVE (15 December 1931). P: First National. C: Marilyn Miller, Ben Lyon, W. C. Fields. Production was completed in 26 days in October 1931. 76m.

15. MAN WANTED (23 April 1932). P: Warner Brothers.
    C: Kay Francis, David Manners, Guy Kibbee. 63m.

16. THE JEWEL ROBBERY (13 August 1932). P: First
    National. C: William Powell, Kay Francis, Helen
    Vinson. 68m.

17. THE CRASH (8 October 1932). P: First National. C:
    Ruth Chatterton, George Brent, Paul Cavanaugh.
    58m.

18. SIX HOURS TO LIVE (16 October 1932). P: Fox Film
    Corporation. C: Warner Baxter, Mariam Jordan,
    John Boles. 78m.

19. SCARLET DAWN (12 November 1932). P: Warner
    Brothers. C: Nancy Carroll, Douglas Fairbanks,
    Jr., Lilyan Tashman. 58m.

20. LAWYER MAN (7 January 1933). P: Warner Brothers.
    C: William Powell, Joan Blondell, Claire Dodd. 68m.

21. GRAND SLAM (18 March 1933). P: Warner Brothers.
    C: Paul Lukas, Loretta Young, Frank McHugh. 65m.

22. ADORABLE (19 May 1933). P: Fox Film Corporation.
    C: Janet Gaynor, Henry Garat, C. Aubrey Smith.
    83m.

23. THE DEVIL'S IN LOVE (21 July 1933). P: Fox Film
    Corporation. C: Loretta Young, Victor Jory, Vivi-
    enne Osborne. 71m.

24. FROM HEADQUARTERS (2 December 1933). P: War-
    ner Brothers. C: George Brent, Margaret Lindsay,
    Eugene Pallette. 63m.

25. FASHIONS OF 1934 (17 February 1934). P: First Na-
    tional. C: William Powell, Bette Davis, Frank
    McHugh. 78m.

26. FOG OVER FRISCO (2 June 1934). P: First National.
    C: Bette Davis, Donald Woods, Lyle Talbot. 68m.

27. MADAME DU BARRY (13 October 1934). P: Warner
    Brothers. C: Dolores Del Rio, Reginald Owen,
    Victory Jory. 77m.

28.   THE FIREBIRD (3 November 1934). P: Warner
      Brothers. C: Verree Teasdale, Ricardo Cortez,
      Lionel Atwill. 74m.

29.   THE SECRET BRIDE (22 December 1934). P: Warner
      Brothers. C: Barbara Stanwyck, Warren William,
      Glenda Farrell. Working title: CONCEALMENT.
      64m.

30.   A MIDSUMMER NIGHT'S DREAM (Roadshow, October
      1935; general release, 8 October 1936). P: Warner
      Brothers. D: Max Reinhardt, William Dieterle. C:
      James Cagney, Dick Powell, Joe E. Brown. In pro-
      duction: December 1934-March 1935. NC:
      $1,300,000. DG: $1,543,447. Roadshow: 132m.
      General relsease: 117m.

31.   DR. SOCRATES (19 October 1935). P: Warner
      Brothers. C: Paul Muni, Ann Dvorak, Barton
      MacLane. In production: June-July 1935. 70m.

32.   THE STORY OF LOUIS PASTEUR (22 February 1936).
      P: First National. C: Paul Muni, Josephine Hutch-
      inson, Anita Louise. Working title: ENEMY OF
      MAN. In production: August-September 1935. 87m.

33.   THE WHITE ANGEL (4 July 1936). P: First National.
      C: Kay Francis, Ian Hunter, Donald Woods. 91m.

34.   SATAN MET A LADY (8 August 1936). P: Warner
      Brothers. C: Bette Davis, Warren William, Alison
      Skipworth. Working title: MEN ON HER MIND.
      The second filmed version of THE MALTESE FAL-
      CON. 74m.

35.   THE GREAT O'MALLEY (13 February 1937). P: War-
      ner Brothers. C: Pat O'Brien, Sybil Jason, Hum-
      phrey Bogart. 71m.

36.   ANOTHER DAWN (26 June 1937). P: Warner Broth-
      ers. C: Kay Francis, Errol Flynn, Ian Hunter.
      72m.

37.   THE LIFE OF EMILE ZOLA (2 October 1937). P:
      Warner Brothers. C: Paul Muni, Joseph Schild-
      kraut, Gloria Holden. NC: $1,000,000. DG:
      $1,500,000. 116m.

38. BLOCKADE (17 June 1938). P: United Artists. C:
     Madeleine Carroll, Henry Fonda, Leo Carrillo. NC:
     $692,086.64. WWG: $718,693.79. 84m.

39. JUAREZ (10 June 1939). P: Warner Brothers. C:
     Paul Muni, Bette Davis, Brian Aherne. 127m.

40. THE HUNCHBACK OF NOTRE DAME (29 December
     1939). P: RKO Radio Pictures. C: Charles Laugh-
     ton, Cedric Hardwicke, Maureen O'Hara. 115m.

41. DR. EHRLICH'S MAGIC BULLET (2 March 1940). P:
     Warner Brothers. C: Edward G. Robinson, Ruth
     Gordon, Otto Kruger. 103m.

42. A DISPATCH FROM REUTER'S (19 October 1940). P:
     Warner Brothers. C: Edward G. Robinson, Edna
     Best, Eddie Albert. 96m.

43. ALL THAT MONEY CAN BUY (17 October 1941). P:
     RKO Radio Pictures. C: Edward Arnold, Walter
     Huston, James Craig. Working title: THE DEVIL
     AND DANIEL WEBSTER. The title was changed one
     day before tradeshowing to HERE IS A MAN and re-
     leased as ALL THAT MONEY CAN BUY. The film
     is now known as THE DEVIL AND DANIEL WEBSTER.
     106m.

44. SYNCOPATION (22 May 1942). P: RKO Radio Pic-
     tures. C: Adolphe Menjou, Jackie Cooper, Bonita
     Granville. 88m.

45. TENNESSEE JOHNSON (20 February 1943). P: Metro-
     Goldwyn-Mayer. C: Van Heflin, Ruth Hussey, Lio-
     nel Barrymore. 9,295ft./103m.

46. KISMET (20 October 1944). P: Metro-Goldwyn-Mayer.
     C: Ronald Colman, Marlene Dietrich, James Craig.
     Technicolor. 9,003ft./100m.

47. I'LL BE SEEING YOU (5 January 1945). P: United
     Artists. C: Ginger Rogers, Joseph Cotten, Shirley
     Temple. FG: $1,244,253. 85m.

48. LOVE LETTERS (26 October 1945). P: Paramount.
     C: Jennifer Jones, Joseph Cotten, Ann Richards.
     101m.

49. THIS LOVE OF OURS (2 November 1945). P: Univer-
     sal. C: Merle Oberon, Charles Korvin, Claude
     Rains. 90m.

50. THE SEARCHING WIND (9 August 1946). P: Para-
     mount. C: Sylvia Sidney, Robert Young, Ann
     Richards. 107m.

51. DUEL IN THE SUN (17 April 1947). P: Selznick Re-
     leasing Organization. D: King Vidor, Joseph von
     Sternberg and William Dieterle uncredited. C: Jen-
     nifer Jones, Joseph Cotten, Gregory Peck. NC:
     $5,255,000. DG: $11,300,000. Technicolor.
     124 1/2m.

52. THE ACCUSED (14 January 1949). P: Paramount.
     C: Loretta Young, Robert Cummings, Wendell Corey.
     101m.

53. PORTRAIT OF JENNIE (22 April 1949). P: Selznick
     Releasing Organization. C: Jennifer Jones, Joseph
     Cotten, Ethel Barrymore. Part color. 86m.

54. VOLCANO (1949, U.S. release, 5 June 1953). P:
     United Artists. C: Anna Magnani, Rossano Brazzi,
     Geraldine Brooks. DG: $48,332.15. 106m.

55. ROPE OF SAND (23 September 1949). P: Paramount.
     C: Burt Lancaster, Paul Henreid, Claude Rains.
     DG: $2,250,000. 104m.

56. PAID IN FULL (March 1950). P: Paramount. C:
     Robert Cummings, Lizabeth Scott, Diana Lynn. 105m.

57. DARK CITY (October 1950). P: Paramount. C:
     Charlton Heston, Lizabeth Scott, Viveca Lindfors.
     98m.

58. SEPTEMBER AFFAIR (February 1951). P: Paramount.
     C: Joan Fontaine, Joseph Cotten, Francoise Rosay.
     DG: $1,425,000. 104m.

59. PEKING EXPRESS (August 1951). P: Paramount. C:
     Joseph Cotten, Corinne Calvet, Edmund Gwenn. A
     remake of SHANGHAI EXPRESS. DG: $1,100,000.
     90m.

60.   BOOTS MALONE (January 1952). P: Columbia. C:
      William Holden, Johnny Stewart, Stanley Clements.
      103m.

61.   RED MOUNTAIN (May 1952). P: Paramount. C:
      Alan Ladd, Lizabeth Scott, Arthur Kennedy. DG:
      $2,000,000. Color. 84m.

62.   THE TURNING POINT (November 1952). P: Para-
      mount. C: William Holden, Alexis Smith, Edmund
      O'Brien. Color. 85m.

63.   SALOME (September 1953). P: Columbia. C: Rita
      Hayworth, Stewart Granger, Charles Laughton. DG:
      $4,750,000. Color. 103m.

64.   ELEPHANT WALK (June 1954). P: Paramount. C:
      Elizabeth Taylor, Dana Andrews, Peter Finch. DG:
      $3,000,000. Technicolor. 103m.

65.   MAGIC FIRE (29 March 1956). P: Republic. C:
      Yvonne de Carlo, Alan Badel, Peter Cushing. Tru-
      color. 112m.

66.   OMAR KHAYYAM (August 1957). P: Paramount. C:
      Cornel Wilde, Michael Rennie, Debra Paget. DG:
      $1,200,000. Technicolor. 101m.

67.   HERRIN DER WELT, PART I (1959). P: Franco-
      London-Continental-CCC. C: Martha Hyer, Carlos
      Thompson, Micheline Presle.

68.   HERRIN DER WELT, PART II (1959). P: Franco-
      London-Continental-CCC. C: Carlos Thompson,
      Wolfgang Preiss, Sabu.

69.   IL VINDICATORE (1959). P: Hesperia-Verdar. C:
      John Forsythe, Rossana Schiaffino, Nerio Bernardi.

70.   DIE FASTNACHTSBEICHTE (1960). P: UFA. C:
      Hans Soehnker, Gitty Daruga, Goetz George.

71.   THE CONFESSION (1964). P: Unreleased. C: Ray
      Milland, Ginger Rogers, Barbara Eden. Shot in
      Jamaica. Production started: 13 April 1964. Color.

Chapter 4

JOSEPH KANE

by Harry Sanford

There was a man whose life and career in the film business included just about everything there was to do; a man of action, who knew better than most, the importance of making pictures <u>move</u>. His name was Joe Kane.

Veteran stuntman-actor George DeNormand once said of him: "I doubt if there was anybody in the business who could move people any better in action films than Joe. He was a helluva guy! He might kill you in the process, but he always got the job done on time and on budget."

"My father," Joe Kane recalled, "Francis Inman Kane, was born in England and was a graduate of Sandhurst, the British equivalent of West Point. He became a second lieutenant in the armed forces of Her Imperial Majesty, Queen Victoria. One of the two prized mementos he left us was his commission signed by the Queen, the other, a marriage certificate bearing my mother's name from Old Christ Church on Wall Street, New York. He resigned his commission and came to America to the Dakota Territory to take up land. He met my mother in New York. She had come from Scotland. They became citizens of the United States when the territories were admitted into the Union on 2 November 1889."

The elder Kane was stricken with tuberculosis shortly after and moved on West to San Diego, California. It was here that young Joseph Kane was born on 11 March 1894. In that city, three months later, Francis Kane died. Together with his mother Marie and his older brother,

---

Opposite: Joseph Kane.

143

Joseph moved all around California. In so doing, he received no real formal education. What Kane didn't learn
about the alphabet from his mother, he learned from bill-
boards and posters. He became an avid reader and to the
end read everything he could lay his hands on.

The years passed. Joe Kane drifted into the picture
business. His first job was as an extra at the old Balboa
Studios in Long Beach. The studios were owned and operated by the Horkheimer brothers, a pair of real characters.
Fatty Arbuckle, Buster Keaton, Cullen Landis, and famed
director Henry King worked there. The company made
everything--comedies, Westerns, and dramas. The brothers
often met the payroll with a roll of the dice, cleaning out
any and all takers in their skillful games. Existence for
creative genius was perilous in those days.

The Westerns were shot on Signal Hill. It has now
become an oil field which, to the casual sightseer, appears
as either a landmark or a blot. From the top of the hill
there was a vast sweeping view of the surrounding country
which was mostly unpopulated, filled with ravines and gullies.
Kane hired on as a rider in Western chase scenes for $5 a
day. The extras would ride back and forth as outlaws being
pursued by the posse. As they reached a wide sandy place
in the trail, for an extra 50 cents, they would tumble heavily to the ground on cue. Today such a stunt costs at least
$300 a fall--one fall! Anything else has to be negotiated,
and the price goes up accordingly.

When World War I broke out Kane reported to his
draft board with a bad case of mononucleosis that developed
into hepatitis. Upon recovering, he was called into service
for the duration of the conflict, serving at Camp Kearny
near San Diego. When he was released, Joe decided that
he still liked movies even it if meant falling off horses. He
got a call from the studio, this time to play sideline music
for an independent company leasing space for the Horkheimer brothers.

"Before I went into the Army, I'd been trying to become a professional musician, a cellist, but not very successfully. I got some work playing in a theatre orchestra
and also at a cafeteria; the latter earned me lunches and
dinners. At least it kept me eating regularly. Mostly, I
was called as a relief for another cellist who was unfortunately an alcoholic. He had fallen from the position of first

cellist at the New York Metropolitan Opera to a movie theatre in Long Beach.

"One night I was struggling with a mimeographed
score when he came in late.   In anger, the leader flung him
the piccolo part, sheets of music filled with dots representing a cascade of notes.   He sat on the edge of the pit and
without tuning his instrument rippled it off as easily as
'Home Sweet Home. '   That taught me one thing: talent is
essential in a competitive world.   A musician like that could
accomplish instantly what would take weeks for me. "

Kane reported to producer-director Milburn Morante
who liked his cello playing because he stuck to old well-
known melodies understood and appreciated by everyone.
"I'd been trying my hand at writing and did a story called
'Cloaker' (later retitled 'Diamond Carlisle') which I gave
him to read.   He liked it and bought it.   Tom Gibson, a
professional writer, put it into a screenplay form with
George Chesebro in the starring role.   Morante decided to
shoot it in and around Fish Camp, near Yosemite. "

Kane wanted to go along but Morante demurred saying that the budget would not allow it.   He decided upon another means of going: he got a job as location chef for the
company.   "I had no trouble after making a rule that when
we had eggs for breakfast they could only be served scram-
bled.   Lunch and dinner were easier because I had more
time to prepare them. "   Between sessions in the cookhouse
Kane penned THE MENACING PAST (Rollo, 1922), a Northwest Mounted Police story.   What with cooking and writing,
Kane's musical career came to an end.   George Chesebro
who over the years appeared in hundreds of Westerns, many
of them directed by Kane himself, was again the male lead
in Kane's second story for the screen.   The cameraman was
Lesley Selander.

The Morante company decided to depart from Balboa
Studios and moved into Hollywood.   Kane, now with some
practical experience under his belt, was able to land a
better job as an assistant to producer Barney Goodman, who
had an office on Beechwood Drive, better known as "Poverty
Row. "   One morning Kane was left in charge.   A tall handsome young man came in looking for a job as an actor.
Goodman had been planning a Western series.   Kane thought
this man would do and told him to wait.   Looking at his
watch, the man said he would be back in an hour because

he had an appointment at the Fox Film Corporation. He
never came back. Frank Borzage saw him and a few days
later he was cast opposite Janet Gaynor in SEVENTH HEAV-
EN (Fox, 1927). His name was Charles Farrell.

Goodman did a series of Westerns with an actor
named Bill Bailey. The director on this was Paul Hurst
who later became a well-known character actor. Kane was
Hurst's assistant, doing any job needed to complete the picture. This was, of course, long before the unions controlled
every phase of production. "When he'd shoot chase scenes
with the outlaws and good guys, I'd wear a black hat and the
wardrobe of the main heavy; then afterwards, I would switch
to the white hat and clothes of the leading man.

"We'd race up and down hills, across stream beds
and over rocky terrain. The leading actors either couldn't
or wouldn't take these hazardous rides. Paul refused to
have assistants who couldn't fork a horse. The horses knew
the sound of his long drawn-out 'come onnnnnnnn' and nothing
could stop them until they passed the camera. Forty years
later when I was directing LARAMIE TV series at Universal,
the gang seemed surprised when occasionally I would climb
aboard a horse and take off at a gallop. That was when I
began to suspect the years were creeping up on me."

Hurst quit soon after the Bill Bailey Westerns and
turned full time to acting. Joe next became associated with
Western producer-director star Leo Maloney in various func-
tions, primarily with Maloney's writer, Ford Beebe, and
also doubled as a second assistant director. When the cutter quit, Kane took over the job as film editor and edited
the next fourteen Maloney Westerns at Pathé. "Woody Van
Dyke was making a series of Westerns with Tim McCoy at
M-G-M but had a cutting room next to mine at the old Consolidated Film Lab in Hollywood. Also nearby was J. P.
McGowan, famous as a director for the HAZARDS OF HELEN
railroad serials. The Lab fixed him up with a cutting room
on the roof which was fireproofed because he always had a
lighted cigar in his mouth. In those days the films were nitrate and highly flammable. I had been in a film fire once
and would not go in his room. If I wanted to see McGowan,
I'd stand in the doorway and talk.

"As sound came in, we were recording on discs and
had to synchronize the scenes in the projection room. Once
in synchronization, the start marks had to be maintained and

we'd scratch them on preceding scenes when the cutting was
done.   The one we did was OVERLAND BOUND [Presidio,
1929] and Leo went to New York to sell it.   The sound
wasn't very good.   It was all right in the projection room
but in a packed house the sound was absorbed by the bodies
and the theatre, and it became faint.   He sold it anyway.
Leo was a heavy drinker.   As a result he once nearly died
of pneumonia.   He had been on the wagon for nearly a year
but went on a binge to celebrate.   It lasted three days and
some of his new-found friends dumped him in front of his
hotel.   The hotel doctor gave him a shot of morphine to
stop a fit of hiccups.   The shot worked. The hiccups stopped.
Leo Maloney died. ''

     His first decade in the business had put Joe Kane on
the fringes of filmmaking.   During his Pathé days he began
to edit and cut serials for Spencer Bennet, who felt that in
Kane he had found one man whom he could trust to do a good
job.   Bennet was accustomed to cutting in the camera; that
is, he would shoot just what he felt he needed and not half-
a-hundred takes so that an editor would have to spend days
putting it all together like a Chinese puzzle.   Kane's reputation as a first-rate editor increased and he soon found himself working for such well-known directors as Gregory La-
Cava, Tay Garnett, Russell Mack, and Al Rogell.   When
Charles Rogers and Harry Joe Brown went into business,
Joe Kane went into business.   Joe Kane went along with the
tandem, first to RKO, then to Paramount where things were
run on a strictly assembly-line basis.   As soon as a picture
was photographed, cutting, scoring, dubbing, previewing,
and printing were scheduled in rapid succession.   Only
Cecil B. DeMille and Josef Von Sternberg were excepted:
their pictures were handled in a different way.

     Fate, or what have you, took a hand in Joe Kane's
life at this point.   Harry Joe Brown left Paramount to go
over to Warner Brothers and later to Universal.   Charles
Rogers informed Kane that he was to be his number-one
assistant.   With such a prospect before him Kane took a
month's vacation from Paramount.   He never went back.
During the interim, Paramount decided that Rogers, without
Harry Joe Brown in double harness, wasn't fully able to
run the operation, so Rogers was made a studio associate
producer and given Val Paul as an assistant.   Having been
promised the assistant's job to Rogers, Kane resigned as a
cutter at Paramount's Marathon Street lot.   The spot was
quickly filled and Kane was out.   Moreover, cutters in those

days stayed on until they died or were fired for cause--us-
ually the only way that an opening would occur.

"I was on the beach kidding myself that I was twenty,
although the year was 1933 and I was thirty-nine. My real
friend was Harry Joe Brown, who tried to get me into Warner's." Not even Brown could budge the rigid system. Until Kane went to Warner Brothers in 1957 to direct three
segments of CHEYENNE with Clint Walker, his stint at Paramount was his last with a major studio for more than twenty
years. One must eat to live and like many in his profession
Kane hunted around looking for work wherever he could get
it. Nat Levine and Mascot beckoned and Kane heeded the
call, glad for anything that would provide a paycheck. Levine was quartered in a small office complex on Santa Monica Boulevard across the street from the Hollywood cemetery.
Kane was assigned to shoot some additional footage for a
Ken Maynard Western then in production entitled IN OLD
SANTE FE (Mascot, 1934). David Howard, the director on
the picture, had already left and the price to get him back
to finish up was more than Levine wanted to pay. Gene
Autry and his singing group were also featured in the film.
The picture was Kane's first association with Maynard, and
his last. The association with Autry, however, would con-
tinue for a number of years.

"I made the mistake of trying to kid with Ken. I
found out later that serious men who succeed in big business
consider levity a waste of time, if not worse. Anyway,
when I handed Ken the revised portion of the script I said I
understood he needed a few minutes to memorize that much.
I started away but suddenly found myself whirled around facing a furious man holding a six-gun aimed at my middle.
Ken had decided I was being sarcastic. He had a violent
temper and a low boiling point. At first I thought he was
putting on an act but he wasn't. His eyes told me that.
He invited me to take the other gun from his belt. I guess
they were really loaded." Gene Autry intervened and got
the fuming Maynard to one side. Kane, still amazed by the
whole thing, walked off. When Maynard cooled down, the
scene was shot and that was the last Joe Kane ever saw of
Ken Maynard.

Within a few months, Nat Levine moved Mascot to
the old Mack Sennett lot in Studio City. This lot had been
used by many of the most famous people in filmdom:
Charlie Chaplin, Fatty Arbuckle, Buster Keaton, Andy Clyde,

Mable Normand, and the Keystone Kops. Sennett had failed
to adjust to the sound era and the once-proud giant of the industry was flat broke and finished for good. Kane edited
several films for Levine directed by William Nigh and Phil
Rosen, once fairly important directors but who for one reason or another were now reduced to working for independents
like Mascot. Levine, for the most part, was quite impressed
with the work Joe Kane was turning out. If given the chance,
Nat thought Kane might be able to do more. He decided to
give him an opportunity to direct. The year was 1935, and
Mascot was being merged with several other independent
companies including Monogram and Consolidated Film Laboratories. The former was headed by Trem Carr and Consolidated by a bald-headed, tobacco-chewing Yankee named
Herbert J. Yates. The new corporation was called Republic
Pictures and Nat Levine headed up production.

Joe Kane and Gene Autry had at least one thing in
common, TUMBLING TUMBLEWEEDS (Republic, 1935). The
picture was Autry's first starring feature and it marked
Kane's debut as a full-fledged director. To say that the
picture, Autry, and the song were a success would be putting it mildly. Kane followed TUMBLEWEEDS with another
Autry opus, MELODY TRAIL, and then found himself co-
director on THE FIGHTING MARINES (Mascot, 1935) which
was distributed through the Republic exchanges. Reaves
"Breezy" Eason worked on MARINES. "Serials were mad;
the pace was frantic. Breezy and I directed on alternate
days. On our respective days off we'd study and prepare
for the next day."

Kane then directed Gene Autry in SAGEBRUSH
TROUBADOR (Republic, 1936). Another serial came along,
DARKEST AFRICA (Republic, 1936) and Joe again co-
directed with Breezy Eason. In THE FIGHTING MARINES
the leads were Grant Withers, who was to appear later in
many pictures that Kane directed, and Adrian Morris,
younger brother of Chester Morris. MARINES was a mystery concerning a gyroscope invented by a young Marine and
coveted by a mysterious criminal known only as the Tiger
Shark. In the last chapter the mystery man was the commanding officer's houseboy, played by one-time silent matinee idol, Jason Robards, Sr.

In DARKEST AFRICA, Clyde Beatty, the world-
famous animal trainer, was the lead. Beatty was no actor,
but his feats of daring with lions and tigers more than made

up for his deficiencies. The plot had to do with a search for a
missing white goddess in the lost city of Jorba. Manuel King,
then 11 and billed as the world's youngest animal trainer, aided
Beatty in his quest for the lost city. It took twelve chapters to
find it and when it ended everyone was relieved, Joe Kane in
particular.

UNDERSEA KINGDOM (Republic, 1936), Kane's third
and last serial, starred Ray "Crash" Corrigan and concerned
the discovery of the lost city of Atlantis. Magnificently
photographed by William Nobles and Edgar Lyons, UNDER-
SEA KINGDOM is considered by some to be one of the best
Republic serials.

Kane's next assignment was three independent
Westerns in a row, produced by one-time stuntman Paul Malvern. John Wayne was the star. Wayne had fallen on hard
times after the failure of THE BIG TRAIL (Fox, 1930), his
first starring role. The pictures, THE LAWLESS NINETIES
(Republic, 1936), KING OF THE PECOS (Republic, 1936),
and THE LONELY TRAIL (Republic, 1936), were shot on location at Lone Pine, with the majestic Mt. Whitney in the
background. "Wayne was very cooperative and no trouble,"
Kane stated evenly.

"By that time Nat Levine had sold Mascot to Herb
Yates to form Republic. Yates thought he had Wayne in the
deal, but found out he had him only for the one series.
Afterwards, Wayne went to Universal with Trem Carr, signing a contract which turned out to be misleading. When
Wayne went, they told him he would have full say on stories,
cast, director, and location. Again, as is so often the case,
Wayne did not read the details. He trusted the word of
others and found out that he was just a hired hand and had
to take what they gave him. One day he confided to me that
after that fiasco, he'd never trust anybody again and would
trample anybody that got in his way." Those words, spoken by
a bitter, resentful John Wayne, were to haunt Joe Kane nearly
ten years later in a manner he would never have anticipated.

Recalling some of the events of that time, Kane told
of shooting a scene where Wayne was to ride up to a well,
dismount, take a dipper to draw some water, and drink. "I
prepared to jerk the dipper away with a wire and told the
prop man to get ready. Pauley (Malvern) shook his head.
He was a crack shot in spite of his thick glasses, and he
and Wayne had actually decided to shoot the dipper out of

Duke's hand with a rifle. I refused to direct the scene and
Pauley took over. He took aim and fired, and the slug
went right through the dipper without taking it out of Wayne's
hand. They filled another dipper with water and prepared to
do it again. This made it doubly dangerous because water
can deflect a bullet. They made the scene and felt very
honest and proud. I thought it was idiotic. It could have
backfired and that would have been the end of Wayne, right
there. "

In THE LAWLESS NINETIES, the second independent
Western directed by Kane, George Hayes played a character
without a beard. Later on he played Windy Halliday in the
Hopalong series and grew his famous brush. When Republic
lured him away to appear in the Roy Rogers series, Harry
Sherman, who produced the Cassidy films, claimed to have
copyrighted the name and character Windy. To avoid a lawsuit Hayes changed his nickname to "Gabby" and played the
same character till he retired.

By 1938, Joe Kane had already directed, in addition
to the three John Wayne solo Westerns, three "Three Mesquiteers," a railroad yarn entitled PARADISE EXPRESS (Republic, 1937), sixteen Autry Westerns, and three serials.
Kane got a slight change of pace with BORN TO BE WILD
(Republic, 1938) which starred Ralph Byrd (the screen's Dick
Tracy), with Doris Weston and Ward Bond in supporting
roles. It was a modern-day melodrama of truck drivers
fighting racketeers. "They just substituted vehicles for
horses--otherwise the plot was the same," according to
Kane.

In the meantime the studio had taken on a new star,
Roy Rogers, billed earlier as Dick Weston and born Leonard
Slye. Gene Autry had kicked up his heels more than once,
causing the Republic brass quite a little concern. One afternoon Gene telephoned Kane and told him not to break his
back getting ready for the next picture as Autry intended not
to be there to shoot it. Autry was a man of his word. He
took off on tour, followed by process servers all over the
South in an effort to restrain him from doing any kind of
work other than that specified by Herbert J. Yates.

"Gene was so popular below the Mason-Dixon line
that people simply surrounded the process server and walked
him out of town. " Finally Yates capitulated. Autry, however, balked three more times, each time getting what he

wanted. Yates' mistake was in thinking Autry was broke.
Gene was never hurting. He had over $50,000 stashed in a
Chicago bank. Before coming to pictures, he'd done better
than all right on radio and records. "Gene was easy to
work with. He knew when to argue and when it wasn't
worthwhile. He guessed it wasn't important to make a fuss
about the kind of pictures we were making. They were
strictly commercial, aimed at a ready presold market that
ate them up like hotcakes. " Yates had brought in the young
Rogers as a lever to use against Autry. While it failed to
work in that regard, it was nonetheless the beginning of Roy
Rogers' career.

ARSON RACKET SQUAD (Republic, 1938), with Bob
Livingston, again momentarily took Kane out of the saddle
with a story of policemen versus arsonists. GOLD MINE IN
THE SKY (Republic, 1938) and MAN FROM MUSIC MOUN-
TAIN (Republic, 1938), a pair of Autry Westerns, followed
and were to be Joe Kane's last association with the singing
cowboy. He directed BILLY THE KID RETURNS (Republic,
1939), with Roy Rogers, and began a forty-four-picture streak
interrupted only twice with non-Westerns: THE GREAT
TRAIN ROBBERY (Republic, 1939), which starred Bob Steele
and Milburn Stone and had to do with an attempt to hold up
an express train; and RAGS TO RICHES (Republic, 1939),
which starred Alan Baxter. During the early 'forties, due
to the fact that Autry entered the Air Force, Roy Rogers
switched from the period Westerns he had been making to
the contemporary cowboy mode Gene Autry had popularized.
Kane's forty-second picture, THE COWBOY AND THE SEN-
ORITA (Republic, 1944), introduced a new leading lady cast
opposite Rogers named Dale Evans. Following the death of
Rogers' first wife, Roy and Dale were married.

Nothing in Joe Kane's career at this point suggested
the spectacular. He made excellent, fast-paced Westerns
that moved, although the later "dude" Westerns had musical
sequences that almost overwhelmed the story. Yet for all
of that, it may be stated without fear of contradiction--based
solely, if you wish, on box-office receipts--that Rogers was
a top moneymaker for Republic thanks largely to Joe Kane's
ability behind the camera.

One of the Republic executives, Sol C. Siegel, later
became a very important producer at Paramount, 20th
Century-Fox, and M-G-M. Sol and his brother Moe had
been with Brunswick Records in New York when Herbert

Yates bought out that company. They were lured to Hollywood where Moe became an administrator and Sol went into
production. "Sol really learned the business in a hurry,"
Kane said. "I did a number of low-budget pictures for him
along the way and he eventually became involved with the
more important films Republic was beginning to make."

Among the prestigious films Siegel produced were
ARMY GIRL (Republic, 1938) and THE MAN OF CONQUEST
(Republic, 1939). The latter starred Richard Dix as Sam
Houston. Kane, like any man of ambition, hoped that he
might get a crack at doing a really big picture but such was
not the case--at least not yet. Instead, Siegel brought in
George Nichols, Jr. from RKO.

MAN OF CONQUEST was a smash hit with the critics
and at the box office. Its major action highlight was the famous battle of San Jacinto, where Houston led the Texans in
routing Santa Ana's army. Siegel knew that this sequence
required a deft and knowing hand to make it all come off.
Without hesitation he enlisted Kane to direct the second unit
action, with Yakima Canutt rigging the stunts. Kane's work
on this big-scale production, if only as a second unit director,
had significant influence on his future.

Then Siegel produced THE DARK COMMAND (Republic, 1940) which starred John Wayne, Claire Trevor and
Walter Pidgeon. Based on a W. R. Burnett novel, it was
a Civil War story with Pidgeon as Will Cantrell. Many
drama and action sequences were combined to make this a
superior film, directed by Raoul Walsh, whom Republic borrowed from Warner Brothers. Kane worked with the second
unit. "Walsh received me in a very friendly way and told
me the company was all mine. Now Walsh was famous for
his action work, and I felt a little silly about the whole
thing. He just walked away, drove off in his car, and didn't
show up until I'd finished. He knew it would embarrass me
if he stuck around. A wonderful guy."

Perhaps the most famous scene from the picture was
a leap by four men and a team of horses hitched to a wagon
off a bluff into Lake Sherwood. In the picture, Wayne,
Gabby Hayes, and two other men are being pursued by
Pidgeon, Joe Sawyer, and their band of renegades. Yakima
Canutt doubled Wayne, while Cliff Lyons doubled Hayes, and
Joe and Bill Yrigoyen doubled the other pair.

"The whole business dropped thirty-five feet into the water," Kane explained. "To protect the horses, the entire front end of the wagon was made of balsa wood and the harness was breakaway. Everyone got out safely. The horses swam to shore and commenced eating grass--maybe to quiet their nerves. The ironic part was that Sol thought we'd better shoot a scene showing the horses reaching shore and in that scene we almost drowned one of them."

The camera work was done by Jack Marta and special process photography by Bud Thackery, who had shot his footage with a 25mm. lens, shooting straight down and cranking up the camera to double speed. This was matched and interjected with Marta's panoramic shots. The effect on the screen was of falling twice the distance because it looked twice as far due to the 25mm. lens. When seeing the finished picture, some production people at 20th Century-Fox thought the horses really went off a seventy-foot embankment, and figured to do likewise themselves for one of their pictures. They actually sent two horses off such a height and killed them in the process. It was regrettable, of course, but Fox did not have a Joe Kane or a Yakima Canutt to ramrod the shot for them. Canutt and Kane knew such a distance would kill the horses because of their heavy posteriors. They would turn over and break their backs. This is precisely what happened.

Careless actions, such as the one at Fox, led to the foundation of the Society for the Prevention of Cruelty to Animals, aided by the Hearst newspapers. The Society brought legislation regarding the use of animals in pictures, including the banning of the running W. "That was a device to spill horses," Kane explained. "People who knew what they were doing never hurt a horse, because it was a matter of choosing your horses and preparing the ground. It had about the same result as a football player being tackled. But some inexperienced people used horses not suited to falling, and they did it in rocky terrain. So I guess it was a good thing it stopped. Later, animals were trained to fall when pressure was applied by the reins on their necks. Pity the poor actor who got on one and made the signal by mistake."

The fifty-year-old Kane was working steadily. He directed Roy Rogers in one vehicle after another with little fanfare. He had a chance to reflect. He was doing fine. The money was good, and his position at Republic was quite

secure. He knew his business and made a good product that
spelled income for the studio. But Joe Kane still wanted a
crack at the big time. He wondered if it would ever come.
The year 1945 would mark the tenth anniversary of Republic
Studios, and plans were being made to celebrate the event.
The number-one star was John Wayne. He still owed the
studio a commitment on a three-picture deal. Wayne had begun to come into his own after STAGECOACH (United Artists,
1939) and had made a number of big pictures for studios
other than Republic. Paramount starred him in REAP THE
WILD WIND (Paramount, 1942), directed by Cecil B. De-
Mille. Universal had starred him with Marlene Dietrich in
SEVEN SINNERS in 1940, then cast him in the fourth and
best remake of THE SPOILERS (Universal, 1942), which
featured the best-known screen fight ever filmed, with Wayne
outlasting bad guy Randolph Scott. However, Scott got even
in PITTSBURGH (Universal, 1942) by lambasting Wayne and
winning Marlene Dietrich to boot.

Duke then did a pair of films for RKO: A LADY
TAKES A CHANCE (RKO, 1943) with Jean Arthur, and TALL
IN THE SADDLE (RKO, 1944) with Ella Raines. Wayne may
have been somewhat lost with Joan Crawford and Philip Dorn
in REUNION IN FRANCE (M-G-M, 1942) but he was making
big box-office pictures for major studios. At Republic he
had done IN OLD CALIFORNIA in 1942, then a big war film,
THE FLYING TIGERS in 1942, followed by IN OLD OKLA-
HOMA in 1943, with Martha Scott and Albert Dekker. There
was a spectacular race with oil-filled wagons through a burning canyon for IN OLD OKLAHOMA. Kane was picked to direct the second unit, and Yakima Canutt to rig it. The locale was Piria Canyon in Utah, near Kanab.

"Fox was shooting BUFFALO BILL [20th-Fox, 1944]
in the same area and they raised hell with us, demanding
we get out. They said that the two pictures would look
alike if we both used the same location." Kane found out
that it was Federal land. He called Washington. The Department of the Interior sent one of their field agents out
and, upon hearing the facts, ruled in Republic's favor.
"Yak rigged the fires with pipelines and holes drilled like
giant lawn sprinklers, with gasoline pumped under high pressure. Desert brush was piled in front and the towering
flames looked as if the brush itself was burning, out of
control. The lines were not straight, but staggered in sec-
tions, overlapping one another, set far enough apart to allow the wagons to race through." Later Kane and Canutt

teamed up again to shoot a flaming canyon fire, this time
on Iverson's ranch at Chatsworth, for the FIGHTING SEA-
BEES (Republic, 1944) which starred Duke Wayne, Susan
Hayward, and Dennis O'Keefe. The story had the Americans
releasing flaming oil down a ravine to trap an invading Japanese army. It was fantastic and Kane added more kudos to
his list of credits.

Ten long years of waiting and working finally paid off.
Joe Kane was called into Yates' office and was informed that
he was at last to receive his long-awaited chance to do a
major feature. "After twenty-three years in the business, I
had my opportunity to make a big picture, FLAME OF THE
BARBARY COAST [Republic, 1945], and get Duke Wayne as
the leading man. I remembered Duke from years ago and
sure didn't expect any trouble. We'd gotten along fine before and, though we hadn't worked together for nine years,
we used to see each other around the lot. But I certainly
had a rude awakening. Wayne had been through a great deal,
including a divorce from his first wife, and I suppose he
couldn't be blamed too much. He had been lied to, put upon
in the past by people he trusted and got burned." Kane
later remembered Duke's words that he would trample anyone who got in his way. "I was sorry he thought it necessary to make it tough on me."

One cannot tell Joe Kane's story further without
bringing in Herbert J. Yates' relationship to Vera Hruba
Ralston, Republic's leading lady, of sorts. Vera, just plain
Hruba, was an ice skater of some merit from Czechoslovakia,
who had come to the United States before the outbreak of
World War II, along with her mother, father (who later re-
turned to Prague), and a brother, Rudy. She was featured
in one of Republic's programmers doing a skating routine.
She was perhaps the third-best skater in pictures, with only
Sonja Henie and Belita her superiors.

Yates, then in his sixties, saw Vera and fell in love
with her. Along with his deep affection, Yates had the idea
that he could make her into a great star. Perhaps he recalled William Randolph Hearst's similar situation with Marion Davies, and thought he could improve upon it. He did
end up marrying Vera. He put her in one film after another, even though, at first, she had trouble with English
and spoke with a thick halting Czech accent. Troublesome
as that was, it was not insurmountable. The crux of the
problem was that Vera had scant talent and couldn't act,

but Yates wasn't going to let a little thing like that deter
him. George Sherman, who got stuck in a couple of early
pictures, abruptly quit the studio rather than do any more
with her. The remaining staff directors at Republic, including Joe Kane, were forced to use her time after time,
though fully aware of her limitations. Yates once even had
her billed as the world's most beautiful woman, but that idea
came to a screeching halt when exhibitors refused to use the
posters and one-sheets featuring her.

Other contract directors like Allan Dwan, John Auer,
and R. G. Springsteen were forced by Yates to use Vera
whether they wanted to or not. John English, the director,
had enough, and told Vera just how good she really was. It
might be added that John English never worked at Republic
again. Joe Kane had the dubious honor of having Vera in a
total of eleven pictures.

"She really wasn't a bad gal personally," Kane recalled. "Everybody liked her, but the situation was next to
impossible. She was not box office. Yates insisted on
block sales, and sold Vera's pictures that way. I could
hardly get a big male star, because he knew if he signed,
Vera most likely would be cast opposite him. Yates
wouldn't let me cast a big female star in any picture because usually Vera wanted the role whether she was right
for it or not." Resistance by exhibitors to Vera continued.
Republic sales people claimed that Vera lost $1 million each
time her films were released. Even a giant like John Wayne
came up short with Vera hanging on like an anchor.

Vera at least wasn't in Joe Kane's first big picture.
In 1944, the studio had an original story treatment for
FLAME OF THE BARBARY COAST by Prescott Chaplin.
Kane was to direct and was also the associate producer, a
term insisted upon by the taciturn Yates, who maintained
that it was his money and that whoever was a so-called
producer was only acting in the capacity of a supervisor.
Kane contracted Borden Chase to write the screenplay for
this first of the Wayne-Republic bombshells. 'Wayne insisted on starting 5 July 1944, otherwise he would be able
to walk out of his contract and still be paid for the picture.
That gave us only five weeks to do the screenplay and prepare the film."

In the story a Montana cowboy went to San Francisco
to collect a debt, met the Flame, who was the queen of the

Barbary Coast, and fell in love with her. Kane wanted
Claire Trevor but Wayne requested Ann Dvorak who had recently returned from England where she had gone at the outbreak of the war when her husband Leslie Fenton, a British
subject, was called to the colors. She had driven ambu-
lances and performed magnificently in the auxiliary service.
She delivered a fine performance as Flaxen Tarry. The distinguished Broadway actor Joseph Schildkraut (who would be
associated with Kane off and on at Republic for the next
four years) was cast as Tito Morell, Wayne's rival in the
film.

Borden Chase, working under great pressure due to
Wayne's attitude, managed to bring in a screenplay and Kane
got the picture started on schedule. Also in the cast were
William Frawley, Virginia Grey, Paul Fix, Russell Hicks,
Jack LaRue, Marc Lawrence, and Jack Norton. It was a
handsome production, well-staged and well-acted, and did
nicely at the box office. There was an unusual earthquake
sequence rigged by Canutt with special effects staged by the
incomparable Lydecker brothers, Howard and Theodore.

Wayne, however, didn't seem to like any of it and
went out of his way to be testy and disagreeable. "It was
almost impossible to create a good script and prepare a big
production in five weeks," Kane sighed. "Wayne, he didn't
care. I guess he figured it couldn't be done and he wouldn't
have to do the picture. He obviously didn't care that my
failure to deliver, no matter whose fault, would have probably finished me at Republic. I had no major credits, just
a string of Autry and Rogers Westerns. I would have been
back to the cutting room if I could even get that.

"Borden Chase was my hero on that picture. Borden
was a tough guy who had worked as a sandhog digging sub-
way tunnels in New York before he became a successful
writer. I have only met two men in this business who I
thought had real fire in them, Borden Chase and Yakima
Canutt. Both were bad men to fool with, but the greatest
to know as friends."

Kane went from the dramatic BARBARY COAST to a
comedy, THE CHEATERS (Republic, 1945), starring Joseph
Schildkraut. It was this story by Albert Ray and Frances
Hyland that brought Schildkraut back from Broadway to Hollywood and into a contract with Republic. If they would purchase the property from Paramount, Schildkraut would sign.

It was a charming, warm, well-played film, one of Kane's
best. Schildkraut delivered a virtuoso performance as a
run-down actor invited into the home of a scheming rich
family at Christmas time. Also cast were Billie Burke,
Ona Munson, Ruth Terry, Eugene Pallette, Bob Livingston,
and Raymond Walburn.

The trouble-free period of THE CHEATERS was followed by a real merry-go-round with Yates, who began ne-
gotiations with Wayne on a new picture deal. Yates sur-
mised that Wayne's name and box-office draw would be a
good coattail for Vera to grab hold of and ride on to stardom. The planned production was DAKOTA (Republic, 1945),
based on a story idea by Carl Foreman who later became
much more famous in his association with Stanley Kramer
in HIGH NOON (United Artists, 1952) and on his own with
such blockbusters as BRIDGE ON THE RIVER KWAI (Columbia, 1957) and THE GUNS OF NAVARONE (Columbia,
1961). Carl Foreman was also among the Hollywood Ten.
Kane, given the directorial assignment, put writer Lawrence
Hazard to work on the screenplay from Howard Estabrook's
adaptation.

Yates went to New York. Duke Wayne came into
Kane's office and turned the picture down, cold. "What
could I do?" Kane shrugged. "I wired Yates and immediately a wire came back ordering both Hazard and myself to
New York. It was still during the war and getting available
space was none too easy, and getting transportation was
none too easy either." Kane and Hazard finally arrived and
to Kane's utter surprise, Wayne along with producer Edmund Grainger were also in New York. Wayne had a meeting scheduled with Yates, so he, Grainger, and Kane walked
together from their hotel to Yates' office. "The last thing
Wayne said to me," Kane continued, "as he left to go in the
elevator to see Yates was that he would not do the picture
with Vera under any circumstances. Grainger and I went
back to the hotel to wait with Hazard. Soon we got a call
from Yates' office and went over once more. Wayne had
already left and we did not see him again in New York."

What went on behind the closed doors of Yates' office
is open to speculation. But Yates informed Kane and Hazard
that Wayne would do the picture. "The worst part of it was
that Wayne flatly told me at the studio that he was not going
to do it! Now if you know Duke, you know he usually means
what he says. So, of course, I had Hazard stop all work on

the script.   Then Yates says it's go with almost no time to
start.   I protested that with such a deadline we would have
no time to make necessary script revisions.   Yates just
waved aside my objections and said to get moving.   I wired
Yak immediately and told him to start shooting the second
unit (a burning wheat fire that was shot in the San Joaquin
Valley) and hoped we could do something with the script.   We
speculated what Yates gave Wayne to bring him around. "

    The picture, in which Dakota homesteaders become
victims of ruthless racketeers, started and things didn't improve.   Wayne was difficult on the set, objecting to the dialogue and trying to direct the other actors.   He even told
veteran cameraman Jack Marta how to do his job.   Kane
was unhappy about the situation but did his best with the
picture.   In addition to Wayne and Vera, the cast included
Walter Brennan, Ward Bond, Ona Munson, Hugo Hass, Paul
Fix, Mike Mazurki, Grant Withers, and Jack LaRue.   The
picture should have been better, but Vera was a drag.
There were some good action scenes and Kane gave it all
he had, but the property itself, like Vera, just didn't measure up.

    Duke's attitude, Vera, and the lack of time to revise
the script properly did not help Kane's position and his feel-
ings toward Wayne hardened.   "It's no use saying I like
Wayne.   I don't like him so much that I haven't seen a picture of his since.   I was really unhappy with the whole situation and told Paul Fix that I'd never work with Wayne
again.   I think he heard about it and returned the compli-
ment.   Doing DAKOTA with him was like pulling teeth.   The
fact that he was a big star didn't mean a thing to me.   And
I'm damn certain I don't mean a thing to him.   I used to
see him on the lot and we'd nod, no trouble or anything,
just nothing.   Later, for a tour promoting a picture called
ROCK ISLAND TRAIL (Republic, 1950), Wayne got on the
train in Illinois and went along with us for publicity value. "

    For Joe Kane it would seem that the web woven by
Yates, Wayne, and Vera would entangle him even more.   His
next production was IN OLD SACRAMENTO (Republic, 1946),
a third remake of his original story DIAMOND CARLISLE,
done with George Chesebro back in the 'twenties.   He had
remade it in 1940 as THE CARSON CITY KID with Roy
Rogers.   The third time would probably be the best, but
problems set in.   Kane had a chance to get Randolph Scott
for the lead, but decided in favor of William "Wild Bill"

Elliott, the studio's Red Ryder. Looking at it now, the
choice was highly debatable to say the least. Scott was a
big-name star while Elliott was better known to moppets at
the Saturday matinees. The Red Ryder pictures were solid
moneymakers and Elliott was among the top ten Western
favorites, but in scope and name value he was not in Randy
Scott's league.

But Republic Studio brass had seen something in the
grim-faced Elliott akin to William S. Hart, whom Elliott
resembled a great deal. In fact, Elliott later tried in vain
for years to get the studio to do Hart's life with himself in
the title role. Kane wanted color but Yates, piqued, vetoed
that idea and decreed black and white. Elliott played Johnny
Barrett, who donned a mask to become a bandit called
Spanish Jack. Constance Moore was the leading lady and
support was in the capable hands of Eugene Pallette, Lionel
Stander, Grant Withers, Ruth Donnelly, Jack LaRue, and
Hank Daniels, Jr. It was a well-mounted film with some
good musical numbers and fine singing by Connie Moore.
At the fade, Elliott reformed but it was too late. He was
shot, and died in the arms of Miss Moore, with young
Daniels hovering in the background to comfort her.

The shock of seeing Wild Bill finished off in that way
may have caused many young admirers to shriek in dismay.
This was Elliott's first major starring role and, while he
was effective, he seemed at times a bit stiff and ill at ease,
particularly in his love scenes with Miss Moore. One of the
stories that has always persisted about Elliott was that he
was tired of making "B" Westerns and, noting his mounting
popularity and growing fan mail, demanded that Republic do
better by him. "Not so," Joe Kane countered. "One day
Wild Bill called me aside on the set and really lit into me.
I could not believe what he was saying. He told me that if
I thought I was doing him a favor by getting him to do this
picture rather than Randy Scott, I should forget it! He had
been perfectly content and much happier being Red Ryder.
What the devil could I say? Later on he changed his mind.
Other than that one time, I never had any problems with
Wild Bill. "

OLD SACRAMENTO did pretty well at the box office,
even though the Republic sales office didn't quite know how
to promote it. Had they put a massive effort behind Elliott
as was done for John Wayne in STAGECOACH, they might
have built him into a fairly important property. Instead,

Joe Kane on the set of THE PLAINSMAN AND THE LADY
(Republic, 1946), relaxing with Vera Hruba Ralston. Photo
courtesy of Joe Kane.

they just let the picture out to find its own level. Joe Kane
closed the year with a really good Western, also starring
Elliott, entitled THE PLAINSMAN AND THE LADY (Republic,
1946). This was a lavish, handsomely mounted production
about the pony express, and was greatly aided by George
Anthiel's vibrant dramatic musical score. The film was
well received by Western fans, and most critics thought well
of it. Also in the cast were Joseph Schildkraut, Gail Pat-
rick, Andy Clyde, Paul Hurst, Raymond Walburn, and Don
"Red" Barry, another well-known cowboy hero playing, this
time, a killer named Feisty dressed all in black. The leading lady was none other than (Yep, you guessed it!) Vera.

This is not intended to be a vindictive tirade against
Vera Ralston; it is rather a statement made in terms of Joe
Kane and her merits as an actress in any accepted sense.

But for her relationship with Yates, she would have had difficulty even getting inside a studio, much less starring in
pictures. Duke Wayne, who appeared with her in DAKOTA,
repeated his folly later in one of his own productions, THE
FIGHTING KENTUCKIAN (Republic, 1949), perhaps figuring
Vera had improved. She hadn't! Probably the only reason
Wayne used her was the fact that Yates underwrote the entire
production.

In PLAINSMAN AND THE LADY Vera wasn't that bad.
Carefully photographed by Reggie Lanning, costumed by
Adele Palmer, with make-up by Bob Mark and direction by
Joe Kane, Vera got through it rather well. The picture did
business and Kane got his next assignment, WYOMING (Republic, 1947), with Bill Elliott, Vera, John Carroll, Gabby
Hayes, Albert Dekker, Virginia Grey, Grant Withers, Harry
Woods, and Madame Maria Ouspenskaya, whom one would
not normally expect to see in a Western. Lawrence Hazard
did the screenplay with Gerald Geraghty. It was an action-
packed story of a cattle baron and his efforts to keep out
encroaching homesteaders. Vera had a double role, first as
Elliott's wife and later as his grown-up daughter. John Carroll provided the love interest and Albert Dekker was the
principal heavy.

WYOMING was no exception. Joe Kane again demonstrated that he had few peers in the making of the action-
adventure pictures. John Alton's photography was vivid,
though for close-ups on Vera he seemed to be shooting
through a mile of gauze in order to highlight her face. In
order to explain how Vera had grown up with an accent, the
story had her leave for Vienna as a little girl and return
years later to the Wyoming ranch with Madame Ouspenskaya,
who had her own Russian accent and looked the same as she
had in the beginning of the picture--ancient! One memorable
scene was a tremendous fight between Elliott and Dekker in
a hotel lobby. Fred Graham doubled Dekker and Ben Johnson, who went on to become a fine actor and Academy
Award winner, doubled Elliott. For sheer impact, the fight
ranks with those in THE SPOILERS (Universal, 1942), PAN-
HANDLE (Monogram, 1948), and SHANE (Paramount, 1953).

"My daughter Louise was ten years of age. She
played Vera as a little girl. She was a fine little horse-
woman and had a lot of fun making the picture. This was
also the last picture Gabby Hayes made for Republic. The
place didn't seem the same without him. " It was also the

last time for Maria Ouspenskaya, who shortly after met a
tragic death--smoking in bed.

OLD LOS ANGELES (Republic, 1947) was next. What
should have been a fast-paced story with all the color and
drama of early California turned out rather uneven. Bill
Elliott, Catherine McLeod, Joseph Schildkraut, John Carroll,
and Andy Devine were featured. The fault lay in the script
and dialogue which was at times dull. The actors did what
they could with it. Andy Devine appeared a simple boob
and his lines, meant to be funny, weren't. There were
some nice musical numbers done by Catherine McLeod, a
Frank Borzage discovery who failed to live up to all the
ballyhoo although she was a very talented young actress.

One thing that was really emphasized was the pas-
sionate lovemaking between Elliott and Miss McLeod--1947
style. Red Ryder never did anything like that! John Carroll
was the heavy, but he seemed at times to be totally disin-
terested. Schildkraut did a good job. "Joe was a great
character," Kane recalled. "We were making Westerns and
they were the last thing in the world Schildkraut wanted to
do. I could not blame him. He was very unhappy with
Yates and the entire set-up. But he and I were very good
friends and no matter the role, he always did his best."

The critics faulted the screenplay by Clements Ripley
and Gerald Drayson Adams. Ripley, in better days, had
scripted JEZEBEL (Warner's, 1938). Kane did what he
could with the picture but it wasn't one of his best. Whatever OLD LOS ANGELES may have lacked, Kane made up
for it in THE GALLANT LEGION (Republic, 1948). The
story by a trio of writers, John K. Butler, Gerald Geraghty,
and Gerald Drayson Adams, dealt with a lawless element attempting to abolish the Texas Rangers and make West Texas
a separate state under their control. Bill Elliott, Adrian
Booth, Joseph Schildkraut (his last picture for Republic),
Bruce Cabot, Jack Holt, Adele Mara, and Andy Devine were
cast. Kane had tried three years earlier to make IN OLD
SACRAMENTO in color, but Yates had refused. Now he
was to do his first picture in that medium, using the studio's
Trucolor process. The picture was known as THE PLUND-
ERERS (Republic, 1948) and starred Rod Cameron, Ilona
Massey, Adrian Booth, and Forrest Tucker. The screen-
play was by James Edward Grant, a well-known screenwrit-
er who worked on and off for many years for Duke Wayne.
Indians, cavalry, cowboys, saloon girls, gunslingers, and

enough fights to keep everybody happy were blended into a
most satisfactory outdoor drama. "It was a fun picture and
the public seemed to like it," Kane said. The picture saw
a Sioux uprising save an Army officer from arresting a
young outlaw who eventually saves his life.

As 1949 rolled around, a pair of color Westerns ap-
peared, done very much in the familiar Kane manner: ac-
tion, adventure, and movement. The first was THE LAST
BANDIT (Republic, 1949) and starred Bill Elliott, Adrian
Booth, Forrest Tucker, Andy Devine, Jack Holt, and Grant
Withers. The second film was BRIMSTONE (Republic, 1949),
with Rod Cameron, Adrian Booth, Walter Brennan, Forrest
Tucker, "Big Boy" Williams, Jim Davis, Jack Lambert,
and James Brown. Shot on location near Sacramento,
BRIMSTONE was a fast-moving Western.

"I made a lot of Westerns," Joe Kane commented.
"But I honestly never thought of myself as strictly a Western
director. Don't get me wrong, I liked to do them. I figured that I could do other things if I got the opportunity."
Liking them or not, in 1950 Joe Kane directed three more
Westerns. The first was ROCK ISLAND TRAIL (Republic,
1950). It was based on Frank Nevins' novel, A Yankee
Dared, and was the story of the Rock Island Railroad's efforts to extend across the Mississippi in opposition to marauding Indians and a crooked riverboat operator. Shot in
color on location in Oklahoma, the picture starred Forrest
Tucker, Adele Mara, Adrian Booth, Bruce Cabot, Chill
Wills, Jeff Corey as a young Abraham Lincoln, and Barbara Fuller. The producer on the picture was Paul Malvern, with whom Kane had worked in the mid-'thirties directing Duke Wayne's "B" pictures. Republic spent what
was for them a considerable sum, not only on the film itself but also to publicize and promote it. There were
plenty of fights; one in a tavern where Tucker and Cabot dip
floor mops in a boiling cauldron of soup and wop each other
all over the establishment.

THE SAVAGE HORDE (Republic, 1950), in black and
white, followed and was Kane's last picture with Bill Elliott.
Elliott was presently to leave Republic to do a series of low-
budget films for Monogram-Allied Artists. With his departure, all his hopes of major stardom rode into the sunset. SAVAGE HORDE had it all in spades. Along with Elliott portraying reformed gunslinger John "Ringo" Baker
were Adrian Booth, Jim Davis, Grant Withers, Noah Beery,

Jr. , Barbara Fuller, Roy Barcroft, Marshall Reed, Stuart
Hamblen, and Bob Steele as Dancer, a cold-blooded, vicious
gunslinger.

"I remember Bob as Curley in OF MICE AND MEN
[United Artists, 1939] and he was a nasty, mean little hell-
raiser in that one," Kane said. "So I knew he could do the
job. I think it only cost $300,000 to make, if that. But I
was satisfied with our results. "

CALIFORNIA PASSAGE (Republic, 1950), written by
James Edward Grant, closed out the year. Starring Forrest
Tucker, Adele Mara, Jim Davis, Charles Kemper, Bill Williams, Peter Miles, and Estralita, it was the story of two
partners in a saloon in love with the same girl.

Still another Western followed--OH! SUSANNA. This
historical Western was the story of a cavalry company which
guarded the Sioux territory from marauding gold rushers,
who masqueraded as Indians. It starred such familiars as
Rod Cameron, Adrian Booth, Forrest Tucker, Chill Wills,
and James Lyon.

Kane got his chance at a non-Western in FIGHTING
COAST GUARD (Republic, 1951), written by Charles Marques
Warren and veteran Ken Gamet. It was Republic's followup to SANDS OF IWO JIMA (Republic, 1950). If there were
any doubts about Kane's ability to change horses in mid-
stream, this completely erased them. COAST GUARD was
a highly exciting story of the nation's oldest service during
World War II. It had a strong cast headed by Brian Donlevy,
Ella Raines, Forrest Tucker, John Russell, Richard Jaeckel
and Hugh O'Brian. With superb editing, it was a winner all
the way.

"It was funny," Kane remarked. "COAST GUARD
was the first non-Western I'd done in ten years and I had,
of course, wondered if I'd ever do anything else. The next
two were modern-day stories. I still looked over my shoulder every once in a while to see where the horses were. "
Gerald Drayson Adams scripted Kane's next film, THE SEA
HORNET (Republic, 1951), with old familiars Rod Cameron,
Adele Mara, Adrian Booth, Richard Jaeckel, Chill Wills,
Jim Davis, Ellen Corby, Grant Withers, and William Ching.
It was a fast-paced story with plenty of action, fights,
chases, and romance, with Cameron having to decide which
of two lovelies to choose: Adele Mara or Adrian Booth.

The problem was settled for him when Miss Booth was revealed to be the wife and crooked partner of bad guy Jim
Davis.

Kane's next film had as a background Senator Estes
Kefauver's Senate Investigating Crime Committee. Bob Con-
sidine, the Hearst columnist, worked on the screenplay. To
her credit, Vera Ralston backed off from the leading role,
feeling that she was totally wrong for the part. Claire Trev-
or was cast instead and gave a memorable performance in
HOODLUM EMPIRE. In this film a nation-wide gambling
syndicate got the role of the usual bad guys with black hats
in Kane's Westerns.

In 1948, Republic released one of its biggest money-
makers of all time, WAKE OF THE RED WITCH, which
starred John Wayne, Gail Russell, Gig Young, Adele Mara,
and Luther Adler. Duke later took, as the name of his own
production company, Batjac, the name of the shipping lines
owned by his chief rival in the picture, Luther Adler. The
author of the book on which the picture was based was Gar-
land Roark. He had written several period stories set in
the Dutch East Indies. The studio figured that it was time
for another one. It purchased FAIR WIND TO JAVA (Republic, 1953) and intended to give it big-budget treatment. By
this time, however, John Wayne had left Republic for good
in a dispute with Yates over filming THE ALAMO, which he
would remake on his own nearly seven years later. Famed
war correspondent Richard Tregaskis was assigned the
screenplay. Meanwhile, Kane and Yates came to a head
over the project. "Truly," Kane said, "it could have been
called the KANE MUTINY and I even considered quitting the
studio after eighteen years. It got that bad. We had sent
Tregaskis to Java to gather data, and he came back with a
ton of interesting material. But the trouble started when
we began to cast the picture." The female lead in the book
was a tiny fourteen-year-old native girl called Kim Kim.
"Guess who Papa Yates decided was to play the role? Yep
--Vera! I was ready to walk out. My agent told me things
were slow and to stay put. Maybe I should have quit, but
it takes a lot to dislodge a man with family responsibilities
when he'd been there as long as I had. I finally agreed to
do the picture with Vera and Fred MacMurray in the role
of Captain Boll, master of the Gerrymander."

The studio threw out most of the book and made it a
nineteenth-century pirate yarn instead. They used as a

Joe Kane and Walter Brennan while making SEA OF LOST
SHIPS (Republic, 1954).   Photo courtesy of Joe Kane.

climax the great Krakatoa volcanic eruption of 27 August
1883 that killed over 50,000 people in the gigantic tidal
waves that followed.   Kane located a large four-masted sail-
ship in Seattle.   "It was ideal because, in addition to its
sails, it had an auxiliary diesel power plant.   My idea was
to shoot aboard ship on the way to Hawaii and use one of
the islands for the Java location."   Yates rejected this suggestion.   By now he and Vera were married and they
planned to take a delayed honeymoon trip to Europe on the
maiden voyage of the S.S. United States.   Such a location
would postpone their travel plans.   Eventually the picture

was shot on the back lot with location scenes at Paradise
Cove.   Half a sailing ship was built on a sound stage,
mounted on rockers, surrounded by a huge painted panoramic backdrop of sea and clouds.   "The whole thing cost a
fortune to build.   Also included was the Javanese village and
the palace of villain Robert Douglas with the most elaborate
furnishings ever used at Republic.   We hired a Javanese
dancer named Saroka.   She practically lived with Vera in
order to teach her the delicate hand and body movements of
Javanese girls.   Vera went on a crash diet and really
slimmed down, but she was still far from what the part
really called for. "   The picture cost over $1, 250, 000 and
did not live up to expectations at the box office.

Novelist Gwen Bristow had written several best sell-
ers including Tomorrow Is Forever which was made into a
highly successful picture.   She hit it big with a Literary
Guild winner, Jubilee Trail, and M-G-M bought an option on
the screen rights.   Herbert Yates decided that he wanted to
make a picture based on the novel.   The giant Culver City
lot was having problems with the project and somebody in
the legal office evidently failed to notice when their option
ran out.   There are conflicting stories that Republic bought
the property from M-G-M directly, and others that they
purchased it when Metro failed to renew their option.   In
any case, a sum in excess of $100,000 was paid for the
novel, a huge sum for Republic or for anybody in those
days.   Republic began a strong campaign to exploit the picture, expanding publicity and advertising budgets.   A number
of people were mentioned for the leading roles, that of
Florinda Grove, the dancehall queen from New Orleans, and
John Ives, the California trader.   Gloria Graham and Van
Heflin were frequently mentioned, with Miss Graham, a recent Academy Award winner for THE BAD AND THE BEAU-
TIFUL more than interested in the part.

Such was not to be the case!   Herb Yates had it all
planned and packaged with Vera, and only Vera, to play
Florinda.   When the smoke cleared and production began,
Vera was the star, with old Republic standby Forrest Tucker cast as John Ives.   Nothing was spared to make this a
glossy, panoramic, sweeping drama of early California with
romance, tragedy, adventure, and action.   A rousing score
by Victor Young helped set the pace, and Jack Marta's
smooth and vivid Trucolor photography was outstanding.   "I
wanted to shoot it in Cinemascope, " Kane said.   "Fox, who
owned the rights to the process, was asking $25, 000 a pic-

ture.   Theatres all over the country were equipping their
projectors with the lenses and building new and wider screens.
But Yates was having a private quarrel with Spiros Skouras,
Fox president, and wouldn't do it.   If he had done as I asked,
he might have had a real financial success."   JUBILEE
TRAIL (Republic, 1954) was nonetheless a moneymaker and
generally well-received by the public.   Vera gave one of her
better performances, although she was thirty pounds over-
weight and showed it.   Standing next to huge Buddy Baer,
quite virile as Nicoli the Russian, known as The Handsome
Brute, Vera looked almost as big as the one-time heavy-
weight contender.

One of the pictures that Yates really spent money on
was TIMBERJACK (Republic, 1955).   "The whole thing at
times was a nightmarish headache," Kane said.   "We thought
a logging yarn might do well, remembering Warner's VAL-
LEY OF THE GIANTS [Warner's, 1938], and so we put
Bruce Manning on salary to come up with a script.   My wife
Margaret and I accompanied him to British Columbia to
scout locations and local color.   We were intrigued to see
East Indian lumber truck drivers wearing turbans and, upon
inquiry, learned that several big timber companies were
owned by wealthy East Indians.   They were, however, mostly operated by Scotch-Canadians."

Manning developed a story about an East Indian family in British Columbia and the conflicts arose from differ-
ing social and moral codes.   He had a $50,000 deal with a
ten-month time limit, which meant that if it took longer to
produce a script satisfactory to all concerned, they'd have
to pay him more.   An outline was submitted and he was
told to do a treatment.   Two months later the treatment was
turned in and he was told to go ahead with the screenplay.
Weeks later he turned in the first draft and it was approved.
Manning then did the final draft and received the balance of
his money.   "It turned out," Kane lamented, "that nobody
had read any of his previous drafts when submitted and,
upon seeing the final shooting script, they thought it was
terrible and tossed it in the wastebasket.   They could have
come to the same decision based on the outline, because
what they objected to in the first place was the basic idea
of the story.   Had that been done, it only would have cost
$10,000 and the scouting trip.   But that isn't the way things
were done in Hollywood, and has led me to believe that
heads of picture companies either hadn't ever learned to
read or were simply too damn lazy.   It was easier to spend

$50,000 of the stockholders' money than to sit down and scan over a short outline."

One of Kane's most interesting productions was the remake of Zane Grey's famous novel THE VANISHING AMERICAN, which had originally been done in 1925 by Paramount with Richard Dix in the title role. "I assigned Alan LeMay to the screenplay and asked Yates for Barbara Stanwyck as my leading lady. I wanted to shoot the picture in color. Yates refused. In Barbara's case, the $100,000 she asked for was considered big money then, and was more than Yates would pay. We settled on Audrey Totter, who did a fine job." Scott Brady (Bronx accent and all) did the blue-eyed Indian lead. Perhaps for this reason color was ruled out. Forrest Tucker, Gene Lockhart, Jim Davis, Lee Van Cleef, and Charles Stevens (a real-life grandson of Geronimo) were all cast. The picture was filmed in Utah and the crisp black and white photography of Jack Marta was very effective. "The picture did fairly well," Kane recalled, "and again was liked by the critics." But by now the nationwide resistance to Republic pictures was gathering steam. Yates insisted on block sales, as did all other studios where they could, and that meant a picture starring Vera, a dead loss. "My final big-budgeteer picture was THE MAVERICK QUEEN [Republic, 1956]. The studio was scraping the bottom of the barrel to get a big moneymaker and they finally let me have color and Naturama and Barbara Stanwyck in the starring role as Kit Bannion. The novel had been put together from notes by Zane Grey's son, Romer, after the author's death."

It is doubtful that Zane Grey had anything to do with THE MAVERICK QUEEN. The story is of an outlaw queen in Wyoming, her Virginia family ruined by the Civil War, who falls in love with a Pinkerton detective claiming to be one of the Younger brothers. She dies after warning him against a jealous gang member.

Kane took his company to Silverton, Colorado, at an elevation over 10,000 feet. For a train robbery sequence, they used rolling stock from the old Durango-Silverton railway, the same one used in AROUND THE WORLD IN EIGHTY DAYS (United Artists, 1956). "It was a real pleasure to work with a grand trouper like Missy," Kane said of Barbara Stanwyck. "She'd do anything, and you had to darn-near hogtie her to keep her from breaking her neck doing a dangerous stunt." Although the picture went well at

the box office, losses in general for Republic were heavy
and things were going from bad to worse. By 1956 the
studio was becoming a whisper. The only thing that kept
plant operations going was the leasing of the studio facilities
to Revue, the television production company owned by Music
Corporation of America.

Although Kane did a couple more low-budget films
for Republic, his association soon came to an end. He negotiated with the Revue people to do some of the WAGON
TRAIN television episodes and, while waiting for a contract,
went over to Warner Brothers to do the three segments of
their CHEYENNE series I've already mentioned. In the
meantime, Herb Yates contacted Kane and told him that he
had obtained financing for several more quickie pictures and
that Kane would receive $5,000 per picture and sixteen per
cent of the profits. Kane mulled it over and let twenty
years of loyalty overrule his better judgment. Two hours
later the WAGON TRAIN people called and asked him to
come with them. Being a man of his word, Kane reluctantly
turned them down. He had barely hung up the phone when
Warner Brothers called, also wanting his services. He
turned them down as well. Kane was never to see any profit as a result of the pictures he made with Yates. There
were eight more films in all, several of them with Rudy
Ralston, Vera's brother, as producer. There isn't much
more to say. With the completion of the last picture for
Republic, Kane's association with Yates ended, and the little
valley lot folded forever.

Revue moved its production company to Universal
Studios when the parent company MCA bought the lot. The
Columbia Broadcasting System leased the Republic studio
and later renamed it CBS-TV Center.

"The Republic story was long and confused," Kane
reflected. "It was a public corporation owned by the stockholders, but whenever I hear that old cliché about corpora-
tions not being owned by the top brass but by thousands of
little faceless shareholders, I have to laugh. Yates did as
he pleased and the stockholders had about as much to say
as a native in Timbuktu." While Yates stayed in New York
and left studio operations to people like Sol and Moe Siegel,
Al Wilson, and Jack Baker, things were fine. But when he
found Vera and began to run things directly, disaster was
the result.

With the fall of Republic, Kane looked around, but twenty years in one organization had isolated him from the rest of the studios. And the idea of starting all over at his age was not an easy thing to do. Kane went into television work on a full-time basis, filming shows such as BONANZA and RAWHIDE.

Joe Kane died at the age of eighty-one on 25 August 1975 at Santa Monica hospital. He had spent fifty years of his life doing what he loved most: making pictures. There were good times and bad times, good breaks and bad. William Witney, one of the finest action directors in Hollywood, said this of his friend "Uncle" Joe Kane: "As a kid I was his script clerk, and I can tell you flat-out, Joe Kane was one of the most prolific action directors that ever lived. Just look at his films and you will realize how good he really was. " Veteran stuntman-actor Fred Graham made this sage observation: "Joe Kane was a gentleman and a professional. There's no higher tribute you can pay a man than that. "

Joe Kane was a craftsman of the highest order. He was truly a motion picture director in the fullest sense of the word. He was a visual man who used the screen as a broad canvas to make his pictures. He provided sweeping adventure and tense conflict. His Westerns were the kind that moved and that had flair and style. Even if some of the scripts were at times lacking, Kane's touch, his feel, his sense of timing and pace more than made up for any deficiencies. And when he had it all together, few if any could match him for the kind of picture he was making. Joe Kane made films that were enjoyable to watch. What more could anyone ask for?

JOSEPH KANE

A Film Checklist by Karl Thiede

Assistant Director /Film Editor

1.   THE HIGH HAND (12 September 1926). P: Pathé. D: Leo Maloney. C: Leo Maloney, Josephine Hill, Paul Hurst. 5, 679ft. /63m.

2. THE OUTLAW EXPRESS (14 November 1926). P:
    Pathé. D: Leo Maloney. C: Leo Maloney, Joan
    Renee, Melbourne MacDowell. 5,479ft. /61m.

3. THE LONG LOOP ON THE PECOS (9 January 1927).
    P: Pathé. D: Leo Maloney. C: Leo Maloney,
    Eugenia Gilbert, Frederick Dana. 5,977ft. /66m.

4. THE MAN FROM HARDPAN (6 March 1927). P:
    Pathé. D: Leo Maloney. C: Leo Maloney, Eugenia
    Gilbert, Rosa Gore. 5,814ft. /64 1/m.

5. DON DESPERADO (8 May 1927). P: Pathé. D: Leo
    Maloney. C: Leo Maloney, Eugenia Gilbert, Fred-
    erick Dana. 5,804ft. /64 1/2m.

6. TWO-GUN OF THE TUMBLEWEED (17 July 1927). P:
    Pathé. D: Leo Maloney. C: Leo Maloney, Peggy
    Montgomery, Josephine Hill. 5,670ft. /63m.

7. BORDER BLACKBIRDS (28 August 1927). P: Pathé.
    D: Leo Maloney. C: Leo Maloney, Eugenia Gilbert,
    Nelson McDowell. 5,326ft. /59m.

8. THE DEVIL'S TWIN (11 December 1927). P: Pathé.
    D: Leo Maloney. C: Leo Maloney, Josephine Hill,
    Don Coleman. 5,478ft. /61m.

9. THE BOSS OF RUSTLER'S ROOST (22 January 1928).
    P: Pathé. D: Leo Maloney. C: Don Coleman,
    Ben Corbett, Tom London. 4,833ft. /54m.

10. THE APACHE RAIDER (12 February 1928). P: Pathé.
    D: Leo Maloney. C: Leo Maloney, Eugenia Gilbert,
    Don Coleman. 5,755ft. /64m.

11. THE BRONC' STOMPER (26 February 1928). P:
    Pathé. D: Leo Maloney. C: Don Coleman, Ben
    Corbett, Tom London. 5,408ft. /60m.

12. THE BLACK ACE (2 September 1928). P: Pathé. D:
    Leo Maloney. C: Don Coleman, Jeanette Loff,
    Billy Butts. 5,722ft. /63 1/2m.

13. YELLOW CONTRABAND (28 October 1928). P: Pathé.
    D: Leo Maloney. C: Leo Maloney, Gretel Yoltz,
    Eileen Sedgwick. 5,686ft. /63m.

14.   . 45 CALIBRE WAR (17 February 1929). P: Pathé.
      D: Leo Maloney. C: Don Coleman, Ben Corbett,
      Al Hart. 4,790ft. /53m.

15.   HIS FIRST COMMAND (28 December 1929). P: Pathé.
      D: Gregory La Cava. C: William Boyd, Dorothy
      Sebastian, Gavin Gordon. 5,850ft. /65m.

16.   OVERLAND BOUND (15 April 1930). P: Syndicate
      Pictures. D: Leo Maloney. C: Leo Maloney,
      Allene Ray, Jack Perrin. 5,040ft. /56m.

17.   NIGHT WORK (3 August 1930). P: Pathé. D: Rus-
      sell Mack. C: Eddie Quillan, Sally Starr, Frances
      Upton. 8,394ft. /93m.

18.   HER MAN (21 September 1930). P: Pathé. D: Tay
      Garnett. C: Helen Twelvetrees, Marjorie Rambeau,
      Ricardo Cortez. 7,508ft. /83m.

19.   BIG MONEY (26 October 1930). P: Pathé. D: Rus-
      sell Mack. C: Eddie Quillan, Robert Armstrong,
      James Gleason. 7,698ft. /85 1/2m.

20.   LONELY WIVES (22 February 1931). P: RKO-Pathé.
      D: Russell Mack. C: Edward Everett Horton,
      Esther Ralston, Laura La Plante. 90m.

21.   SWEEPSTAKES (10 July 1931). P: RKO-Pathé. D:
      Albert Rogell. C: Eddie Quillan, Marion Nixon,
      James Gleason. 77m.

22.   THE BIG GAMBLE (4 September 1931). P: RKO-
      Pathé. D: Fred Niblo. C: William Boyd, Dorothy
      Sebastian, Warner Oland. 63m.

23.   SUICIDE FLEET (20 November 1931). P: RKO-Pathé.
      D: Albert Rogell. C: William Boyd, Robert Arm-
      strong, James Gleason. 87m.

24.   PRESTIGE (22 January 1932). P: RKO-Pathé. D:
      Tay Garnett. C: Ann Harding, Adolphe Menjou,
      Melvyn Douglas. 71m.

25.   YOUNG BRIDE (8 April 1932). P: RKO-Pathé. D:
      William A. Seiter. C: Helen Twelvetrees, Eric
      Linden, Arline Judge. 76m.

26. IS MY FACE RED? (17 June 1932). P: RKO Radio
     Pictures. D: William A. Seiter. C: Helen Twelve-
     trees, Ricardo Cortez, Robert Armstrong. 66m.

27. 70,000 WITNESSES (2 September 1932). P: Para-
     mount. D: Ralph Murphy. C: Phillips Holmes,
     Dorothy Jordan, Charles Ruggles. 72m.

28. MADISON SQUARE GARDEN (7 October 1932). P:
     Paramount. D: Harry Joe Brown. C: Jack Oakie,
     Marion Nixon, William Collier, Sr. 74m.

29. THE BILLION DOLLAR SCANDAL (6 January 1933).
     P: Paramount. D: Harry Joe Brown. C: Con-
     stance Cummings, Robert Armstrong, James Gleason.
     78m.

30. STRICTLY PERSONAL (17 March 1933). P: Para-
     mount. D: Ralph Murphy. C: Marjorie Rambeau,
     Eddie Quillan, Dorothy Jordan. 70m.

31. SONG OF THE EAGLE (28 April 1933). P: Para-
     mount. D: Ralph Murphy. C: Charles Bickford,
     Richard Arlen, Mary Brian. 83m.

32. I LOVE THAT MAN (9 June 1933). P: Paramount.
     D: Harry Joe Brown. C: Nancy Carroll, Edmund
     Lowe, Robert Armstrong. 75m.

33. GOLDEN HARVEST (22 September 1933). P: Para-
     mount. D: Ralph Murphy. C: Richard Arlen,
     Chester Morris, Genevieve Tobin. 70m.

34. SITTING PRETTY (24 November 1933). P: Paramount.
     D: Harry Joe Brown. C: Jack Haley, Ginger
     Rogers. 80m.

35. NO MORE WOMEN (23 February 1934). P: Para-
     mount. D: Albert Rogell. C: Edmund Lowe,
     Victor McLaglen, Sally Blane. 72m.

36. HERE COMES THE GROOM (22 June 1934). P: Para-
     mount. D: Edward Sedgwick. C: Jack Haley, Mary
     Boland, Patricia Ellis. 64m.

37. LITTLE MEN (14 December 1934). P: Mascot. D:
     Philip Rosen. C: Ralph Morgan, Erin O'Brien-Moore,

Junior Durkin. 72m.

38. McFADDEN'S FLATS (29 March 1935). P: Paramount.
D: Ralph Murphy. C: Betty Furness, Richard
Cromwell, Walter C. Kelly. 65m.

39. THE HEADLINE WOMAN (15 May 1935). P: Mascot.
D: William Nigh. C: Roger Pryor, Heather Angel.
70m.

Director

40. MELODY TRAIL (14 October 1935). P: Republic. C:
Gene Autry, Smiley Burnette, Ann Rutherford. 60m.

41. TUMBLING TUMBLEWEEDS (9 November 1935). P:
Republic. C: Gene Autry, Smiley Burnette, Lucile
Browne. 57m.

42. THE FIGHTING MARINES (23 November 1935). P:
Mascot-Republic. C: Grant Withers, Adrian Morris,
Ann Rutherford. 12 chapters.

43. THE SAGEBRUSH TROUBADOUR (2 December 1935).
P: Republic. C: Gene Autry, Barbara Pepper,
Smiley Burnette. 54m.

44. DARKEST AFRICA (15 February 1936). P: Republic.
D: B. Reaves Eason, Joseph Kane. C: Clyde
Beatty, Manuel King, Elaine Shepard. NC:
$119,343. 12 chapters.

45. THE LAWLESS NINETIES (15 February 1936). P:
Republic. C: John Wayne, Sheila Mannors, Ann
Rutherford. 55m.

46. KING OF THE PECOS (9 March 1936). P: Republic.
C: John Wayne, Muriel Evans, Cy Kendall. 54m.

47. THE LONELY TRAIL (25 May 1936). P: Republic.
C: John Wayne, Ann Rutherford, Cy Kendall. 55m.

48. UNDERSEA KINGDOM (30 May 1936). P: Republic.
D: B. Reaves Eason, Joseph Kane. C: Ray Corrigan, Lois Wilde, Monte Blue. NC: $99,222. 12
chapters.

49. GUNS AND GUITARS (22 June 1936). P: Republic.
     C: Gene Autry, Dorothy Dix, Smiley Burnette. 56m.

50. OH, SUSANNA! (19 August 1936). P: Republic. C:
     Gene Autry, Smiley Burnette, Frances Grant. 59m.

51. RIDE, RANGER, RIDE (30 September 1936). P: Re-
     public. C: Gene Autry, Smiley Burnette, Kay
     Hughes. 59m.

52. GHOST TOWN GOLD (26 October 1936). P: Republic.
     C: Robert Livingston, Ray Corrigan, Max Terhune.
     55m.

53. THE OLD CORRAL (21 December 1936). P: Republic.
     C: Gene Autry, Smiley Burnette, Lon Chaney, Jr.
     56m.

54. PARADISE EXPRESS (22 February 1937). P: Republic.
     C: Grant Withers, Dorothy Appleby, Arthur Hoyt.
     58m.

55. ROUND-UP TIME IN TEXAS (28 February 1937). P:
     Republic. C: Gene Autry, Smiley Burnette, Maxine
     Doyle. 58m.

56. GIT ALONG LITTLE DOGIES (22 March 1937). P:
     Republic. C: Gene Autry, Smiley Burnette, Judith
     Allen. 62m.

57. GUNSMOKE RANCH (5 May 1937). P: Republic. C:
     Robert Livingston, Ray Corrigan, Max Terhune. 56m.

58. COME ON, COWBOYS (24 May 1937). P: Republic.
     C: Robert Livingston, Ray Corrigan, Max Terhune.
     57m.

59. YODELIN' KID FROM PINE RIDGE (14 June 1937). P:
     Republic. C: Gene Autry, Betty Bronson, Smiley
     Burnette. 60m.

60. PUBLIC COWBOY NO. 1 (23 August 1937). P: Re-
     public. C: Gene Autry, Ann Rutherford, Smiley
     Burnette. 59m.

61. HEART OF THE ROCKIES (6 September 1937). P:
     Republic. C: Robert Livingston, Ray Corrigan, Max

Terhune. 56m.

62. BOOTS AND SADDLES (4 October 1937). P: Republic.
     C: Gene Autry, Judith Allen, Smiley Burnette.   59m.

63. THE OLD BARN DANCE (29 January 1938). P: Re-
     public. C: Gene Autry, Smiley Burnette, Helen
     Valkis. 60m.

64. BORN TO BE WILD (16 February 1939). P: Republic.
     C: Ralph Byrd, Doris Weston, Ward Bond. 66m.

65. ROUGH RIDERS' ROUND-UP (13 March 1938). P:
     Republic. C: Roy Rogers, Mary Hart, Raymond
     Hatton. 58m.

66. ARSON RACKET SQUAD (28 March 1938). P: Repub-
     lic. C: Robert Livingston, Rosalind Keith, Jackie
     Moran. 65m.

67. UNDER WESTERN STARS (20 April 1938). P: Repub-
     lic. C: Roy Rogers, Smiley Burnette, Carol Hughes.
     65m.

68. GOLD MINE IN THE SKY (4 July 1938). P: Republic.
     C: Gene Autry, Smiley Burnette, Carol Hughes.
     60m.

69. MAN FROM MUSIC MOUNTAIN (15 August 1938). P:
     Republic. C: Gene Autry, Smiley Burnette, Carol
     Hughes. 58m.

70. BILLY THE KID RETURNS (4 September 1938). P:
     Republic. C: Roy Rogers, Smiley Burnette, Mary
     Hart. 56m.

71. COME ON, RANGERS! (25 November 1938). P: Re-
     public. C: Roy Rogers, Mary Hart, Raymond Hat-
     ton. 57m.

72. SHINE ON HARVEST MOON (23 December 1938). P:
     Republic. C: Roy Rogers, Mary Hart, Stanley
     Andrews. 57m.

73. FRONTIER PONY EXPRESS (19 April 1939). P: Re-
     public. C: Roy Rogers, Mary Hart, Monte Blue.
     58m.

74. SOUTHWARD HO! (19 May 1939). P: Republic. C:
     Roy Rogers, Mary Hart, George Hayes. 58m.

75. IN OLD CALIENTE (19 June 1939). P: Republic. C:
     Roy Rogers, Mary Hart, George Hayes. 57m.

76. IN OLD MONTEREY (14 August 1939). P: Republic.
     C: Gene Autry, Smiley Burnette, George Hayes.
     73m.

77. WALL STREET COWBOY (6 September 1939). P: Re-
     public. C: Roy Rogers, George Hayes, Raymond
     Hatton. 66m.

78. THE ARIZONA KID (29 September 1939). P: Republic.
     C: Roy Rogers, George Hayes, Sally March. 61m.

79. SAGA OF DEATH VALLEY (22 November 1939). P:
     Republic. C: Roy Rogers, George Hayes, Donald
     Barry. 58m.

80. DAYS OF JESSE JAMES (20 December 1939). P:
     Republic. C: Roy Rogers, George Hayes, Pauline
     Moore. 63m.

81. THE DARK COMMAND (15 April 1940). P: Republic.
     D: Raoul Walsh. Second unit director: Joseph Kane.
     C: John Wayne, Claire Trevor, Walter Pidgeon.
     94m.

82. THE CARSON CITY KID (1 July 1940). P: Republic.
     C: Roy Rogers, George Hayes, Bob Steele. 57m.

83. THE RANGER AND THE LADY (30 July 1940). P:
     Republic. C: Roy Rogers, George Hayes, Jacque-
     line Wells. 59m.

84. COLORADO (15 September 1940). P: Republic. C:
     Roy Rogers, George Hayes, Pauline Moore. 57m.

85. YOUNG BUFFALO BILL (5 October 1940). P: Re-
     public. C: Roy Rogers, George Hayes, Pauline
     Moore. 59m.

86. YOUNG BILL HICKOK (21 October 1940). P: Repub-
     lic. C: Roy Rogers, George Hayes, Jacqueline
     Wells. 59m.

87. THE BORDER LEGION (5 December 1940). P: Republic. C: Roy Rogers, George Hayes, Carol Hughes. 57m.

88. ROBIN HOOD OF THE PECOS (14 January 1941). P: Republic. C: Roy Rogers, George Hayes, Marjorie Reynolds. 59m.

89. THE GREAT TRAIN ROBBERY (28 February 1941). P: Republic. C: Bob Steele, Claire Charleton, Milburn Stone. 61m.

90. IN OLD CHEYENNE (28 March 1941). P: Republic. C: Roy Rogers, George Hayes, Joan Woodbury. 58m.

91. SHERIFF OF TOMBSTONE (7 May 1941). P: Republic. C: Roy Rogers, George Hayes, Elyse Knox. 56m.

92. NEVADA CITY (20 June 1941). P: Republic. C: Roy Rogers, George Hayes, Sally Payne. 58m.

93. RAGS TO RICHES (31 July 1941). P: Republic. C: Alan Baxter, Mary Carlisle, Jerome Cowan. 57m.

94. BAD MAN OF DEADWOOD (4 September 1941). P: Republic. C: Roy Rogers, George Hayes, Carol Adams. 61m.

95. JESSE JAMES AT BAY (17 October 1941). P: Republic. C: Roy Rogers, George Hayes, Gale Storm. 56m.

96. RED RIVER VALLEY (12 December 1941). P: Republic. C. Roy Rogers, George Hayes, Sally Payne. 62m.

97. THE MAN FROM CHEYENNE (16 January 1942). P: Republic. C: Roy Rogers, George Hayes, Sally Payne. 60m.

98. SOUTH OF SANTA FE (17 February 1942). P: Republic. C: Roy Rogers, George Hayes, Linda Hayes. 55m.

99. SUNSET OF THE DESERT (1 April 1942). P: Repub-

lic.   C: Roy Rogers, George Hayes, Lynne Car-
ver.   54m.

100.   ROMANCE OF THE RANGE (18 May 1942).   P: Re-
       public.   C: Roy Rogers, George Hayes, Sally
       Payne.   63m.

101.   SONS OF THE PIONEERS (2 July 1942).   P: Repub-
       lic.   C: Roy Rogers, George Hayes, Marie Wrix-
       on.   61m.

102.   SUNSET SERENADE (14 September 1942).   P: Repub-
       lic.   C: Roy Rogers, George Hayes, Helen Par-
       rish.   58m.

103.   HEART OF THE GOLDEN WEST (11 December 1942).
       P: Republic.   C: Roy Rogers, George Hayes,
       Smiley Burnette.   65m.

104.   RIDIN' DOWN THE CANYON (30 December 1942).   P:
       Republic.   C: Roy Rogers, George Hayes, Linda
       Hayes.   55m.

105.   IDAHO (10 March 1943).   P: Republic.   C: Roy
       Rogers, Virginia Grey, Smiley Burnette.   70m.

106.   KING OF THE COWBOYS (9 April 1943).   P: Repub-
       lic.   C: Roy Rogers, Smiley Burnette, Peggy
       Moran.   67m.

107.   SONG OF TEXAS (14 June 1943).   P: Republic.   C:
       Roy Rogers, Sheila Ryan, Barton MacLane.   69m.

108.   SILVER SPURS (12 August 1943).   P: Republic.   C:
       Roy Rogers, Smiley Burnette, Phyllis Brooks.
       68m.

109.   MAN FROM MUSIC MOUNTAIN (30 October 1943).
       P: Republic.   C: Roy Rogers, Ruth Terry, Paul
       Kelly.   71m.

110.   IN OLD OKLAHOMA (6 December 1943).   P: Repub-
       lic.   D: Albert Rogell.   Second unit director:
       Joseph Kane.   C: John Wayne, Martha Scott, Al-
       bert Dekker.   Reissued as WAR OF THE WILD-
       CATS.   102m.

111. HANDS ACROSS THE BORDER (5 January 1944). P:
      Republic. C: Roy Rogers, Ruth Terry, Guinn 'Big
      Boy" Williams. 73m.

112. THE FIGHTING SEABEES (10 March 1944). P: Re-
      public. D: Edward Ludwig. Second unit director:
      Joseph Kane. C: John Wayne, Susan Hayward,
      Dennis O'Keefe. 100m.

113. THE COWBOY AND THE SENORITA (12 May 1944).
      P: Republic. C: Roy Rogers, Mary Lee, Dale
      Evans. 78m.

114. THE YELLOW ROSE OF TEXAS (24 June 1944). P:
      Republic. C: Roy Rogers, Dale Evans, Grant
      Withers. 69m.

115. SONG OF NEVADA (5 August 1944). P: Republic.
      C: Roy Rogers, Dale Evans, Mary Lee. 75m.

116. FLAME OF THE BARBARY COAST (28 May 1945).
      P: Republic. C: John Wayne, Ann Dvorak, Jo-
      seph Schildkraut. 91m.

117. THE CHEATERS (15 July 1945). P: Republic. C:
      Joseph Schildkraut, Billie Burke, Eugene Pallette.
      87m.

118. DAKOTA (12 December 1945). P: Republic. C:
      John Wayne, Vera Ralston, Walter Brennan. 82m.

119. IN OLD SACRAMENTO (31 May 1946). P: Republic.
      C: Bill Elliott, Constance Moore, Hank Daniels.
      89m.

120. THE PLAINSMAN AND THE LADY (15 November
      1946). P: Republic. C: Bill Elliott, Vera Ral-
      ston, Gail Patrick. 87m.

121. WYOMING (1 August 1947). P: Republic. C: Bill
      Elliott, Vera Ralston, George Hayes. 84m.

122. OLD LOS ANGELES (25 April 1948). P: Republic.
      C: Bill Elliott, John Carroll, Catherine McLeod.
      88m.

123. THE GALLANT LEGION (25 July 1948). P: Repub-

lic.   C: Bill Elliott, Joseph Schildkraut, Bruce
Cabot.   88m.

124.   THE PLUNDERERS (1 December 1948).   P: Republic.
       C: Rod Cameron, Ilona Massey, Adrian Booth.
       Trucolor.   87m.

125.   THE LAST BANDIT (25 April 1949).   P: Republic.
       C: Bill Elliott, Adrian Booth, Andy Devine.   Tru-
       color.   80m.

126.   BRIMSTONE (15 August 1949).   P: Republic.   C:
       Rod Cameron, Adrian Booth, Walter Brennan.   Tru-
       color.   90m.

127.   ROCK ISLAND TRAIL (19 May 1950).   P: Republic.
       C: Forrest Tucker, Adele Mara, Adrian Booth.
       Trucolor.   90m.

128.   THE SAVAGE HORDE (22 May 1950).   P: Republic.
       C: Bill Elliott, Adrian Booth, Grant Withers.   90m.

129.   CALIFORNIA PASSAGE (15 December 1950).   P:
       Republic.   C: Forrest Tucker, Adele Mara, Este-
       lita Rodriguez.   90m.

130.   OH! SUSANNA (28 March 1951).   P: Republic.   C:
       Rod Cameron, Adrian Booth, Forrest Tucker.   Tru-
       color.   90m.

131.   FIGHTING COAST GUARD (1 June 1951).   P: Repub-
       lic.   C: Brian Donlevy, Forrest Tucker, Ella
       Raines.   88m.

132.   THE SEA HORNET (6 November 1951).   P: Republic.
       C: Rod Cameron, Adele Mara, Adrian Booth.   84m.

133.   HOODLUM EMPIRE (15 April 1952).   P: Republic.
       C: Brian Donlevy, Claire Trevor, Forrest Tucker.
       98m.

134.   WOMAN OF THE NORTH COUNTRY (5 September
       1952).   P: Republic.   C: Ruth Hussey, Rod Came-
       ron, John Agar.   Trucolor.   90m.

135.   RIDE THE MAN DOWN (1 January 1953).   P: Re-
       public.   C: Brian Donlevy, Forrest Tucker, Rod

Cameron. Trucolor. 90m.

136. SAN ANTONE (15 February 1953). P: Republic. C:
Rod Cameron, Arleen Whalen, Forrest Tucker.
90m.

137. FAIR WIND TO JAVA (28 April 1953). P: Republic.
C: Fred MacMurray, Vera Ralston, Robert Douglas.
Trucolor. 92m.

138. THE SEA OF LOST SHIPS (1 February 1954). P:
Republic. C: John Derek, Walter Brennan, Wanda
Hendrix. 85m.

139. JUBILEE TRAIL (15 May 1954). P: Republic. C:
Vera Ralston, Forrest Tucker, Joan Leslie. Trucolor. 108m.

140. HELL'S OUTPOST (15 December 1954). P: Republic.
C: Rod Cameron, Joan Leslie, John Russell. 90m.

141. TIMBERJACK (28 February 1955). P: Republic. C:
Sterling Hayden, Vera Ralston, David Brian. Trucolor. 94m.

142. THE ROAD TO DENVER (16 June 1955). P: Republic. C: John Payne, Mona Freeman, Lee J. Cobb.

143. THE VANISHING AMERICAN (17 November 1955). P:
Republic. C: Scott Brady, Audrey Totter, Forrest
Tucker. 90m.

144. THE MAVERICK QUEEN (3 May 1956). P: Republic.
C: Barbara Stanwyck, Barry Sullivan, Scott Brady.
Trucolor. Scope. 90m.

145. THUNDER OVER ARIZONA (4 August 1956). P: Republic. C: Skip Homeier, Kristine Miller, George
Macready. Trucolor. Scope. 75m.

146. ACCUSED OF MURDER (December 1956). P: Republic. C: David Brian, Vera Ralston, Sidney
Blackmer. Trucolor. Scope. 74m.

147. DUEL AT APACHE WELLS (January 1957). P: Republic. C: Anna Maria Alberghetti, Ben Cooper,
Jim Davis. Trucolor. Scope. 70m.

148. SPOILERS OF THE FOREST (5 April 1957). P: Republic. C: Rod Cameron, Vera Ralston, Ray Collins. Trucolor. Scope. 68m.

149. THE LAWLESS EIGHTIES (31 May 1957). P: Republic. C: Buster Crabbe, John Smith, Marilyn Saris. Trucolor. Scope. 70m.

150. LAST STAGECOACH WEST (July 1957). P: Republic. C: Jim Davis, Mary Castle, Victor Jory. Scope. 67m.

151. THE CROOKED CIRCLE (November 1957). P: Republic. C: John Smith, Fay Spain, Steve Brodie. Scope. 72m.

152. GUNFIGHT AT INDIAN GAP (13 December 1957). P: Republic. C: Vera Ralston, George Macready, Anthony George. Scope. 70m.

153. THE NOTORIOUS MR. MONKS (28 February 1958). P: Republic. C: Vera Ralston, Don Kelly, Paul Fix. Scope. 70m.

154. THE MAN WHO DIED TWICE (June 1958). P: Republic. C: Rod Cameron, Vera Ralston, Mike Mazurki. Scope. 70m.

155. BEAU GESTE (August 1966). P: Universal. D: Douglas Heyes. Second unit director: Joseph Kane. C: Telly Savalas, Doug McClure, Guy Stockwell. Technicolor. Scope. 9,405ft./104 1/2m.

156. HERE COMES THAT NASHVILLE SOUND (© 20 September 1966). P: Ambassador Films. C: Randy Boone, Sheb Wooley, Paul Brinegar. Technicolor. 84m.

157. TOBRUK (February 1967). P: Universal. D: Arthur Hiller. Second unit director: Joseph Kane. C: Rock Hudson, Guy Stockwell, George Peppard. Technicolor. Scope. 9,867ft./109 1/2m.

158. TRACK OF THUNDER (September 1967). P: United Artists. C: Tom Kirk, Ray Stricklyn, Faith Domerque. Technicolor. 83m.

159. DID YOU HEAR THE ONE ABOUT THE TRAVELING
     SALESLADY? (March 1968). P: Universal. D:
     Don Weis. Second unit director: Joseph Kane. C:
     Phyllis Diller, Joe Flynn, Bob Denver. Techni-
     color. Scope. 8,746ft. /97m.

160. THE SHAKIEST GUN IN THE WEST (May 1968). P:
     Universal. D: Alan Rafkin. Second unit director:
     Joseph Kane. C: Don Knotts, Don Barry, Barbara
     Rhodes. Technicolor. Scope. 9,065ft. /101m.

161. IN ENEMY COUNTRY (July 1968). P: Universal.
     D: Harry Keller. Second unit director: Joseph
     Kane. C: Tony Franciosa, Guy Stockwell, Anja-
     nette Comer. Technicolor. Scope. 9,599ft. /107m.

162. SEARCH FOR THE EVIL ONE (© 15 August 1968).
     P: Ambassador Films. C: Lee Patterson, Lisa
     Pera, Henry Brandon. Technicolor. 90m.

163. SMOKE IN THE WIND (1971). Unreleased. C:
     Walter Brennan, John Ashley, Dan White.

Witney as he looked in late 1973.　Photo courtesy of the St. Louis Post-Dispatch.

Chapter 5

WILLIAM WITNEY

by Francis M. Nevins, Jr.

Ask any movie lover for the names of the ten greatest
living American directors and, whoever is on the list, it's a
safe bet that William Witney will not be. And yet on his own
turf, within the area in which he has specialized, he is probably the greatest filmmaker alive or dead. What Hitchcock
is to the suspense film and Lubitsch was to the sophisticated
comedy and Ford to the epic Western, William Witney is in
his domain--the pure action film.

The purest variety of action film, and the genre in
which Witney earned a reputation as a visual genius that sur-
vives among connoisseurs to this day, is the serial. Remember those twelve- and fifteen-chapter extravaganzas of
breathless excitement which kids in the 'thirties and 'forties
absorbed on Saturday afternoons, one gorgeous chapter and
one fantastic cliffhanger a week? Remember Flash Gordon,
Zorro, Captain Marvel, The Black Commando, and their
dozens of heroic chapter-play counterparts? If you don't, I
recommend three fine books: Alan G. Barbour's Days of
Thrills and Adventure (Macmillan, 1970), Raymond William
Stedman's The Serials (University of Oklahoma Press, 1971),
and Jim Harmon and Donald F. Glut's The Great Movie
Serials: Their Sound and Fury (Doubleday, 1972). All three
books seem to agree that by far the best serials were those
of Republic Pictures, and that the best Republic serials were
those directed (either alone or in tandem with John English)
by William Witney. In Witney's work at Republic we can
see the art of the serial in action.

A serial is (or should be) an audiovisual fireworks

189

display, a cross between a football game and a ballet, a
panorama of spectacular visual action paralleled by a furious
musical score. The story-lines of serials were frequently
constructed on the house-that-Jack-built model, with an in-
definitely expansible middle that could go on for chapter after
chapter, week after week, without making substantial progress toward any goal. But serial story-lines were rarely
more than pegs on which to hang the action, and the more
action the better. Just as the best football games are those
that contain the most breathtaking plays, so are the best
serials.

The first test of a serial, its visual dimension, depends on the director's skill, on the grace and bounce and
excitement which he and the stuntmen and his other collaborators can put into the film, working without a set of rules,
without a script that spells out what to do--stuntman Fred
Graham has estimated that about half of Republic's serial
stuntwork was improvised on the set--and with no intent to
make any statement other than the images themselves. The
second test of a serial, its aural dimension, demands a
music score that runs in confluence with the physical action,
its soul-pounding themes reinforcing the visual excitement.
Although no serial director controlled the musical scoring
of his films, it happens that a majority of the visually most
impressive chapter plays are also the most impressive to
the ears, thanks mainly to four men--Alberto Colombo,
William Lava, Cy Feuer, and Mort Glickman--whom we
shall meet presently. The third and final test of a serial,
its mythological dimensions, requires that the movie's structure be able to accommodate all the visual and aural fireworks, with a hero and villain each of titanic stature and
contending for stakes worthy of their larger-than-life
grandeur. A mysterious masked rider of the Old West
fighting a tyrant who has the whole territory in his grasp;
an intrepid secret agent battling Nazi spies on land and sea
and in the air; an adventurer catapulted to another planet to
combat a mad emperor who's determined to annihilate the
human race--the possibilities for creating a story-line with
the proper mythological dimension are limitless. In short
then, a serial is (or should be) a cinematic myth about the
triumph of good over evil after a long series of ritual struggles committed to film with the maximum visual and aural
impact.

Of the four studios that turned out significant numbers
of serials during the sound era--Mascot, Universal, Repub-

lic, and Columbia--Republic alone consistently satisfied these
criteria, at least within the Golden Age of Serials, 1936-45.
The studio's competitors referred to it mockingly as Repul-
sive, but it brought and held together a band of the most
gifted action film people alive--writers, editors, cinematog-
raphers, special effects experts, composers, actors, stuntmen, and directors. And the foremost contract director at
Republic, one of the few who stayed with the studio virtually
throughout its existence (with time off for war service), was
William Witney.

Is Witney an auteur as the term is customarily used?
Not if it means a director who controls every aspect of his
films and uses them to express a personal vision of the
world. Witney at Republic was not an individualist on a ego
trip; he was a member of a collective, perhaps the most
creative collective in American movies. He was intimately
involved in the creation of all his serials from the first
rough draft of a script to the editing of the final print, and
there are some themes that recur in many of his films:
the hero as reincarnation of a towering figure from the past,
symbolic death and resurrection prior to the victory over
evil, the celebration of collective work and of the collective
as hero; but there is no consistent personal philosophy in
Witney's serials, and they would have been weakened as serials had he tried to turn them into vehicles for such a philosophy. His films seem to explode with the joy and excitement of an incredibly talented young man who is making
movies and loving it, but Witney insists today that directing
to him was just a $75-a-week job which he would have chucked
without a second thought if something better paying had come
along. He looks on himself as a technician, nothing fancier,
and would probably cut his throat rather than discourse to
intellectuals about his art. He says quite frankly that he
can't understand anyone being interested in his serials. But
today, more than thirty years after they were made, those
serials still bring gasps of wonder from audiences cutting
across all barriers of age, sex, race, wealth, occupation,
and ideology.

Nevertheless, after almost forty years as a director
and despite the explosion of film consciousness over the past
decade, Witney has not been the subject of one significant
reference in English except for serial fan publications and
the three specialized books I've mentioned before. In the
première issue of Movie (May, 1962), in which that magazine's editors divided directors into the categories of Great,

Brilliant, Very Talented, Talented, Competent or Ambitious,
and The Rest, Witney was relegated to bottom line of the
last category--and with his name misspelled to boot.   In one
of the rare foreign discussions of his work, he is patroniz-
ingly described as "a director of honest craftsmanship but
mediocre invention, like many directors of minor films, who
in their time created works containing some popular interest,
at least within the confines of the elementary mythology of
the world of the pioneers" (Filmlexicon Degli Autori e Delle
Opere, Vol. VII. Rome: Edizioni di Bianco e Nero, 1967).
In the graphically stunning and mammoth-sized history of
Republic serials, Jack Mathis' Valley of the Cliffhangers
(1975), Witney's name is mentioned just a handful of times,
and then only in passing, the text giving no sense at all of
Witney as a person nor of his contributions to the art of the
action film.   I hope the present career study will fill this
gap in the literature and pay William Witney a small part of
the tribute that is his due.

What kind of guy is he?   Of medium build, fit and
rugged-looking at sixty, with a craggy face that looks lived
in, and eyes that gleam with devilish delight.   A plain-
spoken and unpretentious man, uninterested in publicity and
almost painfully without ego.   At a film convention packed
with his fans, he refused to wear a name tag and would not
go into the screening room to see any of the serials he
made in his early twenties.   An earthy and non-stop talker,
full of behind-the-scenes stories from his forty years in the
industry, but with harsh words only for those few who didn't
do their jobs.   A compulsive worker, who must be busy at
all times, who demands much of his co-workers but more
of himself.   A lover of liquor, competitive sports and fine
horseflesh.   A tough-minded and resilient man, who came
up the hard way through a depression and a world war, and
developed the beliefs and values that one would expect of a
man who had prospered after such experiences.   A consummate professional and a man's man in a time when he per-
ceives both ideals dying.

It was out of this Howard Hawks-like mystique that
Witney's films sprang.   Listening to him reminisce, one can
almost see it take shape again, the image of the close-knit
fraternity of professionals who make their living by taking
physical risks, who work their butts off day after day with
the utmost in cool competence, then spend half the night
drinking and carousing and indulging in robust and violent
horseplay with each other but in the morning are back at

their jobs and working as a supremely professional collective
once again. Whatever we may think of this quasi-military
mystique of manhood, Witney kept it out of his films, or at
least buried it so deep that only a political hypersensitive
would let it interfere with his enjoyment of the pure visual
experience.

The violence, of course, is not buried at all, and
hardly a minute of a Witney serial goes by without a chase
or fight of some sort. But as Witney points out, violence
is an ambiguous term. The new breed of gore-nography,
where blood and brains spill all over the screen, is not Witney's brand of bourbon (although by his own account, his recent film I ESCAPED FROM DEVIL'S ISLAND is in this
category, with sharks tearing a man's arm off and similar
treats for the tenderminded). Witney's serials portray something completely different: an unrealistic, ritualized, visually pleasing imitation of combat, a ballet of violence which
by its very unrealism would seem to purge viewers' primitive instincts rather than encourage them to take up weapons.

The man who grew to make these serials was born in
Lawton, Oklahoma in 1915, spent most of his boyhood in
Coronado, California, took the Annapolis Naval Academy en-
trance exams in 1933, and while waiting for the results entered the movie industry with a job as office boy at Nat
Levine's Mascot Studio. Mascot's specialty was crude, low-
budgeted but fast-paced serials turned out in a few weeks
apiece by action directors like Otto Brower, Armand Schaefer, the great B. Reaves Eason, and Colbert Clark, Witney's
brother-in-law, who got him the studio job. Witney stayed
with Mascot during its last two years of existence, working
his way through the positions of janitor, prop boy, guide,
and electrician, and absorbing from Eason and other directors all that there was to know about the art of making a film
move. Late in 1935 Mascot and some other small studios
merged with Herbert Yates' Consolidated Film Laboratories
into a new organization called Republic Pictures. Along with
Levine himself, directors Eason and Joseph Kane and many
of Mascot's ablest technicians, Witney went with the merger.
He worked as a script clerk on the earliest Republic serials
--which were produced by Levine and turned out by virtually
the same people who had made the last Mascot chapter plays
--and was rapidly promoted to film editor, receiving his
earliest screen credits in that capacity on the studio's fourth
and fifth serials, ROBINSON CRUSOE OF CLIPPER ISLAND
(Republic, 1936) and DICK TRACY (Republic, 1937).

Early in 1937 Witney as film editor went along to St.
George, Utah for location shooting with the cast and crew of
Republic's next chapter play, THE PAINTED STALLION.
The directors assigned to this project were the same pair
that had directed DICK TRACY: the prolific but undistinguished Ray Taylor (1889-1952), veteran of countless silent
and sound serials, and Alan James, then about sixty years
old and best known for directing Ken Maynard Westerns in
the early 'thirties. While on location in Utah, THE PAINTED
STALLION began to come apart at the sinews, plagued by
incessant rainfall and human ineptitude that combined to
throw shooting way behind schedule. Finally the front office
dismissed Taylor and told young Witney that he had just become the director in charge.

Sound like the old Hollywood musical plotline about
the trembling understudy replacing the star on a moment's
notice? Maybe, but that's the way it happened, and Witney
with James' help completed twelve chapters in noble style.
THE PAINTED STALLION was set in the New Mexico territory of the early 1820s, shortly after the revolt of Mexico
from Spanish rule, and starred Ray Corrigan as American
scout Clark Stuart and Julia Thayer as a mysterious Indian
girl who aids Stuart and his companions (including Davy
Crockett, Jim Bowie, and an adolescent Kit Carson) in their
fight against the tyrannical governor of Santa Fe. Silent and
early-talkie cowboy star Hoot Gibson had a major role as a
wagonmaster, and the young Duncan Renaldo, later to become famous as the Cisco Kid, played a renegade leader.
Witney's intense love of horses manifested itself in some
magnificent riding sequences, especially where Miss Thayer
and her pinto stallion escape pursuers by making a spectacular leap across a wide abyss. Directorial credit was shared
by Witney, James, and Taylor, in that order. This was the
first of twenty-three consecutive serials directed in whole or
in part by William Witney, making up the most stunning cycle of pure action films in the history of moving pictures.

Witney's second chapter play and his final collaboration with "Smokey" James was SOS COAST GUARD (Republic,
1937), which starred Bela Lugosi as Boroff, mad-scientist
inventor of a disintegrating gas called Arnatite, and Ralph
Byrd as Coast Guard Lieutenant Terry Kent, who vows vengeance after Boroff, in trying to smuggle his gas out of the
country, murders Kent's brother. The brother, incidentally,
was portrayed by Thomas Carr, who later became a director
himself and turned out Westerns for Republic, serials for

Columbia and many series episodes for television. Boroff's
giant zombie henchman, Thorg, was enacted by Richard
Alexander (Prince Barin in the first two of Universal's three
Flash Gordon serials), and the female lead, newswoman-
aviatrix Jean Norman, was played by Maxine Doyle, who
became Mrs. William Witney shortly after filming was completed and remained the director's wife until her death of
throat cancer in May 1973. The film's best sequences grow
out of the wreck of the S. S. Carfax in Chapter One, in
which it's virtually impossible to tell that the entire ship is
a miniature model, courtesy of Howard Lydecker and his incomparable special effects department. For the scenes of
the disintegrating gas at work, Witney photographed the melt-
ing of film emulsion so as to make an entire mountain appear to dissolve before the viewer's eyes--a technique he'd
learned at Mascot where Brower and Eason had used it for
the destruction of an underground civilization in the last
chapter of THE PHANTOM EMPIRE (Mascot, 1935). Raoul
Kraushaar, who had also arranged the background music for
THE PAINTED STALLION, was credited with the haunting
score for Witney's second serial, although he got a certain
amount of assistance from Beethoven's Egmont Overture,
Liszt's Les Preludes, and the stock music library of prior
Republic productions.

    Before shooting began on the studio's next chapter
play, producer Nat Levine made a contribution to serial history that outstripped anything he'd done at Mascot. He
teamed Witney with John English (1903-1969). English, too,
had started out as a film editor, working for M-G-M until
the death of Irving Thalberg, afterwards working at any minor studio that would give him a job. Like the best people
in every other area of the action film, he wound up a member of the Republic collective, in creative partnership with
Witney. But English's relationship with Witney went much
deeper: they remained close friends all their lives, and
English was godfather to Witney's son. English preferred to
direct indoor scenes, full of dialogue that would advance the
story, while Witney's forte was spectacular outdoor action.
(Their taste in clothes corresponded to their filmmaking
tastes, with English always coming to work nattily attired
while Witney, who was out in the boondocks most of the day,
went into the field wearing the sloppiest clothes he could
find.) Together the two men formed the most perfect collaboration of action directors in the world.

    Their first project together was ZORRO RIDES AGAIN

(Republic, 1937), starring John Carroll as James Vega, great-grandson of the original Zorro, who takes up the ancestral black suit when the California-Yucatan Railroad is menaced by El Lobo and his outlaws. Carroll's baby-faced good looks stood him in good stead when he had to act the incompetent fop as James in order to conceal his second identity as Zorro, but the oafish-hulk image of Richard Alexander was completely wrong for El Lobo. (El Lobo's real name in the script was Brad Dace, and apparently no one could decide whether the character was supposed to be an Anglo or a Mexican, so Alexander used his Brooklynesque accent interspersed with an occasional and wildly unconvincing Spanish phrase.) But Duncan Renaldo was excellent as the masked man's faithful servant, and Noah Beery, Sr. deliciously fruity as the villainous financier who is masterminding the sabotage on the railroad. Whenever Zorro came on screen in an action sequence he was portrayed by the great Yakima Canutt, king of the 1930s stuntmen. The setting of this Western adventure in modern times gave Witney plenty of opportunity to stage action in speeding trains, trucks and planes, as well as the chance to shoot an abundance of fluidly beautiful horseback chases. The fistfights and other scenes of violent physical contact are still apprentice work, and the climax in which Zorro's horse tramples El Lobo to death is quite amateurish. But Whitney was learning his craft rapidly, and would soon be absolute master of his genre. Alberto Colombo supervised the excellent music score.

The same score, augmented of course by the Rossini William Tell Overture, punctuated the action in Republic's next and now legendary chapter play, THE LONE RANGER (Republic, 1938). Legendary, because it and its sequel THE LONE RANGER RIDES AGAIN (Republic, 1939) were withdrawn from circulation after a few years and almost all of the prints destroyed. The most complete existing version I know of consists of scratchy and choppily re-edited segments of thirteen out of the original fifteen chapters, subtitled in Spanish, with the masked man called El Llanero Solitario and the name of his Indian companion changed to Ponto since tonto in Spanish means fool. The story-line, diverging almost totally from that in the famous radio and television series, centers on the device of concealing until the last chapter the identity of the hero, rather than that of the villain as was done in so many other serials. At the end of the Civil War, five Texas Rangers band together to lead a revolt against the tyrant Jeffries and his tax-collecting

Gestapo who have turned the state into a private empire.
Whenever they get into a tight spot, one of the quintet slips
away to reappear in the mask of The Lone Ranger.   During
the fifteen chapters one after another of the five Rangers is
killed, until at the end, with Jeffries' domain destroyed,
only one is left.   The five suspects were played by Herman
Brix (better known as Bruce Bennett), Lee Powell, George
Letz (better known as George Montgomery), Hal Taliaferro
and Lane Chandler, with Chief Thundercloud in the role of
Tonto and Stanley Andrews (who later became The Old Ranger, narrator of the TV series DEATH VALLEY DAYS) as
Jeffries.   The Colombo score became the basis of the background music for the radio and television series in later
years.   The action never slackens for a minute, and the
film is full of Witney's magnificently fluid horseback sequences in which animal, rider and landscape merge into a
single unit, breathtaking to watch.   The scene in Chapter
One where all five Rangers and Tonto escape Jeffries' army
in a stagecoach, one man on each of the six horses of a
yoked-together team, is perhaps the most visually forceful
tribute to collectivity ever created by the Republic collective.
Yakima Canutt once again did a magnificent job as the
masked hero, although Witney told me that in this and similar assignments Canutt did have one problem.   Yak, it
seems, was a tobacco chewer, and every so often he'd start
to get rid of a chaw and forget he was wearing a mask that
covered his nose and mouth as well as his eyes.   Canutt's
remarks as the plug descended into his digestive apparatus
would not, I'm told, have been appreciated by the Hays Office.

      Witney and English returned to a contemporary set-
ting and military heroics with their next work, THE FIGHT-
ING DEVIL DOGS (Republic, 1938), starring two of the five
Lone Ranger suspects, Lee Powell and Herman Brix, as a
pair of Marine lieutenants who conduct their own twelve-
chapter war against a black-cloaked villain known as The
Lighting, master of fantastic electronic weapons with which
he seeks to rule the world.   This serial is entertaining but
cheaply and hastily put together, using a stupefying amount
of back-projection and lifting many action sequences from
earlier Republic productions like ROBINSON CRUSOE OF
CLIPPER ISLAND, DICK TRACY, and SOS COAST GUARD.
But Witney's next chapter play came back up almost to the
level of his first masterpiece, THE LONE RANGER.

      DICK TRACY RETURNS (Republic, 1938) was the

first of three Witney-English sequels to the original Dick
Tracy serial of 1937 on which Witney had been film editor.
Ralph Byrd portrayed Chester Gould's famous comic-strip
cop in all four serials, but the roles of Tracy's associates
shifted from film to film.   In RETURNS Lynn Roberts took
the role of Tracy's secretary Gwen, Michael Kent was his
assistant Steve Lockwood, Lee Ford played his dumb stooge
Mike McGurk, and Jerry Tucker acted Junior.   The villains
in this serial were loosely based on the infamous Ma Barker
and her sons, but with Ma changed to a male, Pa Stark,
and portrayed by the great serial villain Charles Middleton
(whose performance as the Emperor Ming in the three Flash
Gordon serials at Universal has become a landmark of pop-
film history).   In the first chapter Stark, his five vicious
sons, and their gang murder a young FBI agent, played by
Olympic athlete David Sharpe, who would very quickly make
his mark as one of the great stuntmen.   Tracy mobilizes
the forces of the Bureau against the incredibly diversified
criminal activities of Stark and his gang, battling the min-
ions of evil on land and sea and in the air through fifteen
chapters full of spectacular sequences such as a wild chase
among two trains and a one-man tank, a gigantic fight at a
power house, a speedboat melee, and a battle royal at an
abandoned quarry.   Chapter Seven is especially interesting
for a few moments of "in" humor where a walk-on villain
is gratuitously given the name Zarkoff so that Middleton as
Pa Stark can address some properly Mingian remarks to
him.   Colombo's score is excellent and the movie as a whole
is a fine example of serial art.

          For HAWK OF THE WILDERNESS (Republic, 1938),
Republic's final chapter play of the year, Colombo was replaced as music director by William Lava, and Herman Brix
(Bruce Bennett) returned in his third major role under Witney, this time portraying Kioga, a Tarzan-like noble savage
who is discovered on an uncharted island by a party of ex-
plorers.   The search for a lost treasure, encounters with
hostile Indians and modern pirates and wild animals, and a
blazing volcano give rise to the action, filmed in stunningly
beautiful Mammoth Lakes locations.   The story-line is not
the greatest and the picture is marred by heavy doses of
racism, but Brix is superb in the leading role and Witney
exploits his star's (and stuntman Ted Mapes') athletic prowess to the maximum.

          Next on the Republic schedule came THE LONE
RANGER RIDES AGAIN (Republic, 1939), another "lost"

work but one which--as I can testify from having viewed the
only surviving print, a washed-out duplicate with Spanish
subtitles--shows the collective at its rare worst. The story-
line bears no relation to that of the Lone Ranger radio
series, nor even to the first Lone Ranger chapter play.
This time the masked man is cowboy Bill Andrews (Robert
Livingston), who along with the faithful Tonto (Chief Thundercloud again) and the fiery Juan Vasquez (Duncan Renaldo)
steps into the range war between cattleman Bart Dolan's outlaw band of Black Raiders and the homesteaders. Dolan's
sister was portrayed by Jinx Falken, who later restored the
-burg to her last name and became a radio and TV personality. Witney's riding sequences and Renaldo's performance
are first-rate, but far too many elements of the film are
simply awful, including a mess of inept fistfights, a ridiculous declamatory acting style reminiscent of riverboat melodrama, a hopeless performance by butterball Ralph Dunn as
the villain, and a lame music score by Lava relying heavily
on the William Tell and Light Cavalry overtures. And yet
this was the immediate forerunner to the three masterpieces
of the Witney-English duo!

What makes the difference between THE LONE RANG-
ER RIDES AGAIN and the later serials of 1939? In a word,
choreography. As David Sharpe explained to me, the traditional practice had been to film any fight sequence all at
one time, with the stuntmen tumbling and jumping and punch-
ing and throwing breakaway furniture at each other for two
or three minutes without let-up. This is exhausting work,
even for men in tiptop physical shape, and the inevitable result was that a fight sequence could never retain zip and
grace and bounce throughout its length but would lose momentum as it went along. Witney eliminated this problem by
a device so simple that no one had thought of it before.
The inspiration came to him from watching Busby Berkeley
film a dance sequence. Witney then decided to break down
each of his own fight sequences into dozens of individual
fragments--a punch, a thrown chair, a kick or tumble or
what have you in each fragment--but he'd shoot only a few
of these fragments at a time, as Berkeley had shot his fantastic dance sequences. Then Witney would switch to a non-
strenuous scene, and return to shooting the fight when everybody had rested. It was a brilliant device, the culmination
of Witney's early experience as a film editor, and it's the
reason why his fight sequences remain full of action and
drive and balletic grace from first frame to last. The internal evidence of his films would suggest that the break-

through came early in 1939.   In all of Witney's serials after
THE LONE RANGER RIDES AGAIN, the fight scenes are
among the finest ever put on film.

If serial lovers had to choose the best chapter play
of all time, many would vote for DAREDEVILS OF THE RED
CIRCLE (Republic, 1939).   The three titular heroes--played
by Charles Quigley, Herman Brix, and David Sharpe--are
amusement-park acrobats working for millionaire Horace
Granville (Miles Mander); but in a sense the trio make up a
single integrated hero, with Quigley contributing brains,
Brix brute strength, and Sharpe almost inhuman agility.
(Witney told me he can always spot Sharpe doing a stunt on
the screen, even in long shot, because he moves like a cat.)
Charles Middleton turns in a bravura performance as 39013,
an escaped convict who's out to ruin Granville's business interests one by one in retaliation for the tycoon's role in
sending him to prison.   When Quigley's small brother is
killed in a huge amusement-park fire set by Middleton, the
trio take to the warpath, with periodic assistance from an
unknown ally called The Red Circle.   (Any students of Freud
in the audience might have guessed from the sexual symbolism of the name that The Red Circle was a woman, and it
did turn out to be Carole Landis, who thus serves the same
function in this film that Julia Thayer did in THE PAINTED
STALLION.)   The twelve chapters are brim-full of spectacular action beginning with the first chapter, the cliffhanger
of which shows Quigley on a motorcycle racing through a
vehicular tunnel with a living wall of water pounding behind
him--another of the countless Republic sequences to which
Howard Lydecker and his life-like miniatures contributed.
Lava's furious score for the film was superbly coordinated
to the visual excitement.

DICK TRACY'S G-MEN (Republic, 1939) has a less
impressive Lava score but as visual spectacle again shows
Witney at his best.   Ralph Byrd as Tracy, Phylis Isley
(better known as Jennifer Jones) in the minor role of Gwen,
and Ted Pearson as Steve Lockwood battled the distinguished
actor-director Irving Pichel who portrayed international spy
Zarnoff.   At the beginning of the serial Zarnoff has already
been caught by Tracy and sentenced to the gas chamber.   By
taking an experimental drug he manages to have himself
brought back to life after his execution--although "at a price
no mortal man was ever expected to pay"--and swears vengeance on Tracy.   Tracy sets out to frustrate each of Zarnoff's new schemes of sabotage, and the ensuing action

sequences--a leap from the landing gear shaft of a cabin
plane into a racing speedboat and then back onto the plane,
a dirigible fire, a battle around a diving bell and another in
a lumberyard--are marvelously inventive and exhilarating
every second.

       But Republic's final chapter play of the year is my
personal choice for the number one serial of all time.
ZORRO'S FIGHTING LEGION (Republic, 1939) is blessed

Witney, his co-director John English (r.), and in the center,
Hiram Brown, producer of many of the Witney-English ser-
ials, including ZORRO'S FIGHTING LEGION (Republic, 1939).
Photo courtesy of William Witney.

with spectacular direction, an exceptionally strong story-line,
one of the great serial heroes and the greatest of all serial
villains, a rousing Lava score, and virtual perfection in
every element of chapter play art.   The setting is Mexico
in the 1820s.   The revolution has been won, the harsh laws
have been abolished and the good society is growing.   But
in the province of San Mendolito the long-dormant Yaqui Indian god Don Del Oro has come to life and is directing his
white and Indian followers in a campaign to destroy the republic and replace it with his own dictatorship.   Don Fran-

cisco Vega organizes a fighting force to combat this menace
but is murdered in Chapter One. His nephew Diego takes
Francisco's place, playing the effeminate fop by day and
riding at the head of his legion as Zorro by night. Since
the governing council of San Mendolito is largely composed
of Don Del Oro's followers (in fact the leaders of the council collectively are in a sense Don Del Oro), Zorro's legion
is outlawed and has to combat the local military as well as
the Yaquis and white renegades under the enemy's banner.
After twelve chapters of spectacular footage--swordplay,
acrobatics, breathtaking chases of every description--the
God of Gold literally drops into a fiery pit and the good society is restored. Reed Hadley is magnificent as Diego and
Yakima Canutt no less so behind the black mask, while di-
minutive Billy Bletcher, who was the voice of The Lone
Ranger in the two chapter plays about that hero, contributed
his deep stentorian tones this time to the figure of Don Del
Oro. A sense of exhilaration, of good humor, of joy in
life, and in fighting the good fight, and in making movies
permeates every frame of this absolute masterpiece of its
kind. It's from ZORRO'S FIGHTING LEGION that we learn
what the serial at its best could be.

     The first Republic serial of the following year was
planned as something different, an attempt to minimize
fights and chases and other spectacular action and to stress
a mood of mystery and occult horror. DRUMS OF FU MAN-
CHU (Republic, 1940) was based on the world-famous Oriental fiend created by Sax Rohmer (1883-1959), and the script
was closer to both the spirit and specific incidents in Rohmer's novels than was customary when Republic screenwriters adapted material from other sources. Fu and his
army of dacoits invade California in quest of various exotic
objects (The Dalai Plaque, The Kardak Segment) which,
when put together, will give Fu the key to the location of
the lost sceptre of Genghis Khan, which in turn will make
Fu the absolute ruler of all Asia. Henry Brandon in magnificently sinister Oriental make-up played Fu, while William
Royle was given the role of Sir Denis Nayland Smith, the
evil doctor's nemesis in the Rohmer novels. The undistinguished Robert Kellard had the action lead as Nayland's
young assistant, Allan Parker (a character not present in
any Rohmer story), although Dave Sharpe replaced him in
the stunting sequences. After fifteen chapters Fu's schemes
are defeated and the doctor himself is apparently killed in
an automobile crash, but in the final scene he returns to
Genghis Khan's tomb, somewhat the worse for wear, and

vows that "there will come another day--a day of reckoning
when the forces of Fu Manchu will sweep on to victory."
Allowing the villain to remain alive and unpunished at the
end of a serial was a novelty unappreciated by the Hays
Office, but the censors backed down before the argument
that all of Rohmer's novels ended the same way. So the
path was cleared for the promised sequel, but no followup
serial was made, reportedly because of pressure from the
Chinese government on the State Department. The music
score for DRUMS was prepared by Cy Feuer, who would
later turn Broadway and movie producer with such hits as
CABARET (Allied Artists, 1972) to his credit. Witney has
said that this is his personal favorite among his serials,
largely because it was so different in mood and tone from
his other chapter plays, and because the shooting schedule
and budget were more generous than usual.

        Republic's next serial was ADVENTURES OF RED
RYDER (Republic, 1940), based on Fred Harman's comic-
strip cowboy. Both Witney and English wanted Dave Sharpe
for the lead but they were overruled by studio head Herbert
Yates' insistence that the role go to a young actor named
Don Barry, who had brought a crackling Cagneyesque intensity to his "good badman" roles in two Republic features of
1939, SAGA OF DEATH VALLEY with Roy Rogers, and
WYOMING OUTLAW, a Three Mesquiteers film starring
John Wayne. Although Barry felt he was wrong for the
part, he brought the same ferocity to his role as the cow-
poke who leads the fight against Harry Worth, Noah Beery,
Sr., and assorted cut-throats trying to drive the ranchers
off their property and sell it to the railroad. The situation
is no more than a peg on which to hang large numbers of
Witney's fantastically exuberant action set-pieces, with Dave
Sharpe stunting for Barry much of the time. The serial's
only flaws are a few sequences of speeded-up editing which
gives the effect of Keystone Kops comedy and a Cy Feuer
score which uses the ludicrously inappropriate "Oh Susanna"
as accompaniment to action scenes; but otherwise it's a
model of chapter play dynamism that displays Witney's talent at peak form.

        Unfortunately the next Witney-English serial, KING
OF THE ROYAL MOUNTED (Republic, 1940), has been inac-
cessible for decades, since Republic purchased from the
Zane Grey estate the right to exhibit its films based on his
characters only for a term of years. The heroic Mountie
Sergeant, played by the late Allan Lane, took twelve chapters

of whirlwind action to defeat enemy agents on the trail of
something called Compound X (a combination polio cure and
naval weapon element). Cy Feuer was once again credited
with the music score, as he had been for DRUMS and RED
RYDER.

The final Republic serial of the year, like that with
which the year had begun, was villain- rather than hero-
oriented, but this time the villain was created at the studio
itself. According to Henry Brandon, the original plan for
MYSTERIOUS DOCTOR SATAN (Republic, 1940) was to have
Brandon play a traditional devil in modern dress, complete
with slight horns and a goatee. "We were going to hoke it
up for the kids," Brandon said, but when he was offered a
role in a major production he dropped out of the project.
The excellent character actor Eduardo Ciannelli handled the
title role without any of the originally conceived hokey trap-
pings, playing Satan as a power-mad scientist out to rule the
world by means of an army of robots. The masked hero
standing in his way was called The Copperhead, with bland
Robert Wilcox playing the character in his private identity
and dynamic Dave Sharpe doing the honors under the snake-
skin mask. The original Copperhead had been Bob Wayne's
father, a Robin Hood figure of the old West; but Bob assumes the identity after the ancestral mask, carried in his
breast pocket, stops one of Satan's poison darts from killing
him--the themes of symbolic death, resurrection, and reincarnation brought to life on the screen in one short, word-
less and enthralling scene. Cy Feuer's score is the finest
he contributed to any serial and there are dozens of fine
action sequences, perhaps the most famous being the bank
robbery performed by Dr. Satan's robot (who is portrayed
by ace stuntman Tom Steele and who first appears in a
chapter playfully entitled "Doctor Satan's Man of Steel").
The climactic extreme-low-angle shot of Satan plunging
screaming out of a window and over a cliff in the arms of
his metallic creation is a real stunner.

The new decade got off to a rousing start at Republic with THE ADVENTURES OF CAPTAIN MARVEL (Republic, 1941), starring Olympic weightlifter and Western hero
Tom Tyler, and with Dave Sharpe as stunt double performing the most spectacular flying leaps of his career. Frank
Coghlan, Jr. played Billy Batson, the young radio operator-
newscaster on whom an ageless Oriental wizard has be-
stowed the power to turn himself into a superman by repeating the magic work SHAZAM! The masked villain known

as The Scorpion is trying to recover the component parts of
an occult device which can both turn base metals into gold
and disintegrate any person or object in its path.   Marvel's
battles against The Scorpion cover the ground from Siam to
California and back again, with the emphasis not so much
on physical combat (who can last long against a super-
powered hero?) but rather on heart-stopping acrobatic work,
the finest footage of its kind ever filmed.   Unfortunately the
script is full of chaotic transitions and unexplained incidents,
and the Cy Feuer score is much too lethargic to do justice
to the action sequences.   But purely on the directorial level
CAPTAIN MARVEL ranks among Witney's finest achievements.

        Spectacular leaps through the air, although this time
with the aid of swinging vines, punctuate the action once
more in JUNGLE GIRL (Republic, 1941), which was very
loosely based on a novel by Edgar Rice Burroughs and was
the first of several Republic serials with a female lead.
Frances Gifford played the heroine, Nyoka Meredith, with
Tom Neal as the good white hunter who helps her clear her
father's reputation and discover a diamond treasure.   Trevor Bardette (in a dual role) and Gerald Mohr are the guys
in the black pith helmets, and vicious-looking Frank Lack-
teen portrays Shamba, their native co-conspirator.   For the
vine swingings and fistfights and other strenuous activities
demanded of Nyoka, Dave Sharpe in wig and miniskirt shared
the honors with top stunt girl Babe De Freest, who did the
scenes in which Nyoka's legs would be clearly in view.

        The next Witney-English effort, KING OF THE TEXAS
RANGERS (Republic, 1941), returned to the tradition of the
contemporary Western and to the far older tradition, going
back to Houdini and to Nat Levine's practices at Mascot, of
signing real-life athletic heroes to portray similar roles in
serials.   Southern gridiron great Slingin' Sammy Baugh
played Ranger Tom King and Duncan Renaldo his Mexican
counterpart, Lt. Pedro Garcia, battling a small army of
Axis spies whose headquarters is a dirigible hovering over
Texas.   Exploding oil fields, trains bursting through tunnels
in the midst of an avalanche, plane collisions, fights and
leaps of all sorts punctuate the non-stop actionfest.

        The year's final Republic chapter play was also the
last of the studio's Dick Tracy films and the last Witney-
English collaboration.   DICK TRACY VERSUS CRIME, INC.
(Republic, 1941) pits Ralph Byrd as the iron-jawed sleuth

against The Ghost, a vengeful master criminal armed with
death rays and a device for making himself invisible, who
has declared total war on the city of New York. Many cliffhangers in this fifteen-chapter epic are borrowed from the
three earlier Tracy serials, but the cannibalized footage is
among the most exciting actionwork from the older films, so
that CRIME, INC. constitutes a virtual anthology of The
Best of Dick Tracy and, in many enthusiasts' judgment, the
finest of all the Tracy films. Cy Feuer's score was the
last he contributed to a Republic serial.

The chapter plays of the following year showed certain differences in tone, due mainly to America's entry into
World War II. Before Pearl Harbor, Republic had made
only two serials with an international espionage background--
KING OF THE ROYAL MOUNTED in 1940 and KING OF THE
TEXAS RANGERS in 1941--but six out of the studio's next
eight chapter plays were anti-Nazi. The aural impact of the
wartime serials was greatly enhanced by the scores of Mort
Glickman, who replaced Feuer at the end of 1941. And on
the directorial side, John English dropped out of the partnership with Witney, having grown tired of serials and desirous
of making feature-length pictures on his own. His resignation left a gap in the ranks of the tight-knit men's club of
actors, stuntmen, writers, directors and others who made
up the Republic serial unit, and after discussion with the
front office Witney agreed to assume English's duties as
well as his own and direct the studio's chapter plays solo.

Having had minimal experience directing actors but
five solid years' experience directing action, Witney put his
personal stamp on his first serial alone by making the action
literally nonstop for hours on end and filling every frame
with the visual energy of a maniac. The result, for me at
least, was the finest serial of all time except for ZORRO'S
FIGHTING LEGION. SPY SMASHER (Republic, 1942) employed Kane Richmond in a dual or collective role as the
caped unofficial agent of the government and his civilian-
suited twin brother, both of them working loosely under
Naval Intelligence in a series of campaigns against a German spy known as The Mask. Superb performances by
Richmond, Marguerite Chapman, Hans Schumm, Frank Cor-
saro and the entire cast combined with the eye-popping set-
pieces of action and a thunderous Glickman score (the leit-
motif adapted from the Beethoven Fifth Symphony) to turn
SPY SMASHER into one of Witney's greatest achievements.
Even the few moments of humor in the dead-serious script

are priceless: one sequence is built around a huge billboard
advertising DICK TRACY VERSUS CRIME, INC., and in the
first chapter Spy Smasher slips into a cavern full of counter-
feit money and drawls laconically to the single spy on the
premises: "Got change for a five?"--which might be considered the granddaddy of all the James Bond witticisms.
Witney's low-key and unobtrusive work with Kane Richmond
is so skillful as almost to convince us that the brothers
were played by two different actors.

His next serial was more evenly balanced between
action and dramatic sequences and had nothing to do with the
war effort. PERILS OF NYOKA (Republic, 1942) employed
the same first name for the heroine as 1941's JUNGLE GIRL
(the name had not been used in Burroughs' novel and so could
be re-used by Republic without additional royalty payments),
but except for her name she's a totally different character,
living in what looks like the old West rather than a jungle
and played by a different actress. Kay Aldridge portrayed
the lovely white queen of the desert tribes, hoping someday
to find her long-missing father, and Clayton Moore--who
would later, for TV and feature films, don the mask of The
Lone Ranger--enacted the young doctor who has come to the
desert in search of the lost tablets of Hippocrates, which
are the key to both a cancer cure and a hidden treasure.
The forces of evil are led by darkly beautiful Lorna Gray
as Vultura and good old Ming Middleton as Cassib, assisted
by an army of Arab terrorists and a grotesque pet ape.
Nyoka performs as many Nijinsky leaps and socks as many
villainous jaws as any male hero of a Witney serial, which
isn't surprising since both Miss Aldridge and Clayton Moore
were doubled by Dave Sharpe. Glickman's score is almost
as rousing as his music for SPY SMASHER.

KING OF THE MOUNTIES (Republic, 1942), the second and final chapter play based on the Zane Grey character, once again starred Allan Lane, his adversaries this
time being a nest of Axis spies equipped with a "bat plane"
and headquartered in a dormant volcano. Unhappily, this
serial, like its predecessor KING OF THE ROYAL MOUNTED,
has been withdrawn from circulation for contractual reasons.

Witney's last work for Republic during the early
'forties was an espionage epic, G-MEN VERSUS THE BLACK
DRAGON (Republic, 1943), starring Rod Cameron as secret
agent Rex Bennett, a sort of home-grown James Bond of
World War II. The enemy spies in this fifteen-episoder

were led by Haruchi (Nino Pipitone), who had been smuggled
into the U.S. in a mummy case during suspended animation.
The loose story-line provided plenty of opportunity for whirlwind action, punctuated aurally by gigantic explosions (courtesy of Howard Lydecker and his miniatures) and by another
superb Glickman score. Witney was drafted near the end of
shooting and producer W. J. O'Sullivan had to finish the last
few scenes himself.

     While Lieutenant Witney was serving in the Pacific as
officer in charge of a Marine combat photography unit, most
of Republic's serials were in the hands of Spencer Bennet
(1893-   ), a veteran action director whose best work is
neck-and-neck with the best of Witney, although in 1943
John English left feature films long enough to helm the
studio's DAREDEVILS OF THE WEST (Republic, 1943) and
to share the megaphone with Elmer Clifton on CAPTAIN
AMERICA (Republic, 1943). The war claimed the life of at
least one serial stalwart who had gone into the Marines--
Sergeant Lee Powell, of THE LONE RANGER and FIGHTING
DEVIL DOGS, killed in July 1944 during the Battle of Tinian.
Witney survived his four years of service but came out in
1946 full of scars and scabs, disgusted at violence in all its
forms, and, in his own words, feeling shaky. He didn't
want to go back to Republic, and for a while it looked as
though he wouldn't have to. A deal was in the works whereby he would go over to Universal and be given a high-budget
musical to direct. Then, shortly before the contract were
to be signed, Universal suspended all operations. Witney
was still jobless. He waited till the last day he had left
under the GI Bill to reclaim his old position, then went
knocking on Republic's door. Before he knew it he was
back on a serial again.

     THE CRIMSON GHOST (Republic, 1946), co-directed
by Fred C. Brannon who did the dramatic and dialogue sequences John English used to helm, starred Charles Quigley,
whom Witney had last directed earlier in DAREDEVILS OF
THE RED CIRCLE, and Linda Stirling, who had become Republic's reigning serial queen under the direction of Spencer
Bennet while Witney had been at war. The titular villain,
garbed in full-length black robes and a skull mask, was
after a new invention called the Cyclotrode, which had the
power to short-circuit electric current and bring any city to
its knees. Clayton Moore portrayed the Ghost's second-in-
command. The Glickman score was for the most part a
rehash of themes from earlier serials, but Witney's ballets

of violence were fully up to his pre-service standards.
Nevertheless, his heart wasn't in it any more. A clue to
his postwar attitude to serials may be found in the license
plate on the villains' auto, which consists of three digits
preceded by the letters BS. He asked to be transferred to
another unit, and was assigned to direct Roy Rogers films.
The years with Rogers, he told me, were the happiest of
his life.

Witney's pre-war exposure to feature-length movie
making had been restricted to three Western programmers
plus bits and pieces of other Republic Westerns which had
been credited to their official directors. His first feature,
THE TRIGGER TRIO (Republic, 1938), had been the tenth
picture in Republic's Three Mesquiteers series, which usually starred Bob Livingston, Ray Corrigan, and ventrilo-
quist Max Terhune. It was a routinely entertaining yarn in
which the Mesquiteers become involved with a murder growing out of an attempt to hide the existence of hoof-and-mouth
disease in a herd of cattle. But as if a director of less
than a year's experience and working on his first feature
didn't have worries enough, Witney's problems skyrocketed
when Bob Livingston suffered a fractured skull in an accident just before filming was to begin. Livingston was replaced by iron-jawed Ralph Byrd, who was woefully inappropriate in a Western but who had starred under Witney before in SOS COAST GUARD and would star under him again
in the last three Dick Tracy serials. Two years later Witney had directed another Mesquiteers film, HEROES OF THE
SADDLE (Republic, 1940), the twenty-seventh in Republic's
series, and the best of Witney's three pre-war features,
with Livingston, Duncan Renaldo, and Raymond Hatton in
the leads. The story had the Mesquiteers befriending the
inmates of an orphanage and setting out to break the power
of the institutions' corrupt superintendent. A fantastic insider's joke takes place about halfway through the film when
Livingston suddenly dons the same mask he'd worn the previous year in THE LONE RANGER RIDES AGAIN, breaks
into the orphanage in order to kidnap all its inmates, and is
instantly captured and unmasked, thus becoming the holder
of the world's shortest-lived secret identity. Cy Feuer's
music keeps the fire lit under a number of fine chase sequences. Witney's third and final feature before going into
the Marines, OUTLAWS OF PINE RIDGE (Republic, 1942),
had reunited him with RED RYDER star Don Barry, who
this time played an honest gambler embroiled in territorial
political scheming after he foils a hold-up in a saloon whose

owner has designs on the governor's mansion. It's a routinely professional job, short on action and betraying no hint
that its director had helmed the breath-stopping SPY SMASH-
ER only months before.

          With his pre-war feature experience limited to these
three films and with action-crammed serials constituting the
great bulk of his work, Witney seemed an unlikely choice to
take over the direction of Roy Rogers' films in 1946. Although Rogers' early films from 1938 through 1941 had been
a fine blend of music, action, and exceptionally strong
stories--my favorite is SAGA OF DEATH VALLEY (Republic,
1939) which had helped make Don Barry a star--the series
took a rapid downhill spin when Gene Autry, the most popular singing cowboy of them all, left Republic for war service, and the studio decided that the Rogers series should be
turned into a carbon of Autry's actionless and elaborately
costumed musical comedies, at least until the war was over.
And most of Rogers' films of the early and middle 'forties
fulfilled the studio's prescription to the letter. Once Witney
took over the unit, he worked in collaboration with screenwriter Sloan Nibley (who was and still is married to serial
queen Linda Stirling), set out to change the direction of Roy's
movies, restore a reasonable measure of fast action and
stunting in the serial tradition, and experiment with techniques for making hand-to-hand combat look a bit more realistic than had been acceptable before the war, although still
light-years removed from the current vogue for gore-nography or from the real thing. In the Rogers films of the late
'forties, when people get into fistfights they come out bloodied,
and the fights themselves are less balletic and more bone-
crunching, with hero's fist and villain's jaw really making
contact even when the brawl is taking place on the edge of a
cliff, as in the climactic melee between Rogers and Dave
Sharpe in BELLS OF SAN ANGELO (Republic, 1947).

          It was while working on the Rogers pictures that Wit-
ney perfected the technique of having the combatants slam
away at each other in slow motion and undercranking the
camera as he filmed them so that the speed of their movements seemed perfectly normal on the screen. Such devices as these, plus the easy-on-the-eyes Trucolor process
and the unusual modern-West story-lines and Rogers' natural
charm, made up for the obligatory cowboy songs and the
sickly background music (most of it by Stanley Wilson or R.
Dale Butts) and kept this series on a consistently higher
level than Republic's other action films of the late 'forties,

Witney with Edward J. White, producer of the Roy Rogers films at Republic, which Witney directed. Photo courtesy of William Witney.

which became worse and worse each year. Even though the
front office demanded several country-western ditties per
picture--at the proper moment a bored Witney would call
out "Okay, guys, song time!" and Rogers and the boys would
go into their number--action devotees could be sure that each
Rogers film would have at least two or three sequences that
would make their eyes pop out, such as the chase in THE
FAR FRONTIER (Republic, 1949) where the villains roll oil
barrels from the back of their truck onto the road and Trigger jumps over or sidesteps every barrier on the instant
obstacle course, or the scene in TWILIGHT IN THE SIERRAS
(Republic, 1950) where Roy rescues a man and woman bound
and gagged inside a burning runaway stagecoach. The story-
lines of Rogers' third-period films hold up well almost thirty
years later, with much emphasis on ecological themes and
the problems of disadvantaged groups--Indian tribes, Chi-
canos, ex-convicts--and even more stress on Witney's life-
long empathy with animals.

        Such motifs recur throughout Witney's work of the
late 'forties and early 'fifties, but if I had to pick a single
incident in a single film to represent this side of Witney, it
would be the scene in EYES OF TEXAS (Republic, 1948)
where the villains send out four killer dogs after Roy and
his horse Trigger. At the height of the attack Roy recog-
nizes one of the dogs as an animal he had earlier nursed
back to health, although the other side had subsequently re-
captured the dog and whipped it into savagery again. The
dog in turn remembers Roy, edges away from the rest of
the killer pack and takes his place beside Roy and Trigger
for a counterattack. "Now it's three against three," Roy
says, in a scene that would seem ludicrous in the hands of
almost any other director but is unarguably right in a film
by Witney, for whom man and horse and dog dwell on the
same plane just as man and horse and landscape do when
he is filming a rider on horseback. Witney directed a total
of twenty-seven Roy Rogers features from ROLL ON TEXAS
MOON (Republic, 1946) to PALS OF THE GOLDEN WEST
(Republic, 1951), after which Rogers left Republic and
started making half-hour films for television.

        With Roy's departure, Witney was assigned to sing-
ing cowboy Rex Allen, the newest and last of Republic's
crop, who had been starring in Republic films since 1949.
He directed nine of the Allen films of 1952-53, with time
out halfway through the cycle to make a ridiculous Judy Ca-
nova hillbilly-cum-service comedy, THE WAC FROM WALLA

WALLA (Republic, 1952). Within Witney's nine films with
Allen one can trace the decline of the series Western at Republic. The early entries, like BORDER SADDLEMATES
(Republic, 1952), were the equivalent of the Rogers films in
glossiness, superb action sequences (especially where Rex
rescues Roy Barcroft from being dragged to death by a runaway horse), the love of animals that infuses the whole production, the obligatory educational lecture in mid-film (here
the subject is fox health), and overall mood of good humor
and excitement. The very next Witney-Allen film, OLD
OKLAHOMA PLAINS (Republic, 1952), contains some well-
staged action but is mainly structured around stock footage,
although spectacular footage to be sure--the great race between a troop of cavalry and an experimental tank which
Breezy Eason had shot for Republic's feature ARMY GIRL
in 1938. The later features, like OLD OVERLAND TRAIL
(Republic, 1953), lack even a commitment to first-rate stock
footage, and Witney's last films with Allen relied on indoor
filming interspersed with almost anything that could be
dragged out of Republic's vaults. Late in 1953 the studio
decided that it was no longer economically feasible to make
"B" Westerns and the Rex Allen series ground to a halt.

Over the next few years Witney did some free-lancing
on the side, his most notable work along this line being the
river battle and siege of the Alamo which he directed without
credit for Frank Lloyd's THE LAST COMMAND (Republic,
1954), a film which never leaves the standard patriotic-epic
rut except for Witney's ten minutes of footage. He helmed
seven non-series pictures for Republic, beginning with THE
OUTCAST (Republic, 1954), a superb Western starring John
Derek and Jim Davis. The sixth film of these seven is
Witney's favorite among all his movies, because, in his
words, there's nothing in it but relationships. STRANGER
AT MY DOOR (Republic, 1956), starring Macdonald Carey
and Patricia Medina, deals with the interactions of an outlaw on the run, a preacher of unshakable simple-minded
faith, the clergyman's restless young wife and his hero-
worshipping son; and Witney elicits such vivid performances
from the players that we can see each of the main characters both as he views himself and as he is perceived by
each of the others. There's no playing of favorites, no
privileged viewpoint, until the mawkish climax, which depends on at least three separate and distinct divine miracles
and leaves God in his heaven, the outlaw dying happily in
the shadow of the preacher's unfinished church, "inspira-
tional" music filling the soundtrack, and a sick feeling in

the heart of any moviegoer at the ruination of what might
have been a magnificent film. But the three action sequences, especially the eye-popping scene of a killer horse
going wild in the middle of the picture, are as filled with
maniacal energy as anything Witney did in the serials.

        In 1956 Republic ceased active production, and Wit-
ney's twenty-year association with the foremost purveyor of
low-budget high-octane entertainment came to an end. This
did not mean the end of Witney's career as a theatrical film
director but he was now a free-lance, without a long-term
contract and without the support of the great Republic collective. He turned out juvenile delinquency pictures like THE
COOL AND THE CRAZY (American-International, 1958); an
early version of the Bonnie and Clyde legend for American
International (THE BONNIE PARKER STORY, 1958); low-
budget crime melodramas like THE SECRET OF THE PUR-
PLE REEF (20th-Fox, 1960); a science-fiction film, MAS-
TER OF THE WORLD (American-International, 1961), starring Vincent Price and Charles Bronson and based on two
novels by Jules Verne, although the film was shot almost
entirely indoors and is unsuited to Witney's unique talents;
and even a modest contribution to the beach-bikinis-and-
screaming-teenies genre, THE GIRLS ON THE BEACH
(Paramount, 1965). Between 1964 and 1967 he directed
three Westerns starring the late Audie Murphy, filming in
Arizona and making use of a memorably pervasive ice-blue
color scheme. The best of the trio, ARIZONA RAIDERS
(Columbia, 1965), is a brutal tale of two Confederate veterans who join Quantrill's Raiders and then are forced to become double agents and betray the rest of the gang. Among
the familiar faces in the cast are Republic stunt ace Fred
Graham as Quantrill and Buster Crabbe as the head of the
Arizona Rangers. More recently Witney has contributed to
the black action genre with I ESCAPED FROM DEVIL'S IS-
LAND (United Artists, 1973), a black variant of PAPILLON
with Jim Brown in the lead, and DARKTOWN STRUTTERS
(New World, 1975), a wild comedy-action flick featuring a
gang of black girl cyclists and a black male street gang who
join forces against a Dr. Satan-like villain with plans to use
cloning and artificial insemination to create a race of black
android slaves.

        But theatrical films have constituted only a small
fraction of Bill Witney's workload during the past twenty
years. Some of his energies have been channeled into a
great deal of lucrative second-unit direction, all of it un-

credited except for the comedy MR. HOBBS TAKES A VACA-
TION (20th-Fox, 1962), starring James Stewart. It was in
this capacity that Witney was hired by Alfred Hitchcock to
direct the fox hunt sequence in Hitchcock's MARNIE (Universal, 1964). (Could it have been the fox hunts in Witney's
features like BELLS OF SAN ANGELO and BORDER SAD-
DLEMATES that earned him this job?) But most of his out-
put since the mid-'fifties has consisted of episodes for television series--so many series that he's already forgotten
some of their names.

At the time Republic folded, Witney was no stranger
to the small screen, having spent a good bit of his time between 1954 and 1956 working on two series for Republic's
own TV unit. The thirty-nine-episode STORIES OF THE
CENTURY (1954-55) starred Jim Davis as railroad detective
Matt Clark, who, with a blithe disregard for historical fact,
was credited with having helped kill or capture literally
every outlaw the Old West had ever spawned, from Belle
Starr and Billy the Kid and the James brothers and Geroni-
mo down to obscurities like Milt Sharp and L. H. Musgrove.
Most of the action sequences were lifted from Republic features going back to the beginning of the studio, but Witney
told me that he thought he had made better use of them than
had the productions for which they had first been shot.
Critics and viewers of the time must have agreed, for
STORIES OF THE CENTURY won several awards during its
run and was frequently recycled on local TV stations under
alternate titles like FAST GUNS OF THE WEST. Witney's
second series for Republic's TV unit, however, did not fare
so well. DR. FU MANCHU (1956), which was a sort of
spin-off from the Witney-English 1940 serial, DRUMS OF
FU MANCHU, starred the talentless Glen Gordon in the old
Henry Brandon role and was yanked after thirteen unwatch-
able episodes, of which Witney directed the last four.

From 1956 on, Witney's telefilms proliferated like
mushrooms, and there was hardly a Western or adventure
show on TV to which he did not contribute: WAGON TRAIN,
MIKE HAMMER, RESCUE 8, CORONADO 9, FRONTIER
CIRCUS, THE TALL MAN, TALES OF WELLS FARGO,
BRANDED, DANIEL BOONE, LAREDO--the list goes on and
on. He was hired for some of these series specifically on
account of his prior work--for example, Rex Allen as star
of the thirty-nine-episode FRONTIER DOCTOR (1957-58)
must have been influential in the employment of Witney as
the show's director, and Walt Disney studio executives

probably screened ZORRO'S FIGHTING LEGION before hiring
him for the Disney series ZORRO (1957-58, seventy-eight
episodes), starring Guy Williams. But the majority of Witney's countless assignments as a television director came his
way simply because he had the experience and the talent and
was available.

        Occasionally these jobs didn't work out well, and one
of his less comfortable experiences in television occurred
during the Summer of 1958, which he spent working on
ZORRO for Disney. Caught in the middle between a front
office that demanded he keep to the schedule and a crew that
worked so lackadaisically that it was impossible to keep to
the schedule, Witney became so disgusted that, after completing eight thirty-minute episodes, he walked out.

        Other series served him well, however, including
such perennial favorites as BONANZA (1959-73), the saga of
the Cartwright family and the Ponderosa ranch. Between
1961 and 1967 Witney directed nineteen episodes that ran the
gamut from comedy through psychological and social drama
to straight action. His best BONANZA episode is "The
Gamble," from an original story co-authored by series star
Michael Landon, in which the Cartwrights are framed for
bank robbery and murder by a corrupt sheriff and his deputies, and Landon as Little Joe breaks jail and organizes a
fighting force to save his father and brothers from being
hanged. Witney touches are evident throughout the production, including an abundance of visual echoes of ZORRO'S
FIGHTING LEGION and a villain who hates horses. Two of
Witney's BONANZA episodes are full of social interest:
"The Deserter" is a powerful before-the-fact parable of My
Lai, about an Indian-massacring colonel hunting down a
young lieutenant who deserted rather than take part in the
slaughter, and "The Saga of Squaw Charlie" deals with a non-
violent Indian rights crusader, clearly based on Dr. Martin
Luther King, who is abused and beaten by the white racists
of Virginia City, led by none other than Don Barry from
Witney's RED RYDER serial. Echoes of ZORRO'S FIGHT-
ING LEGION again resound in "The Deadly Ones," with Will
Kuluva playing an older, more tired and costumeless Zorro
figure, still fighting to free Mexico from tyranny but forced
to employ Anglo professional killers in the cause. But not
all of Witney's episodes were this serious, and in "The Bur-
ma Rarity" he showed his skill in directing complex comedies as well. More than any other series with which he
was associated, BONANZA offered Witney the chance to
make use of all facets of his directorial talent.

During the same years Witney also turned out ten episodes of THE VIRGINIAN (1962-71), a long-running ninety-
minute series with a penchant for overblown stories, snail's
pacing and minimal action which even Witney could not defeat.   But in at least one of his episodes, "Beloved Outlaw,"
the actionless but touchingly beautiful story of a teenage girl
and a wild white stallion provided Witney with a perfect vehicle in which to express visually his own lifelong love of
horses.

If there was a single series which seemed to cry out
for Witney as director it was THE WILD WILD WEST (1965-
69).   This Old West variant of the James Bond movies
starred Robert Conrad as a nineteenth-century secret agent
in an Ian Fleming-like milieu of suave repartee, de luxe
settings, gorgeous ambivalent women, grotesque villains,
exotic tortures, and gadgets.   Witney directed the first two
episodes filmed, "The Night of the Deadly Bed" and "The
Night of the Sudden Death," and turned them into miniature
models of his own Republic serials.   "Deadly Bed," for instance, has Conrad as James West going below the border
to battle Florey, a Don Del Oro figure who heads a private
army and dreams of becoming Napoleon V, emperor of Mexico.   A perfectly reproduced Republic cliffhanger preceded
the first and third intermissions so that the sixty-second
commercial break does duty for the traditional week between
chapters.   The spike-studded canopy of the titular bed de-
scends on West at the end of Act One, and as Act Three
closes he is about to be pulverized on a giant gong.   Witney
employs some stunning Lydeckeresque miniatures for the
scenes with the locomotive battering ram with which Florey
plans to wreck the U.S. railroad system.   Non-stop action,
a pounding musical score, and even a visual echo of the
famous BUCK ROGERS sequence of the slaves' revolt in the
furnace room provides further nostalgia in this loving re-
prise of Witney's salad days as a director.   Unfortunately
there were continual disputes between Witney and Robert
Conrad during the filming of the first two episodes of the
series and Witney quit the program.

Another late-'sixties series that offered Witney a job
after his own heart was TARZAN (1966-68), filmed in South
America with Ron Ely in the lead.   Witney had never worked
on a Tarzan picture before, but his three ersatz-Tarzan
serials--HAWK OF THE WILDERNESS, JUNGLE GIRL,
PERILS OF NYOKA--had been far better in terms of spectacular action and visual imagery than the vast majority of

genuine Tarzan movies. For the TV series he directed a
two-part serial and three sixty-minute episodes, of which
the last is the best. "Rendezvous for Revenge" is burdened
with a silly story-line but packed with action, opening with
a scene that is pure Witney: a man in an asbestos suit running amok through the jungle with a flame-thrower, until
Tarzan swings down to save his domain and its animals.

In May of 1973, while Bill was in Mexico directing I
ESCAPED FROM DEVIL'S ISLAND, Maxine Doyle Witney
died of throat cancer. But he bounded back from the loss
of his wife as he has from everything else life has thrown
at him. He remarried later that year, and he and his Mexican bride have spent much of their subsequent time south of
the border, where he helmed several episodes of the short-
lived TV series, THE COWBOYS. More recently he directed
an episode of the Clint Walker Alaskan adventure series
KODIAK and the just-released black action-comedy DARK-
TOWN STRUTTERS. As of this writing he is back in his
beloved Mexico, directing action.

For a while, in the transition period after his first
wife's death, Bill Witney thought of changing careers, of
writing fiction and teaching. He did conduct two-week Summer filmmaking courses at the University of Portland in
Oregon, where he worked the students into the ground but
was told by every one of them at the end of the course that
they had never learned so much about film in so short a
time in their lives. When he spoke about filmmaking at St.
Louis University in November 1973, he not only lit up like
a Christmas tree in front of the audience but lit up the audience just as brightly. He is a born teacher, as he is a
born filmmaker, and I envy anyone who will study under him.
Now he's back behind the megaphone again, carrying on his
forty-year tradition of turning out visual fireworks displays
on film, infused with good humor and love of nature and
physical grace and the boundless energy of a person in an
epileptic fit. But whether he trades in his megaphone for
a lectern or stays outdoors where the action is, he will
continue in motion on one path or another as long as he has
breath. That is the art and the craft and the mystique of
William Witney.

Witney as an actor, playing Gen. Curtis LeMay in a stage
production of The Wild Blue Yonder (1951).   Photo courtesy
of William Witney.

WILLIAM WITNEY

A Film Checklist by Karl Thiede

Director

1. THE PAINTED STALLION (5 June 1937). P: Republic.
    D: William Witney, Alan James, Ray Taylor. C:
    Ray Corrigan, Hoot Gibson, Sammy McKim. NC:
    $109,164. 12 chapters.

2. SOS COAST GUARD (28 August 1937). P: Republic.
    D: William Witney, Alan James. C: Ralph Byrd,
    Bela Lugosi, Maxine Doyle. NC: $128,530. 12
    chapters.

3. THE TRIGGER TRIO (18 October 1937). P: Republic.
    C: Ray Corrigan, Max Terhune, Ralph Byrd. 56m.

4. ZORRO RIDES AGAIN (20 November 1937). P: Repub-
    lic. D: William Witney, John English. C: John
    Carroll, Helen Christian, Reed Howes. NC:
    $110,753. 12 chapters.

5. THE LONE RANGER (12 February 1938). P: Republic.
    D: William Witney, John English. C: Lee Powell,
    Chief Thundercloud, Herman Brix. NC: $168,117.
    15 chapters.

6. FIGHTING DEVIL DOGS (28 May 1938). P: Republic.
    D: William Witney, John English. C: Lee Powell,
    Herman Brix, Eleanor Stewart. NC: $92,569. 12
    chapters.

7. DICK TRACY RETURNS (20 August 1938). P: Repub-
    lic. D: William Witney, John English. C: Ralph
    Byrd, Lynn Roberts, Charles Middleton. NC:
    $170,940. 15 chapters.

8. HAWK OF THE WILDERNESS (3 December 1938). P:
    Republic. D: William Witney, John English. C:
    Herman Brix, Mala, Monte Blue. NC: $121,168.
    12 chapters.

9. THE LONE RANGER RIDES AGAIN (25 February 1939).
    P: Republic. D: William Witney, John English.
    C: Robert Livingston, Chief Thundercloud, Duncan
    Renaldo. NC: $213,997. 15 chapters.

10. DAREDEVILS OF THE RED CIRCLE (10 June 1939).
    P: Republic. D: William Witney, John English.
    C: Charles Quigley, Herman Brix, David Sharpe.
    NC: $126,118. 12 chapters.

11. DICK TRACY'S G-MEN (2 September 1939). P: Re-
    public. D: William Witney, John English. C:
    Ralph Byrd, Irving Pichel, Ted Pearson. NC:
    $163,530. 15 chapters.

12. ZORRO'S FIGHTING LEGION (16 December 1939). P:
    Republic. D: William Witney, John English. C:
    Reed Hadley, Sheila Darcy, William Corson. NC:
    $144,419. 12 chapters.

13. HEROES OF THE SADDLE (12 January 1940). P:
    Republic. C: Robert Livingston, Raymond Hatton,
    Duncan Renaldo. 56m.

14. DRUMS OF FU MANCHU (15 March 1940). P: Repub-
    lic. D: William Witney, John English. C: Henry
    Brandon, William Royle, Robert Kellard. NC:
    $166,312. 15 chapters.

15. ADVENTURES OF RED RYDER (15 June 1940). P:
    Republic. D: William Witney, John English. C:
    Don Barry, Noah Beery, Sr., Tommy Cook. NC:
    $145,961. 12 chapters.

16. KING OF THE ROYAL MOUNTED (20 September 1940).
    P: Republic. D: William Witney, John English. C:
    Allan Lane, Robert Strange, Robert Kellard. NC:
    $137,874. 12 chapters.

17. MYSTERIOUS DOCTOR SATAN (13 December 1940).
    P: Republic. D: William Witney, John English.
    C: Eduardo Ciannelli, Robert Wilcox, William
    Newell. NC: $147,381. 15 chapters.

18. ADVENTURES OF CAPTAIN MARVEL (28 March 1941).
    P: Republic. D: William Witney, John English.
    C: Tom Tyler, Frank Coghlan, Jr., William Bene-
    dict. NC: $145,588. 12 chapters.

19. JUNGLE GIRL (21 June 1941). P: Republic. D:
    William Witney, John English. C: Frances Gifford,
    Tom Neal, Trevor Bardette. NC: $177,404. 15
    chapters.

20. KING OF THE TEXAS RANGERS (4 October 1941). P:
    Republic. D: William Witney, John English. C:
    Sammy Baugh, Neil Hamilton, Pauline Moore. NC:
    $139,701. 12 chapters.

21. DICK TRACY VS. CRIME, INC. (27 December 1941).
    P: Republic. D: William Witney, John English.
    C: Ralph Byrd, Michael Owen, Jan Wiley. NC:
    $175,919. 15 chapters.

22. SPY SMASHER (4 April 1942). P: Republic. C:
    Kane Richmond, Marguerite Chapman, Sam Flint.
    NC: $156,431. 12 chapters.

23. PERILS OF NYOKA (27 June 1942). P: Republic. C:
     Kay Aldridge, Clayton Moore, William Benedict. NC:
     $175,010. 15 chapters.

24. KING OF THE MOUNTIES (10 October 1942). P: Re-
     public. C: Allan Lane, Gilbert Emery, Russell
     Hicks. NC: $139,422. 12 chapters.

25. G-MEN VS. THE BLACK DRAGON (2 January 1943).
     P: Republic. C: Rod Cameron, Roland Got, Con-
     stance Worth. NC: $156,599. 15 chapters.

26. OUTLAWS OF PINE RIDGE (27 October 1943). P: Re-
     public. C: Don Barry, Lynn Merrick, Donald
     Kirke. 57m.

27. ROLL ON TEXAS MOON (12 September 1946). P: Re-
     public. C: Roy Rogers, George Hayes, Dale Evans.
     68m.

28. THE CRIMSON GHOST (26 October 1946). P: Repub-
     lic. D: William Witney, Fred Brannon. C:
     Charles Quigley, Linda Stirling, Clayton Moore.
     NC: $161,174. 12 chapters.

29. HOME IN OKLAHOMA (8 November 1946). P: Repub-
     lic. C: Roy Rogers, George Hayes, Dale Evans.
     72m.

30. HELDORADO (15 December 1946). P: Republic. C:
     Roy Rogers, George Hayes, Dale Evans. 70m.

31. APACHE ROSE (15 February 1947). P: Republic. C:
     Roy Rogers, Dale Evans, Andy Devine. Trucolor.
     75m.

32. BELLS OF SAN ANGELO (15 May 1947). P: Republic.
     C: Roy Rogers, Dale Evans, Andy Devine. Color.
     78m.

33. SPRINGTIME IN THE SIERRAS (15 July 1947). P:
     Republic. C: Roy Rogers, Jane Frazee, Andy De-
     vine. Color. 75m.

34. ON THE OLD SPANISH TRAIL (15 October 1947). P:
     Republic. C: Roy Rogers, Jane Frazee, Andy De-
     vine. Color. 75m.

35. THE GAY RANCHERO (3 January 1948). P: Republic.
    C: Roy Rogers, Jane Frazee, Andy Devine. Color.
    72m.

36. UNDER CALIFORNIA STARS (1 May 1948). P: Repub-
    lic. C: Roy Rogers, Jane Frazee, Andy Devine.
    Color. 70m.

37. EYES OF TEXAS (15 July 1948). P: Republic. C:
    Roy Rogers, Lynn Roberts, Andy Devine. Color.
    70m.

38. NIGHT TIME IN NEVADA (29 August 1948). P: Re-
    public. C: Roy Rogers, Andy Devine, Adele Mara.
    Color. 67m.

39. GRAND CANYON TRAIL (15 November 1948). P: Re-
    public. C: Roy Rogers, Jane Frazee, Andy Devine.
    Color. 67m.

40. THE FAR FRONTIER (29 December 1948). P: Re-
    public. C: Roy Rogers, Andy Devine, Clayton
    Moore. Color. 67m.

41. SUSANNA PASS (29 April 1949). P: Republic. C:
    Roy Rogers, Dale Evans, Estelita Rodriguez. Color.
    67m.

42. DOWN DAKOTA WAY (9 September 1949). P: Repub-
    lic. C: Roy Rogers, Dale Evans, Pat Brady.
    Color. 67m.

43. THE GOLDEN STALLION (15 November 1949). P:
    Republic. C: Roy Rogers, Dale Evans, Pat Brady.
    Color. 67m.

44. BELLS OF CORONADO (8 January 1950). P: Repub-
    lic. C: Roy Rogers, Dale Evans, Pat Brady.
    Color. 67m.

45. TWILIGHT IN THE SIERRAS (22 March 1950). P:
    Republic. C: Roy Rogers, Dale Evans, Estelita
    Rodriguez. Color. 67m.

46. TRIGGER, JR. (30 June 1950). P: Republic. C:
    Roy Rogers, Dale Evans, Grant Withers. Color.
    68m.

47. SUNSET IN THE WEST (25 September 1950). P: Re-
     public. C: Roy Rogers, Estelita Rodriguez, Penny
     Edwards. Color. 67m.

48. NORTH OF THE GREAT DIVIDE (15 November 1950).
     P: Republic. C: Roy Rogers, Penny Edwards,
     Gordon Jones. Color. 67m.

49. TRAIL OF ROBIN HOOD (15 December 1950). P:
     Republic. C: Roy Rogers, Penny Edwards, Jack
     Holt. Trucolor. 67m.

50. SPOILERS OF THE PLAINS (February 1951). P: Re-
     public. C: Roy Rogers, Penny Edwards, Gordon
     Jones. 68m.

51. HEART OF THE ROCKIES (30 March 1951). P: Re-
     public. C: Roy Rogers, Penny Edwards, Ralph
     Morgan. 67m.

52. IN OLD AMARILLO (15 May 1951). P: Republic. C:
     Roy Rogers, Estelita Rodriguez, Penny Edwards.
     67m.

53. SOUTH OF CALIENTE (15 October 1951). P: Repub-
     lic. C: Roy Rogers, Dale Evans, Douglas Fowley.
     67m.

54. PALS OF THE GOLDEN WEST (15 December 1951).
     P: Republic. C: Roy Rogers, Dale Evans, Estelita
     Rodriguez. 68m.

55. COLORADO SUNDOWN (8 February 1952). P: Repub-
     lic. C: Rex Allen, Mary Ellen Kay, Slim Pickens.
     67m.

56. THE LAST MUSKETEER (1 March 1952). P: Repub-
     lic. C: Rex Allen, Mary Ellen Kay, Slim Pickens.
     67m.

57. BORDER SADDLEMATES (15 April 1952). P: Repub-
     lic. C: Rex Allen, Mary Ellen Kay, Slim Pickens.
     67m.

58. IRON MOUNTAIN TRAIL (8 May 1952). P: Republic.
     C: Rex Allen, Nan Leslie, Slim Pickens. 54m.

59. OLD OKLAHOMA PLAINS (25 July 1952). P: Repub-
     lic. C: Rex Allen, Slim Pickens, Elaine Edwards.
     60m.

60. THE WAC FROM WALLA WALLA (10 October 1952).
     P: Republic. C: Judy Canova, Stephen Dunne, June
     Vincent. 83m.

61. SOUTH PACIFIC TRAIL (20 October 1952). P: Re-
     public. C: Rex Allen, Estelita Rodriguez, Slim
     Pickens. 60m.

62. OLD OVERLAND TRAIL (25 February 1953). P: Re-
     public. C: Rex Allen, Slim Pickens, Roy Barcroft.
     60m.

63. DOWN LAREDO WAY (5 August 1953). P: Republic.
     C: Rex Allen, Dona Drake, Slim Pickens. 54m.

64. SHADOWS OF TOMBSTONE (28 September 1953). P:
     Republic. C: Rex Allen, Slim Pickens, Jeanne
     Cooper. 54m.

65. THE OUTCAST (15 August 1954). P: Republic. C:
     John Derek, Joan Evans, Jim Davis. Color. 90m.

66. SANTA FE PASSAGE (12 May 1955). P: Republic.
     C: John Payne, Faith Domergue, Rod Cameron.
     Color. 90m.

67. CITY OF SHADOWS (2 June 1955). P: Republic. C:
     Victor McLaglen, John Baer, Kathleen Crowley.
     70m.

68. HEADLINE HUNTERS (15 September 1955). P: Re-
     public. C: Rod Cameron, Julie Bishop, Ben Coop-
     er. 60m.

69. THE FIGHTING CHANCE (15 December 1955). P:
     Republic. C: Rod Cameron, Julie London, Ben
     Cooper. 70m.

70. STRANGER AT MY DOOR (6 April 1956). P: Repub-
     lic. C: Macdonald Carey, Patricia Medina, Skip
     Homeier. 85m.

71. A STRANGE ADVENTURE (24 August 1956). P: Re-

public. C: Joan Evans, Ben Cooper, Maria English.
70m.

72. PANAMA SAL (18 October 1957). P: Republic. C:
Elena Verdugo, Edward Kemmer, Carlos Rivas. 70m.

73. THE COOL AND THE CRAZY (12 March 1958). P:
American-International. C: Scott Marlowe, Gigi
Perreau, Richard Bakalyan. 78m.

74. JUVENILE JUNGLE (24 April 1958). P: Republic.
C: Corey Allen, Rebecca Welles, Richard Bakalyan.
69m.

75. YOUNG AND WILD (24 April 1958). P: Republic. C:
Gene Evans, Scott Marlowe, Carolyn Kearney. 69m.

76. THE BONNIE PARKER STORY (28 May 1958). P:
American-International. C: Dorothy Provine, Jack
Hogan, Richard Bakalyan. 80m.

77. PARATROOP COMMAND (December 1958). P: American-International. C: Richard Bakalyan, Jack Hogan,
Jimmy Murphy. 83m.

78. VALLEY OF THE REDWOODS (May 1960). P:
Twentieth Century-Fox. C: John Hudson, Lynn
Bermay, Ed Nelson. 63m.

79. THE SECRET OF THE PURPLE REEF (October 1960).
P: Twentieth Century-Fox. C: Jeff Richards,
Margia Dean, Peter Falk. 80m.

80. THE LONG ROPE (February 1961). P: Twentieth
Century-Fox. C: Hugh Marlowe, Alan Hale, Jr.,
Robert Wilkie. Color. 61m.

81. MASTER OF THE WORLD (28 June 1961). P: American-International. C: Vincent Price, Charles Bronson, Henry Hull. Color. 104m.

82. THE CAT BURGLAR (August 1961). P: United Artists.
C: Jack Hogan, June Kennedy, John Baer. 65m.

83. APACHE RIFLES (October 1964). P: Twentieth
Century-Fox. C: Audie Murphy, Linda Lawson,
Michael Dante. Color. 92m.

84. THE GIRLS ON THE BEACH (May 1965). P: Para-
     mount. C: Martin West, Noreen Corcoran, The
     Beach Boys. Color. 80m.

85. ARIZONA RAIDERS (August 1965). P: Columbia. C:
     Audie Murphy, Buster Crabbe, Michael Dante. Tech-
     nicolor. Scope. 88m.

86. 40 GUNS TO APACHE PASS (May 1967). P: Columbia.
     C: Audie Murphy, Michael Burns, Laraine Stephens.
     Color. 95m.

87. TARZAN'S JUNGLE REBELLION (May 1970). P:
     National General. C: Ron Ely, Manuel Padilla, Jr.,
     Sam Jaffe. Feature version of a two-part TV epi-
     sode, THE BLUE STONE OF HEAVEN, which aired
     on NBC, October 6 & 13, 1967. Color. 92m.

88. I ESCAPED FROM DEVIL'S ISLAND (September 1973).
     P: United Artists. C: Jim Brown, Christopher
     George, Paul Richards. Color. 89m.

89. DARKTOWN STRUTTERS (August 1975). P: New
     World Pictures. C: Trina Parks, Edna Richardson,
     Bettye Sweet. Color. 93m.

Lesley Selander

Chapter 6

LESLEY SELANDER

by Harry Sanford

Les Selander was born at Los Angeles on 26 May 1900. He was sixteen when he entered the motion picture industry. His first job was at the Harold Bell Wright Laboratory as a general handy man.

"We'd get the films wet out of a tub," Les recalled, "and drape them over wooden racks. Smelled like hell, but it was a job, and I was glad to get it. The job lasted for a while. But then, like now, there was a cut back and I was laid off. A friend gave me a tip that they were looking for help on a new Will Rogers film, DOUBLING FOR ROMEO (Goldwyn, 1922), and I hot-footed it over to the studio. The job turned out to be that of an assistant cameraman."

Les was not one to sit around and wait for things to happen. He learned at once to operate a camera and soon became quite proficient. When he was unable to find work in that line, he switched to extra work at five dollars a day.

"I would move from place to place," he commented, "wherever there was work. One day I went out to the Hal Roach studio where I met a man who actually shaped my career and who, to my mind, was one of the greatest guys ever in the business. I mean Woody Van Dyke. My first job for him was as a cameraman on a serial. We did everything in those days, you know; it wasn't at all like it is now." Les smiled, his face tan and relaxed, his hair white, thick, his eyes cheerful. "I did seven pictures with a producer named Neal Hart. They were all Westerns. I was the cameraman. I remember we even shot one in Mexico."

229

Les was also the cameraman for THE MENACING
PAST (Rollo, 1922), directed by Milburn Morante. Little or
nothing is known of the film, save that the screenplay was
by Joe Kane, a man who would attain a degree of prominence
in his own right some years hence at Republic studios.

Van Dyke gave Les his break into directing. Woody,
by then, was under contract to Fox Film Corporation, directing entries in their Buck Jones series of Westerns. He
invited Les to join the unit as his assistant director.

"I was everything out there," Les said, "unit manager, location manager, assistant director ... anything you
might think of. But it was one of the happiest times of my
life. I made some lifetime friendships there, too. Woody
Van Dyke, for one. And I got the chance to learn from
Woody how to shoot films. As a director, I still say Woody
was in a class by himself."

Woody had an uncanny ability to shoot fast, on time,
often ahead of time, turning out a first-rate production.
One scene would be in the process of being set up while
Woody, with his back to the preparations, was shooting a
different scene. Instantly he would turn to the new set and
start shooting there, while the other set was cleared and
prepared for yet another scene. It was a continuous, non-
stop process. Some directors who sought to rush things
would have to re-shoot scenes. Others would shoot a scene
from several angles, figuring one camera would get it right.
Still others would camp in the editing room for days, possibly even months, assembling the film. Not Woody. Time
meant money. He did it right the first time, fast, slick,
and professional.

"In those days, Buck had his own people, like Woody,
Duke Green, and Scotty Dunlap. Buck was the greatest
rider I ever saw. He was so good, in fact, that you could
not shoot too close on tracking shots because he was so
smooth in the saddle that it would look like he was on a
prop horse against a process screen."

Van Dyke soon moved over to Metro-Goldwyn-Mayer.
He was replaced at the Buck Jones unit by Lambert Hillyer.
Les stayed on at Fox for the next nine years, until 1932.
During this time, he was an assistant director on only one
film.

It was Woody who invited Les to join him at Metro. "Woody told me to go to the Seventh Street station and meet him in Tehachopi because he wanted me to assist him on a picture. Needless to say, I went ... read the script ... picked the locations, and was put on the payroll at $65 a week."

It was Les Selander's first step in becoming a director. He worked on MANHATTAN MELODRAMA (M-G-M, 1934) and THE THIN MAN (M-G-M, 1934) as Van Dyke's assistant. MANHATTAN MELODRAMA, the film Dillinger had seen the night he was shot, was basically a Clark Gable vehicle. William Powell played a prosecuting attorney who, in the course of the action, wound up getting Gable, a chum since boyhood, convicted and sentenced to death. Myrna Loy was cast as Powell's wife. The teaming of the two was so successful that they immediately went into THE THIN MAN, based on Dashiell Hammett's novel. The two films together required only five weeks to shoot. Metro put Les under contract. He was loaned out to Warner Brothers to assist Howard Hawks on the picture CEILING ZERO (Warner's, 1935).

After Selander returned to M-G-M, Woody told him about Buck Jones' good fortune. Buck had been signed to a generous contract at Universal which would allow him to have his own production unit with which to make his Westerns. Buck was in need of a unit director. Van Dyke had recommended Les. Selander got together with Jones. They remembered each other well from their days at Fox. Buck felt Les to be exactly what he wanted. The following year Les went under contract to Buck, directing his first picture in his own right, Buck's BOSS RIDER OF GUN CREEK (Universal, 1936). Les directed seven more entries in the Jones series, including two of Buck's best Westerns in the sound era, RIDE 'EM COWBOY (Universal, 1936) and LEFT-HANDED LAW (Universal, 1937). A strong camaraderie developed between Buck, Buck's wife Dell, Les and his wife Caroline. The friendship lasted.

When new management took over Universal in 1936, the studio went on a tight budget. Buck's contract came up for renewal in 1937. Buck was being paid $1,000 a week for fifty weeks a year and wanted a raise to $75,000. Universal wouldn't hear of it. Buck quit and signed with an independent producer to do a series of Westerns for Columbia release. Les was out of a job.

William Boyd and Buck had been friends for years. Buck introduced Les to Harry Sherman, the producer of the Hopalong Cassidy Westerns in which Boyd was the star. Sherman liked Selander's style and hired him as his director. Les started with the thirteenth entry in the series, and one of the best Boyd ever made, HOPALONG RIDES AGAIN (Paramount, 1937).

Les found Boyd a bit of a curiosity, as did most people who worked with him. He hated kids. He disliked horses. He was convinced that all he had to do to retain his popularity was smile into the camera or make use of his enchanting laugh.

"I recall how he gave me this ring," Les said, showing a silver ring on his left hand. "Bill was engaged to Grace Bradley. Dorothy Sebastian had given him this ring when they were married. Bill thought it inappropriate that he should wear it when getting married to Grace. So he gave it to me. I thought nothing about it, thanking him. However, the next year I was contacted by the Internal Revenue Service. Bill had deducted the ring as a $5,000 gift on his income tax and they wanted to know why I hadn't declared it. "

Sherman didn't get along very well with Bill. Their conceptions of how the Hoppy role should be interpreted differed radically. Instead of making him the hard-riding, swearing, scrapping, gunslinger of the Clarence E. Mulford novels, Bill played him as a dandy, dressed all in black, in "a monkey suit" as "Pop" Sherman called the outfit. But the series was making money, so he let it be. He decided to branch out. He proposed a series of pictures based on the novels of Rex Beach. He selected Les Selander to direct THE BARRIER (Paramount, 1937), with Jean Parker, James Ellison, and Leo Carrillo. The troupe went on location to Washington's Mount Baker National Forest. The picture was well-received.

In addition to the requisite number of Hoppy pictures for 1938, "Pop" branched off into producing entries in Paramount's ongoing Zane Grey series. He directed one excellent Hoppy film, SUNSET TRAIL (Paramount, 1938), several not so excellent, and one, THE FRONTIERSMAN (Paramount, 1938), which was just plain bad. And he directed two Zane Grey Westerns, MYSTERIOUS RIDER (Paramount, 1938) and HERITAGE OF THE DESERT (Paramount, 1938). SUNSET

Les directing Jimmy Ellison and Jean Parker in a scene
from THE BARRIER (Paramount, 1937).   Photo courtesy of
Lesley Selander.

TRAIL had a plot which found Hoppy pretending to be a dude.
Boyd borrowed Buck Jones' sheepskin chaps to make his satirical performance consummate.   Russell Hayden, "Pop"
Sherman's former production manager, had been promoted
to acting by Sherman the previous year, playing Hoppy's
sidekick, Lucky Jenkins.   Russell was featured in both the
Grey pictures. MYSTERIOUS RIDER starred Douglas Dum-
brille with Sidney Toler as his saddle pard.   HERITAGE OF
THE DESERT was actually the third Paramount version of
the film, the second one having been Henry Hathaway's first
directorial effort in 1932.   Sherman's version starred Donald Woods with Russell and Sidney Toler in support.   Both
Grey films were among the finest of their kind, although
they embodied "Pop" Sherman's formula for Westerns rather
than Grey's.   "Pop" always said you should open big, forget
the middle, and come to a thrilling finish.   That's the way
Les played it.

Boyd was becoming disgusted with the kind of scripts

he was getting, and pictures Les directed with him, like
HIDDEN GOLD (Paramount, 1939), indicate that Boyd wasn't
merely nit-picking. RANGE WAR (Paramount, 1939) was a
memorable Hoppy film primarily because "Pop" made use of
existing sets employed by Cecil B. DeMille in filming UNION
PACIFIC (Paramount, 1939). The truly unusual pictures
Les did in 1939 were the Zane Grey entries, KNIGHTS OF
THE RANGE, which starred Russell Hayden with Jean Parker and Victor Jory, and THE LIGHT OF THE WESTERN
STARS. The latter cast Jory in the role of a hero, or at
least a drunken saddle tramp trying to do right for the first
time in his life. Tom Tyler was a crooked sheriff. And
Alan Ladd was given a small supporting role. There was a
terrific fight at the end of the picture between Jory and Tyler. Les decided to shoot it without benefit of doubles.
"We were doing the fight at the very end of production,"
Les recalled, "and if somebody got a shiner, it wouldn't
matter too much. I didn't want them to get hurt, of course.
But they wanted to do it ... partially, I think, because they
were a couple of real bozos, but also because they felt it
would look better in the picture to have the principals doing
their own stuff. It came off beautifully and no one got hurt.
I won't say it didn't save money; it did. But with 'Pop'
every dollar you could, you made it show up front, on
screen, where it counted most."

Sherman arranged to have the Hoppy pictures shot in
twelve to fourteen days. He began shooting them back to
back for exteriors. This meant that the unit would go on
location to Lone Pine and film all the exteriors needed for
two Hoppy pictures, changing cast members where necessary.
Then the unit would return to Hollywood and shoot the various interiors with separate casts.

United Artists made a deal with Paramount in 1942.
They needed product to fulfill their distribution contracts.
Paramount sold them a package of films outright, which had
been completed but not yet released. Among them were
several Sherman Westerns, including some Hoppy pictures.
"Pop" then decided to sign his own distribution agreement
with United Artists and undertake to finance the films himself, rather than on a percentage basis as he was with
Paramount.

During his tenure with "Pop," Les directed twenty-
nine Hoppy pictures, four Zane Greys, and seven Western
features. FORTY THIEVES, the last Hoppy picture Sherman

produced and Les directed, was released in 1944. Production shedules had diminished to nine days, but costs still
ran high. The screenplays were more to Boyd's liking. In
FORTY THIEVES he actually holds forty armed gunmen at
bay, with no one daring to draw on him. It was an incredible sequence. But Boyd was, in his way, undeniably a capable actor, and many of his scenes in even these later films
are of singular quality. The problem was mostly that the
Hoppy pictures began losing money. Sherman abandoned
them as a poor bet.

Les Selander's finest achievement from his eight-
year contract with "Pop" was undoubtedly his work on BUCK-
SKIN FRONTIER (United Artists, 1942), one of the pictures
included in the sale agreement with Paramount. The cast
was headed by Richard Dix, with Jane Wyatt, Albert Dekker,
Lee J. Cobb, Victor Jory, and Lola Lane in support. Jane
did all of her own riding. The cast made the picture click.
It ended with an action-packed gunfight with masses of extras.
It showed a good profit upon release.

Selander did a series of films for the War Department in 1943, between Hoppy pictures. Sherman negotiated
himself a deal with Twentieth Century-Fox whereby he was
to produce BUFFALO BILL (20th-Fox, 1943). It starred
Joel McCrea, Maureen O'Hara, and Linda Darnell. "Pop"
wanted Les to direct it. Fox disagreed. They insisted on
an established director and assigned William Wellman to the
picture. But Les got to do the second unit on it, going on
location to Montana. He was paid, but he wasn't credited.

"My contract with 'Pop' ended. I was out on my own
again after nearly eight years. I had to find work and I
started looking around. "

Les wound up under contract to Republic Pictures,
an association that would last three years. He made several pictures for the little valley studio in Studio City with
the likes of Sunset Carson, Smiley Burnette, Allan Lane,
and Wild Bill Elliott as Red Ryder, along with a pair of odd
non-series films, THE VAMPIRE'S GHOST and THREE'S A
CROWD, and a Government training film.

When Selander first went to Republic, he was placed
on salary. After he began making ten to twelve pictures a
year, he asked to be paid instead on a per picture basis.
Les gave his Westerns at Republic the same pacing, feel,

and gusto that had been typical of him on the bigger budget
films he had made for Harry Sherman, the Cassidy pictures
and the specials like BUCKSKIN FRONTIER. The pictures
at Republic were aimed, for the most part, at the Saturday
afternoon matinee crowd. The framework was rigid and the
budgets were honed to a sharp edge. Selander worked
around such difficulties and his Red Ryder Westerns with
Bill Elliott, especially, were action-packed, well-photographed
(employing Bud Thackery, Reggie Lanning, and William Brad-
ford as cameramen), and bore the unique stamp of the Republic product at its best.

"I liked doing them," Selander remarked. "I was
paid for it, knew what was expected of me, and did the best
I could. I didn't know then, and I don't know now, how to
work any other way."

When asked about the various cowboy stars at Republic, Selander reflected carefully. "Bill Elliott was a real
gentleman. He was always on time, knew his lines, and in
every sense of the word was a professional. He learned to
ride damned well, considering that when I first saw him at
M-G-M in the early 'thirties, he didn't know one end of a
horse from another."

It was also during this period that Selander met Allan
Lane and Sunset Carson. Allan Lane worked on three
straight Westerns directed by Selander before he took over
for Bill Elliott in the Red Ryder series. "He could be a
fussy guy and you had to let him know who was running the
show. Allan--later nicknamed 'Rocky'--had a big ... ah,
rear end, and you had to be cautious how you photographed
him. When I first saw Rocky, he was wearing light pants
and a dark shirt. Right from the start, Lane would pick a
fence to climb over or get on a horse so his big rear end
was there in full view of the camera.

"I guess Western stars came in all sizes. The first
time I set eyes on Sunset Carson, he was completely decked
out in a cowboy outfit with hand-tooled gun belt, but he
didn't know how to ride a horse. After a time, he became
an excellent rider, but out of the saddle he was still as
clumsy as ever; that, and he had a broad Texas drawl as
big as your fist. Acting wasn't his thing. But he was a
big, good-looking kid and we figured the only way we could
overcome his shortcomings as an actor was action, action,
and more action.

Les going over the script with Allan Lane and producer
Stephen Auer.   The picture is SHERIFF OF SUNDOWN (Republic, 1944).   Photo courtesy of Lesley Selander.

"Monte Hale was a pudgy fella, kind of baby fat, if
you know what I mean.   He had a pleasant voice; a nice guy.
We did several Trucolor Westerns with him and they came
out pretty well. "

Les got a mystery to do at the beginning of the new
season, FATAL WITNESS (Republic, 1945).   It was followed
by a Red Ryder picture and an Allan Lane Western.   "I had
a few weeks off, and I got a call from Sam Katzman.   He
wanted me to direct a serial for him. "   Sam was then in
charge of production on the Columbia chapter plays.   He had
always been known for his ability to make pictures on lower
budgets than anyone else would have dared.   The serial was
titled JUNGLE RAIDERS (Columbia, 1945).   It starred Kane
Richmond with Eddie Quillan and Veda Ann Borg.

"I filmed practically the whole thing up at Lone Pine.
How Sam got a 'jungle' out of that, I'll never know.   It was
my first serial, and my last.   I went back to Republic and
did THE CATMAN OF PARIS [Republic, 1945], which I liked
pretty well. "   Selander is not alone in that feeling.   CAT-

MAN was very well-paced, expertly acted, a horror film
with Carl Esmond. To devotees of the macabre, CATMAN
OF PARIS ranks high all the way round. The year closed
out with NIGHT TRAIN TO MEMPHIS (Republic, 1945) with
Allan Lane, Roy Acuff, and a hillbilly background.

Les did nine more films for Republic in 1946, including work on the new Monte Hale series Westerns. He
was then loaned out to Eagle-Lion to direct THE RED STAL-
LION (Eagle-Lion, 1946), with Robert Paige and Ted Donald-
son. "I was getting $350 a week from Republic. They
loaned me out for a thousand a week. I got my base salary.
Republic got the rest." RED STALLION was a hit, well-
received by general audiences everywhere, proving itself to
be one of Eagle-Lion's most successful pictures.

Selander went back to Republic and made an obscure
picture called LIGHTNIN' STRIKES TWICE (Republic, 1947).
It was followed by a pair of Gene Autry films, SADDLE
PALS (Republic, 1947) and ROBIN HOOD OF TEXAS (Republic, 1947). These were the last films Autry did at Republic.
He moved his entire unit over to Columbia when his Republic
contract ran out.

"Gene was a funny guy. Whenever he wasn't before
the camera, he'd be on the phone to his broker. I remember one time poking my head in his dressing room. He was
saying, 'Okay, buy the radio station, and get the hotel while
you're at it.' Gene knew the stock market, the value of
money and what it could do better than John D. Rockefeller
and J. P. Morgan combined. When it came to his lines,
he learned the wrong script."

Les closed out his contract at Republic with UNDER
COLORADO SKIES (Republic, 1947), a Western with Monte
Hale. He had done twenty-six features for them, in addition to the Katzman serial and THE RED STALLION on loan-
out. He liked his tenure at Republic. "I think part of the
reason our films looked good was because we had fun making them. We would always take ten minutes out to play a
joke on someone. You can't keep working all the time."

Monogram Pictures was undergoing an attempt at ex-
pansion and would presently, and optimistically, change its
name to Allied Artists. Selander's next film was for them--
PANHANDLE (Monogram, 1947). It was the product of two
struggling young writers, John Champion and Blake Edwards.

It starred Rod Cameron, Cathy Downs, Reed Hadley, and
Blake Edwards himself.   There was a lot of publicity about
the film and the reviews, apparently, were uniformly good.
"We ran out of money," Les remarked.   "And the big budget ... ha, it cost $190,000 and we still tapped out near
the end.   We had Cameron, as gunfighter John Sands, killed
during the final shoot-out in the rain.   But the studio wanted
a happy ending, so he lived and was seen walking out of
town in the rain, singing 'The Deacon Went Down to the Cel-
lar to Pray' at the fade."

        RKO contacted Les and worked out a contract for him
to direct GUNS OF WRATH (RKO, 1947) in their Tim Holt
Western series.   RKO was a tight money factory, particularly with Sid Rogell managing the studio.   The trial film
worked out and Les was engaged to do four more for the
next season.   The contract was on a picture-by-picture basis.

        For all that, the Tim Holt Westerns were being made
on better budgets than any other series Westerns with the exception of Gene Autry's new series at Columbia and the Roy
Rogers musicals at Republic.   Holt was a likable player
with an innocent face.

        "He had very bad eyesight, though.   Originally, it
kept him out of the service.   But he kept eating carrots all
the time, and finally he was inducted.   Probably Tim's only
real problem was women.   He was maintaining two or three
women and their apartments, and he was tired a lot of the
time.   But he was a better actor than many would have you
believe, and his pictures are among the finest I worked on."

        When RKO's president, Charles Kroner, died, Dore
Shary took over as head of production.   Shary had produced
CROSSFIRE (RKO, 1947), a hard-hitting message film about
anti-Semitism, directed by Edward Dmytryk, which had
created a sensation.   He plunged the studio headlong into
films on the same theme and other social issues, losing
heavily on every one of them.   The Jane Russell pictures
may have offset this somewhat, but the studio was on shaky
ground.   Shary was released and Howard Hughes took over.
Just exactly what Hughes had in mind is open to speculation.
Some say he intended to use RKO as a write-off against his
other prospering enterprises.   In any case, what Shary
hadn't done, Hughes did, eventually unloading the studio at
a profit to the General Tire Company, which set about liqui-
dating its assets.

No matter what the troubles, the combination of Lesley Selander and Tim Holt made money, one of the few
things that did. Les directed three entries in 1948, six in
1949, six in 1950, and four in 1951 before the series was
abandoned with the suspension of the budget units.

In 1948, Edward Alperson, the former sales manager
at Warner Brothers in the 'thirties, who had helped found
Grand National pictures, hired Les to direct a Western he
was producing for release by Twentieth Century-Fox, BELLE
STARR'S DAUGHTER (20th-Fox, 1948). It starred George
Montgomery, Rod Cameron as a bad man, and Ruth Roman.
It was based on a story by W. R. Burnett. The picture did
business.

Jack Wrather was a multi-millionaire from Texas
who married actress Bonita Granville and became a Hollywood producer. His father had been a wildcatter who had
hit a gusher in West Texas during the boom or bust days in
the oil fields. Using this as sort of a background, Wrather
hired writer Francis Rosenwald to come up with a story.
The result was STRIKE IT RICH (Monogram, 1948), with
Rod Cameron, Bonita Granville, and Stuart Erwin. Les directed. The film was lively and well-made. Shot on location and using hundreds of local people and the Texas National Guard, the picture on the screen looked many times
its actual cost.

Blake Edwards and John Champion, riding the crest
after PANHANDLE, wrote and co-produced another Western,
STAMPEDE (Monogram, 1948), and brought in Selander to
direct. Rod Cameron, Gale Storm, and Johnny Mack Brown
headed the cast. Cameron played a cattle baron making war
on the nestors threatening his land empire. The film was
good, but not the equal, certainly, of PANHANDLE.

Les started out the next season by directing the last
Charlie Chan film in the Monogram series, with Roland
Winters in the role. SKY DRAGON (Monogram, 1949) had
Keye Luke back as the Number One son, exchanging antics
with Mantan Moreland, whose low Negro humor only empha-
sized how far the conception behind the pictures had fallen
since Warner Oland had portrayed the Oriental detective at
Fox in the 'thirties.

Besides the Tim Holt features that year, Edward Alperson had Les back to direct another Western production of

his, DAKOTA LIL. The picture was shot in Cinecolor. It
starred George Montgomery, Rod Cameron, and Marie Windsor. "There were some interesting locations for that film,"
Les said. "I liked Marie. I thought she was a fine girl
and a finer actress. She should have been a big star; she
had it all."

Les had to go on location to Australia to film THE
KANGAROO KID (United Artists, 1950) with stuntman-actor
Jock Mahoney. "The facilities there were rather primitive
by Hollywood standards, but we had fun, loved the people,
and got a kick out of the whole thing. Jock is without a
doubt the best athlete I've ever seen, smooth and sleek as a
cougar."

Scotty Dunlap, whom Les had first met while working
with Buck Jones at Fox, was in charge of production at
Monogram Pictures. He contracted Les to direct SHORT-
GRASS for Monogram release. The picture was based on a
Tom Blackburn novel and starred that familiar trio, Rod
Cameron, Cathy Downs, and Johnny Mack Brown. Apparent-
ly, Dunlap was impressed with the kind of picture Les could
turn in on a Monogram budget and the kind of performance
he could get from Rod Cameron. He followed up SHORT-
GRASS with a Cinecolor Western, again starring Rod Came-
ron, entitled CAVALRY SCOUT (Monogram, 1950). Also in
the cast were Audrey Long, Jim Davis, and James Arness.
It was an above-average entry, but not as tightly plotted as
SHORTGRASS had been.

David Diamond produced I WAS AN AMERICAN SPY
(Allied Artists, 1951), something of a change-of-pace picture for Les, starring Ann Dvorak, Gene Evans, and Richard Loo. It was based on the true story of an American
cafe entertainer in war-torn Manila during the Japanese occupation and her efforts to aid the resistance. It was a
good picture on the whole, and proved Selander was as much
at ease out of the saddle as in.

THE HIGHWAYMAN (Allied Artists, 1951), from the
same year, was Les's first swashbuckler, filmed in Cinecolor. It was based on a poem by Alfred Noyes. "The
Monogram lot was too small, so we shot the picture over
at the Goldwyn studio. It was like a Western, only we used
swords instead of six-guns. It had a nice style and I was
pleased with it." The Hollywood Reporter agreed. "Lesley
Selander's direction is brisk throughout," the review said,

"and under his persuasive hand the players come through
with most believable characterizations. " Variety added:
"Lesley Selander's direction capitalized on the action and he
is most responsible for the good performances. "

The Mirisch brothers, who subsequently produced
films like THE APARTMENT (United Artists, 1960) and IN
THE HEAT OF THE NIGHT (United Artists, 1967), had pro-
vided the financing for CAVALRY SCOUT.   They now engaged
Les to direct two lower medium budget programmers,
FLIGHT TO MARS (Allied Artists, 1951) and FORT OSAGE
(Allied Artists, 1951).   FORT OSAGE, with Rod Cameron

Virginia Houston, Cameron Mitchell and Lesley Selander on
the set of FLIGHT TO MARS (Monogram, 1951).   Photo
courtesy of Harry Sanford.

(of course!), was particularly liked by the often critical Los
Angeles Times.   "It's story by Dan Ullman is solid," wrote
the reviewer, "and well-established melodramatic interest
and the action is forcibly [sic] directed by Lesley Selander. "
The Hollywood Reporter remarked, "Lesley Selander handles
the action very well and draws good performances from the
cast. "

But whatever his successes with these pictures, the rest of the year was spent closing out the final entries in the Tim Holt series and directing four half-hour television Westerns with Russell Hayden and Jackie Coogan. The series was produced by Hayden, who had worked with Les on the Hoppy pictures Harry Sherman produced; he was now a producer himself, also starring as a frontier government agent.

Sixteen years after he had directed Buck Jones' Westerns for Universal, Les was contracted by Universal-International to make a Technicolor Western for them, THE RAIDERS (Universal-International, 1952). "Unfortunately," Les recalled, "the picture was totally miscast because Universal was using up their contract actors." THE RAIDERS starred Richard Conte, Viveca Lindfors, and Barbara Britton. "Don't get me wrong. Richard Conte's a fine actor, but not in a Western; and the same goes for Viveca Lindfors, though she's one superior actress in every way possible. The chemistry of the people and the script didn't really mix, but we tried to make it move as best we could."

Selander returned to Allied Artists to do four pictures in a row. The first was FLAT TOP (Allied Artists, 1952), produced by the Mirisch brothers. Despite an uneven script by Steve Fisher, the cast, headed by Sterling Hayden, Richard Carlson, and Keith Larsen, under Les' direction overcame Fisher's often rambling dialogue and made a respectable picture from it. "Lesley Selander's adroit megging concentrates on the physical," The Hollywood Reporter noted, "wisely skipping over the more personal moments in the lives of the men involved for the sake of emphasizing the lusty action. The result is an engrossing film that never lets down in tenseness."

BATTLE ZONE (Allied Artists, 1952) came next. It was produced by Walter Wanger and starred John Hodiak, Steve McNally, and Linda Christian. The story concerned the activities of a Marine combat cameraman during the Korean War. A good cast and tight direction struggled valiantly against Steve Fisher's routine script, which couldn't make up its mind which direction to take.

FORT VENGEANCE (Allied Artists, 1953) was in Cinecolor, also for Walter Wanger. At the time, however, Wanger was in prison for having shot Jennings Lang, whom he claimed was trying to break up his home life with Joan

Bennett. "I only saw him a couple of times," Les said,
"and he really didn't have a thing to do with the picture."
James Craig, Keith Larsen, and Rita Moreno were cast in
this story of two brothers who flee to Canada to join the
Mounties.

Les closed out the year with COW COUNTRY (Allied
Artists, 1953), starring Edmund O'Brien. Not PANHANDLE
by any means, COW COUNTRY was a sturdy, well-traveled
story by Tom Blackburn that looked a lot better than it was,
due to Selander's direction.

Among Les' seven pictures for the next year was
FORT ALGIERS (United Artists, 1953) with Edward Alperson
producing. But WAR PAINT (United Artists, 1953), produced
by Howard Koch and Aubrey Schenck, was one of Selander's
unusual achievements. Written by Richard Alan Simmons
and Martin Berkley, it was a grim drama of taut suspense.
It was filmed mostly in Death Valley and concerned itself
with a cavalry detachment led by Robert Stack and menaced
both from within and without. Stack gave an exceptional
performance. Boxoffice praised the film: "The veteran
hand of Lesley Selander shows in the able direction which
packs in many vivid action panels and holds attention constantly and a basic purpose to the plot that further bulwarks
the developing drama." Hopefully, Les customarily directed
his films with more expertise than that employed by the reviewers writing English prose about them, even if the tone
was complimentary.

THE ROYAL AFRICAN RIFLES (Allied Artists, 1953)
starred Louis Hayward and Veronica Hurst. The idea behind the film was original: the British forces in East Africa against the Germans during the First World War. According to Selander, however, it didn't come off as well as
it should have. "Dan Ullman's screenplay was sluggish and
uncertain. Hayward, who was one of the great swashbuck-
lers on the screen, did his thing in grand style and there
was some good action at the climax, but the picture was not
all it should have been."

Sterling Hayden, J. Carrol Naish, and Joy Page
starred in FIGHTER ATTACK (Allied Artists, 1953). It
was a Second World War film about an American flyer who
crashes and joins a group of resistance fighters in Italy.
The love scenes between Hayden and Page were vivid, proving that Les could direct the clinches as well as the fights.

"Where I had been doing Westerns galore, now I was on a war kick." DRAGONFLY SQUADRON (Allied Artists, 1954) brought the military cycle full circle to Korea. It was the story of the South Korean air force at the beginning of the Korean conflict. John Champion, an old friend, both wrote it and produced. John Hodiak, Barbara Britton, and Bruce Bennett were the featured players.

ARROW IN THE DUST (Allied Artists, 1954) was also made that year. Sterling Hayden, Coleen Grey, and Jimmy Wakely were starred. Added to the tight budget was a lot of borrowing of footage from an earlier film, NEW MEXICO (United Artists, 1951). Scenes where troopers rolled flaming brush down on advancing Indians, filmed on location in New Mexico in Ansco color, did not match the Technicolor process used for ARROW or the Iverson ranch locations.

THE YELLOW TOMAHAWK (United Artists, 1954) was shot on location in Utah. Produced by Howard Koch and Aubrey Schenck, it was an admirable little programmer.

RETURN FROM THE SEA (Allied Artists, 1954) was one of the best pictures of its kind. Starring Neville Brand and Jan Sterling, it was a touching, poignant story of a twenty-year Navy chief who comes into port, meets a woman, and falls in love. Brand, in a role suggesting a younger Wallace Beery, was never better and Jan Sterling was outstanding as the hard-bitten waitress in a hash house who has seen too much of life. For some reason, Allied Artists just let RETURN FROM THE SEA out on the theatrical market without any promotion and it went past unseen by many people. But it does reveal another side of Selander's directing talent, humor and pathos, tender love and deep emotion.

Les next got a call from Warner Brothers to direct TALL MAN RIDING (Warner's, 1955), with Randolph Scott. The story was based on a novel by Norman S. Fox. Dorothy Malone and Peggie Castle were also in the cast. It was Les' first time on the Warner's lot in twenty years, and it would be his last.

Rory Calhoun and Clark Reynolds together had written a screenplay entitled SHOTGUN which Calhoun hoped to star in. He was under contract to Universal-International at the time. The studio nixed the deal he negotiated with producer John Champion because the film would be released by Allied

Artists.   The impasse was bridged only by Calhoun bowing
out of the film and Sterling Hayden taking his place.   The
picture also featured Yvonne De Carlo, Zachary Scott, and
Bob Wilke.   Filmed on location in Utah with breathtaking
color photography by Ellsworth Fredericks, SHOTGUN (Allied
Artists, 1955) was well-received by critics and fans alike.
And it made money.

     For the next decade, Les divided his time between
motion picture direction and direction of television episodes.
He worked on countless LASSIE units, the FURY series,
and LARAMIE, among others.

     In 1964, Les made three quick, undistinguished
Westerns for United Artists release and was summoned back
to Paramount by A. C. Lyles.   Paramount, of course, had
released many of the Hoppy pictures, but almost no shooting
had been done on the Paramount lot.   Lyles was producing
a series of "A" budget programmer Westerns.   He had recently purchased TOWN TAMER by Frank Gruber and had
assembled an impressive cast: Dana Andrews, Terry Moore,
Pat O'Brien, Lon Chaney, Barton MacLane, Richard Arlen,
Bruce Cabot, and Bob Steele.   Perhaps these players had
seen better days, but they still had name value.   Lyles had
a strict two-week schedule and needed someone who could
shoot fast and well.   Les Selander's reputation was familiar
to Lyles.   He assigned him to direct the picture.   Lyles,
who considered himself another Harry Sherman, could work
wonders on a budget.   His pictures were always in color,
with good production values and veterans who could be
counted on to do a job.   The only consistent weakness the
entries had was their pedestrian scripts.

     A year went by and then Les directed THE TEXICAN
(Columbia, 1966).   It was a remake of PANHANDLE, produced by John Champion, photographed on location in Spain,
and starring Audie Murphy with Broderick Crawford as the
principal heavy.   "We filmed it in Barcelona and were there
nearly three months.   I really enjoyed Spain.   The location
was perfect and the people were great.   I wish I could say
the same about the picture, but I can't. "   TEXICAN could
not compare with the original.   The mixture of Americans
and Spaniards made it look like a European Western.

     Les' last two films were for A. C. Lyles.   FORT
UTAH (Paramount, 1967) came first.   It starred John Ireland, Virginia Mayo, and Scott Brady.   The budget was too

small for the ambitious scope of the screenplay. An all-too
heavy reliance on stock footage from previous Westerns in
shots that scarcely matched was the result. ARIZONA BUSH-
WACKERS (Paramount, 1958) wasn't any better.

Now Les is enjoying retirement to the fullest. At
his physician's recommendation, he can still have two or
three double whiskeys a day. He has remarried and travels
extensively around the world with his second wife. He is
active with the pension committee of the Screen Directors'
Guild. In response to an inquiry about anything special he
might remember from his career, he came up with a surprising reminiscence.

"I was doing a Bill Elliott picture, SHERIFF OF LAS
VEGAS [Republic, 1944], a Red Ryder, and getting ready for
a big fight in a schoolroom. The three bad guys were William Haade, Bud Geary, and Kenne Duncan. They were to
jump Red Ryder in the schoolroom and push the school teacher, Peggy Stewart, into a closet. Well, we had that kid,
Bobby Blake, now Robert Blake, playing Little Beaver. We
wondered what we were going to do with him. I mean, there
were going to be four guys breaking up a room and you
couldn't get a kid involved. One of the gaffers came over
and said, 'Look, why not have him by the blackboard while
the fight is going on? Have him write Red Ryder and, below it, Meanies. Each time Red lands a punch, chalk up a
mark for him, and the same for the heavies. I thought
about it a second and said, yes. We even added to it by
having him throw a globe at one of the crooks just as he was
about to shoot Elliott. Now this might not seem like anything on a little Western. But it showed the care, interest,
and family-like attitude we all had then. We were a team,
even on a budget Western; it made no difference. Things
like that I'll always remember about the business and be
glad I was part of it."

LESLEY SELANDER

A Film Checklist by Karl Thiede

Assistant Director

1. TIMBER WOLF (20 September 1925). P: Fox Film

Corporation. D: William S. Van Dyke. C: Buck
Jones, Elinor Fair, David Dyas. 4,809ft. /53m.

2. DURAND OF THE BAD LANDS (1 November 1925). P:
    Fox Film Corporation. D: Lynn Reynolds. C:
    Buck Jones, Marion Nixon, Malcolm Waite. 5,844ft./
    65m.

3. SOFT LIVING (5 February 1928). P: Fox Film Cor-
    poration. D: James Tinling. C: Madge Bellamy,
    John Mack Brown, Mary Duncan. 5,629ft. /62 1/2m.

4. DON'T MARRY (13 June 1928). P: Fox Film Corpor-
    ation. D: James Tinling. C: Lois Moran, Neil
    Hamilton, Henry Kolker. Production started: 27
    February 1928. 5,708ft. /63m.

5. WIN THAT GIRL (16 September 1928). P: Fox Film
    Corporation. D: David Butler. C: David Rollins,
    Sue Carol, Tom Elliott. Working title: PREP AND
    PEP. Production started: 21 May 1928. 5,337ft. /
    59m.

6. TRUE HEAVEN (13 January 1929). P: Fox Film Cor-
    poration. D: James Tinling. C: George O'Brien,
    Lois Moran, Phillips Smalley. Working title:
    FALSE COLORS. Production started: 30 October
    1928. 5,531ft. /61 1/2m.

7. THE CAT AND THE FIDDLE (16 February 1934). P:
    Metro-Goldwyn-Mayer. D: William K. Howard. C:
    Ramon Novarro, Jeanette MacDonald, Charles Butter-
    worth. In production: September-October 1933.
    8,118ft. /90m.

8. LAUGHING BOY (13 April 1934). P: Metro-Goldwyn-
    Mayer. D: William S. Van Dyke. C: Ramon No-
    varro, Lupe Velez, Ruth Channing. In production:
    November-December 1934. 7,259ft. /81m.

9. MANHATTAN MELODRAMA (4 May 1934). P: Metro-
    Goldwyn-Mayer. D: William S. Van Dyke. C:
    Clark Gable, William Powell, Myrna Loy. In pro-
    duction: March-April 1934. 8,515ft. /94 1/2m.

10. THE THIN MAN (25 May 1934). P: Metro-Goldwyn-
    Mayer. D: William S. Van Dyke. C: William

Powell, Myrna Loy, Maureen O'Sullivan. In production: April 1934. 8,350ft. /93m.

11. PARIS INTERLUDE (27 July 1934). P: Metro-Goldwyn-Mayer. D: Edwin Marin. C: Robert Young, Otto Kruger, Madge Evans. Working title: ALL GOOD AMERICANS. In production: June 1934. 6,565ft. / 73m.

12. WHAT EVERY WOMAN KNOWS (19 October 1934). P: Metro-Goldwyn-Mayer. D: Gregory La Cava. C: Helen Hayes, Brian Aherne, Madge Evans. In production: July-September 1934. 8,104ft. /90m.

13. THE NIGHT IS YOUNG (11 January 1935). P: Metro-Goldwyn-Mayer. D: Dudley Murphy. C: Ramon Novarro, Evelyn Laye, Charles Butterworth. In production: October-November 1934. 82m.

14. SOCIETY DOCTOR (25 January 1935). P: Metro-Goldwyn-Mayer. D: George Seitz. C: Chester Morris, Virginia Bruce, Billie Burke. Working titles: AMBULANCE CALL, ONLY EIGHT HOURS. In production: November-December 1934. 6,109ft. / 68m.

15. SHADOW OF A DOUBT (15 February 1935). P: Metro-Goldwyn-Mayer. D: George Seitz. C: Ricardo Cortez, Virginia Bruce, Constance Collier. In production: December 1934-January 1935. 6,787ft. / 75m.

16. ORCHIDS TO YOU (12 July 1935). P: Fox Film Corporation. D: William A. Seiter. C: John Boles, Jean Muir, Charles Butterworth. In production: May 1935. 6,640ft. /74m.

17. A NIGHT AT THE OPERA (15 November 1935). P: Metro-Goldwyn-Mayer. D: Sam Wood. C: Groucho, Chico, Harpo Marx, Kitty Carlisle. In production: June-July 1935. 8,655ft. /96m.

18. THE BISHOP MISBEHAVES (13 September 1935). P: Metro-Goldwyn-Mayer. D: E. A. DuPont. C: Edmund Gwenn, Maureen O'Sullivan, Norman Foster. In production: July-August 1935. 7,827ft. /87m.

19. CEILING ZERO (25 January 1936). P: First National.
     D: Howard Hawks. C: James Cagney, Pat O'Brien,
     June Travis. In production: October-November 1935.
     95m.

20. THE GARDEN MURDER CASE (21 February 1936). P:
     Metro-Goldwyn-Mayer. D: Edwin Marin. C: Ed-
     mund Lowe, Virginia Bruce, H. B. Warner. In pro-
     duction: January 1936. 5,553ft. /62m.

21. MOONLIGHT MURDER (27 March 1936). P: Metro-
     Goldwyn-Mayer. D: Edwin Marin. C: Chester
     Morris, Madge Evans, Leo Carrillo. In production:
     February-March 1936. 6,072ft. /67 1/2m.

22. FURY (5 June 1936). P: Metro-Goldwyn-Mayer. D:
     Fritz Lang. C: Spencer Tracy, Sylvia Sidney, Wal-
     ter Abel. Working title: MOB RULE. In produc-
     tion: March-May 1936. 8,447ft. /94m.

Director

23. FOR THE SERVICE (6 May 1936). P: Universal. D:
     Buck Jones, Lesley Selander. C: Buck Jones, Clif-
     ford Jones, Edward Keene. 65m.

24. RIDE 'EM COWBOY (20 September 1936). P: Univer-
     sal. C: Buck Jones, George Cooper, William
     Lawrence. 59m.

25. BOSS RIDER OF GUN CREEK (1 November 1936). P:
     Universal. C: Buck Jones, Harvey Clark, Muriel
     Evans. 64m.

26. EMPTY SADDLES (20 December 1936). P: Universal.
     C: Buck Jones, Louise Brooks, Harvey Clark. 62m.

27. SANDFLOW (14 February 1937). P: Universal. C:
     Buck Jones, Lita Chevret, Robert Kortman. 58m.

28. LEFT-HANDED LAW (18 April 1937). P: Universal.
     C: Buck Jones, Noel Francis, Matty Dain. 63m.

29. SMOKE TREE RANGE (6 June 1937). P: Universal.
     C. Buck Jones, Muriel Evans, John Elliott. 59m.

30. BLACK ACES (5 September 1937). P: Universal. D:
    Buck Jones, Lesley Selander. C: Buck Jones, Kay
    Linaker, Fred Mackaye. 58m.

31. HOPALONG RIDES AGAIN (3 September 1937). P:
    Paramount. C: William Boyd, George Hayes, Rus-
    sell Hayden. Production started: 4 June 1937. 65m.

32. THE BARRIER (12 November 1937). P: Paramount.
    C: Leo Carrillo, Jean Parker, James Ellison.
    Production started: 6 July 1937. Lesley Selander
    replaced Edward Ludwig at the last minute. 90m.

33. PARTNERS OF THE PLAINS (28 January 1938). P:
    Paramount. C: William Boyd, Harvey Clark, Rus-
    sell Hayden. 68m.

34. CASSIDY OF BAR 20 (25 February 1938). P: Para-
    mount. C: William Boyd, Russell Hayden, Frank
    Darien. 56m.

35. HEART OF ARIZONA (22 April 1938). P: Paramount.
    C: William Boyd, George Hayes, Russell Hayden.
    68m.

36. BAR 20 JUSTICE (24 June 1938). P: Paramount. C:
    William Boyd, George Hayes, Russell Hayden. 70m.

37. PRIDE OF THE WEST (8 July 1938). P: Paramount.
    C: William Boyd, George Hayes, Russell Hayden.
    55m.

38. THE MYSTERIOUS RIDER (21 October 1938). P:
    Paramount. C: Douglas Dumbrille, Sidney Toler,
    Russell Hayden. 74m.

39. THE FRONTIERSMAN (16 December 1938). P: Para-
    mount. C: William Boyd, George Hayes, Russell
    Hayden. 74m.

40. THE SUNSET TRAIL (24 February 1939). P: Para-
    mount. C: William Boyd, George Hayes, Russell
    Hayden. 60m.

41. SILVER ON THE SAGE (31 March 1939). P: Para-
    mount. C: William Boyd, George Hayes, Russell
    Hayden. 68m.

42. HERITAGE OF THE DESERT (23 June 1939). P:
     Paramount. C: Donald Woods, Evelyn Venable,
     Russell Hayden. 75m.

43. RENEGADE TRAIL (18 August 1939). P: Paramount.
     C: William Boyd, George Hayes, Russell Hayden.
     58m.

44. RANGE WAR (8 September 1939). P: Paramount. C:
     William Boyd, Russell Hayden, Willard Robertson.
     64m.

45. SANTA FE MARSHAL (26 January 1940). P: Para-
     mount. C: William Boyd, Russell Hayden, Marjorie
     Rambeau. 65m.

46. KNIGHTS OF THE RANGE (23 February 1940). P:
     Paramount. C: Russell Hayden, Victor Jory, Jean
     Parker. 68m.

47. THE LIGHT OF THE WESTERN STARS (19 April 1940).
     P: Paramount. C: Victor Jory, Jo Ann Sayers,
     Russell Hayden. 67m.

48. HIDDEN GOLD (7 June 1940). P: Paramount. C:
     William Boyd, Russell Hayden, Minor Watson. 61m.

49. STAGECOACH WAR (12 July 1940). P: Paramount.
     C: William Boyd, Russell Hayden, Julie Carter.
     63m.

50. CHEROKEE STRIP (11 October 1940). P: Paramount.
     C: Richard Dix, Victor Jory, Florence Rice. 86m.

51. THREE MEN FROM TEXAS (15 November 1940). P:
     Paramount. C: William Boyd, Russell Hayden,
     Andy Clyde. 70m.

52. DOOMED CARAVAN (10 January 1941). P: Paramount.
     C: William Boyd, Russell Hayden, Andy Clyde.
     62m.

53. THE ROUNDUP (4 April 1941). P: Paramount. C:
     Richard Dix, Patricia Morison, Preston Foster.
     90m.

54. PIRATES ON HORSEBACK (23 May 1941). P: Para-

mount. C: William Boyd, Russell Hayden, Andy Clyde. 69m.

55. WIDE OPEN TOWN (8 August 1941). P: Paramount. C: William Boyd, Russell Hayden, Andy Clyde. 78m.

56. STICK TO YOUR GUNS (© 19 September 1941). P: Paramount. C: William Boyd, Brad King, Andy Clyde. 63m.

57. RIDERS OF THE TIMBERLINE (© 3 December 1941). P: Paramount. C: William Boyd, Brad King, Andy Clyde. 59m.

58. THUNDERING HOOFS (24 July 1942). P: RKO Radio Pictures. C: Tim Holt, Ray Whitley, Lee White. 61m.

59. BANDIT RANGE (25 September 1942). P: RKO Radio Pictures. C: Tim Holt, Cliff Edwards, Joan Barclay. 64m.

60. UNDERCOVER MAN (23 October 1942). P: United Artists. C: William Boyd, Andy Clyde, Jay Kirby. NC: $103,815.64. WWG: $134,177.99. 6,130ft. / 68m.

61. LOST CANYON (18 December 1942). P: United Artists. C: William Boyd, Andy Clyde, Jay Kirby. NC: $82,808.83. WWG: $136,628.57. 5,542ft. /62m.

62. BORDER PATROL (2 April 1943). P: United Artists. C: William Boyd, Andy Clyde, Jay Kirby. NC: $87,285.09. WWG: $132,406.23. 5,927ft. /66m.

63. BUCKSKIN FRONTIER (14 May 1943). P: United Artists. C: Richard Dix, Jane Wyatt, Albert Dekker. NC: $227,806.41. WWG: $387,222.63. 6,853ft. /76m.

64. COLT COMRADES (18 June 1943). P: United Artists. C: William Boyd, Andy Clyde, Jay Kirby. NC: $101,850.15. WWG: $122,832.19. 6,064ft. /67m.

65. BAR-20 (1 October 1943). P: United Artists. C: William Boyd, Andy Clyde, George Reeves. NC: $85,705.93. WWG: $122,993.70. 4,935ft. /55m.

66. RIDERS OF THE DEADLINE (3 December 1943). P:
     United Artists. C: William Boyd, Andy Clyde,
     Jimmy Rogers. NC: $106,234.43. WWG:
     $116,545.16. 6,294ft./70m.

67. BUFFALO BILL (April 1944). P: Twentieth Century-
     Fox. D: William Wellman. Second Unit Director:
     Otto Brower, Lesley Selander. C: Joel McCrea,
     Maureen O'Hara, Linda Darnell. Technicolor. 90m.

68. LUMBERJACK (28 April 1944). P: United Artists.
     C: William Boyd, Andy Clyde, Jimmy Rogers. NC:
     $117,402.22. WWG: $115,389.25. 64m.

69. FORTY THIEVES (23 June 1944). P: United Artists.
     C: William Boyd, Andy Clyde, Jimmy Rogers. NC:
     $129,925.73. DG: $114,891.40. 60m.

70. CALL OF THE ROCKIES (14 July 1944). P: Republic.
     C: Smiley Burnette, Sunset Carson, Ellen Hall.
     56m.

71. BORDERTOWN TRAIL (11 August 1944). P: Republic.
     C: Smiley Burnette, Sunset Carson, Weldon Heyburn.
     56m.

72. STAGECOACH TO MONTEREY (15 September 1944).
     P: Republic. C: Allan Lane, Peggy Stewart, Wally
     Vernon. 55m.

73. CHEYENNE WILDCAT (30 September 1944). P: Re-
     public. C: Bill Elliott, Bobby Blake, Alice Fleming.
     59m.

74. SHERIFF OF SUNDOWN (7 November 1944). P: Re-
     public. C: Allan Lane, Linda Sterling, Max Ter-
     hune. 56m.

75. FIREBRANDS OF ARIZONA (1 December 1944). P:
     Republic. C: Smiley Burnette, Sunset Carson, Peg-
     gy Stewart. 55m.

76. SHERIFF OF LAS VEGAS (31 December 1944). P:
     Republic. C: Bill Elliott, Bobby Blake, Alice Flem-
     ing. 55m.

77. THE GREAT STAGECOACH ROBBERY (15 February

1945). P: Republic. C: Bill Elliott, Bobby Blake,
Alice Fleming. 56m.

78. THE VAMPIRE'S GHOST (21 May 1945). P: Republic.
C: John Abbott, Peggy Stewart, Grant Withers. 59m.

79. THREE'S A CROWD (23 May 1945). P: Republic. C:
Pamela Blake, Charles Gordon, Gertrude Michael.
58m.

80. TRAIL OF KIT CARSON (11 July 1945). P: Republic.
C: Allan Lane, Helen Talbot, Tom London. 55m.

81. PHANTOM OF THE PLAINS (7 September 1945). P:
Republic. C: Bill Elliott, Bobby Blake, Alice Fleming. 56m.

82. JUNGLE RAIDERS (14 September 1945). P: Republic.
C: Kane Richmond, Eddie Quillan, Veda Ann Borg.
15 chapters.

83. THE FATAL WITNESS (15 September 1945). P: Republic. C: Evelyn Ankers, Richard Fraser, George
Leigh. 59m.

84. THE CATMAN OF PARIS (20 April 1946). P: Republic. C: Carl Esmond, Lenore Aubert, Adele Mara.
65m.

85. PASSKEY TO DANGER (11 May 1946). P: Republic.
C: Kane Richmond, Stephanie Bachelor, Adele Mara.
58m.

86. TRAFFIC IN CRIME (28 June 1946). P: Republic.
C: Kane Richmond, Adele Mara, Anne Nagel. 56m.

87. NIGHT TRAIN TO MEMPHIS (12 July 1946). P: Republic. C: Roy Acuff, Allan Lane, Adele Mara.
95m.

88. OUT CALIFORNIA WAY (5 December 1946). P: Republic. C: Monte Hale, Adrian Booth, Bobby Blake.
Trucolor. 67m.

89. THE PILGRIM LADY (22 January 1947). P: Republic.
C: Lynne Roberts, Warren Douglas, Alan Mowbray.
67m.

90. LAST FRONTIER UPRISING (1 February 1947). P:
     Republic. C: Monte Hale, Adrian Booth, James
     Taggart. 67m.

91. SADDLE PALS (15 June 1947). P: Republic. C:
     Gene Autry, Lynne Roberts, Sterling Holloway.
     72m.

92. ROBIN HOOD OF TEXAS (15 July 1947). P: Repub-
     lic. C: Gene Autry, Lynne Roberts, Sterling Hollo-
     way. 71m.

93. BLACKMAIL (24 July 1947). P: Republic. C: Wil-
     liam Marshall, Adele Mara, Ricardo Cortez. 67m.

94. THE RED STALLION (16 August 1947). P: Eagle-
     Lion. C: Robert Paige, Noreen Nash, Ted Donald-
     son. Cinecolor. 81m.

95. PANHANDLE (31 January 1948). P: Allied Artists.
     C: Rod Cameron, Cathy Downs, Reed Hadley. 84m.

96. GUNS OF HATE (18 June 1948). P: RKO Radio Pic-
     tures. C: Tim Holt, Nan Leslie, Richard Martin.
     62m.

97. BELLE STARR'S DAUGHTER (November 1948). P:
     Twentieth Century-Fox. C: George Montgomery,
     Rod Cameron, Ruth Roman. 85m.

98. INDIAN AGENT (9 November 1948). P: RKO Radio
     Pictures. C: Tim Holt, Noah Beery, Jr., Richard
     Martin. 65m.

99. STRIKE IT RICH (1 January 1949). P: Allied Artists.
     C: Rod Cameron, Bonita Granville, Don Castle.
     81m.

100. BROTHERS IN THE SADDLE (8 February 1949). P:
     RKO Radio Pictures. C: Tim Holt, Richard Mar-
     tin, Steve Brodie. 60m.

101. STAMPEDE (1 May 1949). P: Allied Artists. C:
     Rod Cameron, Gale Storm, Don Castle. 78m.

102. SKY DRAGON (1 May 1949). P: Monogram. C:
     Roland Winters, Keye Luke, Mantan Moreland. 64m.

103. RUSTLERS (14 May 1949). P: RKO Radio Pictures.
     C: Tim Holt, Richard Martin, Martha Hyer. 61m.

104. THE MYSTERIOUS DESPERADO (10 September 1949).
     P: RKO Radio Pictures. C: Tim Holt, Richard
     Martin, Edward Norris. 61m.

105. MASKED RAIDERS (15 October 1949). P: RKO Radio
     Pictures. C: Tim Holt, Richard Martin, Marjorie
     Lord. 60m.

106. DAKOTA LIL (February 1950). P: Twentieth Century-
     Fox. C: George Montgomery, Rod Cameron, Marie
     Windsor. Cinecolor. 88m.

107. RIDERS OF THE RANGE (11 February 1950). P:
     RKO Radio Pictures. C: Tim Holt, Richard Mar-
     tin, Jacqueline White. 60m.

108. STORM OVER WYOMING (22 April 1950). P: RKO
     Radio Pictures. C: Tim Holt, Noreen Nash, Rich-
     ard Powers. 60m.

109. RIDER FROM TUCSON (7 June 1950). P: RKO Radio
     Pictures. C: Tim Holt, Elaine Riley, Douglas
     Fowley. 60m.

110. THE KANGAROO KID (22 October 1950). P: Eagle-
     Lion. C: Jock Mahoney, Guy Doleman, Veda Ann
     Borg. 73m.

111. RIO GRANDE PATROL (November 1950). P: RKO
     Radio Pictures. C: Tim Holt, Jane Nigh, Douglas
     Fowley. 60m.

112. SHORT GRASS (24 December 1950). P: Monogram.
     C: Rod Cameron, Cathy Downs, Johnny Mack Brown.
     82m.

113. LAW OF THE BADLANDS (24 February 1951). P:
     RKO Radio Pictures. C: Tim Holt, Richard Mar-
     tin, Joan Dixon. 60m.

114. SADDLE LEGION (April 1951). P: RKO Radio Pic-
     tures. C: Tim Holt, Dorothy Malone, Robert Liv-
     ingston. 61m.

115. I WAS AN AMERICAN SPY (15 April 1951). P:
      Allied Artists. C: Ann Dvorak, Gene Evans, Doug-
      las Kennedy. 85m.

116. GUNPLAY (May 1951). P: RKO Radio Pictures. C:
      Tim Holt, Joan Dixon, Harper Carter. 61m.

117. CAVALRY SCOUT (13 May 1951). P: Monogram.
      C: Rod Cameron, Audrey Long, Jim Davis. Cine-
      color. 78m.

118. PISTOL HARVEST (July 1951). P: RKO Radio Pic-
      tures. C: Tim Holt, Joan Dixon, Robert Clarke.
      60m.

119. THE HIGHWAYMAN (21 October 1951). P: Allied
      Artists. C: Charles Coburn, Wanda Hendrix, Philip
      Friend. Cinecolor. 83m.

120. FLIGHT TO MARS (11 November 1951). P: Mono-
      gram. C: Marguerite Chapman, Cameron Mitchell,
      Arthur Franz. Cinecolor. 72m.

121. OVERLAND TELEGRAPH (December 1951). P: RKO
      Radio Pictures. C: Tim Holt, Gail Davis, Hugh
      Beaumont. 60m.

122. TRAIL GUIDE (February 1952). P: RKO Radio Pic-
      tures. C: Tim Holt, Richard Martin, Frank Wil-
      cox. 60m.

123. FORT OSAGE (10 February 1952). P: Monogram.
      C: Rod Cameron, Jane Nigh, Morris Ankrum.
      Cinecolor. 72m.

124. ROAD AGENT (March 1952). P: RKO Radio Pictures.
      C: Tim Holt, Richard Martin, Dorothy Patrick.
      60m.

125. DESERT PASSAGE (May 1952). P: RKO Radio Pic-
      tures. C: Tim Holt, Richard Martin, Joan Dixon.
      61m.

126. BATTLE ZONE (26 October 1952). P: Allied Artists.
      C: John Hodiak, Linda Christian, Stephen McNally.
      82m.

127. THE RAIDERS (November 1952). P: Universal. C:
     Richard Conte, Viveca Lindfors, Barbara Britton.
     Color. 80m.

128. FLAT TOP (30 November 1952). P: Allied Artists.
     C: Sterling Hayden, Richard Carlson, Bill Phipps.
     Cinecolor. 83m.

129. FORT VENGEANCE (29 March 1953). P: Allied
     Artists. C: James Craig, Rita Moreno, Keith
     Larsen. Cinecolor. 75m.

130. COW COUNTRY (26 April 1953). P: Allied Artists.
     C: Edmund O'Brien, Helen Westcott, Bob Lowery.
     82m.

131. FORT ALGIERS (15 July 1953). P: United Artists.
     C: Yvonne DeCarlo, Carlos Thompson, Raymond
     Burr. 78m.

132. WAR PAINT (28 August 1953). P: United Artists.
     C: Robert Stack, Joan Taylor, Charles McGraw.
     Color. 89m.

133. THE ROYAL AFRICAN RIFLES (27 September 1953).
     P: Allied Artists. C: Louis Hayward, Veronica
     Hurst, Michael Pate. Cinecolor. 75m.

134. FIGHTER ATTACK (29 November 1953). P: Allied
     Artists. C: Sterling Hayden, J. Carrol Naish,
     Joy Page. Cinecolor. 80m.

135. DRAGONFLY SQUADRON (21 March 1954). P:
     Allied Artists. C: John Hodiak, Barbara Britton,
     Bruce Bennett. 82 1/2m.

136. ARROW IN THE DUST (25 April 1954). P: Allied
     Artists. C: Sterling Hayden, Coleen Gray, Keith
     Larsen. Color. 80m.

137. THE YELLOW TOMAHAWK (May 1954). P: United
     Artists. C: Rory Calhoun, Peggie Castle, Noah
     Beery, Jr. 82m.

138. RETURN FROM THE SEA (25 July 1954). P: Allied
     Artists. C: Jan Sterling, Neville Brand, John
     Doucette. 80m.

139. SHOTGUN (24 April 1955). P: Allied Artists. C:
      Sterling Hayden, Yvonne DeCarlo, Zachary Scott.
      Technicolor. 81m.

140. TALL MAN RIDING (18 June 1955). P: Warner
      Brothers. C: Randolph Scott, Dorothy Malone,
      Peggie Castle. Color. 83m.

141. DESERT SANDS (September 1955). P: United Artists.
      C: Ralph Meeker, Marla English, J. Carrol Naish.
      Color. Scope. 87m.

142. FORT YUMA (October 1955). P: United Artists. C:
      Peter Graves, Joan Vohs, John Hudson. Techni-
      color. 78m.

143. THE BROKEN STAR (April 1956). P: United Artists.
      C: Howard Duff, Lita Baron, Bill Williams. 82m.

144. QUINCANNON, FRONTIER SCOUT (May 1956). P:
      United Artists. C: Tony Martin, Peggie Castle,
      John Bromfield. Color. 83m.

145. REVOLT AT FORT LARAMIE (March 1957). P:
      United Artists. C: John Dehner, Gregg Palmer,
      Frances Helm. Color. 73m.

146. OUTLAW'S SON (July 1957). P: United Artists. C:
      Dane Clark, Ben Cooper, Lori Nelson. 89m.

147. TAMING SUTTON'S GAL (15 September 1957). P:
      Republic. C: John Lupton, Gloria Talbot, Jack
      Kelly. 71m.

148. THE WAYWARD GIRL (22 September 1957). P:
      Republic. C: Marcia Henderson, Peter Walker,
      Katherine Barrett. 71m.

149. THE LONE RANGER AND THE LOST CITY OF GOLD
      (June 1958). P: United Artists. C: Clayton
      Moore, Jay Silverheels, Douglas Kennedy. Color.
      80m.

150. WAR PARTY (March 1965). P: Twentieth Century-
      Fox. C: Michael T. Mikler, Davey Davison,
      Donald Barry. 72m.

151. FORT COURAGEOUS (May 1965). P: Twentieth Cen-
     tury-Fox. C: Fred Beir, Donald Barry, Hanna
     Landy. 72m.

152. CONVICT STAGE (June 1965). P: Twentieth Century-
     Fox. C: Harry Lauter, Donald Barry, Jodi Mitch-
     ell. 71m.

153. TOWN TAMER (November 1965). P: Paramount. C:
     Dana Andrews, Terry Moore, Pat O'Brien. Color.
     Scope. 90m.

154. THE TEXICAN (June 1966). P: Columbia. C: Audie
     Murphy, Broderick Crawford, Diana Lorys. Color.
     Scope. 90m.

155. FORT UTAH (September 1967). P: Paramount. C:
     John Ireland, Virginia Mayo, Scott Brady. Color.
     Scope. 83m.

156. ARIZONA BUSHWACKERS (March 1968). P: Para-
     mount. C: Howard Keel, Yvonne DeCarlo, John
     Ireland. Technicolor. Scope. 86m.

Chapter 7

YAKIMA CANUTT

by Jon Tuska

I

The closest Yakima Canutt has ever come to being an American Indian is his first name. He was born Enos Edward Canutt at Colfax, Washington on 29 November 1896. His lineage was Scottish, Irish, Dutch, and German. While still a youth, he learned to ride and then to use a rope. By thirteen, he was employed as a ranch hand; at seventeen, he joined a Wild West show as a trick rider. The show toured the country. At every available opportunity, Yak entered as a contestant in rodeos. He won the title of World's Champion All-Around Cowboy at the Pendleton Round-Up in Oregon in 1917.

Already at that time he was known as Yakima Canutt. In the Pendleton competition for 1914 an error was made by a reporter. Canutt had been raised in the Yakima Valley of Washington. A photo in a newspaper identified him as the "cowboy from Yakima." It became his moniker. Yak liked it. He retained the Pendleton championship for seven years.

On the rodeo circuit, Yak met Ken Maynard. Maynard also specialized in trick riding. The two were probably the finest of their kind in terms of the amazing dexterity and supple control true of their performances in the arena. Yak also met Tom Mix.

Mix began to work in motion pictures in 1909. He was the most popular Western player on the screen when Ken Maynard went to work for the Fox Film Corporation, where Mix was under contract, making his screen debut in

Yak in action diving into the Kern River lagoon, as he did
in several John Wayne Westerns for Monogram.   Photo courtesy of Movie Star News.

THE MAN WHO WON (Fox, 1923), directed by William Wellman.

　　　　Yak was awarded the Police Gazette Cowboy Championship Belt in 1917, 1918, 1919, 1921, and 1923.   He was
presented the Roosevelt Trophy in 1923.   During the off-
months, he worked as an extra in pictures, and then as a
stuntman.   Ben Wilson was a production supervisor on
Westerns at Universal where Yak frequently worked.   Wilson admired Yak's athletic prowess and his expert horsemanship.   He proposed to feature Yak as a player in a
series of inexpensive independent Westerns to be released
on a state's rights basis as Arrow Productions.   State's
rights pictures were leased for a specified number of years
for an exclusive territory to one or another independent film
exchange servicing the area.   Prior to this Yak's principal
screen credits had been in supporting roles in Neal Hart
Westerns made for independent release by William Steiner.

　　　　Yak's first role was one of support to Ed Lytell in
Wilson's SELL 'EM COWBOY (Arrow, 1924), a story about

a saddle manufacturer.   Yak starred in the next feature,
RIDIN' MAD (Arrow, 1924), and performed all his own
stunts.   Wilson starred himself in THE DESERT HAWK (Arrow, 1924), with Yak as the second lead.   BRANDED A BAN-
DIT (Arrow, 1924), with Yak in the lead, closed out the
year.

        Very few independent films of any kind survive from
the silent era.   This is probably nowhere more true than of
Ben Wilson's Arrow Productions.   I would not wish to imply,
judging from what I have seen of them, that they were personality vehicles.   Dick Hatton, a heavy in low-grade Westerns and serials in the early 'thirties, could as easily star
in an entry like THE CACTUS CURE (Arrow, 1925), with
Yak as a bullying foreman (Yak had the character name Bud
Osborne; it was also the name of a rodeo wrangler who
made a career as a featured player in Westerns), as Yak
could portray a rugged hero in a picture like THE HUMAN
TORNADO (Arrow, 1925).   Neither who was cast nor the
story-line mattered much.   Wilson had contracted to supply
a series of Westerns.   And that is what they were, Westerns,
without distinction.

        Wilson was anything but particular.   If Film Booking
Office was impressed with one of his Westerns, like THE
RIDIN' COMET (F.B.O., 1925) with Yak, he'd sell it to
them to distribute through their exchanges.   But Ben might
also write, direct, and star himself in a Western, as in
WEST OF THE LAW (Rayart, 1926), or take a bit part in a
major studio production like RAINBOW RILEY (First National, 1926).   Yak soon began to free-lance.

        Hal Roach featured Yak in THE DEVIL HORSE (Pathé,
1926).   Rex, King of the Wild Horses, was an unruly black
stallion that became quite popular in a whole series of pictures Roach was producing with him.   Rex played the devil
horse.   It was one of the memorable equestrian films of the
'twenties, primarily for the battle Yak helped stage for the
camera between Rex and a rival painted stallion.   The footage was so exciting it was used over and over as stock for
years, showing up in Ken Maynard's THE STRAWBERRY
ROAN (Universal, 1933), or Yak's use of it in serials like
THE VANISHING LEGION (Mascot, 1931) and THE DEVIL
HORSE (Mascot, 1932); and Yak featured it again in the
Three Mesquiteer Western, HIT THE SADDLE (Republic,
1937).

During the 'twenties, Yak received credit for performing stunts, either for himself or for another player, in some
forty-eight films. It was becoming his specialty. Even
while he was appearing as the lead in independent Westerns
for small producing companies like Big Four Productions,
he found stunt-work assignments on the outside.

Nat Levine came to Hollywood in 1925. He had begun in the film business with theatre-owner Marcus Loew.
His first efforts at independent production were fraught with
problems, but he turned a handsome profit when he co-
ventured a ten-chapter silent serial with Sam Bischoff. It
was budgeted at $70,000 and was titled THE SILENT FLYER.
Universal bought it. Levine had sufficient working capital
as a result to commence making state's rights serials on a
regular basis. He founded Mascot Pictures Corporation.

Nat engaged Yak to stunt for him on his initial chapter play, THE GOLDEN STALLION (Mascot, 1927). It
proved a success. Whatever Nat's difficulties with finding
adequate directors or his tendency to cut corners by employing actors whose popularity had tarnished or who were raw
beginners, it was to Canutt that he was indebted for the hectic, frantic pacing of his serials which led to such immediate and enthusiastic endorsement by matinee audiences. Levine made three serials in 1927, two in 1928. Boris Karloff starred in the initial entry for 1928, VULTURES OF
THE SEA, Yak in the second, THE VANISHING WEST (Mascot, 1928). Harry Webb was Levine's director in 1927.
He was replaced by Richard Thorpe in 1928. Webb had a
drinking problem. Nat didn't like that. Yak never interfered. He did his second unit stunt and action work adeptly
and minded his own business. Harry Webb liked that. He
wouldn't be the last one. Harry had produced a series of
low-budget Jack Perrin Westerns for Aywon release in the
mid-'twenties. After parting with Levine, Harry started
another series with Perrin, this time for John R. Freuler's
Biltmore Productions distributed by Big Four. Harry
brought Yak along. Although he might have a role in a
Western like RIDIN' LAW (Big Four, 1930), Webb relied on
Yak principally for stunting and action sequences.

Yak had contracted bronchial pneumonia during the
Great Influenza. His bronchial tubes bled for days. His
voice altered. It got weak. He had to shout to be heard.
Yak's hard, intense eyes, his chiseled features did not make
him ideal to play heroes, and he did so only sporadically.

After sound came in, his voice necessarily limited him to character roles. He made stunt work his major thrust. He preserved the integrity of his income. He would star in a sound Western like CANYON HAWKS (Big Four, 1930) for the same $125 a week he demanded and received of Nat Levine for working the full three weeks it required to make a serial. The consistency of his Mascot efforts enhanced his reputation as a creative stunt director.

Levine's serials rapidly earned for him a name among exhibitors, patrons, and exchange managers as producing the best chapter plays among serial manufacturers. Never long on logic, their superiority was due to the constant action and truly daredevil stunting. A cutting continuity from any Universal serial from the years 1927-31, put alongside one from a Mascot serial, would reveal the difference: the Mascot thrillers got twice as much into a chapter; things were always happening; and there was always too much plot, not too little. Herbert J. Yates, who had got his start in the tobacco industry, now owned a conglomerate of film laboratories huddled beneath the corporate collective of Consolidated Film Industries. He processed Levine's pictures. He thought Nat a comer.

During the silent era, Levine was accustomed to spending $30-35,000 for a chapter play. The addition of sound for some spoken dialogue, synchronized music, and effects in KING OF THE KONGO (Mascot, 1929) ran him approximately another $5,000. But he had the courage to attempt a sound serial in advance of Universal. Henry MacRae, head of Universal's chapter plays, had to fight studio boss Carl Laemmle and Laemmle's sound engineers before finally winning out in THE INDIANS ARE COMING (Universal, 1930), proving once and for all that sound could be used in making outdoor dramas.

Nat worked hard, and he worked all the time, especially while in production. In this he served as an example to his cast members, who were characteristically asked to work overtime and Saturdays in order to complete the pictures on schedule. Levine strove to be a pathfinder and he was invariably willing to innovate. Ollie Carey, Harry Carey's wife, once told me that as long as Nat ran his office out of his vest pocket he was without equal. Nat himself admitted to me that probably no one was as integral to the success of the Mascot serials as Yakima Canutt.

In 1930, Nat signed Rin Tin Tin to star in a serial
titled THE LONE DEFENDER. Nat paid Lee Duncan, Rinty's
owner, a flat $5,000. Since Rinty had been earning so
much more while a Warner Brothers star in the 'twenties,
Duncan suppressed the actual amount Mascot paid him when,
some time later, he wrote his autobiography. What with
this "star" cost and full sound recording equipment which he
leased from Walt Disney (consisting of one mobile truck unit
for location and a dubbing service which Disney rented out
when not preparing one of his cartoons for Columbia release), expenses were edging dangerously above the $40,000
mark--two to four thousand dangerously. D. Ross Lederman,
who had directed Rinty at Warner's, was engaged for Mascot's second serial that year, PHANTOM OF THE WEST,
starring former F.B.O. player Tom Tyler. To close out
the season, Nat wanted a blockbuster.

Levine engaged both Harry Carey and Edwina Booth,
who had just returned from several months in Africa shooting TRADER HORN for Metro-Goldwyn-Mayer. He had a
jungle story fashioned for the two in hopes of cashing in on
Metro's massive publicity. Carey and Edwina were signed
for one serial each, with an option for two more. Production problems at Metro prohibited them from coming to Mascot to make KING OF THE JUNGLE (Mascot, 1930). The
two were featured for the initial entry the next year, THE
VANISHING LEGION.

The Mascot formula by this time had become established. Each chapter play had its leading player or players;
they could either be familiar names or someone like "Red"
Grange, the football hero, who would guarantee public interest. Flanking the lead players were one or two supporting
actors who could be hired cheaply and yet would add much
to the finished product. The remainder was customarily
made up of free-lance character actors who specialized in
working for the independents. The better known of them
would be placed on a weekly salary, according to the length
of the part; others were paid either weekly or daily, as
needed.

Levine borrowed. He borrowed has-beens from Universal and other studios. He borrowed the two-director
concept from Pathé, with one director working on interiors,
another on exteriors, and Yak on all the action. And he
slashed budgets. Whereas Pathé in the years 1926-29
spent an average of $10,000 an episode, Levine, making

sound serials, spent $5,000 on the first chapter of three
reels and averaged $3,000 for every additional chapter.

Wyndham Gittens was made story supervisor. His
job involved the development of scripts that could be shot in
twenty-one days, that amplified the story characteristics
which appealed to Levine--the super-real and the fantastic,
narrative that pleased the young with plots so loosely conceived that the script need only indicate for action sequences: "See Yak."

In later years, process screens, special effects, and
optical gimmicks would minimize the danger in most stunt
work. But when Yak was working for Levine, such techniques were very primitive and he avoided them. What the
camera recorded and the frequently enthralled viewer perceived was really being done by a man dependent only on
his own amazing dexterity and ingenuity. Canutt's presence
began increasingly to make itself felt with THE VANISHING
LEGION. His exceptional skill at working with horses was
emphasized in the screenplay. Frankie Darro, a talented
action player at twelve and an excellent rider who didn't
need a double, joined the cast for a flat $1,000. He
teamed off with Yak for some astonishing sequences. Levine also signed Rex, the wonder horse, and Yak made his
first usage of stock footage from THE DEVIL HORSE (Pathé,
1928).

Yak, Rex, and Frankie had to combine their abilities
with Harry Carey's reserved and charming screen style to
save the picture and give it what charisma it had. Edwina
Booth was the problem. Although Metro had only paid her
$75 a week and she hadn't had a single line of comprehens-
ible dialogue in all of TRADER HORN (M-G-M, 1931), she
saw herself as a great star. She was in the process of
suing M-G-M for ten million dollars. She claimed she had
contracted a jungle disease in Africa. Gossip on the set at
Mascot had it that she had suffered a miscarriage or an
abortion, and was trying to cover it up. Duncan Renaldo's
wife agreed with the gossip. Duncan had also appeared in
TRADER HORN. He remarked to me much later that the
rumors were groundless. Edwina was driven to location
every morning in a limousine. She remained aloof from
other cast members except Ollie Carey, who drove Harry to
work; Harry never did learn to drive a car. Unfortunately
for Levine, THE VANISHING LEGION had a complex, dramatic part for Edwina. Her acting wasn't even passable.

Yak paid no attention to any of this. He concentrated on the
stunts and the horses. He was also given a credited role.
Breezy Eason joined Mascot with this serial. He and Yak
shared the direction on THE VANISHING LEGION.

Breezy had a serious drinking problem. It had already shown up in the late 'twenties when he had directed
Hoot Gibson at Universal. Nat assigned him to the next
serial, THE GALLOPING GHOST (Mascot, 1931). After it,
he fired him for drinking and absenteeism. It didn't stick.
Nat tried him again the next year for Carey's second serial
with Edwina, LAST OF THE MOHICANS (Mascot, 1932).
This time it did stick. Nat not only fired him, but he kept
him fired until LAW OF THE WILD (Mascot, 1934). Why
did Nat put up with him? Simply because Breezy had talent
as an action director which few in Hollywood could equal.
David O. Selznick thought so too. He assigned all the action sequences in DUEL IN THE SUN (Selznick, 1947), his
colossal high budget Western, to Breezy Eason and another
Mascot alumnus, Otto Brower.

Rin Tin Tin's second serial and his last motion picture was for Mascot. It was called THE LIGHTING WAR-
RIOR (Mascot, 1931). Armand Schaefer directed. Outdoor
cameraman Benjamin Kline was Manny's co-director. Kline
worked closely with Yak. It didn't matter to Yak that he
wasn't credited as a director. He was paid well and Levine
was fully aware of his indebtedness to him. Henry MacRae
borrowed Yak for the chapter play, BATTLING WITH BUF-
FALO BILL (Universal, 1931), with Tom Tyler in the lead
role. It was one of the fastest paced Western serials the
studio made. It has much of the same hectic magic as the
competitive Mascot entries.

When Warner Brothers released THE CLASH OF THE
WOLVES in 1926, with Rin Tin Tin and June Marlowe (Levine again cast June Marlowe in THE LONE DEFENDER
with Rinty), the Photoplay reviewer commented, "This dog
is the most sympathetic and human creature on the screen
today. There are times when we think the dog actually
sheds tears...."

At Mascot, Rinty was an action player and, because
of his age, this meant mostly a dependence on doubles.
Lee Duncan had a whole retinue, including a stuffed wolf
dog for harrowing stunts. THE LIGHTING WARRIOR may
well rank highest among Levine's early serials because of

Yak's brilliant stunts with Rinty and Frankie Darro. Yak
assembled a group of competent stunt performers. Helen
Gibson was among them. She had once shared a room with
Hoot Gibson at the Pendleton Round-Up. Her name was
then Helen Wenger. She never married Hoot, but she assumed his last name. Subsequently she claimed to be his
wife, but she never was. In THE LIGHTING WARRIOR,
she doubled Georgia Hale, the female lead. Georgia had
been Charlie Chaplin's heroine in THE GOLD RUSH (United
Artists, 1925). Richard Talmadge and Cliff Lyons became
understudies to Yak. Later, they would build substantial
careers for themselves as doubles, stuntmen, and second
unit directors.

The sites were carefully selected. Bronson Canyon,
located a short distance from Hollywood, was known for its
"Indian Caves." These were caverns in the canyon walls,
running clear through the mountain in some cases, originally
made while the quarry was active and supplying stone for
the bricks used in the construction of the Los Angeles streetcar system. Motion picture companies had begun in the
late 'twenties to employ the caves for scenic backgrounds.
It was here that Yak created the Wolf Cave, the hide-out for
the mystery figure in the serial known as the Wolf Man.
The Prudential studio outside Kernville was a large lot often
used in the 'twenties and 'thirties in the production of Westerns. It had a town, a series of shacks, the Kern River,
the arroyo featured in Rex pictures like KING OF THE
WILD HORSES (Pathé, 1926) and THE VANISHING LEGION,
a rough and undulating terrain for chases, and a high cliff
overlooking a lagoon for dangerous jumps. The town set
was named Sainte Suzanne for THE LIGHTNING WARRIOR,
and nearly all the exteriors were shot there or elsewhere
on the Prudential lot. Minimal interior sets were located
at Tec-Art studios in North Hollywood and at Universal City
studios.

George Brent, who had come to Hollywood from the
Broadway stage, presented himself to Levine. Nat signed
him as the male lead. Kermit Maynard, working as a
double for his famous brother Ken Maynard, was assigned
to the second unit by Canutt to stand in for George Brent.
A friendship began between Kermit and Yak that lasted until
Kermit's death in 1971.

Rinty's screen farewell was totally in character with
his fabulous career, retrieved from the trenches in France

and brought to the United States by Lee Duncan. The public gave him a unique place among Hollywood luminaries.
Much of Rinty's earnings were lost through unwise invest-
ments. One afternoon, shortly after THE LIGHTNING WAR-
RIOR was completed, Rinty, then fourteen, jumped into his
master's arms and collapsed. Duncan had trained several
offspring and subsequently Nat featured Rin Tin Tin, Jr. in
several serials.

Yak thought very little of the dog. He felt Rinty was
at his best in closeups. Once the dog bit him, missing entirely the protective pad Yak wore on his arm. Rinty's
double struck Yak as a better action player. Duncan would
hit the dog to get him to obey, on one occasion with a chain.
Levine was buying the dog's name, not his ability.

Typical of the stunts Yak prepared for this serial is
the close of the first episode. The camera is mounted on
the front of a runaway wagon with Yak and Helen Gibson
aboard, doubling Brent and Georgia Hale. They are being
pursued by hostile Indians. The camera tracks to where
the wagon hits a stump, mounted on the driver's seat at the
moment of impact. The horses pull forward, taking the lip
and harnesses with them, the wagon rolling back slowly and
gaining momentum as it hurtles down the hillside.

Another perilous moment is when Frankie Darro is
fighting with the Wolf Man in an ore car suspended high up
in the air. Rinty jumps from a wooden beam as the car
passes, landing on the cloaked mystery figure. Frankie is
thrown from the car and hangs on from below. Yak, as the
Wolf Man, sees Yak as George Brent starting toward him,
hanging onto a hook attached to the cable. The Wolf Man
jumps across into an ore car going in the opposite direction.
The loss of his weight causes the car to dump over. In
the nick of time Frankie grabs hold of Rinty. Now the two
are dangling. Yak jumps atop the overturned ore car. He
pulls both boy and dog to safety.

All of this was accomplished only a few feet above
the ground. But the illusion of its being hundreds of feet
in the air is successfully sustained. When the ore car
turned over, audiences gasped and screamed. I heard college students react in this fashion when, at the University of
Indiana, I had occasion as a guest speaker to have this chapter screened for them.

II

We were standing in Yak's study in the Summer of 1975. Everywhere on the walls were action stills of Yak engaged in various feats. I was flipping through the manuscript pages of Yak's autobiography.

"When the late Gabby Hayes was an old man," I said, "I interviewed him. He had worked at one time or another with most of the Western players of the 'thirties and 'forties. He told me he had worked with only one cowboy player worth anything as an action performer. You."

I showed him the page I was at in his manuscript. The chapter heading read, "I Meet John Wayne."

"He didn't think Duke much of a cowboy," I said.

"That's probably because Duke doesn't like horses," Yak said.

Duke Wayne is six feet four inches tall. If you meet him, he looms; he dominates the space around him. Wayne's screen career didn't begin at Mascot, but it just as well might have. He started as a prop boy for Tom Mix in 1927 at the Fox Film Corporation. Jack Ford took a liking to him and employed Duke in several capacities in his Fox pictures. He got his first chance in 1930 when Fox starred him in their 70mm. super Western, THE BIG TRAIL. It turned out a box-office bomb. Fox gave him a fast shuffle. In 1931 he was out looking for work. His agent managed to get him signed on at Columbia Pictures as a contract player. Duke didn't like playing "second" lead to Tim McCoy and Buck Jones in their series Westerns. He was saucy, sullen, hard to get along with, and unhappy. He wanted to star in pictures.

Levine heard about this and thought of a way to take advantage of it. His three serials for 1931 had done so well on a state's rights basis that he felt secure in his decision to increase his production budget by another $15,000, cut the individual budgets on all entries, and thus have four serials for 1932. Distributors were required to contract for all four serials if they were to get any one. So, John Wayne liked being a star. All right, he'd give him his opportunity. With Carey and Edwina Booth on an option for

two more chapter plays after THE VANISHING LEGION, he
offered Wayne a contract while Wayne was still at Columbia,
to make three serials for Mascot at a total compensation of
$2,000. The contract stipulated that Wayne was to be on
call anytime during the three respective months the chapter
plays were in production. The payments were divided into
shares of $666.66 per serial. Wayne agreed. Yak, at
$250 a week, was earning more than the star.

SHADOW OF THE EAGLE (Mascot, 1932) was the
first venture. Duke had to work six days a week, twelve
hours a day. Once the cast and crew worked seven days,
and some days were eighteen hours long. In a single day
there might be as many as one hundred and fourteen camera
setups. Ford Beebe was the director, but Nat had Breezy
Eason handle some of the action.

Out on location, Breezy announced that next day
everyone was to report to Bronson Canyon at six in the
morning. Returning home at some distance for so few
hours did not appeal to Duke. He determined he would stay
on location. The crew had built a fire as a shield against
the late night cold. There was no place to stay, no cabins,
no tents. A few had brought bed rolls. There were no
commissary trucks. There was only bread and cheese and
whiskey.

Duke sat by the fire and pulled out a pint bottle of
whiskey. He was cold and disgusted. His weary body
ached.

Yak sauntered over to the fire and crouched down.
He did not speak. Duke handed Yak the bottle. Yak un-
corked it and took a long pull. He wiped his mouth with
the back of one hand.

"Well, Duke," he said, "it don't take very long to
spend the whole night here."

Wayne chuckled. He took a pull at the whiskey.

"Sure don't," he said.

They both laughed. They became friends.

THE LAST OF THE MOHICANS came between SHA-
DOW OF THE EAGLE and Duke's second serial, HURRI-

CANE EXPRESS (Mascot, 1932). HURRICANE had a railroad setting. Canutt had to work out complex motorcycle
antics for SHADOW OF THE EAGLE. MOHICANS put him
into a Colonial setting with wagon stunts and plenty of water
action in the Kern River. He put his mind to railroad
thrills for HURRICANE.

THE DEVIL HORSE was the final entry for the year.
Levine dropped Edwina after MOHICANS. Having lost her
suit against Metro, she hadn't even money to pay her legal
fees. Harry Carey sought to assist her. Duncan Renaldo
by this time was in serious trouble and about to be imprisoned by the immigration authorities for illegal entry into the
United States. Carey was the star of THE DEVIL HORSE.

Funds fell short. Nat scrapped the idea of using Rex.
Instead he bought a wild three-year-old black stallion from
Tracy Layne. Otto Brower was assigned the direction.
Brower had been an assistant director at Paramount on their
silent Zane Grey series. He had directed Harry Carey and
Hoot Gibson sound Westerns. He had worked with the Tim
McCoy unit at Columbia. Much of THE DEVIL HORSE was
to be shot on location in Arizona. Levine dispatched Brower
with the cast and crew. Carey didn't want to go, so Yak
did all of his scenes for him except for close-ups. Dick
Talmadge, who had been Douglas Fairbanks' double in the
'twenties, went along as Yak's second unit assistant.

The picture is important because its opening chapter
contains one of Yak's most fabulous stunts. Originally
planned with Rex in mind, the stunt very nearly cost Yak
his life. The script called for Yak, dressed as Harry
Carey, to grab hold of the wild stallion's mane with his
hands. He was then to clamp his legs around the horse's
neck, as the animal reared and bucked and continually tried
to shake him off and dash him beneath his hooves. A pit
shot was arranged, placing a camera in an indentation in
the ground with boards on top. It would capture the hooves
rearing and stamping on the earth. Another camera with a
long-range lens focused on the action from in front. The
horse went berserk and shook violently, Yak hanging on for
all he was worth.

It was fantastic footage, but the stallion proved almost impossible to work with and the serial went way over

budget.   Yak was so impressed, however, with the scene of
his encounter with Apache, as the horse was called, that
he put both it and the fight between Rex and the paint into a
later Gene Autry Western, COMIN' ROUND THE MOUNTAIN
(Republic, 1936).   Levine tried to get rid of the stallion by
donating it to the University of Arizona in exchange for the
University's kindness in letting him use a herd of horses it
owned.   The University ultimately didn't thank him for the
favor and sold the horse to a private interest.   Yak had two
uncredited parts on screen in THE DEVIL HORSE.   He was
done in by the stallion in the early chapters, only to re-ap-
pear later on in the serial as another character altogether.
Evidently the incongruity of this was accepted with equanimity
by the audiences for Levine's serials, if in fact it was noticed by them at all.

In 1933, Levine produced five chapter plays.   He also
leased the Mack Sennett studio lot in North Hollywood.   He
had tried his hand at a feature the previous year, PRIDE OF
THE LEGION (Mascot, 1932), with Barbara Kent and Rin Tin
Tin, Jr.   It did business.   Nat thought the time right to em-
bark on feature production as well as increase the number
of serials annually.   Now that he had lot space, he en-
deavored to rent it out when it was not in use for one of his
own productions.   Trem Carr, who had been producing a
series of low grade Bob Steele Westerns for Tiffany release,
with W. Ray Johnston founded Monogram Pictures.   They set
up their offices at Mascot.   Bob Steele starred in MYSTERY
SQUADRON (Mascot, 1933) for Levine, while Trem contracted
Duke Wayne to appear as the lead in a series of Lone Star
Western features for Monogram release.

Duke had just finished starring in a cheap series for
Warner Brothers, sound remakes of silent Ken Maynard
Westerns made originally by First National, now a wholly
owned Warner subsidiary.   Wayne appeared in close-ups,
with Maynard interpolated in medium- and long-range action
footage.   Carr's idea was to budget his Westerns at $5-
8,000 a picture and shoot them in as few as three days.
Duke was paid $2,500 a film.   Yak was to be in charge of
all stunt work, was to double Wayne, and have a featured
role, usually as a villain.   Paul Malvern was put in charge
as the production supervisor.   Robert N. Bradbury, Bob
Steele's father, directed most of the entries and even wrote
many of the original stories.   Armand Schaefer was occa-

sionally borrowed from Mascot, when he was available, if
Bradbury was tied up.

THE THREE MUSKETEERS (Mascot, 1933) was Duke's
last chapter play.   Ruth Hall was the heroine.   The serial
had a French Foreign Legion background.   The troupe went
on location to Yuma, Arizona for the desert footage.   No
sooner had they arrived than the banks closed.   Roosevelt
had begun his hundred days.   The company was suddenly
without funds.   Because it was Mascot, Ruth had to do all
her own make-up.   Exposure and severe sunburn made it
all the more difficult and, as the serial progresses, her
face darkens graphically.

There was a mystery man.   Yak doubled Duke and
stood in at times for the mystery man, El Shaitan, and
several other cast members.   He worked out a number of
transfers from one horse to another and, additionally, some
harrowing sequences back at the Bronson Canyon location.
It was an entertaining serial and probably the best of the
three that Wayne did.

RIDERS OF DESTINY (Monogram, 1933) was Wayne's
initial Lone Star Western.   Cecilia Parker was the girl.
George Hayes had a featured role.   Hayes became a regular fixture as the series progressed, either as an outlaw or
the girl's father, although increasingly he was working his
way into the role of a sidekick.   In WEST OF THE DIVIDE
(Monogram, 1934) his support of Duke was sympathetic.   In
THE LUCKY TEXAN (Monogram, 1934) he added much to
the comic effect of a chase involving a Model T, a railroad
handcar, and horses.

Yak, of course, was a heavy in LUCKY TEXAN.
During the chase sequence, Yak was to be pumping away on
the handcar.   Duke was to ride up alongside, do a transfer
from his horse to the handcar, fight it out with Yak, and
finally throw Yak off into a ditch.   Duke felt he could do
the leap, but he was worried that he might miss the handcar and break both his legs.   Duke stood around on the set
getting up his courage.   He wanted to show Yak he was his
equal.

"Well," Yak said finally, "are you gonna do it?   Or

would you rather <u>double</u> <u>me</u>?"

It was frequently the case that Yak wound up chasing
himself during the last reel, playing both himself and doubling Duke.

While they were shooting SAGEBRUSH TRAIL (Monogram, 1933), Yak began to notice that Wayne was following
him around all the time. At last, he stopped in his tracks.
He asked Duke why.

"I'm trying to get down that walk," Duke said.
"You roll on the balls of your feet. I want to walk like
that."

If Duke imitated the way Tom Mix mounted a horse:
straight of frame all the way up; if he studied Buck Jones'
look of granite resolve from the time when they worked together on RANGE FEUD (Columbia, 1932); his ambling lope
and his horsemanship once in a saddle, huddled close to the
saddlehorn, he owed to Yakima Canutt.

Jack Mulhall, Francis X. Bushman, Jr., and Raymond Hatton were cast as the Three Musketeers in the Levine serial. With it, Nat began his promotion of the concept of a trio of heroes in action films. It prompted William Colt MacDonald to write his Three Mesquiteer novels
which Levine eventually brought to the screen at Republic.
But even more far-reaching in its impact was Levine's exploitation of the musical Western. Nat was visibly impressed
by what Ken Maynard had been doing at Universal. When
Junior Laemmle ousted Ken from his Universal contract,
Maynard and his wife went on a European trip. Nat contacted Ken in London via long distance telephone. It was
Nat's intention to produce a series of musical Westerns in
both serial and feature form. Ken agreed to Levine's offer
of $10,000 a week for each week that he worked. Nat
wanted Ken for an undetermined number of pictures.

But signing Maynard wasn't the significant thing.
The truly important decision Levine made was to bring Gene
Autry to Hollywood. Perhaps no personality in the history
of the cinema presents a greater paradox to critic, historian,
or modern viewer alike than Gene Autry. One quality about

Autry must be kept in mind above all: he divorced himself
utterly from reality. No one before him developed quite the
thoroughgoing and consistent fantasy world he did, as no one
for better than a decade and a half was the same again in
Western programmers. I am not speaking here so much of
the musical content of the Autry films as I am of the prospect of Gene Autry as a Western hero.

Nat Levine had a reputation for giving young, inexperienced talent a chance with his company. "I received a
dozen letters from Autry during 1933," Nat once commented
to me, "asking for an opportunity to work for me in anything I would suggest in pictures. Autry's name value at
the time was limited to a ... radio station in Chicago, practically an unknown with questionable ability. On one of my
trips East, I stopped off in Chicago, not to meet Autry but
for business I had with my distributor. But I did get to
meet Autry and he virtually begged me for an opportunity to
come to Hollywood and work in pictures. While he was nice-
looking, it seemed to me he lacked the commodity necessary
to become a Western star: virility! I wasn't impressed
and tried to give him a nice brush-off, telling him I would
think about it. For a period of six months he wrote to me
continually, conveying that he would do anything for the opportunity."

Autry had a recording contract with American Records. Herbert J. Yates was president of the company.
Yates' laboratories were still processing all of Levine's
film and Yates knew Nat well enough to loan him money.
Autry enlisted Yates to put in a good word for him. Yates
informed Nat that Gene was selling a lot of records. When
Ken Maynard signed with Mascot, Levine went ahead and put
Autry on salary with a three-year option. It was Levine's
notion to use Autry, who could sing, to support Maynard,
who really could not.

"Gene was completely raw material," Levine continued, "knew nothing about acting, lacked poise, and was
awkward. A couple of days after his arrival I had him at
my home and invited my production staff to meet him. The
next day all of my associates questioned my judgment in
putting him under contract. They thought I was slipping.
But I persisted, and for the first four months he went
through a learning period. We had at that time, in our employ, a professional dramatic and voice teacher, and Autry
became one of her pupils. He wasn't much of a horseman

either, so I had Tracy Layne and Yakima Canutt teach him
how to ride."

The riding lessons didn't win Yak over. He didn't
particularly like Autry, although subsequently he was more
than willing to acknowledge the singing cowboy's acumen in
industries unrelated to motion pictures.

Autry had a singing role in the Ken Maynard feature,
IN OLD SANTA FE (Mascot, 1934), and had a bit acting
part in Maynard's serial, MYSTERY MOUNTAIN (Mascot,
1934). By that time Maynard's unruly ways had got the
better of Levine. Ken was dropped. Levine took a desperate chance. He chose to star Autry in his next serial, THE
PHANTOM EMPIRE (Mascot, 1935). It proved almost as
successful at the box office as had MYSTERY MOUNTAIN.

It would be useless speculation to conjecture what
would have happened to Mascot had it not merged in 1935.
The company was both reputable and profitable, which is
why Yates wanted it. Yates' Consolidated laboratories also
did the lab work for Monogram Pictures. By 1935, Monogram had nineteen company-owned exchanges and twenty
franchisees for the distribution of their pictures. What
Yates proposed came to this. Mascot, Monogram, and Consolidated should combine their assets. Monogram would
bring the John Wayne Westerns and their distribution network to the merger. Mascot would contribute their serial
production, the projected singing Westerns with Gene Autry,
and their lease on the Sennett lot. Yates would provide
additional capital and a total laboratory service. The parties
involved thought the merger a good idea and by March 1935
Republic Pictures was born. Mascot completed its serial
production for that year under its own logo, but its last
chapter play, THE FIGHTING MARINES (Mascot, 1935), was
distributed via the Republic exchanges. Gene Autry's first
feature, TUMBLING TUMBLEWEEDS, was a Republic release, referred to in the publicity as a "Mascot brand name."
John Wayne's first Western for the new company was WEST-
WARD HO (Republic, 1935).

Yak was still free-lancing. But now he was placed
in charge of stunt work and second unit direction on the
Wayne and Autry Westerns and the four Republic serials
produced annually by Levine. He continued for some years
to sign a series of short-term contracts. There was little
Yak could do with Autry, but it was the intention of the

production people--namely Levine, director Armand Schaefer,
and the writers--to keep plenty of action in the films. This
Yak was capable of doing.

Duke Wayne wanted his movie fights realistic. Duke
refused to pull his punches. "I was makin' Yak Canutt and
any other man with whom I fought really sore, black and
blue," Wayne recalled later. "They didn't like it but
couldn't do anything about it. " It was director Robert N.
Bradbury who hit on a solution. "He said," Wayne continued, "that he thought if he placed the camera at a certain
angle it would look as if my fist was making contact with
Yak's face, though my fist was passing by his face, not
even grazing it. We tried it out one day, and when we saw
the rushes we saw how good it looked. Bradbury invented
this trick, which he called the pass system. Other stuntmen and directors picked up on it, and it became the established way of doing a fight. " When sound effects were added,
the fights in the Duke Wayne Westerns became the most realistic on the screen.

Yak taught Duke numerous stunts. He taught him
how to float over a horse's head when the horse buckled beneath him as if shot; how to make a transfer from horse to
horse, horse to stage, or train to horse or horse to train;
how to ride up alongside another man on horseback and jump
him; or how to drop in a slump from a horse when supposedly bushwacked. Duke came greatly to admire Canutt.
He would remark to friends that if only he were the stuntman Yak was, he could quit acting. He complained teasing-
ly about how Yak was still getting paid more than he was.

The scriptwriters for the Republic serials, like their
predecessors at Mascot, let Yak work out all the action sequences, no matter what the setting. Yak perfected the
running W for tripping horses in falls. He only injured one
animal in his entire career. He invented tricks such as
rigging a wagon with fine wire so that it could disintegrate
on cue. With wires, he could make dangerous stunts safe,
like climbing up a suspension bridge as it collapsed. For
THE VIGILANTES ARE COMING (Republic, 1936), a serial
starring Robert Livingston, Yak devised an elaborate stagecoach stunt for the eighth or ninth episode. The hero was
to ride up alongside a moving coach and transfer onto it.
He would then be knocked off onto the tongue of the wagon
between the racing horses. He would grab hold of the shaft,
lower himself down between the horses' pounding hooves and

The running W was a Canutt specialty making for effective
horse tumbles during action sequences.   Photo courtesy of
Movie Star News.

let go.   As the coach would roll over him, he would grab
onto the luggage carrier, pulling himself up, only to climb
again over the top of the coach.   Levine, once he saw how
brilliantly it was executed in the dailies, thought him crazy
to put a stunt like that into a late episode.   Nat wanted it
in the first chapter.

Yak repeated it frequently in other Republic productions and in Westerns for other companies.   When John
Ford was readying STAGECOACH (United Artists, 1939) for
the screen, he viewed a print of RIDERS OF THE DAWN
(Monogram, 1938).   Jack Randall, brother of Robert Livingston, was the star.   At the conclusion of RIDERS there is
a terrific race across the salt flats.   Yak does his famous
stagecoach trick, doubling for Randall.   Ford decided to

lift the idea of the race for his own picture and contracted
Yak in the bargain to perform the stunt for him.

Yates was not a man to have partners. The merger
completed and the company consolidated with a fixed market
for its product, he went about eliminating the men he had invited to join him. Trem Carr was first. Yates bought out
both him and Ray Johnston. Before newly organizing Monogram, Carr went to work for Universal Pictures, now under
different management itself, as a producer. When Duke
Wayne's Monogram contract expired in early 1936, Trem invited him to Universal to star in a series of non-Westerns
he was producing. Duke was pleased by the prospect.

Next Yates moved against Nat Levine. He bought out
his interest in 1937. Levine never again became intimately
associated with producing theatrical films after the close of
the 'thirties. Gene Autry went on strike against Yates and
Republic for more money. All Yates had was the Three
Mesquiteer series Levine had started with Robert Livingston,
Ray Corrigan, and Max Terhune. Yates attempted to fill the
gap by releasing, and then both producing and releasing,
A. W. Haeckle's independent Westerns, with Johnny Mack
Brown in one series and Bob Steele in the other.

Yak branched out into working for other companies to
keep busy. He did second unit work on some of the Tex
Ritter singing Westerns for Grand National and even had a
substantial part as a ranger in RIDERS OF THE ROCKIES
(Grand National, 1937). When Trem Carr resumed Western
production for Monogram release, Yak occasionally worked
for him. Columbia Pictures went into the chapter play field
and Yak handled both the second unit as well as appearing
in a featured role in serials such as THE SECRET OF
TREASURE ISLAND (Columbia, 1938).

Yak thought Yates a hard man with a contract. He
was primarily a businessman interested in little else save
costs. "Working at Republic," Yak remarked to me, "you
were always fighting for something you should have had to
begin with." When word got out that there were to be general pay cuts, Yak took the script of the latest Republic serial to the executives. He told them that he had analyzed
the stunts. They were too difficult. He would only do them
if he received a hundred dollar raise. He got the raise.

It was just as well. Yak's reputation was gaining.

He was hired to double Clark Gable in GONE WITH THE
WIND (M-G-M, 1939) during the scenes of the burning of
Atlanta.   And he was in charge of Ford's action sequences
for STAGECOACH.   It was Ford's first Western of the
sound era.   Ford budgeted it at $220,000, but it actually
cost $531,374.13.   Upon release, it grossed $1,027,000.
It has become a classic.

Ford, who had specifically chosen Wayne to work in
the film, belittled him incessantly.   This rankled Yak.   Duke
tells the story of how, one day, Ford invited him to screen
rushes and evaluate Andy Devine's acting as the stage driver.

"I thought," Duke related, "that Andy held the reins
too loosely and told Ford I thought so.   Ford said to me
that it was an important point and he wanted everyone to
hear it.   Well, he called everybody to him, the cast, the
technical crew, the wardrobe workers, the grips, even the
electricians.   'I want you all to know,' he told them, 'that
Duke thinks this is a great picture and that we're all doing
one helluva job--but he can't stand Devine's performance.'"

Ford felt, even then, that Duke too often took the
point of view of the director rather than that of an actor.
Ford wanted to develop Wayne as an actor.   At night when
on location, in their motel room Duke would rehearse his
lines with Yak as his critic.   He didn't like Ford keeping
after him the way he did.

The race across the salt flats was shot a short distance outside Victorville in California.   Ford told Yak that
he was an expert on how fast horses could run and, therefore, how fast the camera car should be moving during the
chase.   Yak insisted horses couldn't run that fast.   Ford
would hear nothing of it.   He tried racing the camera car
across the flats at that speed and the horses couldn't keep
up.   Ford became agitated.   He suggested Yak shoot the
sequence, any way he wanted.   When Ford saw the rushes
of the horse falls, he was elated; but when he saw Yak's
stunt of falling beneath the stagecoach horses he feigned outright disbelief.

Ford called on Yak's engineering skill to assist him
in the sequence where the stage must be floated across the
Kern river.

Once the film was completed, the cast and crew were

assembled for a party. Bert Glennon had been the cinematographer. Ford overheard someone remark that it was an excellent Western.

"Thanks to Yakima Canutt," Glennon responded.

"It was the first time I worked for John Ford," Yak commented to me, smiling, "and it was the last."

III

STAGECOACH was previewed at the Village Theatre at Westwood. Duke saw to it that the Republic brass attended, particularly Sol and Moe Siegel. Duke spotted them sneaking out of the theatre afterwards, so he knew they had come. And why not? Duke was again back at Republic after a stint at Universal; he was the best Western player the studio had. Now he was suddenly in a major Western. No one said anything to Duke the next day, nor again on the next. At last, Duke broke down and asked Sol Siegel what he thought of the picture.

Yak, in the center in the plaid shirt, heading up the second unit for MAN OF CONQUEST (Republic, 1939). Photo courtesy of Movie Star News.

"If it's a Western they want to make," he returned
succinctly, "let them come to Republic to learn how to make
it."

Duke had four more Three Mesquiteer pictures to
make before concluding the 1939-40 season. His Republic
contract had four more years to run. Duke's agent got
Yates to let him appear in pictures for other companies.
By 1941, Wayne himself got Yates to agree to pay him ten
per cent of the gross profits on his films in addition to his
salary.

In late Fall 1939, Duke made ALLEGHENY UPRISING
for RKO, which once more co-starred him with Claire Trevor. Yates felt the time was ripe for Republic to attempt a
major motion picture. The property he selected was THE
DARK COMMAND, based on a novel by W. R. Burnett.
The budget was set at $750,000 and Raoul Walsh was con-
tracted to direct. After a decade, this picture reunited
Duke with the director who had worked with him on his first
bid for stardom in THE BIG TRAIL. Claire Trevor was
signed and by contract received top billing; Duke was second; Walter Pidgeon was third.

Republic insured the production with Lloyd's of London for $670,000. A delay caused by Claire Trevor falling
ill brought about a suspension of production on 23 December
1939 after a month of shooting. Republic had paid $30,000
for the insurance and was paid $250,000 by Lloyd's as a
settlement for the delay. Production was resumed on 1
February 1940 and completed in sixteen days at a total cost
in excess of a million dollars, or twice as much as STAGE-
COACH had cost.

Yak headed up the second unit. He surpassed himself in a stunt where he and three other stuntmen went over
a cliff and into a ravine in a buckboard. Yak used a ninety-
foot chute, well-soaped, and breakaway harnesses on the
horse team. He also supervised the tense burning of
Lawrence, Kansas, with which the picture concludes, utiliz-
ing techniques he had learned while at work on GONE WITH
THE WIND.

Warner Brothers in the late 'thirties began a series
of high budget Westerns. Errol Flynn's first was DODGE
CITY (Warner's, 1939). After several pictures in this
same romantic and optative mood, Warner's decided to cast

Flynn as General George Armstrong Custer in THEY DIED
WITH THEIR BOOTS ON (Warner's, 1942). Raoul Walsh
was the director.

Walsh had had a lot of trouble with the stunts during
battle sequences. People were getting hurt. Walsh called
in Breezy Eason to assist him. Breezy got Yak. Yak
doubled Flynn. Together with Breezy, he masterminded the
elaborate stunting. There were over three hundred running
Ws in the course of the film and only once was a horse so
much as stunned. Yak and Breezy would rehearse the action
so that all Walsh had to do was shoot it. Errol Flynn in
his autobiography, My Wicked, Wicked Ways (Putnam's,
1959), tells of how he violently objected to the use of running Ws while filming THE CHARGE OF THE LIGHT BRI-
GADE (Warner's, 1936). He complained to the Society for
the Prevention of Cruelty to Animals. It wasn't running Ws
that he remembered about THEY DIED, though. It was the
death of Bill Meade, who was thrown from his horse and
fell on top of his sabre. Eason was sensitive enough to
Flynn's attitude to enlist Yak; the gesture seemed to pacify
Flynn.

Breezy Eason, in addition to the chariot race in BEN-
HUR (M-G-M, 1926), handled the land rush in CIMARRON
(RKO, 1931), the jousting in ROBIN HOOD (Warner's, 1938),
the burning of Atlanta in GONE WITH THE WIND, and the
battle scenes in SERGEANT YORK (Warner's, 1941). He
once gave a cogent summation of directing action: "You can
have a small army of people charging across the screen,
and it won't matter much to the audience. But if you show
details of the action, like guns going off, individual men
fighting, or a fist hitting someone in the eye, then you will
have more feeling of action than if all the extras in Hollywood are running about. That is why real catastrophes
often look tame in newsreels. You need detail work and
close shots in a movie. Only then does it come to life."

In the early 'forties, Republic decided to increase
series Western production, particularly now that Duke Wayne
was becoming a name star and Gene Autry was inducted into
the Air Force. Yates personally negotiated with Bill Elliott
for him to leave Columbia and join Republic. He promised
Elliott full star treatment. After completion of VENGEANCE
OF THE WEST (Columbia, 1942), Elliott's last series Western with Tex Ritter, and his third and last serial, THE
VALLEY OF VANISHING MEN (Columbia, 1942), directed by
Spencer Gordon Bennet, Elliott accepted Yates' offer.

Gabby Hayes had been a sidekick to Roy Rogers. He
was now assigned to the Elliott Westerns. His place in the
Rogers Westerns was then taken by Smiley Burnette, who
had always been Gene Autry's "stooge." The Sons of the
Pioneers, a group Roy had helped found, appeared for the
first time in one of Roy's starring features in RED RIVER
VALLEY (Republic, 1941). Roy urged the Republic management to promote alcoholic, peculiar Pat Brady of the Pioneers into the role of a comic sidekick. The proposal was
not met with enthusiasm. In films like HEART OF THE
GOLDEN WEST (Republic, 1942), besides station wagons and
steam-powered river boats, both Gabby and Smiley were in
comic support, with the Sons of the Pioneers for musical
backup. After Elliott's first season, Gabby was reassigned
to the Rogers unit for a couple of years.

Donald Barry had starred in the serial THE ADVEN-
TURES OF RED RYDER (Republic, 1940). Beginning that
same year, billed as Don "Red" Barry because of the serial,
he was given his own Western series. It lasted for two
seasons. Barry wanted to emulate James Cagney. He kept
asking Yates to let him star in gangster-type roles which
were more or less the kinds of parts he had been playing
when he first came to Republic. Barry's contract paid him
the same whether he was cast as hero or villain.

Yates tried to start another singing cowboy in 1943 by
signing Eddie Dew and co-starring him with Smiley Burnette,
but the series proved unpopular and was hastily dropped.

When Bob Livingston's contract expired with Republic,
he joined Producers' Releasing Corporation for a series that
was intended to capitalize on his serial THE LONE RANGER
RIDES AGAIN (Republic, 1939), called the "Lone Rider." It
was obvious exploitation. Bob was soon replaced by a virtual unknown, George Houston, who added singing to the role.
Livingston, in the meantime, returned to Republic to star
briefly in a new series with Smiley Burnette after which he
turned to playing villains or in character roles for Republic
and then for other studios.

Tom Tyler finished up the Three Mesquiteer series
in the old Livingston/Wayne role of Stony Brooke for one
more season before Yates admitted defeat and scrapped it.
RIDERS OF THE RIO GRANDE (Republic, 1943) and OUT-
LAW TRAIL (Monogram, 1944), the final entries respective-
ly in the Mesquiteer series and the ill-fated Trail Blazer

series at Monogram, in both of which Bob Steele was one of
the leads, marked the demise of the trio concept in Western
production.

Most of these Westerns at Republic were shot on ac-
celerated seven-day schedules. Yak was in charge of all the
second units on every picture and chapter play. As many as
seventy scenes from various pictures were shot in a single
day. Yak had to chart his crews' assignments and oversee
all the action.

Livingston was replaced in his solo series with
Smiley Burnette by tall, athletic Sunset Carson. About Carson's only qualifications were his Texas drawl and his winning a championship cowboy title in Buenos Aires in 1941.
He was a wretched actor whose delivery of the simplest dialogue proved an embarrassment. Yates was so unsure of
him on the basis of his screen test that he released his
first pictures with Smiley Burnette being given top billing.
But Carson caught on with audiences, especially in the South.
To compensate for his total incompetence as a believable
player, his pictures were packed with an extraordinary
amount of action and very strong plot-lines.

In 1944 Yak was signed to a four-year contract as a
full director. He was given one of the Carson pictures to
direct, SHERIFF OF CIMARRON (Republic, 1945). He found
Sunset nervous and indifferent to acting. For the first four
days Carson was sober. The fifth day he showed up hopelessly drunk. Near the end of shooting, there was a fight
sequence. Once it had been shot, Sunset disappeared from
the set. Yak found him sitting outside on a step, crying.
He turned up his tear-wreathed face and confessed that he
thought his arm had been broken.

One of the best Carson Westerns, ROUGH RIDERS
OF CHEYENNE (Republic, 1945), featured Monte Hale in a
strong supporting role (Hale would soon succeed Carson),
leading lady Peggy Stewart with her derrière resplendent in
tight riding breeches, and fantastic action sequences typical
of the films. Ted Mapes, doubling for Sunset, actually
jumps from an overhanging limb onto the top of a moving
stagecoach. Alcoholism and sexual dissipation created such
adverse publicity around Sunset Carson that finally, if reluctantly, Yates was compelled to fire him.

Thanks to Yak's streamlined second units, Republic

was able to transform the reckless, continuous action for-
mat of Mascot and polish it to an incredible degree.   It was
this tremendous technical capacity that allowed the studio to
make a starring series with a character actor like Donald
Barry into moderate box office, that entertained so consistently that by keeping Sunset Carson riding no one guessed
what was missing.   And it is a measure of just how bad
Eddie Dew was to reflect that, with all this going for him,
he didn't make it!

Bill Elliott's first film was CALLING WILD BILL
ELLIOTT (Republic, 1943), directed by Spencer Gordon Bennet.   Bennet had been right behind Elliott coming from Columbia.   The two were frequently teamed over the next two
years at Bill's behest.   The studio did right by Elliott.
Not only was his name used in the title to the picture but,
like Autry and Rogers, Bill played himself in the story.
Spencer stressed action.   Yak doubled Elliott.   In one sequence, Bill had to jump from the roof of a hacienda onto
his pinto below.   Yak constructed a wooden platform at the
back of an adobe arch out of camera range.   The camera
tracked Elliott running across the stucco roof to the arch.
Bill stood poised above his horse.   Then he jumped off the
arch onto the platform.   A split second before Elliott landed
on the platform, Yak continued the jump onto the back of
the horse.   On screen, it appeared to be a single action.

Yak liked Elliott, as did almost everyone who worked
with him.   For the 1944-45 season the studio starred Bill
in a continuing series of Westerns based on the Red Ryder
comic strip, the role Donald Barry had played in the serial.
A young Bobby Blake played Bill's juvenile Indian sidekick,
Little Beaver.   The Republic management went all out to
promote the series.   These were Elliott's last "B" Westerns
before Yates elevated him to "A" status in IN OLD SACRA-
MENTO (Republic, 1946).   They were mounted with blazing
action, excellent stunting, strong plots, and much human
interest.

Once Elliott started in top productions, there was no
thought of his resuming series Westerns.   Gene Autry had
returned.   Yates had been preparing himself for this moment and felt well-armed.   It was true that his efforts in
behalf of Donald Barry and Sunset Carson had come to little.
But with Duke Wayne and now Bill Elliott, he was marching
forward into the ranks of the majors.   Yates had seen a
production of OKLAHOMA in New York and had put out a

general memo that the studio's Roy Rogers Westerns were
to be extravagant musicals. When Yak broke both his legs
performing a stunt in one of Roy's pictures, he was glad of
the chance to leave stunting increasingly to others and concentrate on direction. Yates was able to control Roy.
Gene's first picture after he was back was SIOUX CITY SUE
(Republic, 1946), released in November and produced on a
modest budget. Throughout the war, Yates had been re-
releasing eight Autry Westerns a year. Gene's contract was
again coming up for renewal. Yates warned him that he had
best not be unreasonable in his demands. Military life,
however, had changed Autry.

          "I don't think I ever appreciated money until I had
been in service," Autry once confided to me. "I learned
what it was like to work for almost nothing, and I didn't
like it."

          Autry made four Westerns for Republic that were re-
leased in 1947, the last being ROBIN HOOD OF TEXAS (Republic, 1947). All were firmly in the tradition of what I
call the Autry Fantasy, where everything adverse in life can
be readily overcome with either a joke or a song. Yates
gave Roy Rogers his first "A" budget feature in MY PAL
TRIGGER (Republic, 1946) and promoted Monte Hale into
starring vehicles of his own as a singing cowboy, including
OUT CALIFORNIA WAY (Republic, 1946) in cinecolor, which
featured Roy and Dale Evans, Allan Lane, Bobby Blake, and
Donald Barry as guest stars. Autry felt that as a Western
property he was worth more than any player on the screen.
He refused to put up with Yates' attempt to humble him and
negotiated himself an excellent package with Columbia Pictures. He also signed a lucrative radio contract and was
able quickly to regain his preeminence in the field. Yates,
of all people, apparently understood the least about the secret magic of the Autry Fantasy.

          Allan Lane had appeared as Tim Holt's partner in
crime in THE LAW WEST OF TOMBSTONE (RKO, 1937).
He played mostly nice young men in all kinds of films until
he came to prominence as a Western star when he replaced
Bill Elliott as Red Ryder in 1946. He continued in the
series with Bobby Blake through 1947 when Republic sold
out the property to Eagle-Lion and developed Allan into a
performer in his own right under the name Rocky Lane.

          There may have been a bit of irony in dubbing him

"Rocky." He was most difficult to direct. Yak got assigned to one of his pictures. He told him: "I'm the director. You're the actor. Remember that." All went well until the third day. Lane kicked up a storm. Yak only got him back in line by threatening to go to Yates and have him replaced on the picture. Yak tried to avoid working on Lane's pictures.

Ben Johnson was Bill Elliott's double for his high budget Westerns. Yak was called in to supervise a stunt where Ben was to leap from atop a stagecoach to the ground, a variation of Yak's original stunt of a decade earlier.

"Sorry," said Johnson, "but old Ben would like to stay around a while yet."

Yak determined to do the stunt himself. He got as far as pulling himself up on the luggage carrier. But he had gained twenty pounds. Johnson took the stunt from the pull-up to completion. Yak retired totally from stunt work. When his contract expired in 1948, he returned to free-lancing.

Rocky Lane became an expert rider and did most of his own fights. He had a specially vicious round with Roy Barcroft in CODE OF THE SILVER SAGE (Republic, 1950), in which Barcroft complained about how mean Rocky could be and how, sometimes, when he didn't pull his punches, he only laughed at the physical damage he caused. Republic had an ample supply of stock footage from their prior Westerns. When the script required Rocky to leap onto the back of a wagon, or jump from a tree onto a moving wagon, a cut of a double doing it from a Sunset Carson or Red Ryder picture was used. The problem was that Rocky wore dark blue shirts. The stock shot frequently featured a light-colored shirt. But by that time no one cared anymore. Films like Rocky's COVERED WAGON RAID (Republic, 1950) drew their central sequence--the raid--from former wagon train raids in several Republic Westerns. Yak had done his work too well. It was all recorded on celluloid for perpetual reuse.

Yet, despite the slickness and polish of the post-war theatrical product, the "B" Western never regained the dust-choked crudity which, in retrospect, seems a charm peculiar to the 'thirties and earlier. I must disclose my affinity for that crudity. It is entirely personal, to be sure. The Re-

public formula Westerns of the 'forties and early 'fifties
were quite adeptly made and other studios often fell short
of them in all departments. But the stark, barren quality
of the previous decades was lost. The players just didn't
have the magnitude and screen presence of William S. Hart,
Tom Mix, Buck Jones, Ken Maynard, Hoot Gibson, or Tim
McCoy. Even the old Duke Wayne Westerns for Monogram
and early Republic have an atmosphere lacking in the Roy
Rogers vehicles of the 'forties, no matter the enormous
contrast in budgets. Nor do the series Westerns after 1939
have the passion and devil-may-care optimism of the earlier
films.

These aspects are time-bound. Republic, with its
stuntmen and streamlined approach, sacrificed immediacy for
sophistication. The formula, in becoming rote, lost the intensity of belief which preoccupied the product in the 'twenties and 'thirties. More than ever before, the thinking was
in terms of so many units for a given season, and individual
entries were taken less and less seriously. Above all, the
post-war players were the product of studio development and,
unlike their predecessors, took no pride in making Westerns.
Under the aegis of the Autry Fantasy (or their interpretation
of it), added to little love for the West was no interest at
all in it. The spirit of the frontier had truly receded beyond recall.

Yak was charged with running a herd of sheep off a
cliff for THE DEVIL'S DOORWAY (M-G-M, 1950). He felt
the censors would insist on its deletion. And he wasn't
wrong. He had to reshoot the sequence.

He became associated with top-flight productions,
handling second unit. He worked on IVANHOE (M-G-M,
1950), with Robert Taylor; KNIGHTS OF THE ROUND TABLE
(M-G-M, 1953), again with Taylor; EL CID (Allied Artists,
1961), with Charlton Heston and Sophia Loren; SPARTACUS
(Universal, 1962), directed by Stanley Kubrick; FALL OF
THE ROMAN EMPIRE (Paramount, 1964); and HOW THE
WEST WAS WON (M-G-M, 1964), which included John Ford
as a director of the Civil War episode and Duke Wayne cast
as General Sherman.

Undoubtedly, Yak's finest achievement was directing
the chariot race in the remake of BEN-HUR (M-G-M, 1959).
The reader will recollect that Breezy Eason directed it in
the original. Yak asked Metro to be allowed to use six key

men. He wanted a one-year contract. Metro requested that
Yak use Italians on location in Italy. A series of hassles
ensued. Yak finally got what he demanded. His son Joe
Canutt stunted in the race. Yak constructed a handle on the
back of Joe's chariot for him to hang onto when his chariot
was supposed to leap over another chariot. The horses had
been specifically trained for the stunt. Joe grabbed onto the
front instead. The chariot thundered and lurched. He was
nearly killed. But he had the Canutt luck. His lot was a
few stiches in his chin.

We were sitting in Yak's trophy room. Yak was pet-
ting his German Shepherd. He was older, of course; he had
quit smoking. But his voice had that same distinctive nasal
intonation.

"I ran into old man Yates when I was in Italy," he
said. "He had sold Republic. Now he was living comfor-
tably with Vera Ralston, whom he'd married. He threw his
arms around me and treated me like a long lost friend. He
told me that when I got back to California, I should come
and visit him. When I did get back, I said, 'What the hell!
I might as well go and see him.' And I did. I went out to
his house and told the servant who I was and that I had
come to visit Mr. Yates."

Yak paused and a smile played around the corners
of his mouth.

"The servant came back," he went on. "I was told:
'Mr. Yates can't be disturbed.' It was probably Vera's
doing. During his last years, she wouldn't permit anyone
from the old days to see him."

Yak reclined in his chair. "I never did see him
again."

YAKIMA CANUTT

A Film Checklist by Karl Thiede

Yakima Canutt was second unit director on the Mascot serials from 1927-1935. He was then head stuntman at Republic from 1935-1948.

Director and Second Unit Director credits

1. THE TOPEKA TERROR (26 January 1945). P: Repub-
    lic. D: Howard Bretherton. Second unit director:
    Yakima Canutt. C: Allan Lane, Linda Sterling,
    Earl Hodgins. 55m.

2. SHERIFF OF CIMARRON (28 February 1945). P: Re-
    public. D: Yakima Canutt. C: Sunset Carson,
    Linda Sterling, Olin Howlin. 55m.

3. SUN VALLEY CYCLONE (10 May 1946). P: Republic.
    D: R. G. Springsteen. Second unit director: Yakima
    Canutt. C: Bill Elliott, Bobby Blake, Alice Flem-
    ing. 58m.

4. UNDER NEVADA SKIES (26 August 1946). P: Repub-
    lic. D: Frank McDonald. Second unit director:
    Yakima Canutt. C: Roy Rogers, George Hayes,
    Dale Evans. 69m.

5. ANGEL AND THE BADMAN (15 February 1947). P:
    Republic. D: James Edward Grant. Second unit di-
    rector: Yakima Canutt. C: John Wayne, Gail Rus-
    sell, Harry Carey, Sr. 100m.

6. TWILIGHT ON THE RIO GRANDE (1 April 1947). P:
    Republic. D: Frank McDonald. Second unit director:
    Yakima Canutt. C: Gene Autry, Sterling Holloway,
    Adele Mara. 71m.

7. THAT'S MY MAN (1 June 1947). P: Republic. D:
    Frank Borzage. Second unit director: Yakima Ca-
    nutt. C: Don Ameche, Catherine McLeod, Roscoe
    Karns. 104m.

8. NORTHWEST OUTPOST (25 June 1947). P: Republic.
    D: Allan Dwan. Second unit director: Yakima
    Canutt. C: Nelson Eddy, Ilona Massey, Joseph
    Schildkraut. Color. 91m.

9. WYOMING (1 August 1947). P: Republic. D: Jo-
    seph Kane. Second unit director: Yakima Canutt.
    C: Bill Elliott, Vera Ralston, John Carroll. 84m.

10. G-MEN NEVER FORGET (31 January 1948). P: Re-
    public. D: Fred Brannon, Yakima Canutt. C:

Clayton Moore, Roy Barcroft, Ramsay Ames. NC: $151,554. 12 chapters.

11. OKLAHOMA BADLANDS (22 February 1948). P: Republic. D: Yakima Canutt. C: Allan Lane, Eddy Waller, Mildred Coles. 59m.

12. DANGERS OF THE CANADIAN MOUNTED (24 April 1948). P: Republic. D: Fred Brannon, Yakima Canutt. C: Jim Bannon, Virginia Belmont, Anthony Warde. NC: $150,130. 12 chapters.

13. CARSON CITY RAIDERS (13 May 1948). P: Republic. D: Yakima Canutt. C: Allan Lane, Eddy Waller, Frank Reicher. 60m.

14. ADVENTURES OF FRANK AND JESSE JAMES (21 June 1948). P: Republic. D: Frank Brannon, Yakima Canutt. C: Clayton Moore, Steve Darrell, Noel Neil. NC: $149,805. 13 chapters.

15. SONS OF ADVENTURE (28 August 1948). P: Republic. D: Yakima Canutt. C: Lynn Roberts, Russell Hayden, Gordon Jones. 60m.

16. RED STALLION IN THE ROCKIES (2 May 1949). P: Eagle-Lion. D: Ralph Murphy. Second unit director: Yakima Canutt. C: Arthur Franz, Jean Heather, Jim Davis. Cinecolor. 85m.

17. HELLFIRE (26 June 1949). P: Republic. D: R. G. Springsteen. Second unit director: Yakima Canutt. C: Bill Elliott, Marie Windsor, Forrest Tucker. Trucolor. 90m.

18. THE DOOLINS OF OKLAHOMA (July 1949). P: Columbia. D: Gordon Douglas. Second unit director: Yakima Canutt. C: Randolph Scott, George Macready, Louise Allbritton. 90m.

19. DEVIL'S DOORWAY (15 September 1950). P: Metro-Goldwyn-Mayer. D: Anthony Mann. Second unit director: Yakima Canutt. C: Robert Taylor, Louis Calhern, Paula Raymond. 7,590ft./84m.

20. IVANHOE (20 February 1953). P: Metro-Goldwyn-Mayer. D: Richard Thorpe. Second unit director:

Yakima Canutt. C: Robert Taylor, Elizabeth Taylor, Joan Fontaine. Technicolor. 9,590ft. /106 1/2m.

21. KNIGHTS OF THE ROUND TABLE (15 January 1954).
     P: Metro-Goldwyn-Mayer. D: Richard Thorpe.
     Second unit director: Yakima Canutt. C: Robert
     Taylor, Ava Gardner, Mel Ferrer. Color. Scope.
     9,513ft. /106m.

22. ZARAK (January 1957). P: Columbia. D: Terence
     Young. Assoc. D: Yakima Canutt. C: Victor Ma-
     ture, Michael Wilding, Anita Ekberg. Technicolor.
     Scope. 99m.

23. BEN-HUR (November 1959). P: Metro-Goldwyn-Mayer.
     D: William Wyler. Assoc. D: Andrew Marton, Ya-
     kima Canutt, Mario Soldati. C: Charlton Heston,
     Jack Hawkins, Stephen Boyd. Technicolor. 70mm.
     19,062ft. /212m.

24. SPARTACUS (October 1960). P: Universal. D:
     Stanley Kubrick. Second unit director: Yakima Ca-
     nutt. C: Kirk Douglas, Jean Simmons, Peter Usti-
     nov. Technicolor. 70mm. 22,086ft. /196m.

25. EL CID (December 1961). P: Allied Artists. D:
     Anthony Mann. Assistant director: Yakima Canutt.
     C: Charlton Heston, Sophia Loren, Raf Vallone.
     Technicolor. 70mm. 184m.

26. HOW THE WEST WAS WON (November 1962). P:
     Metro-Goldwyn-Mayer. D: Henry Hathaway, John
     Ford, George Marshall. Second unit director: Ya-
     kima Canutt. C: Carroll Baker, Lee J. Cobb,
     Henry Fonda. Technicolor. Cinerama. 13,739ft. /
     152m.

27. THE FALL OF THE ROMAN EMPIRE (March 1964).
     P: Paramount. D: Anthony Mann. Second unit di-
     rector: Yakima Canutt. C: Sophia Loren, Stephen
     Boyd, Alec Guinness. Technicolor. Scope. 180m.

28. THE SON OF CAPTAIN BLOOD (April 1964). P:
     Paramount. D: Tulio Demicheli. Assistant director:
     Yakima Canutt. C: Sean Flynn, Alessandra Panaro,
     Jose Nieto. Color. Scope. 88m.

29. SONG OF NORWAY (December 1970). P: Cinerama
     Releasing Corporation. D: Andrew L. Stone. Se-
     cond unit director: Yakima Canutt. C: Toralv
     Maurstad, Florence Henderson, Christina Schollin.
     Color. Scope. 150m.

30. RIO LOBO (December 1970). P: National General.
     D: Howard Hawks. Second unit director: Yakima
     Canutt. C: John Wayne, Jorge Rivero, Jennifer
     O'Neill. Color. 114m.

Lewis Milestone reading a copy of All Quiet on the Western Front. Photo courtesy of Wisconsin Center for Theatre Research.

Chapter 8

LEWIS MILESTONE

by David L. Parker & Burton J. Shapiro

Before his Hollywood days, he was named Milstein, like his younger cousin, concert violinist Nathan Milstein. He was born 30 September 1895 near the Black Sea port of Odessa in the Ukraine. Five years later, Milestone's father, a wealthy manufacturer, took his family to live in Chisinau, capitol of Bessarabia, an area which became part of Rumania after 1918.

Upon completing high school in 1912, Lewis was enrolled against his wishes in a mechanical engineering school in Mitweide, Saxony. Later, trade sources listed "Gard University, Belgium." Profoundly interested in the theater, bored with his classes, Milestone took the money his father sent him the following Christmas for a trip home for the holidays, and emigrated to the United States with two classmates. They disembarked in Hoboken with only six dollars left among them.

Milestone had an aunt in New York City. From her he borrowed $100. The three young men divided the money. Milestone's two companions set out for Boston, the city in which some of their relatives lived. When Lewis ran out of money, he cabled his father for more. The reply read, "You are in the land of liberty and labor, so use your own judgment."

The eighteen-year-old found work sweeping floors for a raincoat manufacturer and then for a lace-making company. Briefly he tried selling. His luck changed when he was hired as an assistant in a theatrical photographer's studio and paid seven dollars a week. Milestone learned the special qualities of the still camera, posed the clients, worked in the darkroom, developing and printing the film.

His intense interest in his work and his diligence led to a
promotion to the job of salesman with an increase in salary
and opportunity for earning commissions.

When the United States entered World War I, Milestone joined the Army in September of 1917. When he had
completed basic training he joined the photographic division
of the Army Signal Corps, and was assigned to New York
City for twelve months. Here he served with Gordon Holl-
ingshead (who would be assistant director on BOBBED HAIR
[Warner's, 1925], written by Milestone) and future Hollywood
directors Wesley Ruggles and Victor Fleming.

When he was assigned as film editor to the Army's
lab and medical museum in Washington, D. C. he worked
with Josef von Sternberg (then Joe Sternberg of Brooklyn)
and Richard Wallace, both of whom would serve apprentice-
ships as film cutters before directing.

The training films that they made, FIT TO WIN, FIT
TO FIGHT, THE TOOTHBRUSH, and POSTURE, Milestone
has termed "terrible." For an Army film shot in a Washington park, Milestone played the part of a German soldier.
Provoked by his German uniform, a bunch of young boys
threw rocks at him.

Three months after the end of the war, in February
1919, he was discharged. In the Signal Corps, Milestone
had become acquainted with an independent film producer,
Jesse D. Hampton. Now he asked him for a job. The only
one available was that of a cutting room assistant at $20 a
week. Milestone accepted it and used his savings for a train
ticket to Hollywood. He arrived completely broke. For a
year he worked in the cutting room, again sweeping floors,
running errands, and splicing films. He worked as a gag
man for comedian Harold Lloyd. Then he came to the attention of Henry King, who had directed FUGITIVE FROM
MATRIMONY, a 1919 drama for Hampton starring H. B.
Warner, and was contracted to do two more vehicles with
the actor. King made Milestone his film editor and general
assistant on two films, DICE OF DESTINY (Pathé, 1920) and
WHEN WE WERE 21 (Pathé, 1921).

The first was a favorably accepted program picture
vehicle for the redoubtable British star, flawed by multiple
coincidences in its story-line; the latter--the last of King's
seven films with H. B. Warner--was a hackneyed triangle

plot, tepidly acted, and nearly stolen out from under Warner
by his screen rival in love, James W. Morrison.

Milestone shifted to Fox Film Corporation and to a
raise to $28 a week. Then, as assistant editor for the
Japanese matinee idol Sessue Hayakawa, he made $40 a
week. Later he worked for Richard Wallace, who had become a cutter for the Mack Sennett Studio and for Thomas
A. Ince. Ince's editor, Del Andrews, credited with the
scenario for THE BRONZE BELL (Paramount, 1921) and the
second unit direction of the horseracing sequences in THE
HOTTENTOT (First National, 1922), was a director of
Westerns with Hoot Gibson, Fred Thomson, and Bob Custer,
as well as comedies with Alberta Vaughn. Reportedly, he
helped young Milestone master motion picture technique.
Like Milestone, he would adapt scenarios for director William A. Seiter. Andrews later co-authored the scenario for
Milestone's THE RACKET (Paramount, 1928) and served as
editor for him during BETRAYAL (Paramount, 1929).

Milestone became a close friend of Seiter, an adept
director of light comedies and romances, who was reportedly as interested in golf as in filmmaking. When Seiter
worked, Milestone did editing at night and was present on
the set during the day, directing pickup shots. He was Seiter's assistant director on THE FOOLISH AGE (Robertson-
Cole, 1921) and Seiter's co-author on UP AND AT 'EM
(Robertson-Cole, 1922). Both films starred Doris May, who
had achieved popularity in Henry King's Army comedy,
23-1/2 HOURS LEAVE (Famous Players-Lasky, 1919).
Milestone was assistant editor on Harry Beaumont's film of
Sinclair Lewis' MAIN STREET (Warner's, 1923), and then
he served as assistant director to Seiter on LITTLE CHURCH
AROUND THE CORNER (Warner's, 1923), adapted from a
1902 play. An interesting cast, Pauline Starke, Claire
Windsor, Hobart Bosworth, and an adroitly managed mine
explosion aided the soapy tale of a preacher who stops a
riot through the miracle of making a mute girl speak, in a
situation reminiscent of Lon Chaney's THE MIRACLE MAN
(Paramount, 1919).

"A celluloid disaster" was the verdict of Warner
Brothers' brass after the screening of footage shot for their
first Rin Tin Tin feature. Milestone was hired as film editor to convert the rolls of exposed film into something hopefully resembling a motion picture. The result, WHERE
THE NORTH BEGINS, was released in July 1923. Cheaply

made, it was distinguished by its mobile camera, apt com-
positions, and the nobility of its canine star who saves the
French Canadian hero and heroine from Alaskan dangers.
Milestone's reputation as a "film doctor" was assured.

With "silk hat comic" Raymond Griffith, Milestone
adapted the scenario for J. W. Horne's THE YANKEE CON-
SUL (Associated Exhibitors, 1924) from a stage musical of
1904. "A remarkably fine comedy," wrote Photoplay,
"one you should by no means miss." That same April 1924
issue reviewed William Seiter's DADDIES (Warner's, 1924)
as "a good version of the clever stage play." Again Milestone was the assistant director. His next 1924 credit was
as Seiter's co-author on LISTEN LESTER (Principal, 1924),
a Broadway musical comedy updated by adding bootleggers
to the merry old widower, breach of promise suit, and
packet of incriminating letters. A cast of "names" of wan-
ing appeal and costly sets rented to give production values
to a Florida hotel setting disguised the minor nature of the
effort. Photoplay found it "fast and full of tricks," but its
feeble comedy, overly frequent chases, and weak resolution
left it no credit to those on the credits.

Better was the final 1924 Seiter-Milestone programmer, HELEN'S BABIES (Principal, 1924), spare of incident
but lively and pleasant. Bachelor Edward Everett Horton
attempts to double as a babysitter for his niece, child star
Baby Peggy, in a story adapted from an 1876 children's
book, and appealing greatly to children.

The screen treatment from which the scenario was
constructed and the slot of assistant director were attributed
to Milestone for Seiter's THE MAD WHIRL (Universal, 1925).
Evidently influenced by the film version of the novel FLAM-
ING YOUTH (First National, 1923), this society romance
travels at high speed until its happy ending in which May
McAvoy crusades against the evils of drinking cocktails and
her parents decide to act their age.

In 1925, William Seiter directed his wife, Universal's
leading feminine star Laura LaPlante, in two comedy romances, DANGEROUS INNOCENCE (Universal, 1925), on
which Milestone had done the adaptation from a novel, and
THE TEASER (Universal, 1925), representing the ninth and
final collaboration between the two, with Milestone as assistant director.

The films are characteristic of most of those in which Milestone was involved at the time, in that they begin promisingly, sustain a brisk rhythm until the story approaches its resolution, and then linger too long before the finale, leaving an impression of inordinate length.

Milestone's first solo scenario credit came with BOBBED HAIR (Warner's, 1925), an adaptation of a satire constructed much as was Naked Came the Stranger, by many playful collaborators writing a chapter apiece. In the 1925 book, each of the twenty authors, ranging alphabetically from Louis Bromfield to Alexander Woollcott, hoped to put his protagonists in such situations that the following author would find it almost impossible to extricate them. Not surprisingly, the film was involved and disorienting, but its director Alan Crosland kept the silly slapstick moving, and the required vitality was forthcoming from a cast headed by Mack Sennett alumna Marie Prevost, soon to be the star of Milestone's directorial debut film, SEVEN SINNERS (Warner's, 1925), which followed.

Milestone offered his original story idea to Jack Warner only on the condition that he be allowed to direct it: a comedy about seven crooks impersonating servants at a vacant mansion during a strike of security guards. Two of them, Marie Prevost and Clive Brook, have a change of heart, serve a jail term, and become burglar alarm salesmen at the fadeout. Milestone's assigned scenarist on this and a second Marie Prevost film was an ambitious young writer, Darryl F. Zanuck. Milestone had wanted to be a film director for a long time because he felt it was the easiest job in the world. The SEVEN SINNERS plot recalled the stage version of SEVEN KEYS TO BALDPATE for some because of characters who plot to outwit each other without doing much harm. Film Daily deemed Milestone's direction "excellent," and Photoplay, approving of the "good cast," called it "hilarious." New York Times reviewer Mordaunt Hall found it "quite diverting and it would have been even better if the humor were lighter in some sequences, and if a touch of satire had been included at the finish. It is the best feature exhibited at Warner's for several weeks."

A short three months later Warner's released THE CAVEMAN (Warner's, 1926), Milestone's second feature as director. The film shared a socialite and a coal-shoveler with Eugene O'Neill's play The Hairy Ape, but little else. The story (termed "ridiculous" by Photoplay) has Marie

Prevost pass off Matt Moore as an eccentric professor, who
becomes a social lion. Before the seven reels have run
their course, the socialite exposes the fraud; he abducts her
in his coal wagon, and they wind up at the altar. The New
York Times critic found it "delectable." Milestone systematically combined satirical comments on snobbery with suspense and slapstick in a smooth manner which elicited favorable reviews. An unfaltering, flowing continuity was also
characteristic of his next directorial effort, THE NEW
KLONDIKE (Paramount, 1926).

The title refers to the crazed land boom of the moment. It starred Thomas Meighan who with an idled forty-
man crew needed a director willing to gamble on a title and
a locale for which a script had not yet been developed. Not
for the last time Milestone took such a chance. The story
which emerged on location concerned a baseball player
dropped by his team during Spring training in Florida, who
makes a fortune in the realty business until he is sold a
swamp by a swindler. Some choice satire and a strong
sense of local color enliven the Meighan vehicle. A ball-
player rounds the bases unobstructed as other players studying real estate maps forget him. Tom recovers his money,
wins the girl, Lila Lee, and is hired as the manager of the
team from which he was fired. "Fairly humorous," said
The New York Times, "with amusing incidents." The film
was released by Paramount in March 1926, a day before a
special New York showing of the company's FASCINATING
YOUTH in which Milestone appeared briefly as himself in a
society drama showcasing that year's graduates of the Paramount School for Stars.

He began FINE MANNERS (Paramount, 1926), a society comedy-drama with Gloria Swanson in one of the roles
she did well--a shabby working girl who devotedly loves an
uptown socialite. Swanson and Milestone quarrelled, and
the film was finished by Richard Rosson.

It was during this period that Milestone's reputation
as a "film doctor" was so high that Warner's--which was
paying him $400 a week--continually loaned him out to pro-
ducers with films which needed rescuing, at $1,000 a week.
Milestone felt that he was being exploited and quit; Warner's
sued him for breach of contract and won. To satisfy the
verdict the studio had won against him, he had to go through
bankruptcy for nearly a year. Unable to work, he lived in
a couple of rooms with friends Myron and David Selznick,

the latter then a M-G-M script reader. When free of his
monetary and legal obligations, Milestone signed a four-year
contract with an independent producer just starting out, Howard Hughes.

Milestone's first effort for Hughes was TWO ARABIAN
KNIGHTS (United Artists, 1927), a coarse, gleeful comedy
co-authored by James T. O'Donohue, the scenarist of the
film version of WHAT PRICE GLORY? (Fox, 1926), one of
Milestone's favorite plays. Both concerned the feuding,
double-crossing rivalry between a career Army sergeant and
a private, centering on the favors of an attractive woman (in
this incarnation, an Arabian girl of rank). The principals
were the stage star of WHAT PRICE GLORY?, Louis Wolheim, in his film debut, William Boyd, and Mary Astor.
The doughboys (here POWs captured on the Western Front
during World War I) escape the Germans disguised as Arabs
on a steamer bound for Jaffa. In a series of picaresque
escapades, the soldiers foil their adversaries--who include
the girl's father, her fiancé, and a gang of cut-throats--and
escape from Palestine with her, still fighting each other.

Milestone's direction stressed the vulgar and earthy
comedy but eschewed slapstick for perceptive characterizations and a knowing outlook on life. Despite patently deriva-
tive elements, Photoplay found the film "Original! Proving
that there can be something new in war comedies." Milestone received the first citation for best comedy direction
from the Academy of Motion Picture Arts & Sciences. The
film remains one of his favorites.

Milestone's next film, THE GARDEN OF EDEN
(United Artists, 1928), from a Viennese stage comedy-drama
of two years earlier, was adapted by Hans Kraly, one of
Ernst Lubitsch's favorite scenarists, whose credits included
ROSITA (United Artists, 1923), FORBIDDEN PARADISE
(Paramount, 1924), THE PATRIOT (Paramount, 1928), and
SO THIS IS PARIS (Warner's, 1926). Described as a Lubitsch
plot with von Stroheim touches, it was another in the infinite
number of variations on CINDERELLA. This time the heroine, Corinne Griffith, was a chorus dancer in Budapest, and
an impoverished baroness, Louise Dresser, was her fairy
godmother. Prince Charming was an urbane hotel guest
smitten by Griffith's skill at the piano. The role was played
by Charles Ray, attempting to shake the mannerisms of his
country boy films. The film is notable for its handsome
mounting (particularly the grotesque settings designed by

William Cameron Menzies) and the way Corinne Griffith's
sense of humor and beauty are captured through outstanding
photography. In the United States it grossed $757,378 for
United Artists.

Howard Hughes produced Milestone's next film and
liked it well enough to remake it in 1951. THE RACKET
(Paramount, 1928) appeared at the end of a year of under-
world melodramas launched by von Sternberg's UNDER-
WORLD (Paramount, 1927), the film to which the others
were compared at the time. With the release of THE
RACKET, the Milestone film became a high mark to which
the other films were compared until the coming of sound.
In making silent adaptations of stage plays such as THE
RACKET, Milestone has said that he felt no lack in not having sound because the silent cinema had developed into a
self-contained, expressive storytelling form. THE RACKET
opens with a gruesome lighting effect preceding a gangland
street battle. Thomas Meighan portrays a police captain
who must work alone against the flashy bootlegger king,
Louis Wolheim. It was written by Chicago society reporter
Bartlett Cormack--one of the characters is a newspaperman
replete with his bottle of Scotch and a copy of H. L. Menck-
en, played by the lively comic "Skeets" Gallagher--and was
one of the earliest of the more realistic gangster films.
With candor, Milestone's restrained, firm direction seriously exposed intricate links between policemen and racketeers.
THE RACKET was nominated for best picture in the 1927-
28 Academy Awards.

Hughes loaned him out as Warner's had done. In
1927, when the Russian émigré director Viachetslav Tour-
jansky worked too slowly for Joe Schenck on RED TEMPEST,
a John Barrymore-Louis Wolheim drama of the Russian Revolution, Milestone assumed the direction for a time. He
quit in disgust, and the film, released as TEMPEST (United
Artists, 1928), was finished by Sam Taylor. It was a dull,
unbelievable affair with excessively broad comedy, and ham
acting by Wolheim and Barrymore.

It was at this time that Milestone was being grouped
with other young directors who had served their apprentice-
ship as script-writers and assistant cutters and directors to
long-established filmmakers and were making comedies and
dramas thought to be influenced by Lubitsch's MARRIAGE
CIRCLE (Warner's, 1924), von Stroheim's FOOLISH WIVES
(Universal, 1922), and Chaplin's A WOMAN OF PARIS

(United Artists, 1923). Harry d'Abbadie d'Arrast and Frank
Tuttle were among them. Paul Rotha summarized their
movies as "slick, facile, flashy, well-photographed, display-
ing here and there ... Germanic influence in their camera
angles. They are always rapid in pace ... briskly cut."
For those who saw him as an imitator of Lubitsch comedy,
Milestone had a surprise in store with his next pictures.
His aversion to doing the same thing twice would earn him
the description of "the chameleon."

Milestone's last silent film, BETRAYAL (Paramount,
1929), was released with a synchronized musical score and
sound effects. A tragic Hans Kraly triangle set in the Swiss
Alps (but partly shot at Lake Tahoe), it lurches from the
charming early sequences between an intelligent heroine,
Esther Ralston, and a visiting bohemian artist, Gary Cooper,
to the roughed-in incidents of her death in a toboggan crash
and of the subsequent anguish of her husband, Emil Jannings,
that one of his sons is actually the bohemian artist played
by Cooper. Milestone ineffectively attempts to dramatize
the mayor's passing thoughts about murdering the boy by
pushing him off a glacier. It was as unconvincing as the
cramped, studio-built village and the artificial snow. Jannings fell back on familiar mannerisms to compensate for
the sketchy development of the characterization. Later he
picked up his Academy Awards for best actor in THE WAY
OF ALL FLESH (Paramount, 1927) and THE LAST COM-
MAND (Paramount, 1928) and immediately left for Germany
for good.

After seeing the producer's cut of his next officially
listed film, NEW YORK NIGHTS (United Artists, 1929), the
director asked that his name be taken off it. At first it
was, but by the time of its release Milestone's name was
back on the credits. Rumors circulated implying that much
of the backstage triangle tale had been directed by someone
else.

NEW YORK NIGHTS was produced by Joseph Schenck
as the first sound vehicle for his wife Norma Talmadge, a
popular star of more than two hundred and fifty silent films.
As the faithful wife of an alcoholic songwriter, Gilbert Roland (who had been Armand to Talmadge's Camille in a
1927 film), she must acquiesce to the advances of a lecher-
ous racketeer producer if her husband's song--actually co-
authored by Al Jolson--is to be plugged in a show. Roland
and Talmadge part, but are reconciled in night court (she's

there because of a shooting at a wild party she attended;
he's there for vagrancy). When he faints on the spot, she
buys him his first meal in days. "Gee," proclaims the
Mexican Roland gratefully, "theese Cheenks are goood
coooks." One murder later, the producer is apprehended
by the police. Talmadge forgives Roland at the fadeout. Its
inadvertent comedy aside, NEW YORK NIGHTS is no better
nor worse than dozens of early sound melodramas. Shot
with a single, stationary camera, it offers only the novelty
of having lines once written out in titles--such as a reproach-
ful "So you lied to me!"--now declaimed aloud by Norma
Talmadge in a fine (if overly-emphatic) speaking voice which
was the result of more than a year of daily elocution lessons.
The film grossed $711,838 in the United States. After one
more sound film Norma Talmadge retired. Lewis Milestone
began working on what would be his greatest film, and possibly the screen's greatest indictment of war, ALL QUIET
ON THE WESTERN FRONT (Universal, 1930).

Someone at Universal had been sufficiently impressed
by the Western Front trench scenes in TWO ARABIAN
KNIGHTS to offer the directorial assignment on the film
adaptation of the Remarque bestseller to Milestone. He accepted. A virtually unprecedented freedom from studio interference was allowed this first major production of Universal's new head, the twenty-one-year-old Carl Laemmle, Jr.,
who had promised the author that the film would remain faithful to the book drawn from Remarque's war experiences.

The scripting, preparation, and filming would take
nine months. Milestone and playwright Maxwell Anderson
worked long weeks on Catalina Island, revising and rewrit-
ing, the director envisioning the scenes as if the film were
to be silent, the writer subsequently adding lines of dialogue to it. Later the veteran stage author-director George
Abbott was brought onto the writing team with Anderson,
Milestone, and Del Andrews. The film retained the elo-
quence of the silent film, avoided many of the defects of the
early talkies and even remains most powerful in its silent
version today.

During his time in Washington during the First World
War, Milestone had seen actual combat footage. To simulate the European settings he shot on a mesa near Laguna
to disguise the California location. Sequences were done at
the Irving Ranch fifty miles outside of Hollywood, at the
Pathé backlot in Culver City, as well as at Balboa. The

première found Milestone's version cut from 18,000 to
12,423 feet. Subsequent reissues used versions running
from 105 to 93 minutes.

Contrary to pre-release speculation, the film was an
immediate critical and popular success. Veteran critic
James Agate wrote, "I have never known an audience to be
so deeply, discriminatingly moved."

Howard Hughes acquired filming rights to the rowdy
newspaper comedy, THE FRONT PAGE. He offered it to
Milestone who enthusiastically accepted. Hughes rejected
Milestone's choices for the role of reporter Hildy Johnson
(James Cagney or Clark Gable), so Pat O'Brien, who had
played the role in Chicago, made his film debut as Hildy.
Milestone solved the problem of translating a stage play into
cinema without changing dialogue, action, or setting. His
cast speaks more quickly than in any other version; cutting
is rapid, even within speeches; his camera is constantly in
motion, not only in an introductory tracking shot which had
become his personal signature but also in creating an illusion of spaciousness within the four-walled sets by covering
the headlong action with a series of panning shots. The
debonair Adolphe Menjou, in a bit of switch-casting as the
ruthless editor, is more gentle at times than his stage
counterpart, but sustains a convincing characterization.
O'Brien and Menjou are matched by the lesser characters
in abbreviated roles--Edward Everett Horton, Frank McHugh,
Walter Catlett--and Milestone plays a brief bit himself.
The film grossed $537,508 in the U.S. and won an Academy
Award nomination for Best Picture of 1930-31. Milestone
headed the list of "10 Best Directors of 1930-31" in a poll
of 300 periodical critics conducted by Film Daily. His influence in the film capital during the early sound period was
enormous.

On the strength of this success, Milestone sought
greater independence in his projects.

For three months in 1931 David Selznick tried all
over Hollywood to get financing and distribution for his proposed independent production unit with Lewis Milestone. A
deal with RKO for the production of seven films a year fell
through when Milestone accepted a job as production head
for United Artists, a fact which was announced in April,
1932.

A month later Cecil B. DeMille informed Milestone and the other members of their proposed Directors' Guild-- Frank Borzage and King Vidor--that in the past three months there had been no progress in obtaining financing and distri- bution in the industry for small, independent producing units under the creative control of the filmmakers. The studios were not yet ready to relinquish any artistic control to the directors.

In his memoirs, Why Me? (Doubleday, 1969), William Gargan says that he had supporting roles in two features made at Paramount's Long Island studio. About the second, a Claudette Colbert comedy called MISLEADING LADY (Para- mount, 1932, adapted from a 1913 stage play), Gargan re- members it as having been directed by Milestone, although the film was signed by Stuart Walker, a stage producer who had been dialogue director on some early Columbia sound films and was a director for Paramount in the early 'thirties. (The New York Times issue of 19 April 1932, reviewing MISLEADING LADY, carries on the same page a news item in its "Picture and Players" column about Mile- stone arriving in Hollywood to direct several pictures for United Artists, including RAIN and a Ben Hecht original story for Al Jolson "after a sojourn in New York City," so there may be something in these recollections.) Gargan states that he had impressed Milestone on this picture and that he was offered $1,500 a week to play the part of Sgt. O'Hara in RAIN (United Artists, 1932). Gargan, who was appearing on Broadway in Phillip Barry's THE ANIMAL KINGDOM at the time, got out of his run-of-the-play con- tract and accepted the offer. Shooting took ten weeks and Gargan made $15,000.

Walter Huston's characterization of the grim Calvinist in William Wyler's A HOUSE DIVIDED (released by Univer- sal in January 1932) had been a minor sensation. The Hu- ston role in Wyler's film was along the lines of Eugene O'Neill's play DESIRE UNDER THE ELMS (1924), in which Huston had successfully appeared in a Broadway revival of 1928. Perhaps these portrayals seemed to Milestone to be akin to that of the obsessed Reverend Davidson of RAIN. Huston was signed for the part.

Joan Crawford, one of the top box-office attractions by 1932, had shown dramatic promise in GRAND HOTEL (M-G-M, 1932), and was encouraged by United Artists to attempt a role beyond the dramatic range which she had

Milestone directing Joan Crawford in the famous conversion scene from RAIN (United Artists, 1932). Photo courtesy of Views & Reviews Magazine.

demonstrated she was capable of handling until then, the
role of Sadie Thompson. Her performance received mixed
reviews. Seen today, it has moments of conviction and
power, but it has the feel of something composed in the
editing room out of miniscule bits from hundreds of takes,
and the interlarded shots of other players in her scenes
show an irregular rhythm untypical of Milestone's work,
suggesting the exigencies of this project.

"Before we ever shot a scene," Gargan recalls in
his autobiography, "Milestone would call in a bevy of car-
toonists and they would sketch the scene. Then the actors
would be blocked in with the cameras, and we would begin
rehearsing...."

In a newspaper interview in 1940, Lewis Milestone described the mechanics of his work: when the sets have been built, he blocks out action and lines in great detail, employing extras as stand-ins for his cast. Five hundred-odd sketches with corresponding dialogue attached are built into storyboards for each sequence in the film. Milestone adopted this fairly usual practice for a difficult sequence in ALL QUIET ON THE WESTERN FRONT and has used it ever afterwards.

"I have no patience with the growing method of having every camera shot sketched beforehand so that director, cameraman, and actors can work by rote," complained screen writer Dudley Nichols in 1943. "It destroys the spontaneity of feeling which is the essence of film art."

Nonetheless it allows Milestone to go to the film editor with the storyboards and say, "this is the way I saw it."

In a mid-'forties memo, David Selznick compared an associate unfavorably to Milestone, whom he praised for presenting his crew with a total plan for each day's work, complete with each camera position to be used for each part of the scene to be shot instead of wasteful duplication of set-ups and camera angles characteristic of less competent craftsmen.

Gargan's favorite scene in RAIN was the one in which he tried to get Sadie to escape and to wait for him in Australia: "It took place at night in the rain (pipes overhead pumped salt water from the ocean down on us), and the electricians and the cable carriers were in constant danger from electrical shock ... we walk(ed) around the porch of a circular house and the cameras followed us in a complete circle, which was what made the scene difficult. Milestone wanted it in one continuous take. We began one night at nine, and we finally satisfied Milly on the fifteenth take, at four the next morning. Then we discovered at the next day's rushes there was a scratch on the entire negative. Two days later we shot it again, and this time we got it on the fifth take."

"I was haunted by my inferiority to famous Sadie Thompsons of the past," wrote Joan Crawford in A Portrait of Joan (Doubleday, 1962). "Mr. Joe Schenck thought I worried unnecessarily. He told me to listen to my director, but Lewis Milestone frightened me. I wasn't wise enough

about acting to understand how brilliant a man this was or
how talented a director. He had worked out blueprints for
every scene, precisely what I was to do and how to do it;
but to me, no actress worthy of the name could be a puppet
in anyone's hands. I was no Method actress, I was an emotional one--in RAIN, far too emotional. "

Milestone was pleased with Huston's performance, but
in the scene in which Davidson pursues Sadie down a stair-
case, reciting the Lord's Prayer over and over, contemporary
audiences giggled. "When Sadie wilts before Davidson, "
wrote the New York Times reviewer, "it no longer seems
plausible. " The play had seemed dated and Milestone's efforts to give it its original power--incessant rain, sticky
claustrophobic quarters--had made it seem slow and lacking
in spontaneity and too theatrical. Today its stylization may
be more acceptable to audiences viewing it on TV.

HALLELUJAH, I'M A BUM (United Artists, 1933),
Milestone's next film, was a further experiment in freeing
the sound film from the restrictions of the "potted theatre
play. " A French boulevard comedy was adapted by Ben
Hecht to the personality of Al Jolson, who had signed a two
million dollar contract with United Artists to make four
films. To the depths of a Depression America, it opened
as banks were closing and unemployment reached a record
fifteen million persons. Somewhere in the rhyming couplets
and lyrics and music which make up eighty per cent of the
track is a reference to "Hoover's Cossacks. " The score by
Rodgers & Hart extended the techniques they had used for
Rouben Mamoulian's LOVE ME TONIGHT (Paramount, 1932),
as the characters sing their opinions. In his autobiography
(Musical Stages, 1975), composer Richard Rodgers recalls
his excitement over the project, but admits that the very
real setting of the Depression defeated their attempts to in-
still gaiety in the satire. One of Jolson's songs, "You Are
Too Beautiful (For One Man Alone)" slowly achieved the
status of a "standard" over the years.

The characters include a playboy mayor of New York
(originally Roland Young, but illness led to his replacement
by Frank Morgan) and Manhattan hoboes played by Jolson
(drawing $25,000 a week) and his tiny black friend (Edgar
Connor). They are joined by silent comic Harry Langdon as
a garbage collector and Keystone Kop alumnus Chester Conk-
lin as a cab driver. Madge Evans is the twenty-ish love
interest to fifty-ish Jolson. Their romance drags down the

last third of the fantasy, but the first two-thirds contain
many moments of Milestone's rhythmical camera movement
with music looking back to René Clair and forward to the informal, shot-outdoors production numbers of musicals in the
early 'fifties, and expressing kinesthetically the film's whim-
sical thesis of the freedom of vagrancy.   The film grossed
$1,280,625 in the United States, but costs had run well over
a million and it was not a success.   It was easily Jolson's
best film performance, restrained and clever, but no more
films were made under his contract with United Artists.
Time had found Milestone's direction undistinguished.   The
New York Times thought it excellent.   Vanity Fair condemned
the picture.   Reviews were as mixed as they had been for
RAIN.   But Milestone had succeeded in at least one phase of
the experiment: he established a harmony between picture
and track.   Rhymed couplets, music, and blocking of actors'
movements were all combined by his camera movement and
editing into a single irresistible film rhythm.

        Milestone's next film was also a comedy, this time
made for Columbia where he had been promised fifty per
cent of the film's profits.   It could be called a screwball
GRAND HOTEL at sea, interspersed with a few serious vig-
nettes, all designed as a showcase for a large number of
the 'thirties' rich supply of Hollywood character actors:
THE CAPTAIN HATES THE SEA (Columbia, 1934).

        Walter Connolly is the irascible skipper of a steamer
full of pleasure cruise passengers: a large, disorderly widow (Alison Skipworth); a hard-boiled tramp carrying valuable bonds and pretending to be a librarian on vacation
(Wynn Gibson) with a private detective (Victor McLaglen) on
her trail.   What Otis Ferguson called "the only true steamer
orchestra I ever saw except on a real steamer" is ... The
Three Stooges!   Leon Flynn is an incompetent steward.

        The nominal star, John Gilbert (brought back to work
at Milestone's insistence), as an author who can't keep off
the bottle, provides the framing device for the series of incidents which make up the cruise.   The audience sees the
greetings and leave-takings through Gilbert's hazy viewpoint
at the ship's bar; droll, mocking, slightly biting, abruptly
serious with the death of a general on his way to lead a
revolution in his country and an attempted suicide.

        The film was shot on a rented ship off Southern Cali-
fornia with the handicaps of overcast skies, strong winds,

Milestone on the set of THE CAPTAIN HATES THE SEA
(Paramount, 1934) with Alison Skipworth, Florence Rice,
Victor McLaglen, and the Three Stooges (Curley, Larry and
Moe) in the background.   Photo courtesy of the Museum of
Modern Art.

and a tipsy contingent of cast members.   "There was that
feeling about [the film]," wrote Ferguson "that everybody
read the script and said 'this is going to be fun' and made
it so ... a cruise story to end cruises forever."

     The New York Times review found some of the inci-
dents funny, but was confused by the lack of a definite story-
line.   Many critics praised the good cast and the never-
slackening pace.   But Otis Ferguson told the story when he
titled his second enthusiastic piece (written two years after
the film's release), "Best Neglected Film."

     For Paramount Milestone directed two musicals which
he has dismissed as "insignificant."   The first, PARIS IN
THE SPRING (Paramount, 1935), was a vehicle for Mary
Ellis, the studio's proficient contender in the operatic sweepstakes launched by Grace Moore's success in ONE NIGHT

OF LOVE (Columbia, 1934). Milestone's film borrowed
Moore's leading man, Tullio Carminati, for Miss Ellis and
the style of Ernst Lubitsch for the antique farce, now re-
furbished with a new musical score. The title song, introduced by Ellis in the film, became one of the most popular
of 1935, but the film containing it did not, although the proficient Ellis had had a stage career ranging from Shakespeare to the Metropolitan Opera to O'Neill and the original
ROSE MARIE. Nevertheless, Milestone's direction impressed
critic Graham Greene: "There is one moment in this film
when you have ... a sense of the absurd, unreasoning happiness of a kind of poignant release ... as the Count scram-
bles across the roofs to his mistress' room; happiness and
freedom, nothing really serious, nothing really lasting, a
touching of hands, a tuneful miniature love." Elsewhere
Greene praised Milestone's deft way of transforming nonsense into an enchanting, genuinely fantastic musical.
Others noted that the parts were better than the whole.

Ida Lupino, the blonde ingenue of PARIS IN THE
SPRING, also appeared in Milestone's second musical for
Paramount, ANYTHING GOES (Paramount, 1936); she brought
to it a curt intensity, a knowing glance, and a real sense
of fun. Bing Crosby was less stiff than in earlier films, if
not as casual as in later ones. Leather-lunged Ethel Merman belted out "I Get a Kick Out of You" early in the film
while riding a hoop through a nightclub. She and Crosby
sang some new lyrics for "You're the Top," presumably because Cole Porter's original lyrics might prove too sophisticated for middle America or for the censor. "The whole
number was staged with an editor's eye," Don Miller noted
in a 1963 reassessment of the film version. "It contains
considerable filmmaking sense ... its merits are (mostly)
due to Lewis Milestone." The lavish production included a
Chinese extravaganza on an English dock which was combined with a chase to bring the story to a close. Contemporary reviewers found Charlie Ruggles not the equal of his
role's originator, Victor Moore, and were divided as to
whether Milestone's deliberate style paced the comedy quickly enough.

After the musicals Milestone worked at Paramount
for nearly three months without being assigned a film to
produce and direct according to his contract. He convinced
production head Ernst Lubitsch that a film could be made
from a pulp thriller, THE GENERAL DIED AT DAWN
(Paramount, 1936). The resulting melodrama, from an

original script by the socially conscious playwright Clifford
Odets, was set in the Shanghai of 1927, where a fierce strug-
gle had taken place between Chiang Kai-Shek and the Com-
munists. It resembled a "Terry and the Pirates" comic
strip as much as the decorative photography of Josef von
Sternberg's SHANGHAI EXPRESS (Paramount, 1932), or the
China of Frank Capra's BITTER TEA OF GENERAL YEN
(Columbia, 1933).

Milestone's warlord (Akim Tamiroff, wearing false
upper eyelids to appear Chinese) is opposed by Gary Cooper
as a laconic, tall American trying to smuggle gold into Shanghai for the purchase of arms for an uprising against the warlord. Madeleine Carroll, the prototypical Hitchcock blonde
in distress, projects fire and fright in a complex characterization which is probably her best film performance. Milestone is seen momentarily as a truck driver. Novelist John
O'Hara appears briefly as an English journalist.

The introductory sequences, which play without dialogue, are highly promising. Kites float down among the
dead of a Chinese village. High grass is pushed aside and
trampled by advancing troops. A scarred general with
gratified expression rides down the bumpy road in a sleek,
expensive car of American make. Deliberate pacing makes
the menace almost palpable. In the second sequence, in a
billiard room, the half-obscured figures force us to listen
to the coughs and whispers of the soundtrack. Carroll is
seen clearly for the first time as she leans forward into the
light in a dramatic introduction. Milestone match-dissolves
from a billiard ball to the doorknob which will open into the
next setting. Progressively, the potentially profound elements fall away as the film opts for exciting, preposterous
adventure. Milestone amused himself with such directorial
touches as ceremonial swords splitting the screen into four
panels of simultaneous action by four of the protagonists,
and the serpentine tracking of a camera through the Chinese
junks. Clifford Odets' speeches, while on the side of the
downtrodden, were seen as verbal fireworks for the sake of
fireworks. As one wag quipped, "Odets, where is thy
sting?"

It would be more than three years before another
Milestone film would be seen. Among the unrealized projects was a film based on Vincent Sheean's autobiography,
Personal History (Houghton-Mifflin, 1935), an account of
the journalist's experiences in China, Russia, and Spain,

which was to be filmed for producer Walter Wanger. (Some
of the author's background was suggested in Wanger's fic-
tional film, FOREIGN CORRESPONDENT [United Artists,
1940], directed by Alfred Hitchcock.)

With Clifford Odets, Milestone prepared a screenplay
for DEAD END (United Artists, 1937) for Samuel Goldwyn,
only to see the production turned over to William Wyler.
During shooting Goldwyn retained Milestone to stand by to
take over from Wyler at a moment's notice.

On 29 June 1937, Milestone signed a contract with
Hal Roach to develop a film from the novel ROAD SHOW,
with the first four weeks devoted to the preparation of the
picture and ten subsequent weeks of shooting to be followed
by two weeks of cutting, as a minimum, at a weekly salary
of $5,000.

After ten weeks of shooting, Roach declared ROAD
SHOW was being developed into a serious drama and fired
Milestone, claiming it would cost the studio $420,661 to
scrap what had been done and to remake the film.

In January 1938 Milestone, claiming he was wrong-
fully dismissed as director of ROAD SHOW, sued for $90,000,
including salary arrears, penalties under state law for being
discharged without having been paid off, $55,000 in damages,
seven per cent interest from 10 January 1939 and all court
costs. In an initial decision, the director won his breach
of contract lawsuit. (At one time John Barrymore had
signed a contract with Roach to play the lead in ROAD SHOW,
but he became ill and was replaced before filming began by
Adolphe Menjou. The film remade by Hal Roach was released in 1941, an oddball comedy of an escapee from an
asylum traveling with a carnival, enhanced by a cast of old-
time pros and diminished by its obvious low budget.)

Instead of allowing the litigation over $90,000 with
Milestone go to trial--with a good chance of the studio losing the lawsuit--Roach decided to offer part financing of
Milestone's production, OF MICE AND MEN, in lieu of dam-
ages. Milestone's salary, determined as a portion of the
rest of the capital invested, wound up as eighteen per cent
of the gross. Roach estimated that he would break even
and perhaps make some money instead of having to pay off
Milestone in the courts. And so Roach's "best laid plans"
of making ROAD SHOW resulted in the production of the
Steinbeck play as a film.

During the three months before the studio gave Milestone the green light for OF MICE AND MEN (United Artists, 1940), he took on a film project in much the same way he had accepted THE NEW KLONDIKE (Paramount, 1926): Pat O'Brien, loaned to Paramount by Warner Brothers, was idled with the rest of his cast and crew when the script they had been slated for was purchased by another studio at the last moment. Milestone remembered a fist fight at a New York lunch club in the prohibition era, between Walter Catlett and his friend Louis Calhern, that resulted in both of them being barred from the club for life.

The occurrence was used as the opening sequence of the film and Milestone shot it while he and writer Donald Ogden Stewart invented the rest of the tale (making the friends a play's star and its producer), keeping ahead of filming on the script, writing it for the cast at hand.

In an era when the psychological drama was a rare offering on the American screen, Stewart and Milestone attempted a study of the mind of an actor (Pat O'Brien) with specters in the wings, and a guilt complex over an incident that happened eighteen years earlier when he lost his wife and daughter because of his alcoholism. His life begins when he is reunited with his daughter, Olympe Bradna.

For the first half of the melancholy drama, the cast's labor of love (notably Roland Young), the atmosphere of the Lambs Club, and delicately and subtly written passages conceal the melodramatic hokum which emerges at the end when Pat O'Brien witnesses his daughter's triumph on the stage, and dies of a heart ailment in his dressing room. THE NIGHT OF NIGHTS (Paramount, 1939) is an unusually interesting amalgam of good and bad, at its worst in the play within the play, "Laughter," which is supposed to be a smash but in the sampling offered sounds like rubbish. A trade periodical summed it up accurately if unkindly: "generally excellent direction, all-around good production ... better-than-average programmer ... limited appeal."

John Steinbeck's 1937 book had become a hit Broadway play in a version adapted and directed by George Kaufman. Working with screenwriter Eugene Solow, whose previous work ran to titles like THUNDER IN THE NIGHT (Fox, 1935), CRASH DONOVAN (Universal, 1936), and WHILE THE PATIENT SLEPT (First National, 1935), Milestone finished a film adaptation and showed it to Steinbeck, who personally revised it for him.

The difficulties in casting the play are manifest in
every revival including that of 1975.   The only member of
the Broadway cast selected for the film was Leigh Whipper
as the aging black farm worker, although Lon Chaney, Jr.
had played Lennie, the good-hearted, feeble-minded giant on-
stage in California.   When the veteran cowboy actor Bob
Steele walked into Milestone's office, the director thought the
brazen Curley had stepped out of the book.   The husband-
and-wife playwrights Sam and Bella Spewack insisted that
Betty Field, who had appeared in one of their plays, was
the only possible choice for the part of Curley's frivolous,
bored wife.   For the leading role of George, Lennie's
thoughtful guardian, Burgess Meredith brought with him the
poetic, stylized acting he had used in Maxwell Anderson
verse plays on Broadway and in his film debut in WINTER-
SET (RKO, 1936).   Stylization and symbolism is evident in
what Charles Bickford brought, with his strength and presence, to the role of the ranch foreman, Slim.   Milestone
shot quickly, economically, on a modest budget.   As he
would with Louis Gruenberg, Milestone convinced another
distinguished composer to write his first film score, Aaron
Copland.   It remains one of the strongest written in Hollywood, simple and affecting.

The film opens with what may be the first use of a
pre-main title sequence, as two men escape from a posse
by hopping a freight train.   As they slide a panel shut to
conceal their presence, the quotation from Robert Burns
appears on the panel followed by the credits.   From that
point on the adaptation is scrupulously faithful to the play,
but enlarging its space beyond the Salinas Valley ranch to
the fields in which the farm hands husk barley, and the
cafe in town where they spend their pay.   Steinbeck releases
a new quality in Milestone's work, a strong feeling for life
on the farm and the people who inhabit it, presented com-
passionately, allowing even the worst of them a measure of
human dignity.

There are the characteristic Milestone trucking shots,
irresistibly, forcefully moving with or against the action,
bringing their own feeling of inevitability to the unfolding
drama.   Less obvious is the director's use of camera viewpoint within a scene, accenting the shifting struggle of the
moment, both the outward and the inward tensions of the
characters.   The film garnered an Academy nomination for
best picture in a year which included, among other nomi-
nees, THE WIZARD OF OZ, MR. SMITH GOES TO WASH-

INGTON, STAGECOACH, GOODBYE, MR. CHIPS, NINOTCH-
KA, and GONE WITH THE WIND. It is a good picture for
any year, and was in constant release for a dozen years
following its première; a frequent offering early on TV, it
is still a favorite in repertory cinemas today.

At RKO Milestone now got his own producing unit--
his own art director, star (Ronald Colman), and scripter
(playwright John van Druten)--for two light romantic comedies adapted from French boulevard plays.

The first, finally called LUCKY PARTNERS (RKO,
1940), after being known as CHANGE YOUR LUCK in production, manifests nothing characteristically Milestone, except for pans connecting two groups of people in the same
scene to avoid cutting from an action to a reaction shot,
and one insider's joke: when Ginger Rogers' fiancé (Jack
Carson) picks her up to kiss her goodbye, Milestone cuts to
a close-up of her feet not touching the ground, which is
similar to the shot used to signify Betty Field's death by
choking in OF MICE AND MEN. Otherwise, this routine
triangle comedy could have been directed by any one of
dozens of directors who could get the requisite number of
pages of dialogue shot each day.

In an interview with Charles Higham and Joel Greenberg, Milestone said, "this particular pair of comedies were
of the kind you did if you hoped to stay in motion pictures,
in the expectation that the next film might give you a chance
to redeem yourself."

The script was adapted from one of the nearly one
hundred plays Sacha Guitry wrote for himself to perform.
In this one, Bonne Chance, the typical Guitry premise is
capriciously absurd: Colman, a Greenwich Village sketch
artist (with detachable goatee), shares a sweepstakes ticket
winning with a clerk in a bookstore (Rogers) to go on a
"platonic honeymoon" before her marriage to an insurance
agent from Poughkeepsie (Carson).

Although Carson wears glasses identical with those
of Ralph Bellamy's insurance agent in HIS GIRL FRIDAY
(Columbia, 1940) that same year, he is no Bellamy (or bel
ami), and the screenplay cannot compete in the screwball
comedy cycle with THE AWFUL TRUTH (Columbia, 1937)--
the inspiration for its closing courtroom sequence--or with
MY FAVORITE WIFE (RKO, 1940), with which it shares
honeymoon hotel sequences.

Colman and Rogers, exuding their familiar charm, behave as would house guests trying to be pleasant on a long weekend. Ginger looked lovely in a gown by Adrian photographed by her favorite cameraman, but this is not easily confused with entertaining comedy. Dmitri Tiomkin's score judiciously commented on the action in the manner employed frequently by Preston Sturges' later comedies.

In walking a line between the laws of probability and the censors, Milestone, the master of clean, spare story-telling, at times is unable to achieve a coherent continuity amid all the slamming bedroom doors.

The second comedy of the package, MY LIFE WITH CAROLINE (RKO, 1941), derived from a frivolous triangle play by one of Guitry's competitors, Louis Verneuil, was more successful. This time Colman was a rich New York publisher whose work kept him away from his wife (Anna Lee) so that the sculptor next door (Reginald Gardiner) and another sympathetic admirer (Gilbert Roland) have a chance to alienate her affections. The rotund character actor Charles Winninger played Caroline's father.

The acting was polished, the repartee sometimes sophisticated, the direction adroit, and it had a cleverly analyzed musical score. But the end result was static, deadly, with too much reliance on a great deal of flat small talk to carry the mildly amusing comedy.

In neither film is the outcome ever in doubt. Neither Carson nor Gardiner is a serious threat to Colman. In NO MINOR VOICES (M-G-M, 1948), a similar triangle comedy he directed eight years later, Milestone was able to inject more suspense with a more awesome rival to the husband for the wife's affections.

Milestone was asked to collaborate with the émigré Dutch documentary filmmaker Joris Ivens on a documentary to be made from the scant 15,000 feet shot after the Nazis attacked the U.S.S.R. in June of 1941. Milestone felt the subject was worthwhile and agreed. The resulting forty-minute compilation, OUR RUSSIAN FRONT (REPORT FROM RUSSIA), was an "incomplete, but true" account of the Russian war effort.

The commentary, narrated by Walter Huston, notes that "there are no 'noncombatants' in this war," and the film

shows children standing guard while their fathers set out on
secret guerrilla raids and villagers put their homes to the
torch to deny them to the invading armies. The footage was
all taken from actual newsreels. The following year Milestone would be dramatizing similar events in Russia in THE
NORTH STAR (RKO, 1943).

HOSTAGES (Paramount, 1943), THIS LAND IS MINE
(RKO, 1943), HANGMEN ALSO DIE (United Artists, 1943),
THE SEVENTH CROSS (M-G-M, 1944)--in 1942-44 Hollywood
made a number of melodramas about guerrilla resistance to
the Nazis in occupied countries: Yugoslavia, [CHETNICKS,
20th-Fox, 1943]; France, [JOAN OF PARIS, RKO, 1942];
Poland, [NONE SHALL ESCAPE, Columbia, 1944]; Russia,
[DAYS OF GLORY, RKO, 1944], and several set in Norway:
[FIRST COMES COURAGE, Columbia, 1943], [THE MOON IS
DOWN, 20th-Fox, 1943], [THE AVENGERS, Paramount,
1943], [COMMANDOS STRIKE AT DAWN, Columbia, 1942].
Lewis Milestone made two in this cycle, NORTH STAR and
EDGE OF DARKNESS (Warner's, 1943).

EDGE OF DARKNESS was started by Milestone in his
first collaboration with scriptwriter Robert Rossen when
their projected MOBY DICK was scrapped. The unlikely
Norwegians of the cast speak in Rossen's stylized English--
the only Norwegian heard is sung in an anthem--and the
complex tragedy of Norway is reduced to simple melodrama,
but as melodrama it is very often stirring as a classic action morality play.

The film opens with a Nazi patrol boat spotting a
Norwegian flag flying over a supposedly occupied town. Investigating, they find its streets filled with Nazi and Norwegian bodies; the only signs of life are a crazed Norwegian
and the gathering sea gulls. A flashback depicts the events
leading to the carnage: passive resistance of the underground led by Errol Flynn through the burning of the school-
teacher's books; the stealthy discussions in the pews of the
church; the rape by a Nazi soldier of the underground leader's fiancée (Ann Sheridan); the condemned leaders digging
their own graves in the town square; and finally with the aid
of British weapons, the uprising, staged by Milestone with
every cinematic resource available to make it as exciting
as any ever filmed. Exteriors shot near Monterey, in
Northern California, aided the verisimilitude of the Burbank
interiors.

Sam Goldwyn liked EDGE OF DARKNESS and hired Milestone to direct THE NORTH STAR, from an original screenplay Lillian Hellman had prepared with William Wyler, who had enlisted in the Army Air Force in the intervening time. Halfway through the filming, Hellman left the project. Milestone has recalled that much of THE NORTH STAR finally was being dictated by an adamant Goldwyn when he and Milestone saw things differently. Hellman's script (as published) as an uneven "human" drama was converted into a drama of superheroism in a morass of sentimentality.

The title refers to the name of a small Russian village near the Polish border. The peasants are introduced in a leisurely idyllic sequence verging on operetta style, with some festive Russian dancing preceding an air-raid. Each character acts with staggering consistency. Dana Andrews, a Russian pilot with his co-pilot dead and his gunner badly wounded, aims his plane at the center of the advancing German tanks. Jane Withers is fearful until the moment the cache of arms she is guarding is threatened; then she bravely kills half a dozen Germans before a lucky bullet finds her. Moments later, a Nazi hand grenade--the soldier is shot just after he heaves it--lands next to Farley Granger. He has just graduated from secondary school with highest grades and was on his way to accept a scholarship at a Kiev university. Bravely, he makes his way back to his love (Anne Baxter), and that strong woman breaks into tears only when he asks her whether it is day or night.

James Agee found "the all but unprecedented intention ... to show the conduct of the inhabitants ... during the first days of their war ... to show real people involved in realities (with) a minimum of star-spotlight or story" resulted in "one long orgy of ... sugaring [which] infallibly corrupts a good deal of taste, courage, intelligence. "

As in the other occupied countries films, the Nazi atrocities rouse the villagers to an angry determination to rid their land of the invader. "It could have been a good picture," insists Hellman in her autobiography, An Unfinished Woman (Little Brown, 1969), "instead of the big-time, sentimental, badly directed, badly acted mess it turned out to be. "

THE NORTH STAR was not without effective moments characteristic of Milestone at his best: early in the film Andrews had led his group to the safety of a ditch. Those

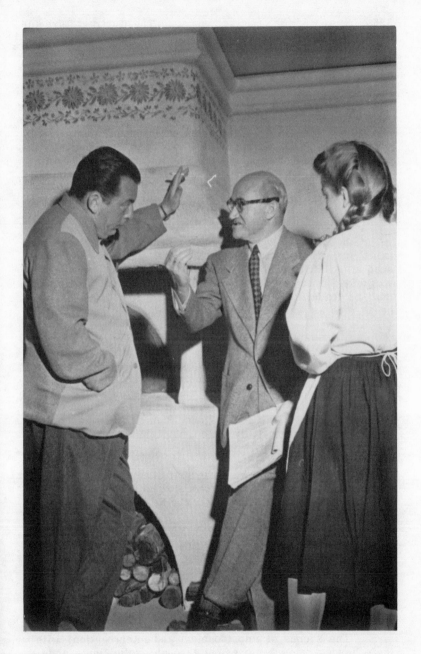

Milestone listening to Sam Goldwyn on how to direct a scene with Anne Baxter for THE NORTH STAR (RKO, 1943). Photo courtesy of the Museum of Modern Art.

who do not heed his warning are killed by the swooping Stukas. As the planes make their last round, Milestone forces us to witness the scene from the viewpoint of those in the ditch. The ear-shattering roar is gone. All is silence. Smoke rises from the overturned, burnt wagon. The frame is filled with a personal awesome discovery of destruction and death. Milestone's camera does not avert its eyes, and he does not cut away but retains the image to allow the audience to feel and to think and to recover a bit.

The later part of the film is too filled with tension and fast action to allow for that reflectiveness which marks much of the best of Milestone's dramas.

In Moscow, the Hollywood conception of Russian peasants was greeted with laughter. When the film was reissued as ARMORED ATTACK in the late 'fifties, a narrator was added over virtually every choral interlude, explaining that the leaders of these Russian people didn't turn out to be as nice as we had thought.

Milestone's last war film, THE PURPLE HEART (20th-Fox, 1944), began with the fact that eight U.S. fliers were captured in China by the Japanese. The drama made from their torture to make them reveal the location of their bases was pure conjecture, but was supported at the time of the film's release by reports of atrocities against war prisoners taken in the Philippines. James Agee found it "well-organized, unusually edged, and solidly acted under Lewis Milestone's direction, his best in years."

Milestone employed as technical advisor, to keep the studio-built Tokyo from becoming surreal, a minister's daughter who had lived in Tokyo during part of the war.

In his autobiography, A Victorian in Orbit (Greenwood Press, 1973), Sir Cedric Hardwicke recounts how tests made of him and C. Aubrey Smith in Oriental make-up as Japanese judges proved so absurd that Oriental actors were hired, including Benson Fong who was perhaps too familiar as Charlie Chan's Number Three Son to be much more real than Hardwicke or Smith.

The scenes of imprisonment and interrogation, with their flowing camera movement through exotic lights and shadows and the deliberate, restrained menace of Richard Loo, combined with the atrocities off-screen into an extra-

ordinary film, hardly less impressive in avoiding monotony
in image and editing within the courtroom sequences.   The
bravado of the ending, in which the sentenced airmen go to
their doom singing "The Army Air Force Song" ("Off we go
into the wild blue yonder") was suggested by studio head
Darryl F. Zanuck.

Lewis Milestone had directed nearly half of an interesting oddity called A GUEST IN THE HOUSE (United
Artists, 1944) when he burst his appendix and was replaced
by John Brahm, with some scenes being shot by Andre de
Toth.   (Some advance synopses carried both names, with
Milestone's later removed.)   The film is a psychological
thriller in which Anne Baxter, as a mentally ill young girl
taken in to live with a family, nearly succeeds in turning
them all against one another; the role has striking similarities to her character in ALL ABOUT EVE (20th-Fox, 1950).

Contemporary critics applauded the film's thoughtful
conception and its appreciation of the subtle interaction of
person and event.   The interaction of performers, camera,
and editing was unusually expressive and almost overcame a
disappointingly anticlimactic ending.   Milestone has said that
his conception differed with Brahm's in that while he wished
to scare the characters, Brahm wished to scare the audience.   Uneven editing indicated the signs of the changing
conception throughout the melodrama.

Milestone's next film, A WALK IN THE SUN (20th-
Fox, 1946), was made independently, and is at once a most
stylized and an honest war film.   Here is war not as excitement and ultimate triumph--there are no large-scale
battles and the face of the enemy is never seen--but war
as infinitely boring and unrelated to a larger view.   In trying to solve the problem of conveying the gist of the de-
scriptive passages in Harry Joe Brown's book without adding
to the dialogue, Milestone hit upon using the ballads sung
on the soundtrack to express the "inner voice" of the action.
"They came across the sea/to sunny Italy/to take a little
walk in the sun. "

Its non-heroic, semi-documentary style submerged
not only its well-known leads, such as Milestone's friend
Dana Andrews, but even familiar comedy actors like Huntz
Hall and Sterling Holloway in differentiated characterizations of foot soldiers moving in and out of the camera's
range.

The title derives from its span of time and action:
a few hours from the landing of the Lee Platoon of the Texas
Division at Salerno in 1943, until they achieve their military
objective, the taking of a farmhouse held by the Nazis six
miles into the country.

From the beginning, in its movement of camera and
men, the film is worked out with meticulous care: the landing in darkness is filmed with a left-to-right sweep of the
boats moving toward the beach. A shell hits the boat; an
officer is badly hurt; the medic (Sterling Holloway) is called
over to pronounce the man dead. We never see the man
before he dies. The reactions of the infantrymen to the
death, in a characteristic Milestone series of close-ups,
serve to introduce the approach and mood which will remain
consistent to the end of the film. After the landing, the
medic meets the sergeant (Dana Andrews) on the beach front.
Their ensuing discussion of war is reminiscent of ALL
QUIET ON THE WESTERN FRONT: as yet they have not
seen war, only experienced its sound. Milestone uses the
soundtrack as a total resource, rather than as subsidiary to
the visual element. The bombing is not seen, but smoke
rises over the dune between them and the sea. The medic
climbs the dune to witness the bombardment. As he saunters
back, smiling, an enemy plane passes over, strafing the
ground, killing the medic. There is a cut to the plane
shooting at the platoon which has taken cover in a wooded
area. When all is silent, the camera pans, right-to-left,
over the immobile soldiers lying on the beach and a second
ballad begins.

These first twenty minutes presage nearly everything
that will happen in the remaining action. Each soldier of
the platoon is differentiated, but not in the hackneyed stereo-
types of a BATAAN (M-G-M, 1943) or GUADALCANAL DI-
ARY (20th-Fox, 1943), in the usual repetitive banter among
soldiers and in "stream-of-consciousness" thoughts on the
track.

Upon subsequent viewings, A WALK IN THE SUN's
values may seem to shift: those who once found its literary
stylization embarrassing may now find it sensitive and lyri-
cal; those who once found it a poetic revelation of what the
cinema could do beyond the conventional action film may now
find it artificial. It remains an ambitious, touching, and
distinguished attempt to show the average man's war.

Rossen, in an interview with Henry Burton, recalled
the initial difficulty selling it to a distributor: "It's good,
but it won't make a dime." The film was first previewed
in a factory district in New Jersey where it was received
enthusiastically. According to Rossen, its conscious lack of
heroics pointed up the real heroism of the average G.I. for
the preview audience. Rossen said that he and Milestone
agreed on the concept and worked harmoniously on the film.

Rossen's interests become more pronounced in a
third, final collaboration with Milestone, a film for Hal Wallis from a story, Bleeding Heart, finally titled THE
STRANGE LOVE OF MARTHA IVERS (Paramount, 1946).

Wallis had liked A WALK IN THE SUN so much that
he asked Milestone to do a film for him. The last of six
properties offered by Wallis was selected by Milestone for
adaptation, and was developed from the prologue of the story
into an original screenplay with Rossen. The result would
be a film redolent of its time, a dramatic sensation of its
year, and a striking contribution to what has come to be
known as film noir.

In a 1975 list of "Great Movies to Watch for on TV,"
Howard Thompson of the New York Times wrote, "the silly
title makes it sound like trash, which it certainly is not ...
strong, original material--what a plot! ... taut, sizzling
melodrama ... well-played, ugly as sin...."

Van Heflin, returning to filmmaking from three years
in the Air Force, portrays a professional gambler returning
to an industrial town he'd once lived in. He uncovers a
dark secret of his childhood companions who now run the
town. Milestone quickly established the Heflin character's
past by having the actor manipulate a half-dollar to and fro
across his knuckles (as might be done in casinos in Las
Vegas) while delivering his dialogue.

Kirk Douglas, in his film debut, was "cast against
type" as the alcoholic weakling who is bound to his dominat-
ing wife by the secret they shared. His complex, sometimes charming villain lends credence to the improbable
chain of murder, assault, extortion, and frame-ups which
ends in the suicide of husband and wife. That ending occurred to the director remembering the true story of a
Hell's Kitchen hood who'd saved his life by thrusting his
thumb against the trigger of a gun pointed at him and firing
the gun himself, but diverting it from any vital spot.

In the title role, Barbara Stanwyck, as the New York Times noted, "is twice the hard-boiled lustful vixen that she played in DOUBLE INDEMNITY [Paramount, 1944]."

Milestone and the cast rehearsed for two weeks before shooting began, to give the cast time to finish individual characterizations and to mesh them to make the dramatization coalesce. (Milestone had also worked as a stage director; this part of his preparation resembles the four weeks of rehearsal before a stage play opens.)

Besides his work with actors and incidents, Milestone lent credibility to the melodrama with a detached, almost uninvolved camera fluidly tracking the reptilian inhabitants of the Pennsylvania town (e.g., his camera holds for a long time while Stanwyck dresses Douglas' wounded hand, so the audience absorbs her capability, hatred). He varies this approach only in the scenes of budding romance between the itinerant gambler, Heflin, and the girl just released from jail. Lizabeth Scott, a Hal Wallis protégé in her second film, gives a sultry but restrained portrait of an emotionally scarred but resourceful woman while delivering some of the film's weakest lines.

To suggest the Scott character's worry about losing Heflin to Stanwyck, Milestone has her repeat a bit of business given Madeleine Carroll in THE GENERAL DIED AT DAWN: a row of stubbed-out cigarettes lined up on a windowsill, to indicate simultaneously the amount of time which has elapsed and her mental state.

THE STRANGE LOVE OF MARTHA IVERS shares with such prestige high budget dramas of the 'forties as KING'S ROW (Warner's, 1942) and ONE FOOT IN HEAVEN (Warner's, 1941), a smoothness of camera movement and transitional devices as an "ideal": the finesse of an optical wipe traveling through the frame at the same speed as a taxi to reveal the next scene; a crane shot which includes three buses and the principals in one boomdown to the Iverstown bus terminal, a locale which will be important again in a later scene. It breaks with those glossy, early 'forties dramas, however, in its unrelenting suspense and lacerating detailing of ethical and physical corruption.

In the scene in which Heflin and Scott meet for the first time there are some awkward shifts of camera position from shot to shot, on the steps of the boarding house and inside a cafe, which are uncharacteristic of Milestone's usually smooth continuity and clean cutting--but these may be the result of Wallis' insertion of large close-ups of his newest star into the continuity after Milestone had completed the director's cut and had left the Paramount studios.

For the obligatory scene of Heflin being beaten up, there is a fresh handling. We assume that it will happen off screen, because the camera stays with Lizabeth Scott after Heflin and his attackers leave, focusing on her self-hatred because of her knowing part in the entrapment. We empathize with her, and see, from her point of view as she leaves the restaurant, a glimpse through the rear window of a passing car of Heflin's bloodied face as he receives another blow, partly obscured and quickly passing out of sight. In this way one of the most ritualized and repeated scenes in film melodrama is given a very personal meaning.

Because of his identification with Remarque's ALL QUIET ON THE WESTERN FRONT, Enterprise Studios asked Milestone to direct a film version of Remarque's novel, ARCH OF TRIUMPH. Milestone found the book very interesting and agreed. The script he developed with Harry Joe Brown indicated that the finished film would run four hours. He asked for time to condense it before shooting but the studio refused: a recent reissue of GONE WITH THE WIND (M-G-M, 1939) had convinced them that length was no problem for a big film. With Ingrid Bergman and Charles Boyer to star in a well-known expensive property, the scale of the production had to be commensurate with the importance of the project. Before the film was released, after a long exploitation build-up, plans for road-showing it were abandoned and the condensation took place in the editing room. The three-and-one-half-hour drama was cut to 137 minutes in Britain, and to 120 minutes in the United States.

The ending of the novel had involved mercy-killing, a taboo subject for the screen at the time, and was changed. Elsewhere the film was less frank than the book. The background of appeasement-era Paris of 1938, teeming with political refugees with no hope and no future, was barely suggested in the version released, which subordinated it to the tragic love story of the two stars. The parts of Ruth Warrick, as an American dilettante, and Charles Laughton as a bestial Nazi menace were drastically shortened in the re-editing. Milestone's friend, Hollywood restauranteur Mike Romanoff, plays himself as the host of the French night club

Scheherezade of Montmartre; the famed basso, Feodor Chali-
apin, who had lost his singing voice following the completion
of Pabst's three-version film, DON QUIXOTE, has an impressive bit as Romanoff's chief chef. Louis Calhern, as a
former White Russian colonel reduced to the post of night
club doorman who is Boyer's confidant, injects some wry
humor and human warmth into the somber story of "the new
European citizen--the refugee without a passport, who has
lost his membership in the human race. "

        ARCH OF TRIUMPH (United Artists, 1948) may have
been originally intended to repeat the mood and success of
Bergman's earlier film, CASABLANCA (Warner's, 1943).
There is great depth of feeling evident in the chiaroscuro
close-ups of Boyer as the trench-coated surgeon and Bergman as the bereted prostitute with dangling cigarette, but
there is an imbalance between the solitary, doomed romance
and the epic setting of a collapsing world. Milestone attempts to avoid a dramatically static quality with a constantly roving camera, and to simulate action with frequent cutting.   These polished techniques cannot conceal the film's
problems. Wrote Otis Guernsey: "[He is] unable to make
an emotion out of a close-up of a gun ... a statuette, a
bunch of flowers. "

        The strong, much-praised musical score was by Louis
Gruenberg, the Russian-born composer prominent for his
operas in the 'thirties, and later for the scores for such
films as THE FIGHT FOR LIFE (Columbia, 1940), SO ENDS
OUR NIGHT (United Artists, 1941), COMMANDOS STRIKE
AT DAWN (Columbia, 1942), and COUNTER-ATTACK (Columbia, 1945).   The plaintive gypsy tunes in the Russian
night club, the subdued melodies, counterpointed with pelting
rain, help to sustain the tragic aura of the film.

        ARCH OF TRIUMPH grossed $1,428,490 in the
United States.   It had cost four million.

        As early as 1946 Lewis Milestone had been attacked
as a leftist by California "Red"-hunters.   He had subsequently been one of the nineteen "unfriendly" filmmakers
called to testify by the House UnAmerican Committee who
declined to "name names, " in November 1946.

        On 12 April 1948, in a curtain speech after his anti-
Communist play premièred in Los Angeles, Myron Fagan
stated that Lewis Milestone had given a party at his home

in September 1947 at which a known leftist had attended.
Hedda Hopper (who appeared in THE CAVEMAN, directed by
Milestone, in her days as an actress) picked up the story in
her gossip column: "Milestone ... born in Chisinau, Russia,
came to this country many years ago. He found many
friends here ... he has a beautiful home in which he holds
leftish rallies, is married to an American, has made a fortune here. But his heart seems to yearn for Russia...."

Unlike others, Milestone kept working during the
"blacklisting" period, but one can only guess to what extent
the charges and his stand affected his career.

NO MINOR VOICES (M-G-M, 1948) was "a little
comedy ... that we tossed off for Enterprise because they
wanted to keep the gates open," Milestone has said. Enterprise was defunct by the time the film opened in New York,
but the comedy produced and directed by Milestone played
art theatres for a number of years thereafter.

The triangle comedy is an early spoof of the psycho-
analytic craze which may have begun with BLIND ALIBI
(Columbia, 1939) and its god-like psychoanalyst, and which
swept the movies in the mid-'forties in the wake of the success of Hitchcock's SPELLBOUND (United Artists, 1945).

In NO MINOR VOICES, the psychoanalytically-oriented
pediatrician (Dana Andrews) is less than god-like, and is
nearly foiled by his jealous instincts, which are engendered
by a painter's (Louis Jourdan) attentions to his wife (Lilli
Palmer).

Unlike the no-contest triangles of LUCKY PARTNERS
and MY LIFE WITH CAROLINE, Jourdan is a worthy rival
for Andrews. Palmer sees through Jourdan, but finds a
great deal of charm in his unconventional artist's view of
life. Each major character has a stream-of-consciousness
soliloquy (heralded by the ringing of bells) which the New
York Times labeled "cubist humor, spoofing à la Gertrude
Stein." Milestone further accents the mind and will of each
with witty blocking and framing and his characteristic pans
from character to character to avoid the harder "feel" of a
cut.

A breakfast-table scene involving the three begins
with cross-cutting between Palmer and Andrews, with Jourdan in every other shot, although he is but a silent witness

to an argument between husband and wife. The impression
is of speed and utility, cut very tightly within spoken phrases,
accenting the emotions the characters keep just below the
surface.

The artist sketches the other characters as they will
become in the future. The denouement finds Andrews looking
at Jourdan's portrait of his wife with a child. He under-
stands what has been lacking in their marriage. The couple
embrace. Jourdan gives his exit line: "The pain is so exquisite, I could live on it for years." The cigar-maker,
who rolls his cigars at his window adjacent to the doctor's
office, and who has witnessed most of the action, draws his
own conclusion: "Everyone sees what they have to see."

Says Milestone, "We had a lot of fun with it. Jourdan showed great promise as a light comedian (even then). "

"Three good main performances in the grand, sweeping style," acknowledged the New York Times critic. "The
ingredients of this long-drawn-out domestic comedy promise
well enough," said Monthly Film Bulletin, "but the handling
of them is over-elaborate. "

Perhaps. But if the fun wears thin before the comedy is over, the fault is more in the script by Arnold Man-
off than in Milestone's realization of it.

"Then I did a much more personal film," recalls
Milestone, "THE RED PONY [Republic, 1949]. " Three of
John Steinbeck's tales, published in a volume of short
stories, The Long Valley, were fitted together to form the
basis of the homespun family drama: "The Promise," about
a mare and a colt owned by the hired man, Billy Buck
(Robert Mitchum); "Leader of the People," about the boy's
grandfather, the garrulous teller of tall tales of the vanished
frontier (Louis Calhern); and "The Gift," an episode in the
maturing personality of the nine-year-old boy (Peter Miles,
the brother of Gigi Perreau, taking his screen name from
the first syllable of Milestone's) whose first knowledge of
tragedy is the death of his beloved pony. To complete the
revelations on relationships in the family, the screenplay
adds a suppressed conflict between his parents which is not
in the previous work of Steinbeck, but was added in his
screenplay adaptation. Shepperd Strudwick is the brooding
father, unreconciled to the grandfather and to his neighbors.
Myrna Loy (whose screen debut had been in Milestone's

THE CAVEMAN) is the cool, tactful mother. The motiva-
tion for these characters is less well-developed than the episodes of the boy and the pony and his faith in the wisdom of
the hired man, which is shattered by the pony's death.

Milestone presents Robert Mitchum with the Motion Picture
Reader Award while they were making THE RED PONY (Republic, 1939).   Photo courtesy of Movie Star News.

Here, at last, one feels Milestone has full independence and full confidence in what he wishes to reveal to
us and his ability to realize it.   There is no artificial cinematic adrenalin injected for fear of losing an audience's attention.   With the exception of the bloody fight between the
buzzard and the boy for the corpse of the pony--criticized
for its violence and horror by those who felt it exceeded
the boundaries of what they mistook for a "children's" pic-
ture--quiet reflection is the tone of the drama.   In retrospect, it seems akin to Michelangelo Antonioni's LA NOTTE
(1961), in eschewing the blandishments of commercial cinema

to concentrate upon what the filmmaker wishes us to consider, without hedging his bet, in any way, on the intelligence and sensitivity of the audience.

Robert Mitchum's laconic Billy Buck is one of his
most sincere, sensitive screen portrayals. Aaron Copland's
wistful, endearing score has become a concert perennial (and
is given a "set piece" of its own in the episode in which the
boy fantasizes himself at the head of a magical parade down
the country lane and into the center ring of a circus tent).

By "Hollywood kid actor" standards, young Peter
Miles is remarkable: unsentimental, restrained, subtle,
although one can imagine an ideal performance with more
flexibility. Only the neighborhood children who tease him--
Beau Bridges, whom Milestone had used earlier in NO MI-
NOR VOICES, is among them--are central-casting-cute, and
remind us of all those other movies (including Disney's SO
DEAR TO MY HEART, in release at the same time) which
seem excessively sentimental by comparison.

The death of the red pony shifts the relationships
among all those who live on the ranch to an uneasy reconcil-
iation and acceptance. Adults must helplessly watch the disillusionment of a boy first discovering the implacability of
nature, the sorrow of aging, and the fallibility of men. And
Milestone, working in color for the first time, brings a subdued glow to the cherished California ranch that marked the
sun-scorched sepia monochrome in OF MICE AND MEN five
years earlier.

In the first of three films for Fox, HALLS OF MON-
TEZUMA (20th-Fox, 1951), Milestone returned to the concerns of his earlier war pictures, the relationships within a
small group of men. When a drug-dependent lieutenant
(Richard Widmark) leads his Marine platoon ashore in a
beachhead attack on a Japanese-held island (Okinawa), he
discovers an unexpected rocket defense which must be located and destroyed within twenty-four hours or it will wipe
out the general attack to take place the next day.

Much of the film depicts the harrowing experiences
of the detail which is ordered forward to capture Japanese
soldiers holed up in a cave, and bring them back for questioning about the rocket launching base.

Flashbacks of the soldiers' civilian pasts are smoothly

integrated, but not as effectively as the dialogue-in-the-
present-which-summoned-up-the-past in A WALK IN THE
SUN.   Nevertheless the writing is capable throughout.   The
somewhat foppish Sgt. Johnson (Reginald Gardiner) is a well-
acted, highly original characterization, and Karl Malden and
Richard Boone (in his film debut) are impressive among a
good cast.

A heightened use of naturalistic sound, shrieking shells,
and well-motivated lighting (in uneven color cinematography)
sustain a "real" feeling of the emphasized brutality and horror of war: flame-throwing tanks; gory hand-to-hand combat;
full minutes of hysterical fear.   Only in the suspenseful interrogation scenes in the last minutes of the film does the
picture look as if it were shot in a studio.

The most disturbing aspect of HALLS OF MONTE-
ZUMA (for those who consider ALL QUIET ON THE WEST-
ERN FRONT the cinema's greatest pacifist statement) is its
amalgam of Milestone's long-term concerns with the elements of the Technicolored recruiting-poster sort of service
tribute film: the "title song" blasts away at the beginning
as the Marines land, and again as smiling Marines march
into battle in the stirring finale.   Before the ending, the
letter of a dead soldier is read aloud, reassuring us that although war is hell, America must be strong and God is on
our side.   It is a long way from A WALK IN THE SUN.

A great commercial success of the previous year was
KING SOLOMON'S MINES (M-G-M, 1950), shot on location
in Africa, and ending with a spectacular brushfire and animal stampede.   Fox apparently hoped to duplicate its success,
as well as make use of its funds "frozen" in Australia,
when in 1951 it sent a unit out to South Australia headed by
Milestone to film KANGAROO (20th-Fox, 1952), the first
U.S. film made in that country.

The script handed Milestone was standard Western
hokum, even mustier than the H. Rider Haggard source of
the M-G-M film.   For a time Milestone urged the studio (now
9,200 miles away) to scrap it in favor of either LAND TAK-
ERS or INHERITORS, novels by the famed Australian journalist Brian Penton, which were full of the real history of
Australia.   The studio replied with a variation of Thomas
Ince's "shoot as written," and Milestone could do little more
than emphasize the epic drought and local color, and limit
the screen time devoted to the impersonation-for-purposes-

of-swindling plot. His use of fine Australian character actors such as "Chips" Rafferty in supporting roles was self-
defeating, in that it threw into sharp relief the unbelievabil-
ity of Peter Lawford (English), Maureen O'Hara (Irish), Finlay Currie (Scottish), and Richard Boone (American) in the
leading roles, and the tenacious aura of Beverly Hills in the
script.

Milestone contented himself with shooting the nineteenth-century tale in as many authentic, historic locations
as possible, in Sydney in poorly employed Technicolor and
against the rugged, exotic background of Flinders Range,
east of Lake Torrens, 3,900 feet above sea level, and in
carrying the use of natural sound to a point where it dis-
pensed with much of the dialogue.

KANGAROO was filled with set-pieces: a bull-whip
fight between two bushrangers (which was absent from the
original script); a Corroboree rain dance by thirsty aborigi-
nal bushmen; a blistering dust storm; a struggle with a wind-
mill whirling out of control; a cattle stampede in the (obligatory) brushfire. A second unit supplied shots of wild kan-
garoos leaping grandly, of mean, wriggling snakes, and assorted Australian scenics.

The sequence which is Milestone's favorite, and is
easily the best in the adventure, comes mid-way: a realistically conceived cattle drive to water during a desperate
drought. Milestone conveys vividly the anguish and frustra-
tion of the cowboys as the "mob" dwindles. Gruesome shots
of cattle dropping, their drivers drooping in the very hot,
dusty air, involve the audience in the painful, physically
and mentally exhausting effort in tough, admirably cinematic
terms.

KANGAROO was released in June 1952 without benefit of previews or re-editing. It was a commercial failure,
even in Fox's chain of theatres in Australia.

LES MISERABLES had been a 1935 success of Zanuck's. Despite the 1951 release of an Italian version by
Riccardo Freda, Milestone was assigned to remake it in
1952. The best known novel of Victor Hugo is partly a historical adventure tale, partly a damning trenchant treatise
on shocking social conditions; it provides enough incidents
for two or three films but in this (estimated to be the ninth
film version) the same incidents (e.g., "The Bishop's Can-

dlesticks") are dramatized again, neither superior nor inferior to the last interpretation.

The strategy of leaping from one famous scene to another, to cover the basic story-line in a scant hour-and-a-
half, works against the believability of Javert's conversion
and suicide at the end, as well as against less critical moments. Milestone had thought Charles Laughton's Javert
"hammy," and the performance he elicits from Robert New-
ton in the same role is uncharacteristically subdued, if still
arch and theatrical.

Milestone steers a middle course between colorful
costume adventure and stark morality drama, employing expert production mounting and skillful model work and a large
cast of familiar Fox players: from the resolute, if monoto-
nous Valjean (Michael Rennie) to the nubile Cosette (Debra
Paget), the sturdy Cameron Mitchell, and Sylvia Sidney, affecting as the dying Fantine.

There are effective cameos by Joseph Wiseman as a
convict; James Robertson Justice as a confidant of Valjean;
Elsa Lancaster as the bishop's unimaginative housekeeper.
But the most moving and precise scene is that with Edmund
Gwenn as the simple charitable bishop.

In the manner of an "illustrated classic," Milestone
extracts the story-line faithfully from the book rather than
the motivations of the characters. There are brisk scenes
of revolutionaries at the barricades, a chase through the at-
mospheric sewers of Paris. (At this point in his novel,
Hugo wrote a five-chapter treatise on the horrors of the
Paris sewers.) Milestone, not allowed to dramatize the
less familiar incidents of the book, looked upon the project
as "just a job" to do and get it over with.

The next film took him to England. MELBA (United
Artists, 1953) seems to have been an effort to duplicate the
success of the British biographical musical of that year,
THE GREAT GILBERT AND SULLIVAN, with which it
shared an outsized characterization by Robert Morley. On
a modest budget, shooting in historic London locations (such
as in Fire Lane, in a building once owned by the Roth-
schilds), Milestone mounted the biographical yarn with elaborate Technicolor, period decoration, and beautiful gowns
which showed his star, the twenty-seven-year-old opera so-
prano, elfin Patrice Munsel, to flattering histrionic and
musical advantage.

The clumsy script eschewed the facts of Dame Nellie
Melba's life--which could have made for absorbing drama--
and settled for a banal rearrangement of the clichés employed in a dozen "singer films" in the Mary Ellis era
twenty years earlier, freshened only by the dramatization of
the inspiration for Peach Melba (but not melba toast).   MEL-
BA opens with the opera star at Windsor Castle singing a request for Queen Victoria (Dame Sybil Thorndike), "Comin'
Through the Rye." She tells the queen the story of her life,
beginning with a flashback to the ranch in Australia.   (Did
KANGAROO get Milestone this job?)

This entry for the art houses relies for its entertainment on the outrageously theatrical impressario, Oscar Hammerstein (Robert Morley), and the larger-than-life Martita
Hunt, a bit of a ballet, and Munsel singing coloratura arias
from eight operas, a new popular song, and last, Mendels-
sohn's "On Wings of Song." The film grossed $269,491 in
the U.S.   Milestone dismisses it as a pot-boiler.

Milestone's second British film, THEY WHO DARE
(Associated Artists, 1955), was more successful, based on a
true occurrence of a trial expedition of World War II to raid
Nazi air bases in Greece.   Its theme bore similarities to
that of A WALK IN THE SUN: four men and how they react under great strain.   As in NO MINOR VOICES there is
an artist sketching caricatures of the officer in charge of
the raid (Dirk Bogarde).

As straight action melodrama, the film is too vague
in the working-out of its details of the strike at the Aegean
Luftwaffe bases and the rescue by submarine.   It is hindered
in its character delineation by the acting of Dirk Bogarde as
a raw young officer who switches unconvincingly from feeling
sorry for himself to a boundless optimism unwarranted by
his predicament, and by Denholm Elliott as a responsibility-
shirking skeptic whose hysterical collapse while awaiting the
submarine on the beach does not ring true.

But in many sequences, such as an escape over the
Greek hills, the script is serviceable and Milestone's eco-
nomical direction (with its connecting pans to reduce the
need for distracting cuts: expressive two-shots and three-
shots, fluid use of dissolves, and optical wipes) is a model
of efficient storytelling.

The same year he directed an Italian/American co-

production known there as LA VEDROVA X (1955) and here
as THE WIDOW, a soap-opera triangle from a Susan York
novel. British box office favorite of the 'forties, Patricia
Roc, is the widow of a European nobleman in love with a
younger man (Massimo Serato), a sportscar racer. She deliberately introduces him to a younger woman (played by a
sensitive rising dramatic actress who had been praised by
Anna Magnani, Anna Maria Ferrero) in order to prove to
him her own superiority. The tragic consequences are fore-
shadowed from the beginning and the materials are familiar,
but sensitive and restrained acting from the principals and
the supporting character actors (notably Akim Tamiroff and
Leonardo Botta) and Milestone's relatively fresh, imagina-
tive treatment make much of the high-powered romance,
which is compelling, if uneven and meandering.

The film, released in the U.S.A. by an art house
distributor of foreign films, apparently got few bookings.
The lone motion picture trade paper review was made on the
basis of a screening at a theatre in Hartford, Connecticut in
1957.

Milestone accepted television work back in California:
two dramas starring his old friend Richard Boone whose
"Palladin" character had origins in his role in KANGAROO
and two ALFRED HITCHCOCK PRESENTS. For Hitchcock's
former associate, Joan Harrison (first a feature film producer, then a TV film producer), Milestone directed a special in the SUSPENSE series. Reportedly he even tried a
car commercial to find out what it was like.

He spent a good deal of time preparing with Kirk
Douglas an epic of CITIZEN KANE-scope called KING KELLY,
which was never produced.

His next excursion into feature films would again be
a war film, again taking place in a limited area, with a
clearly defined military objective. But this was the "police
action" of Korea; some of the rules had changed. Despite
changes made after his departure, PORK CHOP HILL (United
Artists, 1959) would be one of his most courageous, most
thoughtful films.

The source of the film was a book by General S. L.
A. Marshall, U.S.A.R., one of the most distinguished military writers of the time, who used the technique of interviewing soldiers soon after a battle for their experiences.

A new dimension has been added to those familiar in Milestone films from the onset of World War II: a Red loud-
speaker reaches the ears of the UN infantrymen with re-
minders of the peace talks less than seventy miles away at
Panmunjon, playing of taps for dead comrades, and a recording of "Autumn in New York," as part of the psychological brainwashing attempt. The military objective, the hill,
is strategically irrelevant, except psychologically.

The usually heroic black actor Woody Strode is cast
against type as a slacker trying to desert under fire who
threatens to kill his commanding officer (Gregory Peck), who,
himself, is not a stock war film hero but a human, doubting,
uncertain lieutenant with a short life expectancy in battle.
Other solid actors, not yet too familiar on the theatre screen,
include George Peppard, Rip Torn, Harry Guardino, and
seem like real soldiers. In the attack on Pork Chop Hill,
the foolhardy bravery of some (Robert Blake, in a role for
which he thanked Milestone in a 1975 Emmy acceptance
speech) is contrasted with some who are so disorganized
they fail to fire a shot. It is not possible to complain, as
James Agee did of A WALK IN THE SUN, that its movement
and shooting "is worked out with ... vitality and care ...
more nearly related to ballet than to warfare." Here the
confusion of exactly what is going on in a given moment
makes what is seen more convincing. PORK CHOP HILL is
arguably a new kind of war film. Flaws exist; a holdover
from an earlier style of filmmaking is the implacably
smooth, flowing camera-tracking (which seems fake after
the hand-held, tremor-ridden combat photography common on
TV news of the Vietnamese war) and a tendency to take a
"God's eye view" of action seen in mid-ground or in long-
shot, which removes us too easily from identifying with the
combatants. The moment of death is still depicted with a
stuntman's flip-flop, no advance over SERGEANT YORK
(Warner's, 1941).

But its power is undeniable. A soldier, wounded by
a grenade, screams for help. As he is dragged to safety,
the camera does not move but holds on the remainder of
his severed leg. Soldiers caught in breaching the first line
of barbed wire yell to others to advance by climbing over
them. (That kind of sacrifice, when shown by the enemy,
was cited by Americans to prove the enemy's disregard for
human life.)

Although the release cut does not retain Milestone's

intended crosscutting throughout from the peace talks to the
hill and back, most of Milestone's conception is intact.
Those who find the psychological tension less than exhilarating miss his determination to remove the mock heroics from
the grim, realistic tale, to show in a military action so
ironic as to reach the absurd the courage men can bring
forth to die for a cause they but dimly understand, for an
objective they know to be completely pointless. The large
questions of the nature of war in our time are raised, and
the rationalizations spoken in the film's closing moments do
not sweep them away.

PORK CHOP HILL, released in 1959, grossed
$1,845,962 in the United States and $1,737,571 abroad.

The following year Milestone directed Frank Sinatra's
clan (playing themselves) in a spoof of a heist of Las Vegas'
five largest gambling joints on New Year's Eve. Even in a
time when the "caper" film had not yet reached epidemic pro-
portions, OCEAN'S ELEVEN (Warner's, 1960) was too long
in its one-hundred-and-twenty-seven minutes for optimum
comic pace. The robbery is delayed to make room for "in"
jokes among the members of the Rat Pack, and for cameos
by Shirley MacLaine, Red Skelton, George Raft, and Angie
Dickinson. The surprise twist which ends the picture is
clever, but arises not from the preceding film but from left
field.

In trying to combine straight melodrama with personality turns one step away from musical comedy, Milestone
had let his cast indulge themselves in unmotivated behavior
that cancels out any absorption in the raid itself. But Ilka
Chase, Cesar Romero, and the dependable Akim Tamiroff
built amusing characterizations, and the authentic settings
(filmed at the Copa Room of the Sands Hotel while Sinatra,
Lawford, Dean Martin, and Sammy Davis, Jr. were appearing there) reach a new high for loud, saturated Eastmancolor. It offers something for everybody (even witty lines).

After completion of only a seven-minute scene, Sir
Carol Reed left the production of MUTINY ON THE BOUNTY
(M-G-M, 1962) and Eric Ambler's script went with him.
Milestone assumed the director's chair in February of 1961.
He was in Tahiti for more than four months, and was on
the film for a year. The only script he saw was by Charles
Lederer, and it changed sometimes from day to day as it
was rewritten by other scenarists, Borden Chase, Ben Hecht,

John Gay, William L. Driscoll, the film's star, Marlon
Brando, and the president and the production chief of M-G-M.

Both Brando and Milestone have acquired reputations
for being difficult and their work methods and temperaments
are totally opposed. M-G-M had given Milestone command
of the production and Brando command of himself. The
Saturday Evening Post of 16 June 1962 allotted a great deal
of space to Milestone's side of the story, and may have begun a legend which has now evolved in Hollywood about cost
overruns on the film and Brando's part in them: an estimated ten million over its ten million budget. Brando pointed
out bad weather, lack of a suitable script, illnesses, mis-
understandings.

By October 1961, when Fletcher Christian's death
scene was being shot to end the film, Milestone sat in his
office and Brando reportedly directed himself, as he had
throughout the film. (Milestone, and Reed before him, directed the other actors in the other scenes). The film was
a year over its estimated shooting schedule.

Milestone suffered long lapses in the continuity and
filming: characters appear and disappear without a reason,
connecting threads have been chopped out, spectacular episode follows spectacular episode without a moment to think
(no doubt, a deliberate strategy), and there is awesome cinematography, physical mounting, and special effects work.
But the direction is faceless, without a point of view other
than the ubiquitous presence of Brando's Fletcher Christian,
a performance which Milestone has called "horrible."

In connection with MUTINY ON THE BOUNTY, Mile-
stone was afflicted with a disorder that affects his ability to
walk without pain.

In March 1963 Milestone replaced Raoul Walsh on
PT 109 (Warner's 1963) while the story of John F. Kennedy's
experiences as a Navy lieutenant in World War II was in
preproduction. Filming started 27 June under the personal
supervision of Jack L. Warner who fired Milestone on 21
July, claiming "satisfactory progress was not being made."
Milestone, in a press conference, insisted that the script
was not good enough. The resulting film did not refute his
opinion.

In 1965, Milestone was announced as director of the

English story of the three-sketch international espionage melodrama, THE SECRET WAR, a French-German-British co-production, filmed in Germany, Italy, and Africa, and eventually released in the U.S. in 1966 as THE DIRTY GAME. The British segment, full of James Bond gimmickry, starring Henry Fonda as the Russian scientist, "Kourlov," was directed instead by Terence Young, a veteran of James Bond films.

Since then Milestone has directed an episode of the ninety-minute, two-part TV series, ARREST AND TRIAL, "to see how Universal lives," which is "slavery." It was different at Universal for a brief moment when a motion picture was made called ALL QUIET ON THE WESTERN FRONT....

Lewis Milestone's career has been among the most uneven of the major Hollywood directors. His difficulty with huge studios seems to stem from his early association with David O. Selznick, during which he would have had to be responsible for seven films a year. There have been other causes; his independent spirit and reputation for demanding his own way on the set at all times. From the time of ALL QUIET ON THE WESTERN FRONT, some of Milestone's best work has been in war films (though not perhaps THE NORTH STAR, THE PURPLE HEART, nor THE HALLS OF MONTE-ZUMA). A WALK IN THE SUN and PORK CHOP HILL were very advanced independent productions and quite imbued with Milestone's strongest characteristics. A well-constructed script and effective editing were his forte, though the lack thereof seemed to mark his failure at the large studios with RAIN, LUCKY PARTNERS, THE NORTH STAR, KANGAROO, etc. He had tried to make personal films, but the subordinate role he was forced to take under powerful producers made him direct the way he was hired to direct, and to leave rather than fight inch by inch for his first cut of the film. OF MICE AND MEN and THE RED PONY are indicative, again, of the steady hand he was capable of showing in a personal project, but it was only occasionally that he could overcome the mediocrity of the assigned properties with his solid craftsmanship.

The story of Milestone is a story of Hollywood. The sound version of ALL QUIET ON THE WESTERN FRONT remains strong, but the silent version--it still exists--is exceptional. The pacing, the fluidity of camera and actor movement, and the restraint of the acting in many scenes

made a film much stronger, more communicative, than the
dated declamation of some of the dialogue in the sound version.   The popularity of the sound version tended to label
Milestone for the remainder of his career, and saddled him
with the impossible task of duplicating its success at every
turn.   At the same time, ALL QUIET was cut on each reissue and on television, further destroying the intent of the
original.   When Milestone failed commercially, he was
doomed to one- or two-picture contracts, rising to his early
standard only occasionally and only on independent projects.

Typical of many contract directors, he was regarded
unfairly on occasions as a hack, and yet, he always had another good film in him.   As luck would prove, however,
his fine films remained largely anonymous and his floundering reputation sadly remained.   His decline was less real
than assumed.

Andrew Sarris has said of him that "he has never
discriminated against doomed projects."   It is better said
that he has rarely given less than the best he had to offer
to even the most perfunctory of his assignments.   His ju-
dicious clean storytelling is an art a great deal more difficult to achieve than its flowing, effortless unrolling would
indicate.   In an age obsessed with cinema auteurs, there
should still be the ability to appreciate one of Hollywood's
grands seigneurs.

LEWIS MILESTONE

A Film Checklist by Karl Thiede

Director

1.   SEVEN SINNERS (7 November 1925).   P: Warner
     Brothers.   C: Marie Prevost, Clive Brook, John
     Patrick.   6,826ft./76m.

2.   THE CAVEMAN (6 February 1926).   P: Warner
     Brothers.   C: Matt Moore, Marie Prevost, John
     Patrick.   6,741ft./75m.

3.   THE NEW KLONDIKE (15 March 1926).   P: Para-

mount. C: Thomas Meighan, Lila Lee, Paul Kelly.
7,445ft. /83m.

4. TWO ARABIAN KNIGHTS (23 September 1927). P:
United Artists. C: William Boyd, Mary Astor,
Louis Wolheim. NC: $488,968.30. DG:
$743,886.36. FG: $206,000. 8,250ft. /92m.

5. THE GARDEN OF EDEN (4 February 1928). P: United
Artists. C: Corinne Griffith, Louise Dresser,
Lowell Sherman. NC: $757,377.93. DG:
$583,030.74. 7,300ft. /81m.

6. THE RACKET (30 June 1928). P: Paramount. C:
Thomas Meighan, Marie Prevost, Louis Wolheim.
NC: $450,000. WWG: $950,000. 7,646ft. /85m.

7. BETRAYAL (11 May 1929). P: Paramount. C: Emil
Jannings, Esther Ralston, Gary Cooper. 6,614ft. /
73 1/2m.

8. NEW YORK NIGHTS (28 December 1929). P: United
Artists. C: Norma Talmadge, Gilbert Roland, John
Wray. NC: $711,838.28. DG: $620,573.30.
7,447ft. /82 1/2m.

9. ALL QUIET ON THE WESTERN FRONT (N.Y. première, 29 April 1930; general release, 24 August
1930). P: Universal. C: Louis Wolheim, Lew
Ayres, John Wray. DG: $1,500,000. FG:
$1,500,000. 12,423ft. /138m.

10. THE FRONT PAGE (4 April 1931). P: United Artists.
C: Adolphe Menjou, Pat O'Brien, Mary Brian. NC:
$537,507.97. DG: $699,708.70. 8,100ft. /90m.

11. RAIN (22 October 1932). P: United Artists. C:
Joan Crawford, Walter Huston, William Gargan. NC:
$591,532.39. DG: $538,488. FG: $165,571.
85m.

12. HALLELUJAH, I'M A BUM (8 February 1933). P:
United Artists. C: Al Jolson, Madge Evans, Harry
Langdon. NC: $1,280,624.89. DG: $339,072.
FG: $127,720. 82m.

13. THE CAPTAIN HATES THE SEA (22 October 1934).

P: Columbia.   C: Victor McLaglen, John Gilbert,
Walter Connolly.   92m.

14. PARIS IN SPRING (5 July 1935). P: Paramount.   C:
Mary Ellis, Tullio Carminati, Ida Lupino.   83m.

15. ANYTHING GOES (24 January 1936). P: Paramount.
C: Bing Crosby, Ethel Merman, Charles Ruggles.
92m.

16. THE GENERAL DIED AT DAWN (4 September 1936).
P: Paramount.   C: Gary Cooper, Madeleine Carroll,
Akim Tamiroff.   98m.

17. ROAD SHOW (1937).   Unreleased.   Producer: Hal
Roach.   This film was put into production 18 September 1937 and Milestone had shot for ten weeks when
Roach discovered that the film was being developed
into a serious drama, whereas he wanted a comedy.
Roach fired Milestone and scrapped what was shot at
a negative cost of $420,661.   Milestone sued and Roach
counter-sued.   The suit was finally settled by Milestone directing OF MICE AND MEN for Roach.
ROAD SHOW was later made and directed by Roach
at a negative cost of $477,690.92.

18. OF MICE AND MEN (12 January 1940). P: United
Artists.   C: Burgess Meredith, Betty Field, Lon
Chaney, Jr.   DG: $673,027.73.   FG: $239,285.
9,559ft. /106m.

19. THE NIGHT OF NIGHTS (1 December 1939).   P: Paramount.   C: Pat O'Brien, Olympe Bradna, Roland
Young.   85m.

20. LUCKY PARTNERS (30 August 1940).   P: RKO Radio
Pictures.   C: Ronald Colman, Ginger Rogers, Jack
Carson.   101m.

21. MY LIFE WITH CAROLINE (1 August 1941).   P: RKO
Radio Pictures.   C: Ronald Colman, Anna Lee,
Charles Winninger.   81m.

22. OUR RUSSIAN FRONT (February 1942).   P: Artkino.
Producers: Lewis Milestone, Joris Ivens.   Narrator:
Walter Huston.   A documentary trade shown under
the title REPORT FROM RUSSIA.   40m.

23. EDGE OF DARKNESS (24 April 1943). P: Warner
Brothers. C: Errol Flynn, Ann Sheridan, Walter
Huston. DG: $2,300,000. 118m.

24. THE NORTH STAR (© 4 November 1943). P:
Goldwyn-RKO Radio Pictures. C: Anne Baxter,
Dana Andrews, Walter Huston. 105m.

25. THE PURPLE HEART (March 1944). P: Twentieth
Century-Fox. C: Dana Andrews, Richard Conte,
Farley Granger. 99m.

26. GUEST IN THE HOUSE (8 December 1944). P: United
Artists. D: John Brahm, Andre de Toth and Lewis
Milestone uncredited. C: Anne Baxter, Ralph Bel-
lamy, Aline MacMahon. DG: $1,202,841. FG:
$708,066. 10,870ft./121m.

27. A WALK IN THE SUN (March 1946). P: Twentieth
Century-Fox. C: Dana Andrews, John Ireland,
Richard Conte. 117m.

28. THE STRANGE LOVE OF MARTHA IVERS (13 September 1946). P: Paramount. C: Barbara Stanwyck,
Van Heflin, Kirk Douglas. DG: $3,250,000. 117m.

29. ARCH OF TRIUMPH (30 April 1948). P: United
Artists. C: Charles Boyer, Ingrid Bergman,
Charles Laughton. DG: $1,428,489. 10,379ft. /
115m.

30. NO MINOR VOICES (12 November 1948). P: Metro-
Goldwyn-Mayer. C: Dana Andrews, Lilli Palmer,
Louis Jourdan. 8,607ft./96m.

31. THE RED PONY (28 March 1949). P: Republic. C:
Myrna Loy, Robert Mitchum, Louis Calhern. Technicolor. 89m.

32. HALLS OF MONTEZUMA (January 1951). P:
Twentieth Century-Fox. C: Richard Widmark, Jack
Palance, Reginald Gardiner. DG: $2,650,000.
Technicolor. 113m.

33. KANGAROO (June 1952). P: Twentieth Century-Fox.
C: Peter Lawford, Maureen O'Hara, Finlay Currie.
DG: $1,250,000. Technicolor. 84m.

34. LES MISERABLES (August 1952). P: Twentieth Cen-
     tury-Fox. C: Michael Rennie, Debra Paget, Robert
     Newton. DG: $1,100,000. 104m.

35. MELBA (7 August 1953). P: United Artists. C:
     Patrice Munsel, Robert Morley, John McCallum. DG:
     $269,491. Technicolor. 113m.

36. THEY WHO DARE (Released in England in 1953; U.S.
     release in 1955). P: Associated Artists. C: Dirk
     Bogarde, Denholm Elliott, Akim Tamiroff. Techni-
     color. 101m.

37. THE WIDOW (May 1957). P: Distributor Corporation
     of America. C: Patricia Roc, Massimo Serato,
     Anna Maria Ferrero. 89m.

38. PORK CHOP HILL (May 1959). P: United Artists.
     C: Gregory Peck, Harry Guardino, George Shibata.
     DG: $1,845,962. FG: $1,737,571. 97m.

39. OCEAN'S ELEVEN (August 1960). P: Warner Broth-
     ers. C: Frank Sinatra, Dean Martin, Sammy Davis,
     Jr. DG: $5,500,000. Technicolor. Scope. 128m.

40. MUTINY ON THE BOUNTY (November 1962). P:
     Metro-Goldwyn-Mayer. C: Marlon Brando, Trevor
     Howard, Richard Harris. DG: $9,800,000. Tech-
     nicolor. 179m.

41. PT-109 (July 1963). P: Warner Brothers. D: Les-
     lie Martinson, Lewis Milestone uncredited. C: Cliff
     Robertson, Ty Hardin, James Gregory. Production
     started: 27 June 1962. Milestone was fired 21 July
     1962. Technicolor. Scope. 140m.

42. THE DIRTY GAME (April 1966). P: American Inter-
     national Pictures. D: Terence Young, Christian-
     Jaque, Carlo Lizzani, Lewis Milestone uncredited.
     C: Henry Fonda, Robert Ryan, Vittorio Gassman.
     Lewis Milestone was replaced by Terence Young.
     91m.

Chapter 9

EDWARD DMYTRYK

by Nancy K. Hart

Few film directors have attracted both <u>favorable</u> and
<u>unfavorable</u> public attention on quite the scale <u>that</u> Edward
Dmytryk has.

The inescapable air of public discontent that surrounded him came about rather suddenly in 1947 when
Dmytryk was among ten prominent Hollywood figures brought
before the House UnAmerican Activities Committee. He was
cited for contempt of Congress and was fired by RKO where
he was directing at the time.

But in Dmytryk's own words, "That whole business
was, of course, a great personal strain, but it really didn't
have an effect on my career then and doesn't now. " It
seems time has proven Edward Dmytryk correct. His film
career has now spanned fifty-three years and public acceptance of his films grows.

Among his directing credits are THE CAINE MUTINY
(Columbia, 1954), RAINTREE COUNTY (M-G-M, 1957),
WALK ON THE WILD SIDE (Columbia, 1962), THE CARPET-
BAGGERS (Paramount, 1964) and, his latest, THE HUMAN
FACTOR (Bryanston, 1975).

Dmytryk looks at directing more as a way of life
than as a job: "Directing ... there's no job quite like it in
the world. That's why after I finish a picture, I can't even
read a book for three months. My mind is completely
washed out. Even when I was younger, I refused to go into

351

Dmytryk playing solitaire in his trailer while on location. Photo courtesy of the Museum of Modern Art.

another project right away because directing a picture for me is about a year's job. "

Dmytryk's inexhaustible energies are apparent even on first meeting him. He rather directed our first interview, quietly, even-tempered, and very efficiently, as I'm sure he still directs on the set. His first warning to me was, "I don't really want to be hard on you, but do you honestly think you have adequate information with these kinds of questions to write a chapter on my life?"

Then he explained further: "You should be reading a lot of film history books if you're really interested in doing this type of writing. I don't like the film books that merely list chronological facts. You should delve into the character--the human side of a man's film career. "

I think about this statement often as I write about Edward Dmytryk, his life, his friends, and his career. He is definitely not the typical Hollywood director although at our first meeting he seemed at ease and well-placed in the setting of the Brown Derby Restaurant in Hollywood.

He now lives in a pleasant country home outside Los Angeles. "I would not live in Hollywood. I don't go to Hollywood parties either. I guess I'm pretty much of an individual. "

Dmytryk has claimed boxing still keeps him fit and he studies Chinese as a hobby. Of course, films are a big part of his life. He reads novels and scripts, always looking for unique movie possibilities. He has even written a Western. Dmytryk says he is willing to direct any kind of film.

Dmytryk is not a large man physically--at least he does not loom over the set as he appears to do in many production stills I have seen from his movies. He is a short, rather slim man who in no way shows his sixty-eight years. Many of those years have been filled with hard work. Dmytryk explained the activity required of him on a single picture:

"I have to start by working on the script. Rewrite it. Very often, I even type it myself so I know exactly what's in it. It takes anywhere from six weeks to three months to six months for me to work on a script.

"I do all my research work on the picture also.   It
includes studying, picking locations, and so on.   When I was
doing CAINE MUTINY I spent two weeks at the naval base
in Washington just watching 16mm. films of the naval actions
in the Pacific.

"You're constantly thinking of the film from the minute it starts.   You think about the things you'll need, about
scenes, about how they're to be played ... you even dream
about it.

"It takes time to find locations, start casting, the
actual shooting, rehearsals, and work on the set.   I never
work long hours on the set.   I like to work about six or
seven hours a day, because I find it's such tiring work."

Dmytryk may spend only six or seven hours on the
set, but his work on a picture involves much more than that.
"I never go anywhere when I'm working on a picture."

When Dmytryk recently was filming THE HUMAN
FACTOR on location in Italy, outside of the time spent with
his wife and daughter over Easter, Dmytryk devoted all his
time to the picture.

"I would go home to the hotel room, clean up, maybe go out to dinner and return to work on the script or anything else I had to do.

"When facilities are available, two or three nights a
week and Sundays I spend in the cutting room editing my
own pictures.   Even during the shooting of a picture, I have
to worry about cutting it; making sure the dubbing is correct;
working things out with the musicians and sound boys; check-
ing the color balance of the print in the lab ... it's a
twenty-four-hour-a-day job.   You never stop thinking about
it."

Dmytryk has spent many years in the film business
learning the techniques that have brought him to the fine
pictures he is still directing today.   He learned about film
at a very young age.   When he was fifteen, Dmytryk was a
messenger boy at Paramount.   At sixteen, he became a part-
time projectionist; next film editor, then director.

"I've done everything in this business except be an
assistant director.   I started out as a messenger boy.   I

worked in the laboratory. I was a projectionist and then a
cutter, which is a natural progression because all the projectionist does is run the film for the cutter.

"In 1923, at age fourteen, I had to support myself
through high school and into college." Dmytryk's parents
were Ukrainian immigrants who had come to Canada before
Edward was born. His father was a farmer who held land
in both Canada and the Ukraine, so the family commuted between the two countries for several years.

In Dmytryk's own words, "I'm a farm boy. I was
born on a farm in British Columbia. I had to work to make
a living. I didn't know what an inside toilet was until I was
nine years old.

"We all come from different backgrounds. None of
us are born into this kind of work. I remember back in the
old days, everyone in motion pictures was from some different line of work.

"When they started to get college people in the film
business, the college types were people you pointed out--for
example, Arthur Hornwell was a 'Dartmouth man' and it
was something rather fantastic.

"There was no particular respect for the college
graduates. It was just a trademark. We all learned our
trade pragmatically."

Dmytryk was a college man himself. At Hollywood
High School he did so well in science and mathematics that
he was given a scholarship to the California Institute of
Technology. He attended the school for one year and won
five freshman letters for football, basketball, 'track, wrest-
ling, and baseball.

Dmytryk's college education did aid him in his film
career. When he explains the techniques used in MURDER,
MY SWEET (RKO, 1945), Dmytryk says the tricky camera
techniques, dissolves, and use of miniature and enlarge-
ment factors were due to his technical background.

MURDER, MY SWEET, an adaptation of Raymond
Chandler's Farewell, My Lovely, was a complex murder
mystery starring Dick Powell. With this film, critics
started to note Dmytryk's clever directing. He directed

the film for less than $500,000 in forty-four days. Said
Box Office in 1945: "The hair-trigger direction of Edward
Dmytryk milks an ingeniously-contrived screenplay of its
last drop of emotional appeal and uses to great advantage
noteworthy unorthodox camera technique."

        Dmytryk commented that he did use a method of plate
glass in front of the camera for one technique in the movie
which proved dramatically effective. Detective Philip Marlowe (Dick Powell) is sitting at his desk in an office high
atop the city. As the billboard lights across the street
flash on and off, Marlowe sees the reflection of the "Moose"
(Mike Mazurki) in the window. Because of the use of distance from the camera, the plate glass, and effective camera angles, the "Moose" looms huge on the window.

        Although Dmytryk says his mathematics/physics back-
ground may have helped in some of these techniques, he
feels that schools "probably still don't do much except give
you some kind of vague preparation for your career. You
have to learn this business pragmatically."

        Dmytryk's chance to learn came in 1929 when he got
an offer to switch to the cutting room as a handyman. This
was during the confusion caused by the new sound pictures,
and in no time Dmytryk was made a film editor--which he
still affectionately calls film cutter--on the Spanish versions
of Paramount's English-language pictures.

        He cut a number of U.S. features, including the Leon
Errol comedy, ONLY SAPS WORK, directed by Cyril Gardner and Edwin Knoph. In 1930, after being sent to Paramount's studio in Astoria, Long Island, to work on THE
ROYAL FAMILY OF BROADWAY, co-directed by Gardner
and George Cukor, Dmytryk found himself out of work when
returning to Hollywood. A new group was in control at
Paramount.

        It didn't take too long for Dmytryk to be called back
and in late 1931 he started what was to be an eight-year
stay in the cutting room at Paramount, with a short break
to direct a film for a friend.

        Directors like Leo McCarey and George Cukor recog-
nized his skill and requested that he edit their pictures.

        "I was lucky. I was cutting at Paramount and they

initiated the system of having the cutter on the set with the
director. I worked with George Cukor. He came from the
theatre and he didn't know much about cameras. I had to
do the set-ups for him and it did help me when I became a
director myself. In fact, I picked all his set-ups on the
pictures I did for him.

"I also worked with Leo McCarey. Leo had complete
trust in me and he would just shoot the stuff and I would put
it together. As a matter of fact, on one picture, LOVE
AFFAIR (RKO, 1939), he wanted to throw a certain sequence
out because he was so disappointed with it.

"I asked him to let me see what I could do with it.
He said okay and I cut it in such a way that it became one
of the funniest sequences in the picture. Obviously, he
knew the material was there, but it didn't come off until it
was put together in a certain way."

In 1935, Dmytryk took some time off from cutting to
direct a short Western called THE HAWK. At the time he
had no particular ambition to direct.

A magazine reported, "8 May 1935--Edward Dmytryk,
formerly film editor at Paramount, makes his debut as a
director on PRIDE OF THE TRIPLE X, featuring Kazan, the
dog star, for newly formed Affiliated Pictures Corp."

Dmytryk says, "My first film was THE HAWK [re-
named] and there was a dog in it but he by no means was
the star. I made it in five days for $5,000. I just took a
few days off from editing. I don't really consider it my
start as a director. I was doing it for a friend and anxious
for the experience.

"This woman who had written the script, in Long
Beach, had the money and a friend who wanted to get into
pictures. There was nobody in the picture who had a name.
The only one in the picture with any experience, oddly enough,
was the kid, Dickie Jones, who went on to become a kind of
TV star. He (along with the dog, I suppose) were trained
actors."

What Dmytryk considers more of a start at directing
was MILLION DOLLAR LEGS (Paramount, 1939), which he
took over for director Nick Grindé in the last week of shooting when Grindé was in bed because of a throat infection.

MILLION DOLLAR LEGS was a college comedy featuring
Betty Grable. Dmytryk had begun editing the film so knew
right what to do to finish the picture in one week with no
trouble at all. The results were better than satisfactory to
Paramount and they offered Dmytryk $250 a week to direct
a series of low-budget programmers.

So Dmytryk's career as a director began, but he
never forgot the value of his cutting experience.

"Even today, I know exactly how something is going
to go together before I shoot it. I try to give myself as
much latitude as possible, but I feel one-hundred per cent
of the time I at least know how I am going to cut a picture."
And Dmytryk still does edit his own films.

"It's a much easier way to direct when you know how
you will be cutting it. You can plan what you're doing.
You're not shooting blind. Directors who don't know how to
cut will shoot a whole scene in a long shot, then a medium
shot, then close-ups because they don't know how the cutter
is going to put it together. I don't do that. If I know I'm
not going to use a long shot, I don't even bother to shoot it.
If I knew I was going to use close-ups only at the end of
the scene, and not throughout, I would only shoot them at
the end of the scene. If I want a certain angle to shoot a
special piece of business, I only shoot that because it's all
I'm going to use.

"The only time I would shoot a great deal is if it
were with a scene I really didn't know what I was going to
do with for some reason.

"When you do your own editing, you save a lot of
film, time, and compromising with other people. To me
cutting is an essential part of telling the story. Obviously,
I'm prejudiced because I was a cutter. When I direct I'm
using my cuts so that I'm telling the story the way I want
it told--otherwise a director is telling a story the way some
cutter wants to tell it."

Dmytryk feels directing is a natural progression from
cutting. "Assistant directors almost never become directors
because that has nothing to do with directing. The assistant
director is in effect a crew foreman. He's the guy that
sees that the people are there on time, and that everything
you need is there. The assistant director really, and it's

the way the studio likes it, works more for the production
department than he does for the director.

"Actually, it leads to some very tricky divided loyal-
ties as far as assistant directors and so-called 'director's
assistants,' who really side with the director, go. Assistant
directors sometimes work against the director because the
director is always fighting for more time, better scenes,
more money, while the assistant director is fighting for a
schedule, budget, and that kind of thing."

Dmytryk does not use the same assistant director on
his films today and didn't in his early "B" pictures.

He directed four low budget Paramount programmers
the first year, using contract players from the studio.

The first of the four, TELEVISION SPY (Paramount,
1939), was a rather improbable story about an American inventor who perfects long-distance television and, of course,
the foreign agents who try to steal it. At the time of the
picture, reviewers commented that "the actors weren't even
serious about this film."

Next was EMERGENCY SQUAD (Paramount, 1940).
It didn't seem much of an improvement. It was about a girl
reporter who helps the police capture criminals. One critic
said it was the performance of the two dogs which did most
to sustain any interest there could be in the picture.

GOLDEN GLOVES (Paramount, 1940) did have a better
box-office draw. This was probably due to the fact that the
background of this love triangle was boxing, termed "Golden
Gloves," the same name given the Daily News annual amateur boxing contest.

His last film for Paramount, MYSTERY SEA RAIDER
(Paramount, 1940), was an exciting and timely story of a
German submarine during wartime sinking British and French
ships.

Already Dmytryk's films took on political overtones,
although no sides were taken. There is no masking of national identities, the German spy being known as such
throughout, but there is no denouncing of Hitler or Nazism
or Germany in the manner of other war films of that time.
War is only treated as terrible in its effects on the lives of
the leading characters.

In 1940, Sol Siegel took over Paramount's production and all the "B" department people were left to sit out their contracts. It meant one month for Edward Dmytryk and as soon as he was free, Dmytryk did an independent musical for Monogram called HER FIRST ROMANCE (Monogram, 1940). This was the one film Dmytryk was to do on his own before being put under contract by Columbia, scheduled to direct the Boris Karloff features. Although the film was rather simple in the Cinderella fashion, Dmytryk's direction was praised for effectively spacing music, pathos, and comedy. Edith Fellows and Wilbur Evans starred. Alan Ladd had a supporting role.

THE DEVIL COMMANDS (Columbia, 1941) was the first film for Columbia. Starring Boris Karloff, it was the story of an ambition-crazed scientist who constructs an electro-dynamo in an effort to communicate with the dead.

His second at Columbia, UNDER AGE (Columbia, 1941), was one of many films Dmytryk used to teach a lesson. It is the story of racketeers, their use of young girls (never shown but always suggested), and crime. As UNDER AGE warns that crime does not pay, CROSSFIRE (RKO, 1947) warns that prejudice of any type is dangerous, and HITLER'S CHILDREN (RKO, 1943) warns against the Nazi threat.

Many of Dmytryk's films have "preaching" overtones, although always done in a dramatic and tasteful way. "I suppose there is a little of myself in all my pictures. If I thought I was just making too much money with my films and nothing else, I would probably turn a few of those films down."

Dmytryk now directs all his films for a share of the profits. "I always work for a share of the profits. I know, however, it isn't always easy to collect. No matter how successful the picture is, producers keep saying they had so many expenses, there's no real profits.

"Often you have to sue for your proper share. M-G-M has around $35 million in suits for broken contracts.

"The studio system is completely different now than it was in the old days. Contracts are not honored. It's a hard way to work, but maybe it's a part of a whole latter twentieth century morality in this country. Your work

doesn't mean much and it's really difficult to get a law suit
into court, much less out of court.

"In the past, with two or three offers, you knew one
of them had to go. Today you need ten or fifteen offers to
be sure. A lot of people come in with a 'motion picture
package' which you eventually become a part of so the money
can be raised for the film to be made. You could wait from
six weeks to over a year before something develops.

"Today one never says he's on a picture before the
contract is signed. In the old days, I never signed a contract before I was finished with a picture. It's a strange
thing that's happened. If you read anything about this business, the old producers like the Harry Cohns and the Louis
B. Mayers all had somewhat bad reputations and came from
all walks of life. They were button makers or cornet players or whatever, but you could really trust them. It was
just a custom--a way of life.

"A hand-shake was a deal. You didn't have to sign
things. And if for some reason that picture wasn't made,
even though you didn't sign anything, they'd pay you for it.
Sometimes they would offer you another picture, under the
same deal, but if you didn't want it, they would pay you
what the understanding was.

"The price you got for a picture was usually just
the going thing. Any producer could call up the last producer you worked for and ask what a director was paid."

Dmytryk had non-exclusive contracts with many film
companies, which meant that if he was not busy at one studio, he could do a film for another studio. "I had a contract
for five pictures with Fox. I think I actually did six. I
could go to Fox and if they didn't have a picture for me, I
could go to Paramount and ask if they had films for me to
do. All the contract with Fox meant was that they always
had first call on me.

"The same kind of thing happened with Paramount. I
had a four-picture contract once, but I think I only made
two films. They paid me for the other two because they
weren't making many films at the time."

When Dmytryk was under early contract with these
film companies, he didn't get to choose all his films and the
subject matter and type greatly varied.

SWEETHEART OF THE CAMPUS (Columbia, 1941) was a slim offering with Ozzie Nelson and his orchestra taking over a college. THE BLONDE FROM SINGAPORE (Columbia, 1941) was a romantic comedy which most critics termed suitable only for the lower half of a double bill. It was a too complicated plot about an actress-adventuress (Florence Rice) posing as a missionary's daughter.

In CONFESSIONS OF BOSTON BLACKIE (Columbia, 1941), Chester Morris returned as the title character. It was another in the popular series of detective films with laughs and suspense. The plot centered around a piece of sculpture which was stolen and replaced with an imitation piece.

After this film Dmytryk said he would no longer direct "B" pictures, but after being out of work for several months he ran out of money and did two "Lone Wolf" pictures for Columbia and CAPTIVE WILD WOMAN (Universal, 1943).

It was RKO that promised to give Edward Dmytryk better films. He signed a contract and in 1942 got his first assignment. SEVEN MILES FROM ALCATRAZ (RKO, 1942) was a well-built melodrama about two convicts escaping from Alcatraz and becoming involved in a Nazi spy plot. The film was made on a low budget, but did well as a single feature in some spots. Again, Dmytryk's lessons come into play as the convicts change their anti-social ideas when they become enmeshed by the Nazi spy ring, and they capture the spies rather than aid them.

"I honestly don't remember much about my next film, THE FALCON STRIKES BACK [RKO, 1943]," Dmytryk said. "The picture remains a blank to me. If I would see it today it would be a complete surprise. The only thing I vaguely remember about it is one day working on location in Beverly Glen. Why I remember that, I don't know. I don't even remember the scene I was shooting. I couldn't name the cast for you except that [Tom] Conway took over for [George] Sanders as the Falcon."

Tom Conway was George Sanders' brother. Dmytryk's direction of the new Falcon and the whole picture was praised, although critics at the time said that the casting of Edgar Kennedy as a killer might prove the greatest mystery. "It's a mystery to me," Dmytryk said, "I don't even remember the man."

Next, HITLER'S CHILDREN (RKO, 1943) was one of
the better pictures dealing with the Germany of that time.
Dmytryk took over the directing from Irving Reis, who had
trouble getting along with some of the cast. It was Dmytryk's first big money-maker for RKO.

The story is personalized in terms of individuals
caught up in the barbaric political and religious philosophy
of the Nazis. Dmytryk again had his chance to make some
important social points. Talk of sterilization of unfit men
and women; imbedding in children of the idea of dying for
Der Fuehrer; fantastic cruelties of the Gestapo--all are condemned in the film. In fact, the two main characters die
in the end screaming for the German youth to fight for their
freedom.

After placing the actions of the Nazis under the mi-
croscope, Dmytryk came back with a film that did the same
with the Japanese. BEHIND THE RISING SUN (RKO, 1943)
characterizes the Japanese war-makers. Dmytryk utilized
both sedate conversational techniques and violently physical
scenes to stress the points of the film.

Finally came Dmytryk's first "A" picture, starring
Ginger Rogers with a good supporting cast. TENDER COM-
RADE (RKO, 1943) looked at waiting wives whose husbands
were away at war. Besides Ginger Rogers, it also starred
Robert Ryan as the leading man. Ryan, who would appear
in more Dmytryk films, was working at the Pasadena Play-
house and Dmytryk found him and offered him a minor role
in GOLDEN GLOVES.

Dmytryk said there were very few actors and actresses that he didn't like to work with. "I have a number
of favorites of course. I loved working with Bogart, Spencer Tracy. I only made one picture with Gable, but he was
a delight to work with; Van Johnson, Deborah Kerr, Elizabeth Taylor--they were all pleasant to work with.

"Monty Clift, even though he had great personal problems, was a good actor to work with. When he was sober
and not doped up, he was one of the brightest and most
sympathetic human beings I've ever worked with. He was a
very creative actor. Unfortunately, on one picture RAIN-
TREE COUNTY [M-G-M, 1957], we lost months because of
him. He had an accident during the picture, and he was in
pain at the time, so he drank and took dope. You could

never get more than two or three hours of work out of him
a day. But on the next picture I made with him, YOUNG
LIONS [20th-Fox, 1958], he was no problem at all, strange-
ly enough. I was very fond of him. "

    In reflecting on actors and actresses, Dmytryk ex-
plained that Hollywood has altered.

    "The glamour aspect of Hollywood changed tremen-
dously. Glamour is something in your own mind. It's still
a glamour business. It still attracts people. Hollywood itself is certainly not what it used to be. Not in any way.
When I first came to Los Angeles, it was a city of 250,000
people. Hollywood was all there was. Films were the pre-
dominant business. There was a time when motion pictures
were the fourth most important industry in the country. It's
nowhere near that now.

    "In a sense actors and actresses are the same now,
and in a sense they are different. Basically they're the
same type of people. It takes certain characteristics to
make a good actor or actress. But their own attitudes
toward themselves have changed. In other words, when I
started in the business, there was still a hangover from old
theatrical days. Actresses were considered no better than
prostitutes; actors no better than pimps. Nobody in high
society, with rare exceptions, of course, ever invited an
actor or actress to their home. It was a different class.

    "In a sense it was good. Actors and actresses didn't
go around with terribly inflated opinions of themselves or
their work. When some actor can go out and get $400,000
or a million for a few weeks' work, he's got to think he's
either that many more times important than the president
of the U.S. or the people who pay him are idiots.

    "When being paid such fantastic salaries, performers
may develop a huge ego and that is not easy to work with.
Actors used to be much more disciplined. They still are
in Europe to a large extent.

    "If Gable had to be on the set at 9:00 A.M., he was
on the set at 9:00 A.M. There was no question about it.
Not even 9:05 A.M., but 9:00. Some actors like Spencer
Tracy or Van Johnson were always there a half hour ahead
of time. They were there when you needed them. They
never complained about hours.

"I remember a picture I did with Spencer Tracy and
Robert Wagner.   Bob was a nice guy but one of the younger
ones and started to complain about how hard I worked him.
It wasn't a bad complaint, but I had him run at the altitude
we were working on top of the French Alps.   He mentioned
that fact to Tracy, who replied, 'Young man, you ought to
get down on your knees every night and thank God you work
in one of the most overpaid industries in the world.' That
was the attitude of those early actors."

Dmytryk did get the opportunity to work with many
top name stars, whom he most often considered professionals
in the business.   Two such actors were John Wayne and
Anthony Quinn who starred in BACK TO BATAAN (RKO,
1945).   The film was a routine war picture which Dmytryk
did before CORNERED (RKO, 1945), which starred Dick
Powell.

In the film Dick Powell is a Canadian flyer tracking
his wife's killer.   The film is an excellent thriller, but
there are still the warning speeches about the Fascists lurk-

Dmytryk, with megaphone, on the backlot with Dick Powell,
shooting CORNERED (RKO, 1945). Photo courtesy of the
Museum of Modern Art.

ing in our midst. The Motion Picture Herald said, "Edward
Dmytryk, a master hand at melodrama, directed with a splendid sense of timing."

Critics praised Dmytryk for the film and the public
was equally receptive. A 1962 edition of Films in Review
contained thoughts from Edward Dmytryk about the film:

"Dmytryk thinks the last reel and a half of CORNERED
contain some of his best work. He said, 'There was nothing
remarkable in making good in a profession after nearly
twenty years.' He ventured the opinion that cutting is the
only part of a motion picture that is truly cinematic. 'All
the other parts, or arts, are still held by strings to their
original sources--mostly the stage, as are writing and acting. Yes, even photography, although it has gone ahead far-
ther than the other branches. There is too much dependence
on "still composition," which in turn stems from painting.
The eye is made to follow certain lines to certain objects,
and so forth. But this isn't necessarily true of what I call
"dynamic photography." Of course it's important that the
eye should light upon an important object at the right time,
but I don't believe in following specific rules about it. Motion pictures move, and knowing what impression will be
left on the eye, or the mind's eye, is an art in itself. I do
ninety-five per cent of my editing mentally before I shoot a
scene.' "

Next, TILL THE END OF TIME (RKO, 1946) again
warned against Fascism. This time it was a creditable
show that concerns the problems of returning vets, social
adjustments, war widows, and the like. Dorothy McGuire
and Robert Mitchum starred.

It was during this film that Edward Dmytryk met
Jean Porter, who was to become his second wife and to
whom he is still married. She was a member of the supporting cast of the film. Dmytryk's first wife, whom he
married in 1932, was Madeleine Robinson. They had one
son, Michael. The marriage ended in divorce in 1947.

During 1947, Dmytryk did one film, SO WELL RE-
MEMBERED (RKO, 1947), and then CROSSFIRE (RKO, 1947)
which had much to do with the threatened demise of his directing career. In October of the same year the House
Committee on UnAmerican Activities started its investigation
of the film industry.

Dmytryk directing Guy Madison and Ruth Nelson in a scene
from TILL THE END OF TIME (RKO, 1946).   Photo courtesy of Movie Star News.

Although it may have caused problems for Dmytryk
politically, many critics still consider CROSSFIRE Dmytryk's
best picture.   It does pack a strong punch from beginning to
end, striking a heavy blow against anti-Semitism.

The somber and absorbing mood surrounds the story
of American soldiers.   Robert Ryan plays a tough army
man who kills his first victim only because he is Jewish,
and then kills a friend because he knows too much.   His
prejudices are obvious: "The Jew-boy was setting up the
drinks."   "All those Jews played it safe during the war."
"I don't like Jews and I don't like no one who likes Jews."

Robert Young, the police detective in the film, wins

the "preaching" role, although it is done so intelligently and
delicately under Dmytryk's direction that it becomes more a
genuine frankness and sincerity than preaching.   Young says:
"Monte's (Ryan) kind of hating is like a gun."   "Ignorant men
always laugh at things they don't understand."   "Hating is always the same--always senseless!"

    Robert Mitchum also starred in the film for which
Dmytryk received an Academy Award nomination.

    After CROSSFIRE, Dmytryk's long political struggle
began.   In his own words, "Although I feel it had no effect
on my career, it was a great personal strain.   My wife's
friends were telling her to leave me and that kind of thing.
Nothing like that is ever easy."   Although no studio would
hire him, Dmytryk did marry Miss Porter.   "I am, of
course, still married to the same woman today.   Twenty-
seven years.   How could you ever leave a wonderful woman
like that who stuck with you through everything?"

    The problems started during the week of 21 October
1947, when director Sam Wood testified that directors John
Cromwell, Irving Pichel, Frank Tuttle, and Edward Dmytryk
had tried to take over the Screen Directors' Guild in the interest of the Communist Party.

    Dmytryk talked quietly and rather brushed the subject
away at our interview.   At the time of the trials things were
different.   During the first times in court Dmytryk tried
endlessly to make statements on his position, but they were
usually ruled not acceptable in the Committee by the Chairman.

    His first time before the Committee is recorded in
Are You Now or Have You Ever Been? by Eric Bentley
(Harper & Row, 1972), pp. 4-6:

        Edward Dmytryk first appeared before the Com-
        mittee on 29 October 1947.

        Mr. Dmytryk: I was born on September 4, 1908,
        in Grand Forks, British Columbia, Canada.

        Investigator: When and how did you become a
        citizen of the United States?

        Mr. Dmytryk: I was naturalized in '39 in Los
        Angeles.

Investigator: How long have you been a motion
picture director?

Mr. Dmytryk: Since '39.

Investigator: What studios were you associated
with in the past?

Mr. Dmytryk: Most of my years were spent at
Paramount. Now RKO.

Investigator: Would you give the Committee the
names of some of the pictures you have directed?

Mr. Dmytryk: Mr. Chairman, I have a statement
here that I'd like to make.

The Chairman: Let me see the statement. (After
looking at the statement.) It is not pertinent to
this inquiry. The Chair rules it cannot be read....

The Committee questioning went back and forth.
When Dmytryk was finally asked if he was a member of the
Communist Party, he answered: "The Constitution does not
ask that such a question be answered in the way that Mr.
Stripling (the Chairman) wants it answered. What organiza-
tions I belong to, what I think, and what I say cannot be
questioned by this Committee."

Dmytryk was infrequently allowed to complete a sentence. The Committee's attitude toward him as a witness
remained obvious: "The Chair desires to announce at this
time that the Sub-Committee recommends to the full Committee that Edward Dmytryk be cited for contempt...."

Dmytryk's suppressed statement follows, as printed
in Hollywood On Trial by Gordon Kahn (Boni & Gaer, 1948),
pp. 111-112:

It is my firm belief that democracy lives and
thrives only on freedom. This country has always
fulfilled its destiny most completely when its
people, through their representatives, have allowed themselves the greatest exercise of freedom
within the law. The dark periods in our history
have been those in which our freedoms have been
suppressed, to however small a degree. Some of

that darkness exists into the present day in the
continued suppression of certain minorities.   In my
last few years in Hollywood, I have devoted myself,
through pictures such as CROSSFIRE, to a fight
against these racial suppressions and prejudices.
My work speaks for itself.   I believe that it speaks
clearly enough so that the people of the country
and this Committee, which has no right to inquire
into my politics or my thinking, can still judge my
thoughts and my beliefs by my work, and by my
work alone.

The freedom which is so necessary for the fullest
development of a democratic nation is also indis-
pensible for the fullest development of any institution within that nation which deals with ideas and
ideals.   For without the free expression of ideas,
both favorable and critical, no nation can long hope
to remain free.   This principle has been stated
many times before, in far better words than mine.
It is a shame that it should have to be repeated
here before this Committee.

But the intent is clear.   This Committee has demanded that the producers 'clean their own house,'
under the supervision of the Committee's members.
They will name the names and the producers must
make out the blacklist.   But where will it end?
History is all too clear on procedures of this kind.
There is no end.   Is a Committee member anti-
Semitic?   He will force the producers to blacklist
men who are pro-labor.   Is a Committee member
against low-cost housing?   He will force the producers to blacklist men who advocate low-cost
housing.   And thus, even without special legislation, he will succeed in throttling, both artistically
and financially, one of the greatest industries in
the United States.   For he will have succeeded,
through threats and intimidation, in effectively
censoring a screen which has just within the last
few years begun to emerge from a never-never
land into a dim realization of its responsibilities
to the people of this nation and of the world.   As
an added touch of grim humor, this attempt at
censorship is being made just at a time when, as
has been remarked by every responsible critic in
the country, foreign motion pictures are success-

fully challenging ours largely because of their free,
open, and honest approach to the problems that be-
set modern man.

The men who have here been attacked, and countless others in Hollywood who have stood up in
their behalf, have behind them a body of work,
completely open to inspection, which expresses
their point of view.   They have always begged for
understanding and enlightenment.   They have also
preached the elimination of certain institutions,
yes!   They have preached the elimination of the
institution of poverty, of slums, of disease, of
racial intolerance, and of all that bigotry which
prevents men from living in peace and understanding, one with another.

If the Committee succeeds in forcing the producers
to blacklist these men it can only result in the
destruction of the industry in which they are now
employed.   For the loss of these men will inevit-
ably lead to the squelching of the ideas they represent, and which they have freely exhibited to the
people in such pictures as THE BEST YEARS OF
OUR LIVES, PRIDE OF THE MARINES, CROSS-
FIRE, THE FARMER'S DAUGHTER, yes, and
even MARGIE!   The resulting deterioration in the
quality of American pictures cannot fail to result
in the eventual extinction of our industry, both as
an artistic expression and, just as important, as
a successful business enterprise.

I cannot join in this wholesale liquidation of the
principle of free expression but, in company with
my fellow-workers, must stand against it in the
interest of the entire industry.

At the conclusion of the Hollywood hearings on 31
October 1947, the indicted ten purchased newspaper space
to declare: "Not only a free screen, but every free institution in America is jeopardized as long as this Committee
exists....   Our original determination to abolish the Committee remains unchanged. "

The indicted men, who soon became known as "The
Hollywood Ten, " along with various friends also produced a
16mm. short film at the time.   It was the story of the trial
and was used for informational and fund-raising purposes.

Many Hollywood figures of the time spoke up in favor
of "The Hollywood Ten." Dore Shary said while he would
not employ Communists, he didn't feel Dmytryk and Adrian
Scott (the producer of CROSSFIRE) were affiliated in any way
with this subversive organization. Nonetheless, Dmytryk
was fired from RKO for refusing to tell the Congressional
Committee whether he was or had been a member of the
Communist Party, and in the Spring of 1948 he sued the
studio for loss of wages. He later had a suit for loss of
prestige which was thrown out of court. The first suit was
eventually withdrawn.

So Dmytryk was out of work and known as one of the
"Unfriendly Hollywood Ten." Dmytryk still felt high esteem
for the benefits films could offer the public and went to Eng-
land. He signed a contract with Nat Bronston, of Independent
Sovereign Films. The British Ministry of Labor granted
Dmytryk the necessary work permit.

The first film done in Britain, OBSESSION (Eagle-
Lion, 1949), had no real political or social impact like
CROSSFIRE. Dmytryk had not lost his editorial touch, how-
ever, and it did thrill the "who-done-it" fans.

Then Dmytryk directed GIVE US THIS DAY (Eagle-Lion,
1949) and it remains his favorite film. It's a powerful human interest story adapted from Pietro Di Donato's novel,
Christ in Concrete. Constant battles against poverty, depression, unemployment, and more fill the screen. Although
the film was produced in Great Britain, there is nothing
British about it. The locale is New York City slums during
the 1920s; the characters are of Italian descent. It tells of
an Italian bricklayer's life and struggles and eventual acci-
dental death caused by a fall into setting concrete where he
dies with his arms outstretched.

"GIVE US THIS DAY is my favorite picture although
very few Americans know about it. The film was black-
listed in this country when I went to jail. In fact, it's almost impossible to find it now. In this country they called
the film SALT TO THE DEVIL.

"The American Legion forced theatres to quit playing
it. It got the greatest reviews. As a matter of fact, there
are still several books on films which say this is probably
the best motion picture made. I won all the awards in
Europe that year where they saw it ... The Grand Master-

piece Award at Venice; the Paris Press Prize for Direction;
a prize at the Czechoslovakian festival....

"In Italy they still run the film at least once a year
on TV. " Dmytryk spoke tenderly of the "old battered print
dubbed in Italian that they still use. " He also explained
that he was able to obtain a personal print of the film at a
recent film festival in London where they did a retrospective
of Dmytryk films.   It was in payment for Dmytryk's appearance at the festival.

Dmytryk has done much directing in Europe since his
start in 1948.   "Directing throughout the world is much the
same.   The only differences are in approach.   On the continent in Europe the producer is strictly an organizer/financier,
as a producer on Broadway is.   The director handles everything else.   He is in charge of the artistic end of the picture.

"To a large extent that's true in America too, except that when a studio set-up is very strong, and the studios completely controlled the business, there was this constant conflict between some executives in the studios trying
to get more control over the artistic end and the directors
resisting it. "

Again warning me about reading film books, Dmytryk
explained, "If you ever read David O. Selznick's memoirs
you get an idea of this kind of thing.   He should have been
a director.   He wanted to keep control over all the elements
of his pictures.   Selznick wanted me to do a picture for him
but I wouldn't do it, just because of that attitude.   It would
have been a battle from beginning to end. "

Any conflict Dmytryk might have had with producers
was delayed after GIVE US THIS DAY.

Not long after the picture, the Bureau of Immigration in the U.S. told Dmytryk he would have to return to
the U.S. to renew his passport.   Things were going well
for Edward Dmytryk in England--it was a good market for
his films and he had no doubt that he could continue directing there.

Unfortunately, what Dmytryk planned to be a short
visit to the U.S. turned into a continuation of the political
struggle of the previous year.   On 29 June 1950, after a

short trial in Washington, he was convicted for contempt of Congress and sentenced to six months' imprisonment and a fine of $1,000.

Edward Dmytryk served only a few months of his sentence because he signaled the Committee his willingness to inform on former associates.

His first statement was issued from prison in November.

"I declined to answer the question as to my Communist affiliations because of a duty which I thought I owed to all Americans to preserve what I believed was a Constitutional privilege of substance. However, in view of the troubled state of world affairs, I find myself in the presence of an even greater duty, and that is to declare without equivocation where I stand toward my own country. In the discharge of that duty I want to make it perfectly clear that I am not now, nor was I at the time of the hearing a member of the Communist Party, that I am not a Communist sympathizer, and that I recognize the United States of America as the only country to which I owe allegiance and loyalty."

And on 25 April 1951, Edward Dmytryk came before the Committee for the second time. Again the following is from Bentley's book (p. 68):

Mr. Dmytryk: The situation has changed.

Investigator: What do you mean by that?

Mr. Dmytryk: Before 1947 I had never heard anybody say they would refuse to fight for this country in a war against Soviet Russia. Then I saw articles about Party members taking that position: I believe Paul Robeson was one. I signed the Stockholm Peace Petition along with other people. I hoped they were sincere. The Korean War made me realize they were not. The North Koreans would not have attacked the South Koreans unless they had backing of very strong forces: those forces are China and Russia. This made me realize there is a Communist menace, and that the Communist Party in this country is a part of that menace. The next thing was the spy trials, the

Hiss, Coplon, and Greenglass cases, the Klaus
Fuchs case.   This is treason.   I don't say all
Communists are guilty of treason, but I think a
Party that encourages them to act in this capacity
is treasonable.   For this reason I am willing to
talk.

Investigator: I would like to have you state what
the real object of the Communist Party is in Hollywood.

Mr. Dmytryk: They had three purposes: to get
money, to get prestige, and to control the content
of pictures.   The only way they could control the
content of pictures was to take over the guilds and
the unions.

Dmytryk has claimed that he probably wasn't that well
liked by Party members.   He delivered a few lectures, but
didn't give financial support except a little when the hat was
passed around.   Dmytryk lost respect for Party "hacks"
when they tried to tell him what to put in his pictures.

Dmytryk didn't appreciate that kind of thing then and
he doesn't today.   "Studios have no control over you because
you are a contract director, or at least they haven't with
me.   I've been very lucky.   Luckier than most directors.
I've always stayed independent.   I guess I've been a rebel
against the Hollywood way from the beginning.   There's certain pictures I had to do just to live or I wouldn't have done
them normally.   But I've almost never run into conflict.
I've even been able to cast the way I want, although that is
somewhat a matter of compromise."

Recently, at Twentieth Century-Fox, Dmytryk was at
a point that he could choose his own pictures.   The scars
left by his association with Hollywood Communists were not
deep.   The Committee recommended that the film industry
offer to employ him and others who had been helpful in ex-
posing Communists in Hollywood.

One Committee member said, "Mr. Dmytryk, it is
refreshing to find there are people who are willing to assist
our feeble efforts to make a contribution in this world-wide
struggle against Communism.   I think you have made a
great contribution."

It seems the producers were in agreement with the
Committee, and in May of 1951 the King Brothers signed
Dmytryk to direct a film called MUTINY (United Artists,
1952). The use of tint photography made this picture set
during the War of 1812 acceptable, although not one of his
major achievements.

Dmytryk's next home became Columbia. He was
hired by Stanley Kramer to direct four films. The first of
these was THE SNIPER (Columbia, 1952), which Dmytryk
ranks right up there with his favorites. It is the story of
a sex killer whose peculiar perversion is to kill young women at a distance with a rifle. It is told with documentary
touches, rather a new slant for Dmytryk at this point in his
career. Dmytryk attempts to arouse sympathy for the killer
with an abnormal compulsion for this type of killing. The
film suggests sex offenders should be immediately sent away
for treatment instead of being periodically jailed.

The second picture at Columbia was EIGHT IRON
MEN (Columbia, 1952); he was back to war pictures--this
time World War II. Reviews were mixed, although Dmytryk
considered it a good film. Like many other Dmytryk films
at this time, it lacked "name stars," but it is a credible
story depicting the camaraderie enjoyed by men who live
together and die together in battle.

THE JUGGLER (Columbia, 1953) goes a step further
in ways and studies the psychiatric probing of a war-warped
mind. It looks at life in an infant nation, Israel, where it
was filmed. Kirk Douglas starred in this film, which cost
$1,000,000. As the tale unfolds, the viewer sees a man
who tried to find himself in a new land among strangers.
The action involves both the inner and outer emotional conflicts and mental blocks that he must overcome.

With THE CAINE MUTINY (Columbia, 1954) Dmytryk's
fine use of actors and actresses with marquee value became
once again apparent. It was also Stanley Kramer's final
and most important production for Columbia. The color
film was nominated for an Academy Award. This story of
men's minds, emotions, and reactions holds interest throughout. Its cast included Humphrey Bogart, José Ferrer, Fred
MacMurray and Van Johnson. The film was shot in fifty-
four days for three hours of footage and was cut to a little
over two hours for theatrical release, which Dmytryk finds
unfortunate.

After THE CAINE MUTINY, Dmytryk planned to go
back to England to direct films. First he made an off-beat
Western, BROKEN LANCE (20th-Fox, 1954). It starred
Spencer Tracy and Robert Wagner. The film utilized a new
lens from Twentieth Century-Fox and critics of the time
claimed: "The difference is obvious and refreshing. Used
on the endlessly astonishing plains of Western America, they
give a background inseparable from the telling of the story,
and possibly as important. "

Dmytryk says of the film, "Don't underrate a good
Western. If it's done right, nothing beats it for plain
drama. "

THE END OF THE AFFAIR (Columbia, 1955) is another of Dmytryk's favorites. A moving Graham Greene
story, this plot is set in London during World War II.
Deborah Kerr, a young married woman, is involved in an
adulterous affair. If her lover is spared from death in an
air raid, she promises God that she will end the affair.
The Motion Picture Exhibitor said of it: "The plot is an involved one and not assisted by an excess of conversion and
debate on the existence of God and the part He plays in fur-
thering an illicit romance. "

Dmytryk's next film, SOLDIER OF FORTUNE (20th-
Fox, 1955), was done mostly on location in and around Hong
Kong. Starring Clark Gable and Susan Hayward, the film's
greatest virtue is for the viewer to travel in Cinemascope.

Another routine film for Fox, THE LEFT HAND OF
GOD (20th-Fox, 1955) with Humphrey Bogart, was also set
in the Orient. However, unlike its three predecessors,
which were produced on location in Asia, the picture was
made on the studio's back lot. It does possess much authenticity, although the travelogue facets are missing. Bogart changes from an outlaw to a Catholic priest to escape
capture by a ruthless Chinese warlord.

Next, back at Paramount where Dmytryk got his
start, he produced and directed THE MOUNTAIN (Paramount, 1956) with Spencer Tracy and Robert Wagner. It
was the story of two brothers scaling a dangerously icy
mountain, so the picture specializes in suspense and scenery.
It was photographed against the rugged Alps and is a prestige item artistically.

Then came another film with suspense and with expert scenery--this time in the Southern countryside. M-G-M said the film cost $6,000,000, perhaps the costliest in the company's history. The film was RAINTREE COUNTY (M-G-M, 1957), starring Montgomery Clift, Elizabeth Taylor, and Eva Marie Saint.

This film's location hunt was one of the longest on record. A spot was finally found in Kentucky, and they even arranged for the temporary destruction of a railroad. Four railroad lines cooperated in the filming of a realistic enactment of action concerning Abraham Lincoln's funeral train.

A total of four hundred and seventy-eight items were used to dress up the depot set, ranging from the station sign to lanterns and ticket spools. However, just before director Edward Dmytryk shot the scene, one final prop was found to be lacking--an old-style baggage truck.

Another authentic prop was the Green Line steamer "Delta Queen," which was given the necessary "make-up" for its role in the Civil War setting of RAINTREE COUNTY. A cast described as an army and over three thousand five hundred costume changes were also part of Dmytryk's picturesque production.

A newspaper at the time reported that in order to protect Montgomery Clift, Elizabeth Taylor, Eva Marie Saint, and other players who appeared in scenes filmed in a snake-infested swamp near Danville, Kentucky, Dmytryk engaged thirty snake beaters to rid the location of reptiles.

Many other such instances were reported in the filming of the picture. Although Dmytryk is known in many circles for his fine shooting of scenery, he said, "I don't like shooting on location as much as I like shooting in a sound studio. I really don't get to use the sound studios much these days but I do prefer it. Everything is under control. You can do things the way you want them done and not have to worry about outside interference.

"I hate shooting with crowds of people. The picture

---

*Opposite: Dmytryk, hands on hips, directing Gene Tierney and Humphrey Bogart in an exterior from THE LEFT HAND OF GOD (20th-Fox, 1955). Photo courtesy of Movie Star News.

I just made, THE HUMAN FACTOR, which I shot in Naples
for seven weeks, was quite an experience. We had hordes
of people everywhere we went. They were screaming constantly. You learn how to work around this kind of thing
but it's all very hard on the nerves.

"Of course, a couple of streets are usually blocked
off but people are always walking through. You've got a
scene half shot and there are three people walking around
a corner and are right in front of the camera. The cops
aren't very much help.

"One of my favorite pictures, THE SNIPER, shot in
San Francisco, I must say was a little different. The police
had it beautifully controlled. I guess American cops are
tougher than most--even tougher than those in police states.
In Italy it seemed everyone was an anarchist and had no
real respect for law and order."

Dmytryk finds the sound stages in the U.S. ideal
places to make movies. "It is easier to produce a picture
in Hollywood than anywhere in the world, because of superior equipment, labor availability and experience, and studio
organization. U.S. pictures made in England are keeping
the British industry alive and British film workers welcome
U.S. productions because of the jobs they provide."

Making films in Europe isn't always easy, as Dmytryk explained. "When I make pictures in Europe, where I
make practically all of mine today, they're usually co-
produced, which means you get some money from France,
some from Italy, and so on. You can take advantage of the
subsidies in these various countries that way. But that also
means you have to use some German actors, some Italian,
some British, and so on, depending on the countries that
are co-producing the film.

"Some terribly hybrid types of productions do result.
I'll never forget when Max Schell made THE CONDEMNED
OF ALTONA (20th-Fox, 1963). It was a picture of a German family and made by an Italian director, De Sica, but
the interesting thing was that Fredric March was playing
the father; Robert Wagner was playing the younger son;
some French girl was playing the mother; Max Schell, the
only German in the group, was playing the older son and
Sophia Loren, his wife.... All these people were supposed
to be Germans. Even their accents didn't match."

As Dmytryk explained that a director has to get used to working around obstacles when shooting "on location," he also has to make do with different nationality types and many other problems that crop up when making films.

For example, THE YOUNG LIONS (20th-Fox, 1958) has to cunningly shift action between American war camps, wartime Paris, war-torn North Africa, and a horrifying concentration camp. The film never loses impact. It was another war film for Dmytryk to direct, but in this one, right after RAINTREE COUNTY, Dmytryk said at least he had no trouble with Montgomery Clift, who again starred, or with Marlon Brando and Dean Martin.

Dmytryk stayed at Fox and next did WARLOCK (20th-Fox, 1959), with Henry Fonda, Richard Widmark, and Anthony Quinn. Although Dmytryk was not completely pleased with the adaptation of the film from a novel, the good vs. evil syndrome was explored.

THE BLUE ANGEL (20th-Fox, 1959), a remake of Josef von Sternberg's film, was Dmytryk's next Fox film, a story where a showgirl entertainer seduces a school professor. Dmytryk says today he is not sorry he made the picture but realizes it couldn't really match the 1930 version.

After Dmytryk's studies of good vs. evil, his next films seemed to study the more obvious social mores in our society. WALK ON THE WILD SIDE (Columbia, 1962) takes a frank look at prostitution and perversion. The New Orleans French Quarter of the 'thirties, when the picturesque town was wide open, is the principal setting.

Then for a short time Dmytryk's films left the frank study of good and evil and he produced and directed THE RELUCTANT SAINT (Columbia, 1962). This was a charming and humorous story of a simple accident-prone peasant boy who rose to sainthood--supposedly the true story of Saint Giuseppe.

Back, then, to a film loaded with sex and intrigue, as well as frank dialogue and situations--THE CARPETBAGGERS (Paramount, 1964). It recounts the spectacular career of an American business tycoon. This film depicts Hollywood starting in the "Golden Years" and goes on to the turbulent three decades which followed. The film was a chance for Dmytryk to return home to Paramount where he began as an assistant film editor in the 'thirties.

From the author of THE CARPETBAGGERS (Harold
Robbins) also came Dmytryk's next film, WHERE LOVE HAS
GONE (Paramount, 1964).   Again its unsavory subject matter
included murder, infidelity, alcoholism, blackmail, suicide,
and more.   The producer and screenwriter also remained the
same as in the previous film.

Another on-location challenge followed for Dmytryk in
MIRAGE (Universal, 1965), starring Gregory Peck and Diane
Baker.   This time the location was New York City for a
suspense thriller.   Dmytryk had to cope with mobs of people
in Central Park, on bus lines, and in various buildings.
One scene actually had to be changed when crowds couldn't
be kept away.

Dmytryk was worried about authenticity.   He stepped
aside briefly in a scene being shot in Central Park and a
crew of prop men raked up a pile of autumn-colored leaves,
put them in a cardboard box, and sealed it for shipment.
The leaves were sent to Universal's Hollywood studio where
they were duplicated synthetically.   A month later they were
used to match on a Hollywood sound stage floor the exact
scatterings of autumn leaves that appeared in the Central
Park location.

"Shooting on location isn't a vacation," Dmytryk re-
minds us, and ALVAREZ KELLY (Columbia, 1966) was shot
in Louisiana with no small amount of problems.   "The nearest to our locations in which we could put up our people
was on the outskirts of Baton Rouge," Dmytryk said.   "That
meant a forty-mile drive to one location, and sixty miles to
another.   There was no nearer housing.

"Everyone had to be up at 5:30 A.M.   The leaving
time was 6:45 in order to start operations at 8:00 A.M. . . . .
A location week was a six-day week as opposed to a five-
day week in Hollywood."

A newspaper account at the time explained some of
the problems.

There was the weather--all kinds of it.   At first,
they labored with extreme heat and humidity, mingled with
sudden thundershowers which drenched everything and everybody.   Then there were days of overcast when the company
would have to sit and wait for the sun to peep through so
that the color photography would match.   To top it all a

hurricane caught up with the company. They had to huddle
in their motels while a hundred-and-ten-mile-an-hour wind
and rain broke windows and toppled trees and telephone poles
around them.

Apparently, the hurricane did no damage to the in-
sect population in Louisiana. The troupe continued to be
bitten by mosquitoes, fire ants, bees, and hornets. On one
particular location, they were pestered by huge swarms of
yellow-jacket wasps. On another location, they attracted a
plague of flies.

There was absolutely no chance for social life of any
kind. Working under the sun all day, the humidity and other
unpleasantnesses, then the long ride home would leave everyone with no other desire than to get cleaned up, eat, and
get to bed.

"No one who has worked on location has any illusion
that it is any sort of vacation," Dmytryk said. "Breakdown
in equipment, being far from a source of supplies and re-
pairs, are always highly frustrating. Even simple commu-
nications can become a big problem. One of our ALVAREZ
KELLY locations was eighteen miles from the nearest telephone, to which we had to establish a courier service."

Some effective on-location shots were used in ANZIO
(Columbia, 1968) also. This was another "war is hell"
theme often seen in Dmytryk's films. The on-location problems in this film didn't seem as humorous as those with
the actors. Since it wasn't in the script, Dmytryk relegated to the cutting room floor his first take of the landing
scene in ANZIO. The scene showed 6'4" Wayne Preston,
followed by other American Rangers and war correspondent
Robert Mitchum, leaping out of a landing craft as the bow
opened. Preston fell head over heels into the sea.

Dmytryk next did SHALAKO (Cinerama Releasing
Corp., 1968), a rousing Western with Sean Connery and
Brigitte Bardot, followed by BLUEBEARD (Cinerama Re-
leasing Corp., 1972) with Richard Burton.

BLUEBEARD was shot on location in Budapest and
Rome. The setting was a Transylvania-like castle in the
Germany of the 'twenties and 'thirties. The film deals with
the questionable murders of Bluebeard's many wives.

Dmytryk's latest film to date, THE HUMAN FACTOR (Bryanston, 1975), also deals in murder, but this time, the human, touching side. George Kennedy and John Mills star in the suspenseful modern drama of a man who loses his family to a senseless mass-murdering group which is looking for the release of political prisoners. The audience follows George Kennedy as he uses an advanced computer system to track down the killers.

Dmytryk's one-time involvement with the Communist Party in Hollywood obviously has no effect on his career today; he is in a position of choosing any films he desires.

He lives in a quiet home outside of Los Angeles with his wife of twenty-seven years and a young daughter, fourteen. His son Michael, from his first marriage, is working in television. "Michael is now an assistant director in television ... television is something I have never tried. He is working on a long-running series and on those everyone gets to direct, because it becomes a routine thing--the actors know their stuff, they know what they're going to do. In fact, the actors take over in a series. They become the bosses; the directors come and go. Michael is considered one of the best directors."

Edward Dmytryk's son's career in films may just be starting, but his father's is always touching new horizons, too. Yet from such a long and interesting career, Edward Dmytryk told me, "I make it a point never to save a thing." What he has had to say, he has said in the films he has made.

EDWARD DMYTRYK

A Film Checklist by Karl Thiede

Edward Dmytryk started as a film editor at Paramount, but did not edit BELLE OF THE NINETIES (Paramount, 1934), as some sources indicate; LeRoy Stone did.

Director

1. THE HAWK (July 1935). P: Herman Wohl. C:

Yancey Lane, Betty Jordan, Dickie Jones.   55m.

2.   MILLION DOLLAR LEGS (14 July 1939). P: Para-
      mount. D: Nick Grindé, Edward Dmytryk uncredited.
      C: Betty Grable, John Hartley, Donald O'Connor.
      Edward Dmytryk was editing the picture and with one
      week of shooting left Grindé was incapacitated by a
      throat infection.   Dmytryk finished directing the pic-
      ture.   65m.

3.   TELEVISION SPY (20 October 1939). P: Paramount.
      C: William Henry, Judith Barrett, William Collier,
      Sr.   60m.

4.   EMERGENCY SQUAD (5 January 1940). P: Paramount.
      C: William Henry, Louise Campbell, Richard Den-
      ning.   58m.

5.   GOLDEN GLOVES (2 August 1940). P: Paramount.
      C: Richard Denning, Jeanne Cagney, J. Carrol Naish.
      69m.

6.   MYSTERY SEA RAIDER (9 August 1940). P: Para-
      mount. C: Carole Landis, Henry Wilcoxon, Onslow
      Stevens.   78m.

7.   HER FIRST ROMANCE (25 December 1940). P:
      Monogram. C: Edith Fellows, Wilbur Evans, Jac-
      queline Wells.   77m.

8.   THE DEVIL COMMANDS (3 February 1941). P: Co-
      lumbia. C: Boris Karloff, Richard Fiske, Amanda
      Duff.   65m.

9.   UNDER AGE (24 April 1941). P: Columbia. C:
      Nan Grey, Tom Neal, Mary Anderson.   60m.

10. SWEETHEART OF THE CAMPUS (26 June 1941). P:
      Columbia. C: Ruby Keeler, Ozzie Nelson, Harriet
      Hilliard.   67m.

11. THE BLONDE FROM SINGAPORE (16 October 1941).
      P: Columbia. C: Florence Rice, Leif Erickson,
      Gordon Jones.   70m.

12. SECRETS OF THE LONE WOLF (13 November 1941).
      P: Columbia. C: Warren William, Eric Blore,

Ruth Ford.   67m.

13.   CONFESSIONS OF BOSTON BLACKIE (8 January 1942).
      P: Columbia.   C: Chester Morris, Harriet Hilliard,
      Richard Lane.   65m.

14.   COUNTER ESPIONAGE (3 September 1942).   P: Co-
      lumbia.   C: Warren William, Eric Blore, Hillary
      Brooke.   A Lone Wolf film.   72m.

15.   SEVEN MILES FROM ALCATRAZ (8 January 1943).   P:
      RKO Radio Pictures.   C: James Craig, Bonita Gran-
      ville, Frank Jenks.   62m.

16.   HITLER'S CHILDREN (19 March 1943).   P: RKO
      Radio Pictures.   C: Tim Holt, Bonita Granville,
      Kent Smith.   NC: $178,000.   DG: $3,250,000.
      83m.

17.   THE FALCON STRIKES BACK (7 May 1943).   P: RKO
      Radio Pictures.   C: Tom Conway, Harriet Hilliard,
      Jane Randolph.   Working title: THE FALCON COMES
      BACK.   Production dates: 19 January 1943-8 Febru-
      ary 1943.   NC: $118,845.   65m.

18.   CAPTIVE WILD WOMAN (4 June 1943).   P: Universal.
      C: Acquanetta, John Carradine, Evelyn Ankers.
      60m.

19.   BEHIND THE RISING SUN (© 3 August 1943).   P:
      RKO Radio Pictures.   C: Margo, Tom Neal, J.
      Carrol Naish.   88m.

20.   TENDER COMRADE (© 19 December 1943).   P:
      RKO Radio Pictures.   C: Ginger Rogers, Robert
      Ryan, Ruth Hussey.   102m.

21.   MURDER, MY SWEET (© 19 March 1945).   P: RKO
      Radio Pictures.   C: Dick Powell, Claire Trevor,
      Anne Shirley.   Working title and preview title:
      FAREWELL, MY LOVELY.   95m.

22.   BACK TO BATAAN (© 25 June 1945).   P: RKO
      Radio Pictures.   C: John Wayne, Anthony Quinn,
      Beulah Bondi.   Working title: INVISIBLE ARMY.
      97m.

23. CORNERED (December 1945). P: RKO Radio Pictures.
    C: Dick Powell, Walter Slezak, Micheline Cheirel.
    102m.

24. TILL THE END OF TIME (1 August 1946). P: RKO
    Radio Pictures. C: Dorothy McGuire, Guy Madison,
    Robert Mitchum. 105m.

25. CROSSFIRE (15 August 1947). P: RKO Radio Pictures.
    C: Robert Young, Robert Mitchum, Robert Ryan.
    DG: $2,500,000. 86m.

26. SO WELL REMEMBERED (12 November 1947). P:
    RKO Radio Pictures. C: John Mills, Martha Scott,
    Patricia Roc. 114m.

27. THE HIDDEN ROOM (October 1949). P: Eagle-Lion.
    C: Robert Newton, Sally Gray, Naunton Wayne.
    Alternate title: OBSESSION. 93m.

28. SALT TO THE DEVIL (January 1950). P: Eagle-Lion.
    C: Sam Wanamaker, Lea Padovani, Kathleen Ryan.
    Based on the novel, Christ in Concrete. Reviewed
    under the title GIVE US THIS DAY. 118m.

29. MUTINY (14 March 1952). P: United Artists. C:
    Mark Stevens, Angela Lansbury, Patric Knowles.
    DG: $594,564.

30. THE SNIPER (May 1952). P: Columbia. C: Adolphe
    Menjou, Arthur Franz, Gerald Mohr. 87m.

31. EIGHT IRON MEN (December 1952). P: Columbia.
    C: Bonar Colleano, Arthur Franz, Lee Marvin.
    80m.

32. THE JUGGLER (June 1953). P: Columbia. C: Kirk
    Douglas, Milly Vitale, Paul Stewart. 86m.

33. THE CAINE MUTINY (September 1954). P: Columbia.
    C: Humphrey Bogart, José Ferrer, Van Johnson.
    DG: $8,700,000. Technicolor. 125m.

34. BROKEN LANCE (August 1954). P: Twentieth Century-
    Fox. C: Spencer Tracy, Robert Wagner, Jean Pe-
    ters. DG: $3,800,000. Color. Scope 96m.

35. THE END OF THE AFFAIR (May 1955). P: Columbia.
     C: Deborah Kerr, Van Johnson, John Mills. 106m.

36. SOLDIER OF FORTUNE (June 1955). P: Twentieth
     Century-Fox. C: Clark Gable, Susan Hayward,
     Michael Rennie. DG: $2,750,000. Color. Scope.
     96m.

37. THE LEFT HAND OF GOD (September 1955). P:
     Twentieth Century-Fox. C: Humphrey Bogart, Gene
     Tierney, Lee J. Cobb. DG: $3,000,000. Color.
     Scope. 87m.

38. THE MOUNTAIN (November 1956). P: Paramount.
     C: Spencer Tracy, Robert Wagner, Claire Trevor.
     Technicolor. 105m.

39. RAINTREE COUNTY (October 1957). P: Metro-
     Goldwyn-Mayer. C: Montgomery Clift, Elizabeth
     Taylor, Eva Marie Saint. Budget: $6,000,000.
     DG: $5,970,000. M-G-M Camera 65, which is film
     shot on 65mm. negative and then printed on 35mm.
     scope stock. Technicolor. 14,974ft. /166m.

40. THE YOUNG LIONS (April 1958). P: Twentieth Cen-
     tury-Fox. C: Marlon Brando, Montgomery Clift,
     Dean Martin. DG: $5,000,000. Scope. 167m.

41. WARLOCK (April 1959). P: Twentieth Century-Fox.
     C: Richard Widmark, Henry Fonda, Anthony Quinn.
     Color. Scope. 121m.

42. THE BLUE ANGEL (September 1959). P: Twentieth
     Century-Fox. C: Curt Jurgens, May Britt, Theo-
     dore Bikel. DG: $1,400,000. Color. Scope.
     107m.

43. WALK ON THE WILD SIDE (February 1962). P: Co-
     lumbia. C: Laurence Harvey, Capucine, Jane Fon-
     da. DG: $3,000,000. 114m.

44. THE RELUCTANT SAINT (December 1962). P: Davis-
     Royal-Columbia. C: Maximilian Schell, Ricardo
     Montalban, Lea Padovani. Working title: GIUSEPPE.
     105m.

45. THE CARPETBAGGERS (April 1964). P: Paramount.
     C: George Peppard, Alan Ladd, Bob Cummings.
     DG: $15,500,000. Technicolor. Scope. 150m.

46. WHERE LOVE HAS GONE (October 1964). P: Para-
     mount. C: Susan Hayward, Bette Davis, Michael
     Connors. DG: $3,600,000. 114m.

47. MIRAGE (June 1965). P: Universal. C: Gregory
     Peck, Diane Baker, Walter Matthau. DG:
     $1,500,000. 9,771ft./108 1/2m.

48. ALVAREZ KELLY (October 1966). P: Columbia. C:
     William Holden, Richard Widmark, Janice Rule. DG:
     $1,460,000. Color. Scope. 116m.

49. ANZIO (June 1968). P: Columbia. C: Robert Mitch-
     um, Peter Falk, Earl Holliman. DG: $1,400,000.
     Technicolor. Scope. 117m.

50. SHALAKO (November 1968). P: Cinerama Releasing
     Corporation. C: Sean Connery, Brigitte Bardot,
     Stephen Boyd. NC: $1,455,000. DG: $1,310,000.
     Color. 113m.

51. BLUEBEARD (August 1972). P: Cinerama Releasing
     Corporation. C: Richard Burton, Raquel Welch,
     Joey Heatherton. Color. 124m.

52. THE HUMAN FACTOR (November 1975). P: Bryans-
     ton. C: George Kennedy, John Mills, Raf Vallone.
     Technicolor. 95m.

Chapter 10

HOWARD HAWKS

by Jon Tuska

I

It was hot in Palm Springs. The sand from the white dunes swept across the highway, blown by the hot wind. The heat rose in silent eddies from the city streets. It radiated everywhere.

Here it was that Howard Hawks had finally come to live. He is one of the great directors of Hollywood films, as the French especially have hastened to recognize. He is also a gentleman.

He was dressed in light blue shorts and a white shirt as he opened the front door in response to my knock. The effect of the heat was profound. It made you feel light-headed. It clouded your mind and obscured your memory. You walked as if in a daze.

Howard was accustomed to it. He walked very slow-ly. His legs were still tender with blisters from cactus poison.

"I've been in the hospital for the last three days," he remarked, lowering himself into a leather reclining chair and propping up his legs. He was careful. "I was out motorcycling with my son. I made the mistake of riding

---

Opposite: Howard Hawks with his dog Cap while directing COME AND GET IT (United Artists, 1936) for Sam Goldwyn on the Goldwyn lot. Howard was hoping to rent out the dog for $500 a week. Photo courtesy of the Wisconsin Center for Theatre Research.

391

through a clump of poisonous cactus.   I'll be laid up at
least another week, maybe ten days. "

     There were two dogs in the room, one of them a
golden shepherd, the other a hound.   There were no rugs,
only cool stones bordered by masonry.   The hound collapsed
on the floor near Howard's chair.   The shepherd came over
to me, laid his head on my leg, regarding me with sad eyes.
I petted him.   In time, he sauntered philosophically away.
The heat was everywhere in the room.   Your body became
heavy and lethargic from it.

     I recalled that the French director Jacques Rivette
had written of Howard in Les Cahiers du Cinéma when Rivette was still a film critic.   He had said of MONKEY BUSI-
NESS (20th-Fox, 1952):

> Mais l'ennemi s'est maintenant glissé en l'homme
> même: le subtil poison de jouvence, la tentation
> de la jeunesse dont nous savons depuis longtemps
> qu'elle n'est pas la ruse la plus subtile du malin--
> tantôt singe et tantôt basset--lorsqu'une rare intelli-
> gence le tient en échec.   Et la plus néfaste des
> illusions, contre laquelle Hawks s'acharne avec un
> peu de cruauté: l'adolescence, l'enfance sont états
> barbares dont nous sauve l'education: l'enfant se
> distingue mal du sauvage qu'il imite en ses jeux;
> dès que bue la précieuse liqueur, le plus digne
> vieillard s'absorbe dans l'imitation d'une guenon.
> On reconnait ici une conception classique de
> l'homme, qui ne saurait être grand que par acquis
> et par maturité; terme de son progrès, sa vie-
> illesse le juge.

> [But the enemy now creeps within man himself:
> the subtle poison of the Fountain of Youth.   After
> all, for a long time we have known the temptation
> of youth--be it now a monkey, now a hound--is
> only the most subtle wile of the Devil when con-
> fronted by rare intelligence.   Hawks with cruel
> eagerness pursues that most ill-fated of illusions.
> Infancy and adolescence are barbarous states from
> which only education saves us.   The child distinctly
> imitates the savage in his behavior.   Should he
> drink of the Fountain, even the most dignified old
> man will act like a monkey.   We recognize in this
> a classic conception of man.   Greatness is the

result of experience and maturity. At the end of
his journey, a man's old age will be his judge.]

Rivette had called his essay "Genie de Howard Hawks."
Many years had passed since it appeared in May 1953. Now
Howard Hawks was an old man.

"I will tell you a story I have never told anyone," he
said. The Shepherd got up, shook himself, and found a new,
cooler spot on which to slumber. Howard looked at me for
a moment. His eyes were distant. So often in his films,
he has ignored dialogue and concentrated on eyes. "It's a
sequel, really, but I have to tell you the whole story first,
for it to have any meaning. Lauren Bacall's coming to
Hollywood was a mistake on my secretary's part. I only
wanted to find out about her and my secretary sent her an
airplane ticket instead. She showed up in a sweater and
gabardine skirt, very excited, with a high nasal voice. I
couldn't use her. I told her it was her voice. She asked
me what she could do about lowering it. I repeated what I
had heard from other people. For two weeks I didn't see
her. She went back to the apartment where she was staying
and worked on it. When she saw me again, I was amazed.
Her voice had become deep, husky.

"I began to invite her to my home for the Saturday
night parties I had. I always ended up having to drive her
home.

" 'Betty,' I told her, 'this isn't going to work. I
don't always want to take you home. Can't you interest one
of the others in escorting you?'

" 'I've never been very good with men,' she said.

" 'Why not try being insolent?' I suggested.

"The next Saturday night she came over to me and
said she had found a ride home.

" 'How'd you do it?' I asked.

"She said, 'I just walked up to him and asked him
where he bought his tie. He asked me why I wanted to
know. I told him so I could tell people not to go there.
He laughed, and now he's driving me home.'

"It was Clark Gable.

"I got to so like her insolent style that I went to
Jules Furthman when I was back on the Warner lot.   We
were preparing Ernest Hemingway's TO HAVE AND HAVE
NOT [Warner's, 1944].   Furthman and Bill Faulkner were
doing the screenplay. "

I interrupted.

"Duke Wayne told me that originally you had done all
the preparation work on CASABLANCA [Warner's, 1942], but
that at the last minute you went off the picture and Michael
Curtiz directed it in your place.   Duke said you only have
to look at CASABLANCA to see how much of a Hawks picture
it really is.   I wouldn't bring it up, except a number of
critics have claimed TO HAVE AND HAVE NOT was an imitation of CASABLANCA. "

"Well, " said Howard, "Wayne's right.   I did most of
the preparatory work on CASABLANCA.   When it came to
doing TO HAVE AND HAVE NOT, I wanted the picture to be
different.   Ernest had given me screen rights on the novel
some years before, but I just couldn't come up with the
right treatment for it.   With Betty, I thought I might have
it.   I asked Jules if he could write in a part for an insolent
girl.   He didn't see why not.   I gave Betty a screen test
opposite Bogart.   I even wrote that line for her, 'All you
have to do is whistle.   You know how to whistle, don't you?
Just put your lips together and blow. '   Betty was great. "

"They fell in love, " I said.   "Did you try to capture
that in the picture, or later, in THE BIG SLEEP [Warner's,
1946]?"

"No.   I tried to keep it out.   I had told Bogie that I
had a challenge for him, a girl as insolent as he was.   I
didn't figure he would fall in love with her.   But he did.
Of course, that helped Betty.   Bogie played all his scenes
for her.   Under other circumstances, that would have been
an almost impossible thing for anyone to get Bogie to do. "

Howard grew quiet.   Outside the sun blazed mutely.
Its light glared on the white stone fence.

"Did it occur to you that Bogart was falling in love
with someone who was to a certain extent your creation?" I
asked.

Howard nodded.

"I even took Betty aside and warned her. 'Bogie is falling in love with you, Betty. He doesn't know it's just a role.' "

He smiled at me.

"That's what brings me to the sequel. This last year I was invited by the Academy to receive a special award. Wayne was going to give it to me. Betty was there. She came up behind me and kissed me. She said, 'I'm still playing the same role, Howard.' "

John Ford had come to the desert to die. Howard had been at his side. But for Howard the desert, the unceasing heat, the dry, unstirring air had preserved him.

It has always seemed an incongruity to me that Howard, who has placed human relationships first among his elective affinities, should have found himself friends with two such divergent personalities as Hemingway and Faulkner. Hemingway had early perceived the inevitable losses life extracts from you. But Faulkner was light years removed. When he wrote for Howard, he worked, I suspect, by the assignment, giving Howard what he wanted.

"You knew Faulkner rather well."

"Yes, I did," Howard responded. "I was in New York working on SCARFACE [United Artists, 1932]. I read Faulkner. He was employed as a clerk in Macy's book store. I later bought his short story, 'Turnabout,' and made it the basis for the picture TODAY WE LIVE [M-G-M, 1933]. Faulkner by then was living back in Mississippi. I sent him a check and invited him to come to Hollywood to M-G-M, where I was under contract, to assist on the screenplay."

Howard rolled his head to one side to better see me. The heat in the room dried up your energy. You were chilled by it.

"He came to my office. 'I'm Howard Hawks,' I told him. 'I know,' he said. 'I saw your name on a check.' He sat there and smoked his pipe while I took a couple of hours to explain what I wanted. He said nothing until I

finished. Then he stood up. 'Where are you going?' I
asked him. 'I'm going to write your screenplay,' he said.
'It should take me no more than a week.' He didn't know
anything about screenwriting. 'Wait a minute,' I said. 'I
want to know something about you.' He hesitated. 'Have
you got a drink?' he asked. I pulled out a bottle and we
began to talk. When we finished that, we went out and
visited a few saloons. By three in the morning, when the
last cigarette was drowned in a whiskey glass, it was the
beginning of a relationship. We were friends from that day
until his death."

I remembered, as I sat in an easy chair, the air in
the room yawning as it wearily fell to dozing, that Faulkner
had sent Howard a letter once he returned to Oxford, Mississippi after his stint at Metro. "I'm sitting on the porch
with the rain dripping off the eaves, drinking bourbon, and
I hear a wonderful sound--the toilet, and it's due to you."

In his modest and quiet fashion, throughout his career as a filmmaker, Howard Hawks has assembled extraordinary talent around him, all of it to put forth a consistent, cogent point of view. But I knew better than to say as
much. Howard would only deny it.

II

A descendant of a family of wealthy paper manufac-
turers, Howard Hawks was born at Goshen, Indiana on 30
May 1896. He was the eldest of three brothers. Kenneth
Hawks died in 1930 in an airplane crash while directing an
aviation scene. William Hawks, until his death, was a
Hollywood producer for many years.

Howard Hawks moved to Neenah, Wisconsin when he
was two and was relocated to California when he was ten.
He attended elementary and high school in Pasadena. In
1917 he graduated from Cornell University with a degree in
mechanical engineering. That same year, Howard entered
the motion picture industry as a property man at Paramount
Pictures, known then as Famous Players-Lasky. He was
soon promoted to an assistant director.

He joined the Army Air Corps during the Great War
and was stationed in France. At the signing of the Armis-

tice, he held the rank of a second lieutenant. He built airplanes and drove race cars after the war. It wasn't until
1922 that by means of an inheritance Howard re-entered the
picture business, this time as an independent producer and
director of short comedies. They cost about $3,000 to make
and were sold for $6,000. He tried his hand at more ex-
pensive productions and finally associated himself with Jesse
L. Lasky at Paramount. During his time with Lasky, Howard was involved in the making of more than forty films.
He wrote many of the screen stories and even titled several
pictures.

He hired on at Metro-Goldwyn-Mayer shortly after it
was formed, in the hope that he might be assigned to direct
an important picture. When the hope didn't materialize,
Howard quit. Sol Wurtzel, who was in charge of production
at Fox Film Corporation, approached him. Wurtzel had
heard of the fine work Howard had done at Paramount and
decided to put him under contract. THE ROAD TO GLORY
(Fox, 1926) was the first picture Howard directed. It
starred May McAvoy and Rockliffe Fellowes. Howard was
in rather a dark frame of mind. He told the story about a
young girl's reaction to going blind as sustained tragedy. It
was based on an experience he'd had when a girl at a party
he gave went blind as a result of drinking bootleg liquor.
While she was waiting for the doctor, she said, "Just because I'm blind doesn't mean I'm not good in bed." Howard
admired her spirit.

Years later, Howard recalled that Wurtzel was "a
very astute and wise man," but that THE ROAD TO GLORY
was only appreciated by a few critics. "And he said,"
Howard quoted Wurtzel, " 'Look, you've shown you can
make a picture, but for God's sake, go out and make entertainment.' So I went home and wrote a story about Adam
and Eve waking up in the Garden of Eden and called it FIG
LEAVES. It got its cost back in one theatre. And that
taught me a very good lesson; from that time on, I've been
following his advice about trying to make entertainment."

Hawks followed FIG LEAVES (Fox, 1926) with a
comedy, THE CRADLE SNATCHERS (Fox, 1927), which was
fast-paced in what was to become the Hawks style for comic
treatments. The picture was based on a stage play by Russell Medcraft and Norma Mitchell and featured Arthur Lake
and Sally Eilers. PAID TO LOVE (Fox, 1927) came next,
with Virginia Valli, George O'Brien, and William Powell.

F. W. Murnau had just directed SUNRISE (Fox, 1927) and
the executives at Fox were taken with trick photography.
Being of a mechanical frame of mind, Howard tried several
new trick techniques in this picture.   But no sooner had he
experimented with trick photography than he abandoned it.
As in the most effective English prose, Howard came to feel
that simple expression is invariably preferable to all manner
of complexity.   He came to keep his camera for the most
part at eye level.   Anything else, unless it was required for
emphasis, tended to be a distraction and interfered with the
ability of the viewer to remain oblivious to the mechanics
by which personality and incident were being projected on
the screen.

Concerning A GIRL IN EVERY PORT (Fox, 1928),
Howard commented on how it "was the beginning of a relationship I have used in a number of pictures.   It's really a
love story between two men. "   Howard wrote the screenplay.
It was a tale about two sailors who share the same girls in
port.   Louise Brooks, Leila Hyams, and Maria Casajuana
were among the women.   Victor McLaglen and Robert Armstrong played the sailors.   At the end of the picture, the
two men at last renounce women and go off together.   There
is nothing overt in all this.   The picture keeps moving from
port to port.   What seems to be uppermost is that the solid
values which can unite men are alien in terms of the preda-
tory and defensively exploitive instincts of women.   Hawks
was only beginning to detail the complex and tenuous bonds
which hold human beings one to another rather than emphasizing the isolation and disparateness of so many relationships.   It wasn't until much later, and then primarily in his
comedies and RED RIVER (United Artists, 1948), that he
dwelt on what separates people.   Peter Bogdanovich has remarked that in perspective and viewpoint he finds Hawks
most closely related to Ernest Hemingway.   I cannot really
agree with him.   Hemingway was acutely, even painfully
conscious of the ultimate futility of human relationships.
Howard has long chosen to regard the matter in terms of
what brings men and women together.   The option he purchased on Hemingway's The Sun Also Rises (Scribner's,
1926) he never exercised because he couldn't conceive how
it might possibly be made into a comedy, and he had no desire to treat impotence tragically.

Howard's next two films were largely a result of
executing contractual obligations.   FAZIL (Fox, 1928) was a
routine affair and THE AIR CIRCUS (Fox, 1928) not much

better.   Since neither film is very special, I suppose it
will not matter greatly if I bypass them and come to his last
film for Fox and his first cinematic detective story.
TRENT'S LAST CASE (Fox, 1929) was based on the mystery
novel by E. C. Bentley, generally regarded as a classic of
the genre.   The studio was unable to acquire rights to make
a talking version of the story, so it had to be made silent.
Sound films already dominated the American scene.   The
picture, if it was distributed extensively at all in the United
States, was subjected to limited exposure.   Raymond Griffith
and Marceline Day were the principals.

Howard felt that being a contract director unnecessarily constricted his ability to make pictures the way he wanted
to make them.   In the future he would contract to individuals
or studios to make one picture or several after his own
fashion; but he would always retain control over the stories
and casting of his films.   The fact that he didn't have to
depend on directing for a living and that he had extraordinary talent for making financially successful pictures combined to provide him an enviable degree of artistic freedom.

Howard made his first talking picture in 1930 for
Warner Brothers' release.   He worked on the screenplay
and was able to choose his own players.   The story permitted him to introduce themes which he was to vary, in-
vert, and transmute over the next four decades.   THE DAWN
PATROL dealt with the fraternity of men at war, the excitement of mechanical flight, and the confrontation with mor-
tality.   Howard chose to so tell his story that while individuals might come and go, human problems persisted as
an unalterable constant.   It was a time for war pictures.
William Wellman had directed WINGS (Paramount, 1929);
Lewis Milestone was directing ALL QUIET ON THE WEST-
ERN FRONT (Universal, 1930).   Howard Hughes was at work
producing HELL'S ANGELS (United Artists, 1930).

Howard hired for THE DAWN PATROL some of the
same fliers Hughes had previously used in preparing certain
aerial sequences for HELL'S ANGELS.   When it was reported to Hughes that the pilots had been interrogated as to
what they had done for Hughes, he grew worried lest the
Warner film copy identically from the picture in which he
had already heavily invested.   Hughes questioned the pilots
himself.   He learned that there was one striking similarity
between the two pictures: the bombing of an enemy ammu-
nition dump.   Hughes was especially alarmed over the fact

that THE DAWN PATROL would precede HELL'S ANGELS
into general release.

When DAWN PATROL was booked into a San Francisco theatre, Reggie Callow of the Hughes organization and
Joseph Moncure March, story editor on HELL'S ANGELS,
flew up to see it. They thought it an excellent film, but
were impressed by its similarities to a stage play that had
made James Whale's reputation, JOURNEY'S END. Upon
returning to Hollywood, they contacted Whale and he, in
turn, notified the JOURNEY'S END people in London. A
few days later they joined Hughes in a joint suit against Warner Brothers for plagiarism.

The screenplay for DAWN PATROL had been written
by Howard, Don Totheroh, and Seton I. Miller, based on a
story titled "The Flight Commander" by John Monk Saunders.
Hughes very much wanted to get hold of the original story
by Saunders. One day a private detective Hughes had hired
came to Joseph Moncure March's office. He told March
that he had arranged with one of the secretaries at Warner
Brothers to get a copy of the story and show it to them at
her apartment. They went. It was a plant. They were
both arrested. Eventually, consistent with the long time
due process always takes, the plagiarism suit was heard and
the motion denied. Shortly thereafter the charges against
March were dropped.

Hawks thought all the fuss idiotic. He had made, he
felt, a good film with Richard Barthelmess, Douglas Fairbanks, Jr., and Neil Hamilton. JOURNEY'S END (Tiffany,
1930), a Tiffany-Gainsborough release, was of course an
obvious comparison and the critics didn't hesitate to draw it,
nor couple it with the suggestion that perhaps the genre
should die out quickly. Howard's film had none of the
glamour of the remake of 1938 directed by Edmund Goulding with Errol Flynn, David Niven, and Basil Rathbone.
THE DAWN PATROL, as Howard conceived it, was a lean,
straightforward story of British pilots who in a spirit of
hopelessness encounter the inevitability of death as they
systematically prepare for bombing missions over enemy
territory. At times, Hawks piloted a camera plane himself
with the camera up front. He managed to capture several
remarkable aerial sequences.

Hawks' next film in release was THE CRIMINAL
CODE (Columbia, 1931), which starred Walter Huston,

Phillips Holmes, and Constance Cummings. The story was
based on a Broadway stage play that had failed because of
the ending. It was about a district attorney who brilliantly
secures a number of convictions. When his political fortunes reverse, he ends up as warden of the prison where
many of those he prosecuted are serving time. "I got together with ten convicts and said, 'How should this end?' "
Howard related, "and they told me in no uncertain terms."
Howard felt that Walter Huston, who played the district attorney, was one of the greatest actors Hollywood ever had.
"His character was based on a district attorney we had here
in California," Howard went on, "who was finally tried and
sentenced to prison, and they put him in the prison hospital
to protect him because the place was full of men he had
sent there. Finally he said, 'I can't take this any longer.
I want to go out into the yard.' He went out into the yard,
and the scene we did in the picture was just what he did.
Things like being shaved by a man he had sent up for cutting
somebody's throat were all true." The picture taught Howard something rather important, that tragedy can be very
amusing. Perhaps the reader's experience has been the
same as Hawks'. To perceive the humor and folly in human tragedy is to experience a sudden, surprising sense of
freedom.

THE CROWD ROARS (Warner's, 1932) was a transition film. It embodied a love of danger and excitement, the
understated confrontation with violence and death true of
Hemingway's fiction which, without Hemingway's perspective,
became so much a part of the Hawksian world of subsequent
films. Howard knew race cars as he knew airplanes, and
he knew the men who drove them as he had known wartime
fliers. James Cagney was the star. Cagney was tough,
really tough, but he was also capable of an amazing degree
of sensitivity. Howard made use of that. He may even have
had Cagney in mind when he wrote the original story.

Considering the fact that Howard Hughes put nearly
three million dollars into HELL'S ANGELS and tinkered endlessly with it, I suppose he should have been pleased to
find that it only lost $357,807.07. Hughes had a preference
for Lewis Milestone as a director. But when it came to
doing SCARFACE, he decided he wanted the director of THE
DAWN PATROL. He worked out a contract with Howard
whereby Hughes would produce and Hawks direct any property the two agreed upon, and which could be broken by nothing more than a verbal dissent. Hughes gave Howard con-

trol of the picture.   William Wellman had already directed
PUBLIC ENEMY (Warner's, 1931), with Cagney following in
the wake of Mervyn LeRoy's LITTLE CAESAR (Warner's,
1930) starring Edward G. Robinson.   Howard was intrigued
with the idea of a gangster film.   He wanted to alter the
treatment.   The Warner Brothers films had stressed social
conditions as the major cause of criminal violence in the
United States.   It was a silly notion.   Hawks was more Cal-
vinistic.   He told Ben Hecht when he began work on the
screenplay that he wanted to tell the story of Al Capone,
but stylize it so that it took in the whole family, as if the
Borgias were set down in Chicago.   Paul Muni was cast in
the lead.   George Raft was also cast.   It was his first picture.   Like John Ford, with whom he worked at Fox, Howard would frequently select a single physical action to indicate the interior sensations of a character.   He did so with
Raft.   Two or three gang killings in Chicago involved a victim who held a nickel clenched in a palm.   Howard had
Raft flip a nickel in SCARFACE.   It became Raft's trademark.

        "We were influenced a good deal by incestuous ele-
ments in the story of the Borgias," Howard recalled later.
"We made the brother-sister relationship clearly incestuous.
But the censors misunderstood our intention and objected to
it because they thought the relationship between them was
too beautiful to be attributed to a gangster.   We had a scene
in which Muni told his sister that he loved her, and we
couldn't play it in full light.   We wound up playing it in sil-
houette against a curtain with the light coming from outside.
It was a little bit too intimate to show faces--you wouldn't
dare take a chance."

        Hawks thought Paul Muni a great actor.   Muni had
to hit a man in the picture.   He was unaccustomed to fisti-
cuffs.   It occurred to Howard to get a friend of his who was
a prizefighter.   He had him work with Muni for two or
three weeks.   Every time Muni threw a punch, the fighter
blocked it with a hand.   When they came to shoot the scene,
the fighter took the blow straight on and was knocked over
a table.   Muni was petrified at what he had done.   Howard
had to shout at him: "Act!"   He acted.

        Al Capone heard about SCARFACE and sent several
of his associates to see Hawks, requesting a preview of the
picture.   Howard told them to relay to Capone that when the
picture came out, Al could buy a ticket.   Once it was com-

pleted, Howard did screen the film for a few of Capone's
friends.   They thought it was great and related their senti-
ments to Capone.   Howard was invited to Chicago to meet
Capone.

"They met me at the train," Howard said.   "They
were late.   One of the fellows said, 'There was a killing
last night and we had to go to the funeral.'   I said, 'Do I
have to ride with you if there was a killing last night?'
They said I could ride in a different car.   But when we
went into a cafe, they would sit with their backs to the wall
and I had my back to the door.   We had some damn good-
looking girls with us, a bit brassy but very pretty.   When
I saw Capone, we had tea and he was dressed in a morning
coat, striped trousers.   I was with him for two or three
hours."

Capone liked SCARFACE.   He went to see it five or
six times.   Finally he got a personal print of it.   He came
out to California once and visited Howard on the set of a
picture he was directing.   The police arrived and arrested
him.   The reader may think it somewhat of a curiosity that
Capone should have been so taken with the film, particularly
in view of the end the screenplay indicates for the protago-
nist.   The censors were concerned enough to force Howard
to append a new conclusion with Muni being hanged, but the
scene was later dropped.   Although it was filmed in 1930,
all of these perambulations held up release until 1932.

TIGER SHARK (Warner's, 1932) may not have ranked
with SCARFACE for dramatic social impact, but it varied
the theme of A GIRL IN EVERY PORT, adding to it the
tension of a romantic triangle.   Howard was always more
interested in personality than actors and actresses.   And it
was Eddie Robinson's personality which made TIGER SHARK
such a memorable film.   It is incredible when you think that
only two years before, Robinson had made such a reputation
with LITTLE CAESAR; for today LITTLE CAESAR is hopelessly dated and his performance is far too stylized and
time-bound to be wholly convincing.

"When we started TIGER SHARK," Howard said, "it
was written about a very dour man.   At the end of the first
day I said to Eddie, 'This is going to be the dullest picture
that's ever been made.'   Eddie said, 'What can we do?'   I
said, 'Well, if you're willing to try it with me, let's make
him happy-go-lucky, talkative.   You're going to have to keep

talking all through the picture.' Eddie said, 'Fine, let's do it.' So every day I gave him a sheet of yellow paper and said, 'Here's your lines.'" The alteration made the picture everything it was.

Years before, Irving Thalberg had met Howard and talked stories with him. Irving thought Howard the best storyteller he knew. And that is possibly why a Hawks film cannot really age: it consists of a compelling story simply told through personality and the relationships between personalities. It seeks to prove nothing.

Once when Howard was hunting with Ernest Hemingway, Ernest challenged Howard to hit him. Howard hit him. He broke the back of his hand. Ernest just laughed and stayed up half the night working a tomato can into a splint so Howard could go shooting the next morning. In A GIRL IN EVERY PORT, the one fellow always pulls the other fellow's finger; it is a sign of intimacy between a man and a woman, seldom between men. Howard thinks back-patting inane. So in TIGER SHARK he has Richard Arlen cast as Robinson's friend. The symbol of their intimacy is that Eddie will regularly scratch Arlen's back.

The picture opens to a chilling scene of a shark surfacing and snatching off Eddie's hand which is hanging overboard from a life boat. For the rest of the picture, he has a hook. He is mutilated. When he marries and his wife falls in love with Arlen, there is a sequence in which the sound of Eddie crazily shooting sharks from the forecastle is heard while the camera records Arlen and Zita Johann in a clinch. They don't stop even when the shooting stops. The suspense becomes agonizing in anticipation of Eddie opening the door and discovering them.

I cannot exactly say why it is, but Hawks' pictures have a way of growing on you. Each one seems to advance and deepen the perspectives of previous films. TODAY WE LIVE (M-G-M, 1933) was next. It was based, as I've said, on a Faulkner story, a story of friendship between two men in England during the Great War. The story had appeared in the Saturday Evening Post and that's where Howard first read it. Metro contracted Howard after TIGER SHARK. His association with them this time was no more satisfying than it had been before when Thalberg preferred to keep Howard in the story department. Howard sent for Bill Faulkner and hired him to work on the scenario. Faulkner

never did achieve an easy prose style nor the ability to produce a well-made narrative form, although he had a marvelous imagination.   Howard admired Faulkner's considerable
facility for creative storytelling.

Metro interfered.   The studio didn't have a picture
for Joan Crawford.   Louis B. Mayer was intent on saving
her popular image after the adverse effects of her role as
Sadie Thompson in RAIN (United Artists, 1932).   Howard
was informed that TODAY WE LIVE was to be a Joan Crawford vehicle.   The screenplay had to be rewritten to accommodate her.   The original conception was lost, but Howard
and Bill Faulkner had become friends.   Bill had found a
source of income which would permit him to survive and
yet write the kind of unpopular novels he liked.

When, some years ago, Neville Brand, who had
played Al Capone in a television program, micturated on a
bus load of tourists and sightseers being escorted around
Universal City, the incident excited little more than a casual laugh in Hollywood gossip columns.   Lee Tracy wasn't
so fortunate.   He was cast with Leo Carrillo, Fay Wray,
Joseph Schildkraut, Katherine deMille, Henry B. Walthall,
and Francis X. Bushman in VIVA VILLA! (M-G-M, 1934),
with Wallace Beery as Pancho.   David O. Selznick was the
producer.   Ben Hecht worked on the screenplay.   Howard
was assigned to direct.   While the company was on location
in Mexico, Tracy got drunk and micturated off a balcony.
Louis B. Mayer was outraged.   He summoned Lee Tracy
back to Culver City and requested that Hawks also return.
Mayer told Howard he expected him to bear witness against
Tracy; he was determined that Lee Tracy would never again
work in pictures.   Howard refused Mayer's demand.   Mayer
replaced him on the picture with Jack Conway.   Although
Howard had done the story preparation and all the exteriors
and those interiors filmed in Mexico, he received no credit
on the picture when it was released.   Howard had contributed
to the screenplay for RED DUST (M-G-M, 1932), and subsequently contributed story ideas for CAPTAINS COURAGEOUS
(M-G-M, 1937) and TEST PILOT (M-G-M, 1938), all directed by Victor Fleming, but VILLA remains the last directorial effort Howard ever did at Metro.

For TWENTIETH CENTURY (Columbia, 1934), Howard was able to cast John Barrymore, who was still in his
stride after his successes in BILL OF DIVORCEMENT (RKO,
1932) directed by George Cukor and GRAND HOTEL (M-G-M,

Howard Hawks on the set of TWENTIETH CENTURY (Columbia, 1934) directing John Barrymore.   Photo courtesy of Movie Star News.

1932) directed by Edmund Goulding. Ben Hecht and Charles
MacArthur, ultimately Howard's favorite screenwriters, did
the scenario. It was to be Carole Lombard's first comedy
role. Although she did not know it at the time, she also
became simultaneously the first full-fledged Hawksian woman.
Carole was brash, fun-loving, empathetic, caustically outspoken. Standing around on the set of another picture, chat-
ting with the men, when she saw the film's ingenue show up
an hour late after a visit to the office of the producer, she
quipped: "I'll bet she sucks a beautiful cock. She can't
act." But when Lombard came to work opposite Barrymore
she was horribly at sea.

        "She rehearsed and tried to act," Howard recalled.
"Barrymore started holding his nose where she couldn't see
him.

        " 'Look,' I told him, 'until four o'clock in the after-
noon I don't want to hear a peep out of you. After that,
you can say anything you want.'

        "I took Carole out and told her she was doing very
well. She knew all her lines. I asked her how much she
was getting paid, and she told me.

        " 'That's pretty good,' I said. 'What are you getting
paid for?'

        " 'Acting, of course!'

        "I said, 'You've earned all that money today, and I
don't want any more acting.'

        "I knew Carole pretty well. We'd both grown up in
the same little town in Wisconsin. I think she was a second
cousin.

        " 'Carole,' I said, 'what would you do if a man said
---- -- ---- to you?'

        " 'I'd kick him right in the balls.'

        " 'What would you do if a man said ---- ---?'

        "She made a typical Lombard gesture.

        " 'Well,' I said, 'you didn't kick Barrymore.'

"She just stared at me.

" 'Why didn't you wave your arm like that? Look, you go back in there and forget about acting. Kick him right where you said you were going to. Do anything to him you want, just don't act anymore. '

" 'You're serious, aren't you?'

" 'If you don't do it,' I said, 'I'm going to fire you. '

"So we went back.

" 'Let's try a take,' I said.

" 'We're not ready,' Barrymore said.

" 'Who's boss?' I asked.

" 'You are,' he said.

"We started the scene. Barrymore read his line. Carole made a kick at him. He started to dance around. She kept on waving her arms and kicking him. That was the first and only take. We had three or four cameras on it because I didn't know what was going to happen.

"Barrymore made his exit. Then he came back.

" 'That was so perfect,' he said to Lombard. 'That was marvelous. Have you been kidding me all this time?'

"She burst into tears and ran off the stage. He turned to me.

" 'What the hell is going on here?'

"I told him.

" 'The girl is simply marvelous,' he said. 'She's a cinch to be a star. '

" 'Okay,' I said, 'but you've got to help. '

"We made that picture in three weeks. Those two people--all I had to do was turn them loose. ''

Howard so constructed the dialogue that sentences overlapped and characters seemed to be talking at once, as they do in life. It gave the film a sense of frantic pacing, the comedy building in a crescendo. In fact, TWENTIETH CENTURY as comedy ranked as highly as DAWN PATROL had for adventure or SCARFACE for a study of the criminal milieu. The critics, however, had not yet detected anything unusual in any of Hawks' films.

The next two years weren't particularly eventful. In 1935 he directed BARBARY COAST for Samuel Goldwyn, released by United Artists, and CEILING ZERO, released by Warner's First National subsidiary. The important thing about BARBARY COAST was Howard's casting of Walter Brennan, a character about whom I shall have more to say later. CEILING ZERO was about airmail dispatching and starred James Cagney; it was a picture which didn't do much in the way of keeping Cagney happy as a contract player.

THE ROAD TO GLORY was released by Twentieth Century-Fox in 1936. William Faulkner was back in Hollywood working on the screenplay. The story bore no relationship to Howard's earlier effort at Fox. It embodied the idea from THE DAWN PATROL of what it is in war that keeps men going. There is a fatalism in the very air Hawks' characters breathe.

COME AND GET IT, Howard's second film for 1936, found him again working for Goldwyn. Sam was his usual irascible, interfering self. He didn't know how he wanted the picture to end. He kept William Wyler in the wings, poised to take over at a moment's notice if Howard did something of which Sam did not approve. The picture starred Edward Arnold, Joel McCrea, and Francis Farmer. Howard cast Walter Brennan in a character role. Brennan did so splendidly that he won his first Academy Award as a supporting player. In an attempt to find a suitable ending, Howard wrote several scenes and showed them to Sam. Goldwyn's response was simply that directors shouldn't write. Howard was removed from the picture and Wyler finished it, shooting the scenes Howard had written and claiming credit as co-director.

Howard chose Katherine Hepburn as the female lead for BRINGING UP BABY (RKO, 1938). His technique with her was somewhat different from what he had done with Carole Lombard, but the results were equally satisfactory.

Howard was paid $87,500. Hepburn got $72,500 for eight and a half weeks' work, Cary Grant $75,000 for ten weeks. Grant played a scientist in quest of a dinosaur bone. Hepburn was a wealthy heiress who had a pet leopard and whose demented behavior leaves Grant's scientific world in chaos. When Howard came to deal comically with modern life, the lack of order and the ever-present bestiality so apparent in the war films and SCARFACE emerge here in variation as farce, the inevitability of being ridiculous.

ONLY ANGELS HAVE WINGS (Columbia, 1939) followed. It is one of Howard's best pictures. It was based on a true experience. Howard did a lot of flying in these years. One night he had dinner with some Mexican bush pilots who told him of their work. He wrote it down on a piece of paper. One day he went over to the Columbia lot to see Frank Capra. Harry Cohn, who ran the studio under

Hawks in a script conference with Victor Killian and Jean Arthur while filming ONLY ANGELS HAVE WINGS (Columbia, 1939). Photo from The Memory Shop.

his own very close observation, insisted Howard come and
see him before he visit Capra.

" 'Look,' Cohn told Howard, 'I'm stuck.   I've got to
have a story for Cary Grant and Jean Arthur.'

" 'Here's a story I was writing on this morning.'

Howard left Cohn's office and went to see Capra.
When he came back, Cohn was determined.

" 'When can you start?' he asked.

" 'What do you mean?   I haven't got a script written.'

" 'You've got to start ten days from now.'

" 'Okay,' Howard conceded, 'but it's going to cost
you a lot more money.' "

The story concerned an expatriate group of characters in a Central American country where aviation was still
in a primitive state.   Jean Arthur became the Hawksian
heroine typical of the 'forties, tough, aggressively pursuing
Grant, filled with wisecracks.   Howard had a lot of trouble
getting her into the character and, with amusement, relates
how it wasn't until Jean saw Lauren Bacall in TO HAVE
AND HAVE NOT that she really understood what Howard
wanted.   Richard Barthelmess' wife, played by Rita Hay-
worth prior to her star build-up by Harry Cohn, was Cary
Grant's lost love.   ANGELS is Hawks' great romantic film,
permeated by the pessimism of the era, a fitting close to
the decade that he had begun with THE DAWN PATROL.

HIS GIRL FRIDAY (Columbia, 1940) was a remake of
THE FRONT PAGE (United Artists, 1931), originally based
on a play by Ben Hecht and Charles MacArthur.   Howard
Hughes had produced the earlier picture and made a profit
of $164,859.36.   Hecht worked on the screenplay with How-
ard.   The Pat O'Brien role from the Lewis Milestone version was switched to a female played by Rosalind Russell
opposite Cary Grant.   The comedy dialogue is swift.   So
demolishing is the caricature of Ralph Bellamy that he
ended up being Ellery Queen in "B" pictures because it was
so difficult by then to ever take him seriously again.

Howard had heard a legend in Mexico that Pat Garrett

had shot off the face of someone else and let Billy the Kid
escape. He thought it an excellent basis for a Western.
Howard Hughes was anxious to produce it.   Hawks discovered Jane Russell, working in a dentist's office, and Jack
Buetel whom he cast as the Kid.   While production was
starting, Howard caught wind of a story Jesse L. Lasky had
about Sergeant York.   Since Adolph Zukor had forced Jesse
out of Paramount, times had been hard.   Howard got hold
of the story.   Jesse had given him his first important job
in the industry.   It had been the same for Gary Cooper.
Howard contacted Coop and the two of them got together and
sold the idea to Jack L. Warner and Hal Wallis at Warner
Brothers.   Lasky ultimately made two million dollars out of
the deal.

        But a commitment to make SERGEANT YORK (War-
ner's, 1941) put Howard in a bind for completing THE OUT-
LAW for Hughes.   Howard suggested that since Hughes
wanted to be a director anyway, he should finish the picture
himself.   Hughes became intrigued with Jane Russell.   He
had a special brassiere fashioned for her and played up
sexuality in the film.   He even shot two versions of the
picture, one, not for release, with Jane topless.   This combined with censorship problems held up release.   When
Coop won an Academy Award and Howard was nominated for
one for SERGEANT YORK, Hughes became resentful.
YORK, however, proved to be Hawks' biggest commercial
success, due in large measure to the timeliness of the subject on the eve of the Second World War.

                              III

        It would be impossible for me at this point to con-
tinue in a chronological fashion to detail Hawks' films.
With SERGEANT YORK he did more than complete a cycle;
he established his orientations and outlined the basic genres
in which he was to do his finest work.   There is of course
one exception to this, the Western, and so in fairness I
must deal with it separately.   But the Western is certainly
as distinct a genre as are crime and adventure films or
comedies and musicals.   Howard's brilliance as a director
is not to be found in his iconoclasm nor in his innovative
daring; it's rather in the novelty and uniqueness combined
with variations upon a consistent point of view that he
brought to bear on making strictly generic films.

At the request of a high-ranking official in the Army
Air Corps, Howard directed AIR FORCE (Warner's, 1943) to
assist in the war effort. Perhaps the film's most moving
episode was the death scene which Faulkner wrote. Howard
approached it by ignoring what the characters were saying,
even what they were doing, and concentrating instead on the
emotions reflected in their eyes.

Howard had been trying for some time to convince
Ernest Hemingway to write for pictures. After all, he had
been successful in a similar attempt with William Faulkner.
Hemingway resisted.

"Howard," he said, "I don't want to. I don't know
enough about writing for pictures. I'm good at what I'm
doing and I don't want to go to Hollywood."

Howard assured Ernest he wouldn't need to come to
Hollywood. They could go hunting and fishing together and
work on a story. Hemingway was not sure. Maybe he sus-
pected that what interested Hawks most was his personality
and how it influenced the kinds of stories he chose to tell.

"Ernest," Howard said, "I can make a picture out of
your worst book."

"What's my worst book?"

"To Have and Have Not is a bunch of junk."

Hemingway shrugged it off as something he wrote because he needed the money. It wasn't a valid assessment.
But he was positive Howard couldn't turn it into a film.
For ten days the two of them talked about the two characters
in the book and how they met.

If Howard was critical of the novel's structure, he
had a case. But To Have and Have Not is not Hemingway's
worst book. It articulates better than much of Hemingway's
prose how really beat up we are by the course of our lives
and the hopelessness of one man being alone in the modern
world. Howard opted to avoid this perspective. He wanted
to dwell on the love story between Harry Morgan and Marie,
the latter being a former whore to whom Harry is married
at the time of the novel. Harry Morgan loses everything he
values in life and finally he loses his life, too. When Johnson charters Harry's boat and then skips out without paying

him, he inadvertently triggers a series of disasters. Howard reversed this chain of events at the outset by having
Harry Morgan portrayed by Bogart and having him get the
best of Johnson.

The story idea Hemingway worked out with Howard
he sold for $10,000.   Howard acquired screen rights to it
for $80,000.   The percentage terms Howard negotiated with
Jack L. Warner netted him ten times what Hemingway had
earned.   Hemingway didn't like that.

Howard discovered Ella Raines and had her introduced to the screen in CORVETTE K-255 which he produced
but did not direct for Universal in 1943.   The masculine relationships in Howard's films had been one of their most in-
triguing aspects.   Ella Raines was effective as a boyish heroine, but it was Lauren Bacall who became precisely what
Howard wanted, with her smoky passion, sharp tongue, and
insolent sexuality.   In every scene in TO HAVE AND HAVE
NOT, she walks out on Bogart.   She has both character and
integrity.   Jack Warner was quite taken with the repartee
Howard had written for Betty's screen test and rather ada-
mantly insisted that Howard find some way to work it into
the screenplay.   It became Betty's most famous line.

Howard took half of the picture to get around to the
subplot.   The setting was changed from Key West to Vichy
Martinique.   It was Howard's first time working with Bogart.
He was engaged by Bogie's personality and the fact that he
had lost the use of his upper lip so he could not smile.
The screenplay which had begun with two of Hemingway's
characters evolved suddenly into a protracted study of Bogart and Betty's assumption of the role of the consummate
Hawksian woman.

It had been at Howard's instigation that Jack Warner
agreed to a remake of THE MALTESE FALCON (Warner's,
1941) and gave John Huston his chance to direct.   Howard
told Huston he should not deviate from the novel, but follow
it exactly.   After TO HAVE AND HAVE NOT, Howard's
next picture, at Jack Warner's suggestion, was again with
Bogart and Bacall.   He wanted to try his hand at a contemporary detective story.   Most of Hammett's properties
had been used and re-used.   Bill Faulkner concurred with
Howard that, if you couldn't get Hammett, Raymond Chandler
was the best.   For $25,000, Howard purchased screen rights
to Chandler's first novel, THE BIG SLEEP (Knopf, 1939).

Leigh Brackett had written a hard-boiled crime novel. Harry Wepplo of Martindale's book store saw to it that a copy found its way into the pile of thrillers Howard Hawks was accustomed to buy regularly. Howard liked Leigh's dialogue and called her agent. He thought Leigh was a man because she wrote like one. Despite his surprise, Howard signed her for $125 a week. Leigh met Faulkner. Bill

A dialogue conference on the set of THE BIG SLEEP (Warner's, 1946) with Howard Hawks, Sonia Darwin, Howard's secretary Margaret Cunningham, Lauren Bacall, Humphrey Bogart and Louis Jean Heydt. Photo courtesy of the Museum of Modern Art.

was immaculately attired in country tweeds and greeted her in his gentlemanly manner. "We will do alternate sets of chapters," he said. "I have them marked. I will do these; you will do those." In eight days, the script was completed.

Howard chose to concentrate on scenes, not logical continuity. Each scene had to be played to the hilt. Bogart added his own bit of business to dress up a scene where he walks into a book store, and Faulkner added a scene where Bogie presumably seduces a willing Dorothy

Malone in a different book store.   One of the reasons Chandler's novel had structural problems was that he put it together out of unrelated short stories he had written earlier.
When Howard was filming the sequence where Owen's car is
pulled out of the water on Warner's tank sound stage, Bogie
asked him who killed Owen.   After all, if Bogie was the detective and point of view character, he ought to know.   Howard wasn't certain, but he said he'd ask Faulkner.   Faulkner
said he didn't know.   So Howard wired Chandler.   Chandler
replied facetiously that the butler had done it.   In the novel,
it is Brody, played in the film by Louis Jean Heydt, who
kills him.   But Howard never did find out, and that's how it
was filmed.

There is an engaging scene in the novel.   Marlowe
is taken out to a greenhouse to meet General Sternwood, who
brings him into the case.   In the short story version, the
scene runs approximately 1,100 words, whereas Chandler
expanded it to 2,500 words in THE BIG SLEEP.   Chandler
made palpable the physical reality of the humid heat and the
decay.   But it took Howard's sensitivity to human relationships to get the characters beyond talking tough and reveal-
ing momentary affection for one another.   Throughout the
picture Marlowe is able to relate to people in a way he never
can in any of Chandler's novels.   The loneliness in which
Marlowe perpetually dwells is lifted.

In his novel The Maltese Falcon (Knopf, 1930) Dashiell
Hammett described Sam Spade as a blond Satan.   Spade, like
every other character in the book, was out only for himself.
Hemingway had a run-in once with Hammett.   In To Have
and Have Not, Harry Morgan is described as a blond Satan,
but Hemingway was out to show that not even a hard-boiled
blond Satan had a chance.   In casting Bogart, neither John
Huston nor Howard Hawks respected anything of the original
conceptions of Sam Spade or Harry Morgan.   The violence
that both Hammett and Hemingway perceived as an indigenous
by-product of the American system of values, and the pained
isolation in which their characters live, could not be translated into the Bogart personality, although it was decidedly a
part of Bogart's temperament off-screen.   In THE BIG
SLEEP, Bogart was in love.   It was the affirmative elec-
tricity of his relationship with Betty that offset the despair
derived from being constantly lied to by everyone.   Howard
aptly cast Bob Steele as a cold-blooded killer in sharp contrast to the romantic Western roles he had been playing
since the silent era.   But it was through Betty, not in what

she said so much as what she did, that Howard was able to project a forthright honesty, a woman who preferred the company of men, a woman whose virtues were in being outspoken, loyal, a companion rather than a wife, independent but not without affection.

The picture wasn't released right away. Jack Warner was waiting for the gossip columnists to stir up even more popular interest in the Bogart-Bacall romance. Six months after production had been completed, Warner asked Howard to add some scenes between Bogart and Bacall. Howard was racing horses at Santa Anita at the time. He wrote the humorous dialogue himself about race horses which Bogie exchanges with Bacall, filled with sexual innuendo and culminating with Betty's jocular comment that how good she is in the home stretch depends on her jockey.

Howard's later adventure films revealed the same surge of even-tempered optimism that infiltrated his treatment of criminal violence in THE BIG SLEEP, as opposed to his image of social decay at the time of SCARFACE. John Ford's disillusionment with life and his cognizance that his values were increasingly out of place is an experience that Howard escaped. Leigh Brackett did the screenplay for HATARI! (Paramount, 1962), but much of it was improvised on location in Africa because action involving the hunting of wild animals realistically cannot be scripted. Duke Wayne was the star. Howard chose to set the Wayne screen personality against the element of savage jungle life. It made for an entertaining film about human relationships amid danger and excitement.

RED LINE 7000 (Paramount, 1965) became a reversal of HATARI! From familiar actors, the picture went to unfamiliar actors; instead of being able to identify positively with men who love danger, the viewer now becomes estranged. The setting was the race car track. Howard used the story as an opportunity to again vary plot ingredients from what they had been all the way back to THE CROWD ROARS. It was an experiment that was not altogether successful commercially. Yet, no one can be right all the time. Just as Howard has always believed in repeating what has proven successful in the past, by using it in variation, if the variation fails he has never made the error of trying it again.

Howard and John Wayne on location for HATARI! (Paramount, 1962).   Note Howard's RED RIVER belt buckle.
Photo courtesy of the Museum of Modern Art.

IV

When he was driving race cars, Howard in one race
forced another driver coming up rapidly behind him into a
fence.   Racing then was a rough sport.   After the race, the
other driver came over to Howard.   It looked for a time as
if there would be a fight.   The two had a drink.   They became friends.   Howard invited the driver over to his house.
The driver, it turned out, had no place to stay.   He ended
up staying with Howard for five years.   His name was
Victor Fleming.   Howard helped him become a director.

I have already had occasion to mention that Howard
lent Fleming assistance on films like RED DUST, CAPTAINS
COURAGEOUS, and TEST PILOT   He also worked without
credit for some forty days on Fleming's chef-d'oeuvre,
GONE WITH THE WIND (M-G-M, 1939).   Not the least of
his contributions was apt advice about how to handle Vivien
Leigh once she had been selected for the role of Scarlett
O'Hara.   Fleming complained to Howard that try what he

might, he couldn't get Vivien past being precious rather than
a flirty bitch. Howard suggested Fleming have her bend
over and then, with her in that position, kick her as hard as
he could in the derrière. Fleming tried it. He was over-
joyed with the results. It worked as nothing else had.

Hawks was interviewed for Cahiers du Cinèma by
Jacques Rivette and Francois Truffaut in February, 1956

> Je décide de faire un film quand le sujet m'inte-
> resse [Howard said] cela peut être sur les courses
> automobiles ou sur l'aviation, cela peut être un
> western ou une comédie, mais le meilleur drame
> est pour moi celui qui prend pour sujet l'homme
> en danger.... Quand j'ai fait RED RIVER [United
> Artists, 1948], j'ai pensé que l'on pouvait faire
> un western adulte, pour grandes personnes, et non
> pas un de ces quelconques 'cow-boys'.... Et à
> ce moment-la, ils se mirent tous à faire 'des
> westerns intelligents....'

> [I decide to make a film whenever the subject in-
> terests me. It may be on auto racing or on avia-
> tion; it may be a Western or a comedy. But the
> major drama for me is the one which takes for
> its subject a man in danger.... When I made
> RED RIVER, I thought that it might be possible to
> make an adult Western, for mature people, and not
> one of those about mediocre cowboys. And at that
> time, everyone was looking to make intelligent
> Westerns....]

John Ford contended that STAGECOACH (United
Artists, 1939) made Duke Wayne a star, but RED RIVER
proved him to be an actor. How Ford put it was: "I didn't
know that big sonofabitch could act." Hawks had to argue
with Wayne to get him to play the part of Tom Dunson.
"He read the script for RED RIVER," Howard recalled,
"and said, 'I don't know whether I want to play an old man.'
I said, 'You're going to be an old man pretty soon, and you
ought to get used to it. And you also better start playing
characters instead of that junk you've been playing.' So he
said, 'How do I show that I'm old?' and I said, 'Did you
ever see me get up? Just do it that way.' So he did it,
and he saw the film and he said, 'Lord, I'm old.' He
didn't have to do a lot of damn silly things to get that impression across." Ford liked RED RIVER so much that he

Howard working on location with Joanne Dru in RED RIVER (United Artists, 1948). Photo courtesy of the Wisconsin Center for Theatre Research.

immediately began casting Wayne in his own cavalry trilogy, with Duke playing old men more effectively than he had played anything else in his entire career in SHE WORE A YELLOW RIBBON (RKO, 1949) and RIO GRANDE (Republic, 1950).

"When I was casting BARBARY COAST," Hawks said, "they brought in Walter Brennan. I looked at him and laughed. I said, 'Mr. Brennan, did they give you some lines?' And he said, 'Yeah.' I said, 'Do you know them?' And he said, 'With or without?' I said, 'With or without what?' He said, 'Teeth.' I laughed again and said, 'Without.' He turned around and read the lines. I said, 'You're hired.' When we were going to do RED RIVER, there was a line in the scenario; it said, 'The cook's name was Groot.' He said, 'What are we going to do?' I wasn't worried. I said, 'Remember how we met, that "with or without teeth?" Well, I got an idea that you're going to lose your teeth in a poker game with an Indian. And every night he makes you give them back.' 'Oh,' he said, 'we can't do that.' I said, 'Yes, we can.' "

Walter Brennan by the time of RED RIVER had almost become an archetypal figure in Howard's stories, playing very similar parts in both BARBARY COAST and TO HAVE AND HAVE NOT. "I looked forward to doing RED RIVER," Walter Brennan was quoted during production, "not only because it is a fine story and has a fine part for me, but because Howard Hawks is a great director, and I shall never forget what he did for me in the past."

The Indian who won Brennan's teeth was none other than Chief Yowlachie, who had appeared in the first two-color Western, WANDERER OF THE WASTELAND (Paramount, 1924), which starred Jack Holt and Noah Beery, Sr. It was one of the Zane Grey stories that, at Howard's insistence, Paramount had begun filming as a series at the rate of two or three entries a year, certainly one of the best Western series Hollywood produced. Howard cast Pidge, Noah Beery's son, in RED RIVER, and Dobie, Harry Carey's son.

Howard chose a sixty-mile stretch of land for a location, south of Tucson. For approximately $150,000, he had a camp built to house about four hundred persons. The mobile fleet, to attend the picture people and nine thousand cattle, consisted of five water wagons, eight trucks to trans-

port the cattle, and twenty trucks, three buses, and several
other assorted vehicles for the movement of crew and equipment. The feed bill for the stock alone amounted to
$20,000. The final negative cost of the film, after a se-
cond financing, was $2,800,000 and it had a domestic gross
of $3,976,473.86.

Howard signed Broadway actor Montgomery Clift to a
five-picture contract, beginning with RED RIVER. Clift was
enthusiastic about his part and waited with anticipation for
what he felt to be his big scene, when he takes the herd
away from Duke and leaves Duke wounded and stranded on
the trail. After the scene was shot, Clift went to Hawks
and complained that it hadn't turned out to be so big, after
all. Wayne never looked at him. While Clift talked, Duke
continued to stare over his saddle into the distance, leaning
against his horse with his back more or less to Clift. Finally, Duke said simply, "I'm gonna kill you." Hawks
laughed. He chided Clift for ever thinking he could best
Wayne in a scene.

When I talked to Duke Wayne about RED RIVER, he
was quick to remind me that Borden Chase had only rewritten MUTINY ON THE BOUNTY as a Western and that
he knew from the outset that Tom Dunson was a surrogate
for Charles Laughton's Captain Bligh. "When Hawks bought
the story," Wayne told me, "I felt I could play an old man.
He wanted to have Cooper. What he was aiming at was
Cooper and Cary Grant to play Cherry. That was what he
wanted. Now, his idea of the old man was that he was becoming senile and he was afraid. In the last scene, there
was a great chance for me to play a coward. This was
how he conceived of it. He had Walter Brennan in and I
sat there and listened to them. Hawks is a very easy man
to talk to, but Brennan evidently had been giving him the
thing, 'I'll teach this guy to play an old man,' because
Brennan was playing that part when I first met him and he
was about thirty years old. He really always was an old
codger. He said, 'I'll fix it, Mr. Hawks. We'll get some
springs and his legs will do this.' I listened. 'Oh, Christ,'
I thought, 'what have I got myself into?' Hawks said, 'Yep,
that's good, sounds very good.' He sent for a prop man.
I didn't want to say anything with everybody together. I
waited until the following morning and then I went to see
Howard. 'Mr. Hawks,' I said, 'you been down to Texas
lately?' 'Yes, Duke,' he said, 'I've been down there a
little.' I said, 'Have you ever noticed how the older these

strong men are, the top ranchers, how much straighter they
get and how much more personality and power they have as
they reach maturity?' He said, 'I get it, Duke.' I never
had any more trouble. There was another scene. Two
fellas stand up to me. Howard said, 'This is Academy
Award stuff, Duke. Show you're afraid.' I told Howard
that it might be Academy Award stuff to show that I was
afraid, but I wasn't gonna be no goddamn coward. I'd been
strong all through the picture. The kid, Clift, loved me because I was a man he could love. But, sure, I told Howard,
I could be afraid, but not a coward. That's the way we
played it."

Jean-Louis Rieupeyrout in La Grande Aventure du
Western (Editions du Cerf, 1971), one of the very, very few
intelligent books written about American Western films, comments rather aptly that

> ... Dunson va un chemin rocailleux dont les obsta-
> cles humains, aplanis par lui avec une violence
> rare, comptent d'avantage que les obstacles physi-
> ques. De meurtre en bagarre, il campe un type
> d'une antipathie singulière, opposée à la caractéri-
> sation traditionnelle du héros que l'on aime suivre
> en ce genre de films, et pourtant les apparences
> mentent. Dunson finit par convaincre et plaire à
> cause même de sa rudesse née du souci de mener
> à son terme une tâche surhumaine.

> [Dunson travels a rough course in which human
> obstacles, removed by him with a rare violence,
> count for more than physical obstacles. He fixes
> a singular antipathy on murder as a result of a
> brawl, opposing the traditional characterization of
> the hero one loves to follow in this genre of films,
> and yet appearances are misleading. Dunson
> finishes by convincing and pleasing us, because
> his roughness and his anxiety bring to its conclu-
> sion a superhuman task.]

John Ireland played Cherry. He was drunk or late
for call much of the time, so Howard cut his role to almost
nothing. Harry Carey, Sr. had a part as a cattle buyer.

At this point, Howard Hughes entered again on the
scene. He was nursing a lot of grudges. He was still unhappy about THE DAWN PATROL and unhappier still about

THE OUTLAW. He felt that United Artists had mistreated
him during the years the company distributed his pictures
and he was suing for an audit. Once he saw RED RIVER,
he threatened to sue over the fashion in which Wayne and
Clift fight it out at the end of the picture. Hughes' claim
was that Howard had lifted the episode out of THE OUTLAW,
just as years before he had stolen from HELL'S ANGELS.
It was nonsense, but United Artists conceded and had a
short sequence deleted from all the release prints.

Hawks had always admired the astonishing effects
John Ford could get shooting Westerns in all types of weather. In RED RIVER, he got a chance to duplicate such an
effect. When Duke has to pray over Dobie Carey's grave
site on the plains, Howard managed to shoot it during the
brief span of time it took a cloud to pass before the sun,
throwing the scene into gloom.

Some years ago, at the request of an editor, I wrote
an essay on the history of Western films for an anthology.
In the essay I contrasted Howard Hawks' philosophy of making Westerns with Sam Peckinpah's approach. "The Western,"
according to Sam, "is a universal frame within which it is
possible to comment on today." For Howard it has been
otherwise. "To me," Howard has said, "a Western is gunplay and horses.... They're about adventurous life and sudden death. It's the most dramatic thing you can do."

You may feel the Peckinpah principle a bit extreme,
although in the original unreleased version of PAT GAR-
RETT AND BILLY THE KID (M-G-M, 1973) Sam produced
a classic Western by means of it. HIGH NOON (United
Artists, 1952) also fits Sam's principle, even though it was
made clearly a decade before Sam began to direct theatrical Westerns. Neither Hawks nor Wayne particularly liked
HIGH NOON. They felt it lied about the frontier spirit.
Howard decided to make the same story his own way, according to his own principle. When it came to casting, of
course, Wayne was the star, just as Wayne in the end would
be the star of every Western Howard has ever made.

Howard thought Cooper's role in HIGH NOON showed
him to be a coward. He remembered the arguments Wayne
had given him while they had been filming RED RIVER. He
wanted a story about a sheriff threatened by a lawless power who wasn't afraid, who didn't ask for help, but who got
it anyway because he had friends. The friends were Dean

Martin playing a reformed drunk and Walter Brennan playing a feisty old cripple.   Instead of the younger man moving in on the sheriff's old girl friend, Ricky Nelson portrayed a youngster who had to prove himself to be accepted by men he admired.   Ward Bond was rejected in his offer of help because he was too old and had people he had to care about. When he's shot anyway, the tension of RIO BRAVO (Warner's, 1959) begins in earnest.

RIO BRAVO is like an old friend itself, because the more times you see it, the more you come to like it and the splendid camaraderie of its principals.   Angie Dickinson played the honest, aggressive Hawksian heroine who is attracted to Duke and wins him over to her by the fade.

Howard varied his formula for RIO BRAVO when he came to make EL DORADO (Paramount, 1967), this time with Wayne playing an old man and Robert Mitchum as a drunken sheriff.   Mitchum was a good balance to Wayne's powerful screen presence.   There was no such balance in RIO LOBO (National General, 1970), mostly because there was so little money left in the budget after paying Wayne's salary, which had skyrocketed.   Jennifer O'Neill's titillating body was perfect for her role in SUMMER OF '42 (Warner's, 1973), but her neurotic personality and difficulty in acting detracted somewhat from the total impact of RIO LOBO. Like RIO BRAVO and EL DORADO, RIO LOBO was filmed in the Old Tucson town set left over from Wesley Ruggles' ARIZONA (Columbia, 1940), now an Arizona landmark. While in production for RIO LOBO, Wayne had to go to Hollywood to receive his Academy Award for TRUE GRIT (Paramount, 1969).   When he returned to the set, Howard and everyone else, and even Duke's horse, wore a patch over one eye.

Andrew Sarris, the film critic, has commented that Duke Wayne is the preeminent incarnation of the Western hero and that not until he is given his due as a player will the full stature of both Ford's and Hawks' Westerns be appreciated.   Perhaps Greg Ford said it best when he observed that "as Wayne declines in years and physically deteriorates, director Hawks, in compensatory fashion, insistently endows him with greater apparent dignity and self-respect. "   It is so, but Wayne had a part in it.

While John Ford was frequently given credit for RED RIVER, and wasn't above graciously accepting it, Ford could

never have made RED RIVER any more than he could have
made any of Howard's subsequent Westerns. Howard in his
Westerns further concentrated on alternatives for the family
as a basic unit. His relationships were necessarily more
nebulous, more a reflection of men striving toward some
common aim of moderate behavior than spiritual fulfillment.
Romantic love goes begging in Hawks' Westerns. By concentrating on personalities, seldom on acting, Howard has managed within the parameters of his philosophy to produce
Westerns that balance action with meaning in such a manner
as to avoid that disastrous pitfall of what is termed social
significance.

V

Howard collaborated in 1941 with the inimitable Billy
Wilder and his associate Charles Brackett on BALL OF
FIRE. Howard directed. Sam Goldwyn was the producer.
Gary Cooper and Barbara Stanwyck starred. Coop was a
professor whose values underwent a severe alteration when
he was exposed to an erratic show girl. Howard was displeased with the comic pacing and didn't do another comedy
until 1948.

Sam liked BALL OF FIRE so much he wanted it remade with Danny Kaye.

"Goldwyn pestered me and pestered me," Howard recalled. "He offered me $25,000 a week to remake BALL
OF FIRE as A SONG IS BORN. I finally gave in. There
was a way I thought we could do the picture. But Goldwyn
wouldn't let me do anything. It was a horrible experience.
Goldwyn kept interfering no matter how much I insulted him.
Danny Kaye and his wife were separating and he was a bas-
ket case, stopping work twice a day to see a psychiatrist."

Sol C. Siegel, who had long headed up production at
Republic Pictures, moved over to Twentieth Century-Fox
where he became a producer. One of his projects was
Howard's next picture, I WAS A MALE WAR BRIDE (20th-
Fox, 1949), again a comedy, this time with Cary Grant and
Ann Sheridan. The plot was elementary. Grant and Sheridan get married and events conspire to prevent them from
sleeping together. Howard was comfortable directing Grant
and could get him to try anything at all in his scenes. The
picture proved a success.

"Who Goes There?" was one of the finest short
stories of science fiction that John Campbell, the late editor
of Astounding Science Fiction, wrote under his pen name,
Don A. Stuart.   It is a minor classic in the genre.   Howard
bought screen rights to the story and arranged for RKO Radio to finance production.   THE THING was officially produced by Howard Hawks and directed by Christian Nyby.   Before and again after this picture, Nyby was Howard's film
editor.   Howard wanted to give Nyby a chance to direct and
so to the present day disclaims any credit for the film.
Nyby, however, admits enlisting Howard's help and Hawks
did sit in on all the rehearsals and worked extensively on
the script.   THE THING was firmly among the best science
fiction films, a genre that was very much in vogue during the
paranoid 'fifties.   Russell Harlan, who generally photographed
Howard's Westerns, was the cinematographer.   James Arness played the terrible vegetable creature from a distant
world who crashes in a flying saucer into the frozen wastes
of the Arctic only to be discovered by a group of naive
scientists.

Howard both produced and directed THE BIG SKY in
1952, also for release by RKO Radio Pictures.   It was
based on a novel by A. B. Guthrie with the screenplay by
Dudley Nichols; Russell Harlan was the cinematographer,
Christian Nyby the film editor.   Like TIGER SHARK, of
which it was a variation, the plot concerned the friendship
between two frontiersmen played by Kirk Douglas and Dewey
Martin and the torment introduced into their relationship by
Douglas' loss of an infected finger and his involvement with
an Indian girl played by Elizabeth Threatt.   Howard felt in
retrospect that Kirk Douglas was perhaps miscast in a role
which demanded that he inspire more sympathy in the audience than he was readily capable of.

Whatever the distrust of science embodied in BRING-
ING UP BABY or THE THING, Howard further confirmed
his suspicions in his elaborate spoof, MONKEY BUSINESS
(20th-Fox, 1952), with Cary Grant and Ginger Rogers.   The
humor poked at the notion of a Fountain of Youth is more
bitter than the humor in any of Howard's previous comedies.
Howard cast Marilyn Monroe in the picture.   Darryl F.
Zanuck was impressed by her and decided to give her full
star treatment.

"They gave her about four stories," Howard said,
"and they were all failures.   Zanuck wanted to know why.

" 'Because,' I said, 'you did real pictures, and she isn't real. She's just a complete fantasy. There isn't one real thing in her. She ought to do a musical comedy. '

" 'But she can't sing!'

" 'Yes, she can. '

" 'How do you know?'

" 'She goes to cocktail parties in Palm Springs. Nobody will take her home so she comes around and asks if I will. And then she doesn't talk. One time I said, "If you can't talk, can you sing," and she said, yes. We turned on the radio. She sang along. So ... I know she can sing. '

" 'Okay,' Zanuck said, 'make the picture. '

" 'Only if I can get someone like Jane Russell to back up Monroe. '

" 'You can't get her. '

"I told him I thought I could. I had got her started in pictures. Zanuck got her on the phone.

" 'Jane,' I said, 'I've got a picture for you. '

" 'When do we start?'

" 'Wait a minute. There's a part in it that may be better than yours. '

" 'Well, you want me, don't you?'

" 'Yes. '

" 'Okay, I'll do it. '

"She was more help than anybody else could have been, because she would explain to Marilyn what I wanted. Marilyn would say, 'Well, why didn't he say that?' after I'd just explained it all to her six or seven times.

"The camera liked Monroe. The camera made her sexy. But if you worked with her, she could be sitting around with practically nothing on and no one would give her

a second look. If a good-looking girl all dressed up would
pass by, everybody would whistle. They never did that with
Marilyn. She could never get anyone to take her out. "

GENTLEMEN PREFER BLONDES (20th-Fox, 1953)
allowed Howard to use the two chief sex symbols on the
screen at that time with their heavy breasts and full bottoms,
striking contrasts to Bacall's Slim in TO HAVE AND HAVE
NOT, or Sheridan's W. A. C. , or a few years hence, Angie
Dickinson's Feathers in RIO BRAVO. The humor was biting
at Monroe's expense when her heavily endowed body constantly gets in her way and makes her clumsy.

Howard's last picture before his cycle with Duke
Wayne beginning with RIO BRAVO was LAND OF THE
PHARAOHS (Warner's, 1955). It was not a success. How-
ard was lost at sea with the story--above all with the dia-
logue. William Faulkner was at last having some literary
impact on the reading public and had given up screenwriting.
He had certain commitments to his publisher, Random
House, which had stuck with him since the mid-'thirties.
But when Howard asked him to come along and help bail out
the picture, Faulkner consented at once. Faulkner, Harry
Kurnitz, and Hawks worked on the script in Paris, Stresa,
St. Moritz, and Cairo. Faulkner kept asking Howard how
Pharaohs talked and Howard couldn't tell him. Faulkner
left the picture somewhat ahead of schedule and stopped
over in Paris to make needed alterations in the manuscript
of A Fable which his editor Donald Klopfer at Random House
insisted on. "It's the same movie Howard has been making
for thirty-five years, " he was quoted as saying. "It's RED
RIVER all over again. The Pharaoh is the cattle baron, his
jewels are the cattle, and the Nile is the Red River. But
the thing about Howard is, he knows it's the same movie,
and he knows how to make it. " Then Faulkner did what for
him was a very unconventional thing. He helped promote
the film in Memphis at a sales meeting a month before the
picture was to go into release.

It was indicative of his ambivalence toward Hollywood.
Joseph Blotner, whose massive biography on Faulkner is of
itself a triumph of literature, wrote an essay on Faulkner
for Man and the Movies (Louisiana State University Press,
1967) in which he had an opportunity to quote Faulkner on
his experience with the motion picture industry. I believe
the comment is worth repeating. When asked by a student
how you could remain an individual and yet not isolate your-

self from society, nearly twenty-five years after Howard
first gave him a job at Metro-Goldwyn-Mayer Faulkner replied: "There's some people who are writers who believed
they had talent, they believed in the dream of perfection,
they get offers to go to Hollywood where they make a lot of
money, they begin to acquire junk swimming pools and imported cars, and they can't quit their jobs because they have
got to continue to own that swimming pool and the imported
cars. There are others with the same dream of perfection,
the same belief that maybe they can match it, that go there
and resist the money. They don't own the swimming pools,
the imported cars. They will do enough work to get what
they need of the money without becoming a slave to it ... it
is going to be difficult to go completely against the grain or
the current of a culture. But you can compromise without
selling your individuality completely to it. You've got to
compromise because it makes things easier."

VI

         These days Howard Hawks has excited the attention
of cinema critics, on the continent and now increasingly in
the United States. Robin Wood wrote a book about Hawks
as an entry in the Cinema One series, published in 1968.
He expressed a sense of indebtedness to the English literary
critic F. R. Leavis whose books, particularly The Great
Tradition (New York University Press, 1963), have stirred
up some controversy. I am no expert in these matters,
but Leavis strikes me as a man of penetrating intelligence
and a keen perception imprisoned by a narrow taste and denied the gift, or, if you prefer, the skill of lucid self-
expression. Robin Wood's book on Hawks reflects a definite
stylistic affinity with Leavis' prose, but beyond this any
comparison, I think, would be unjustified. The response I
have had to Wood's book is to ponder over the possible
meanings of his complex sentences while learning very little
about either Howard Hawks or the films he has made. The
French are both more persuasive and comprehensible.

         Yet it is ill-advised, I suspect, to engulf Hawks in
elaborate critiques or metaphysical speculations when they
are so alien to him as a person. His cinematic achievement has been to tell a story simply and entertainingly. It
is empty argument to imagine all the possible interpreta-
tions a scene or an entire film might be construed to pro-

ject. Much of Howard Hawks' success has been derived
from the capable professionalism of his entertainments and
their lack of pedantry or moralizing. His stories were conceived from his point of view and embody a condensation of
his experiences or reveal those charming quirks of temperament which combine in some mysterious way to make him
such a gracious and interesting man. I should not want to
say more than that. I agree with him that as a filmmaker
his concerns have been personality and human relationships
that evoke the values according to which he has lived his
own life. If upon occasion the reader should detect that
Howard has related more than once in interviews identical
anecdotes told in almost the same words, it is only an indi-
cation of the way in which he has carefully organized his life
and the patterns which he has imposed upon his recollection
of his past.

"I think a director's a storyteller," Howard once
said, "and if he tells a story that people can't understand,
then he shouldn't be a director. I don't care what they do
as long as they can tell it well."

The beauties of nature which Ford managed to capture in films like SHE WORE A YELLOW RIBBON, THE
SEARCHERS (Warner's, 1956), or CHEYENNE AUTUMN
(Warner's, 1964) are beyond Howard's reach. Backgrounds
have to be sparse in order to highlight personal interaction.

On the way back to Hollywood, the wind was sharper,
blowing across the flat lands and swirling around dunes; the
fine sand beat against the windshield. Actors, actresses,
even topography are so much more recognizable to American filmgoers than the names of directors.

"It's been a lot of fun," Howard had remarked to me
just before I departed, "but it has been a long fight for directors like Ford, Capra, myself. We fought to get credit
and the way we did it mostly was by not going under contract. Never agree to do something until you have things
your own way."

I distrust posterity. I do not know how long Howard's
films will retain their following. But for myself, as I've
said, I cannot watch one of his pictures without enjoying it
the more for having seen it before, no matter how jaded the
years of screening at least two films a day have made me,
no matter what year the picture was produced, nor who was

in it.   John Ford was a painter.   Henry King was a poet.
But Howard Hawks, more than King, more even than Ford,
has a quality of the people about him.   At his very best, he
entertains; he tells us nothing about the times in which we
live, nor is he a visionary.   He tells of men and women
who are not losers and therefore are exceptional enough to
attract our interest; who are flawed and are therefore human enough to engage our sympathies.   Above all, he has
never lost his sense of humor, his amused cognizance that
almost nothing in life deserves being taken seriously for
very long.

HOWARD HAWKS

A Film Checklist by Karl Thiede

Director

1.   THE ROAD TO GLORY (7 February 1926).   P: Fox
     Film Corporation.   C: May McAvoy, Leslie Fenton,
     Ford Sterling.   6,038ft. /67m.

2.   FIG LEAVES (22 August 1926).   P: Fox Film Corpor-
     ation.   C: George O'Brien, Olive Borden, Phyllis
     Haver.   6,498ft. /72m.

3.   THE CRADLE SNATCHERS (5 June 1927).   P: Fox
     Film Corporation.   C: Louise Fazenda, Ethel Wales,
     J. Farrell MacDonald.   6,281ft. /70m.

4.   PAID TO LOVE (14 August 1927).   P: Fox Film Cor-
     poration.   C: George O'Brien, Virginia Valli, J.
     Farrell MacDonald.   6,888ft. /76 1/2m.

In 1928 Hawks signed a six-picture contract with Fox.   He
was to be paid $30,000 each for the first three and $40,000
each for the last three.   Hawks made the first four pictures
and was fired in May, 1929.   On 1 February 1932 it was
announced that Hawks was suing Fox Film Corporation for
$65,000 for the balance of his contract.

5.   A GIRL IN EVERY PORT (26 February 1928).   P:
     Fox Film Corporation.   C: Victor McLaglen, Louise

Brooks, Robert Armstrong. 5,500ft. /61m.

6. FAZIL (4 June 1928). P: Fox Film Corporation. C:
    Charles Farrell, Greta Nissen, Mae Busch. 7,217ft./
    80m.

7. THE AIR CIRCUS (30 September 1928). P: Fox Film
    Corporation. C: Louise Dresser, David Rollins,
    Arthur Lake. Production started: 17 April 1928.
    7,702ft. /86m.

8. TRENT'S LAST CASE (31 March 1929). P: Fox Film
    Corporation. C: Donald Crisp, Raymond Griffith,
    Raymond Hatton. 5,834ft. /65m.

9. THE DAWN PATROL (20 August 1930). P: First
    National. C: Richard Barthelmess, Douglas Fair-
    banks, Jr., Neil Hamilton. Production started: 28
    February 1930. 95m.

10. THE CRIMINAL CODE (3 January 1931). P: Colum-
     bia. C: Walter Huston, Phillips Holmes, Constance
     Cummings. In production: 23 September 1930-No-
     vember 1930. 100m.

11. SCARFACE (9 April 1932). P: United Artists. C:
     Paul Muni, Ann Dvorak, Karen Morley. Production
     was completed in 47 days in August 1931. NC:
     $711,379.92. DG: $691,498.62. 95m.

12. THE CROWD ROARS (16 April 1932). P: Warner
     Brothers. C: James Cagney, Joan Blondell, Ann
     Dvorak. Production was completed in 45 days in
     January 1932. 84m.

13. TIGER SHARK (24 September 1932). P: First Nation-
     al. C: Edward G. Robinson, Richard Arlen, Zita
     Johann. In production: April-June 1932. 80m.

14. TODAY WE LIVE (21 April 1933). P: Metro-Goldwyn-
     Mayer. C: Joan Crawford, Gary Cooper, Franchot
     Tone. In production: December 1932-February 1933.
     10,300ft. /114m.

15. THE PRIZEFIGHTER AND THE LADY (10 November
     1933). P: Metro-Goldwyn-Mayer. C: Max Baer,
     Primo Carnera, Myrna Loy. In production: August-

October 1933.   9,345ft. /104m.

16.   VIVA VILLA! (27 April 1934).   P: Metro-Goldwyn-
      Mayer.   D: Jack Conway, Howard Hawks, Dick Ros-
      son, Art Rosson, William Wellman.   C: Wallace
      Beery, Leo Carrillo, Fay Wray.   In production: No-
      vember 1933-January 1934.   Hawks began work on
      this picture.   All the above directors worked on the
      picture.   Jack Conway was given sole credit.   The
      official press release explained that Hawks had caught
      a tropical fever and he had to be replaced.   The
      same article announced that M-G-M and Hawks had
      agreed to terminate their contract instantly with only
      two months left.   NC: $1,022,000.   10,284ft. /114m.

17.   TWENTIETH CENTURY (11 May 1934).   P: Columbia.
      C: John Barrymore, Carole Lombard, Walter Con-
      nolly.   91m.

18.   BARBARY COAST (27 September 1935).   P: United
      Artists.   C: Miriam Hopkins, Edward G. Robinson,
      Joel McCrea.   In production: June-July 1935.   NC:
      $778,468.92.   DG: $852,000.   90m.

19.   CEILING ZERO (25 January 1936).   P: First National.
      C: James Cagney, Pat O'Brien, June Travis.   In
      production: October-November 1935.   95m.

20.   THE ROAD TO GLORY (4 September 1936).   P:
      Twentieth Century-Fox.   C: Fredric March, Warner
      Baxter, Lionel Barrymore.   Working titles: WOOD-
      EN CROSSES, ZERO HOUR, ROAD TO GLORY.
      101m.

By 1936 Hawks' asking price per picture was $125,000 for
ten weeks maximum work.

21.   COME AND GET IT (13 November 1936).   P: United
      Artists.   D: Howard Hawks, William Wyler.   C:
      Edward Arnold, Joel McCrea, Francis Farmer.   In
      production: June-October 1936.   NC: $1,291,934.27.
      DG: $876,436.14.   FG: $439,658.   On 13 August
      1936, with one week's shooting left, Hawks left the
      picture.   William Wyler took over.   The film's pro-
      ducer, Sam Goldwyn, and Howard Hawks had been
      disagreeing over story angles and concluding episodes.
      Hawks issued a statement saying that he believed

Goldwyn should complete the picture in his own manner. Hawks was paid. The picture up to Hawks'
departure cost approximately $900,000. Wyler re-
made 80% of the picture at an additional expense of
approximately $400,000. 99m.

22. BRINGING UP BABY (18 February 1938). P: RKO
Radio Pictures. C: Cary Grant, Katharine Hepburn,
Charles Ruggles. In production: 3 September 1937-
12 January 1938 (91 days). Budget: $776,776.07.
102m.

Hawks was paid a total of $44,166 by RKO Radio Pictures
in the year 1936 and $130,416 for the year 1937. $87,000
of these two amounts was charged to BRINGING UP BABY.

Hawks was paid $112,500 by Columbia for the year 1939.

23. ONLY ANGELS HAVE WINGS (25 May 1939). P: Columbia. C: Cary Grant, Jean Arthur, Richard
Barthelmess. Working title: PLANE NO. 4. In
production: January-March 1939. 121m.

24. HIS GIRL FRIDAY (18 January 1940). P: Columbia.
C: Cary Grant, Rosalind Russell, Ralph Bellamy.
In Production: October-November 1939. 92m.

25. THE OUTLAW (February 1943). P: United Artists.
(8 February 1946.) P: RKO Radio Pictures. D:
Howard Hughes, Howard Hawks uncredited. C: Jane
Russell, Walter Huston, Jack Buetel. Hawks left
the production of THE OUTLAW to shoot SERGEANT
YORK. Hughes produced the film at a negative cost
of $1,250,000 for release by Twentieth Century-Fox.
Hughes ended up releasing the film on a limited
basis at a running time of 121 minutes. United
Artists then re-released the film in 1943. The running time was 116 minutes and its domestic gross
was $3,050,000. RKO Radio Pictures re-released
the film in 1946. Running time was 103 minutes
with a domestic gross of $1,960,000.

Hawks was paid a total of $142,500 by Warner Brothers in
1941.

16. SERGEANT YORK (27 September 1941). P: Warner
Brothers. C: Gary Cooper, Walter Brennan, Joan

Leslie. In production: March–May 1941. DG:
$6,000,000. 134m.

27. BALL OF FIRE (9 January 1942). P: RKO Radio
     Pictures. C: Gary Cooper, Barbara Stanwyck, Os-
     car Homolka. In production: September–October
     1941. NC: $800,000. DG: $2,200,000. 111m.

28. AIR FORCE (20 March 1943). P: Warner Brothers.
     C: John Garfield, John Ridgely, George Tobias. In
     production: July–September 1942. DG: $2,700,000.
     124m.

29. CORVETTE K-225 (1 October 1943). P: Universal.
     Produced by: Howard Hawks. D: Richard Rosson.
     C: Randolph Scott, Ella Raines, James Brown.
     Working title: CORVETTES IN ACTION. DG:
     $1,000,000. 99m.

30. TO HAVE AND HAVE NOT (20 January 1945). P:
     Warner Brothers. C: Humphrey Bogart, Lauren
     Bacall, Walter Brennan. 100m.

31. THE BIG SLEEP (31 August 1946). P: Warner Bro-
     thers. C: Humphrey Bogart, Lauren Bacall, John
     Ridgely. DG: $3,000,000. 114m.

32. RED RIVER (17 September 1948). P: United Artists.
     C: John Wayne, Montgomery Clift, Joanne Dru.
     NC: $2,800,000. DG: $3,976,473.86. 11,422ft. /
     127m.

33. A SONG IS BORN (6 November 1948). P: RKO Radio
     Pictures. C: Danny Kaye, Virginia Mayo, Benny
     Goodman. Remake of BALL OF FIRE. NC:
     $2,800,000. DG: $2,400,000. Color. 113m.

34. I WAS A MALE WAR BRIDE (September 1949). P:
     Twentieth Century-Fox. C: Cary Grant, Ann Sheri-
     dan, William Neff. DG: $4,100,000. 105m.

35. THE THING (April 1951). P: RKO Radio Pictures.
     Produced by Howard Hawks. D: Christian Nyby.
     C: Margaret Sheridan, Kenneth Tobey, Robert
     Cornthwaite. DG: $1,950,000. 87m.

36. THE BIG SKY (August 1952). P: RKO Radio Pictures.

C: Kirk Douglas, Dewey Martin, Elizabeth Threatt.
DG: $1,650,000. 122m.

37. O. HENRY'S FULL HOUSE (September 1952). P:
     Twentieth Century-Fox. D: Henry Koster, Henry
     Hathaway, Jean Negulesco, Howard Hawks, Henry
     King. C: Fred Allen, Oscar Levant, Lee Aaker.
     A five part movie. Hawks' segment is THE RANSOM
     OF RED CHIEF. DG: $1,000,000. 117m.

38. MONKEY BUSINESS (September 1952). P: Twentieth
     Century-Fox. C: Cary Grant, Ginger Rogers,
     Charles Coburn. DG: $2,000,000. 97m.

39. GENTLEMEN PREFER BLONDES (October 1953). P:
     Twentieth Century-Fox. C: Jane Russell, Marilyn
     Monroe, Charles Coburn. DG: $5,100,000. Color.
     Scope. 97m.

40. LAND OF THE PHARAOHS (2 July 1955). P: Warner
     Brothers. C: Jack Hawkins, Joan Collins, Dewey
     Martin. DG: $2,700,000. Color. Scope. 105m.

41. RIO BRAVO (4 April 1959). P: Warner Brothers. C:
     John Wayne, Dean Martin, Ricky Nelson. DG:
     $5,750,000. Technicolor. 141m.

42. HATARI! (June 1962). P: Paramount. C: John
     Wayne, Elsa Martinelli, Hardy Kruger. DG:
     $7,000,000. Color. 149m.

43. MAN'S FAVORITE SPORT (February 1964). P: Uni-
     versal. C: Rock Hudson, Paula Prentiss, Maria
     Perschy. DG: $2,325,000. Technicolor.
     10,796ft./120m.

44. RED LINE 7000 (November 1965). P: Paramount. C:
     James Caan, Laura Devon, Gail Hire. DG:
     $2,076,837. Technicolor. 110m.

45. EL DORADO (July 1967). P: Paramount. C: John
     Wayne, Robert Mitchum, James Caan. Production
     started: 11 October 1965. DG: $5,424,741.
     Technicolor. 126m.

46. RIO LOBO (23 December 1970). P: National General.
     C: John Wayne, Mike Henry, Bill Williams. Pro-

duction started: 16 March 1970. NC: In excess of
$4,000,000. DG: $4,460,117. Color. 114m.

CONTRIBUTORS

TOM FLINN is book editor for The Velvet Light Trap, a journal of cinema history and criticism. He teaches film at the University of Wisconsin extension at Steven's Point, Wisconsin. Portions of his interview with William Dieterle were previously published in The Velvet Light Trap.

JOEL GREENBERG is co-author of The Celluloid Muse and Hollywood in the Forties. Mr. Greenberg presently resides in Sydney, Australia.

NANCY K. HART is an associate editor of The Magic Lantern, a journal of cinema history and criticism. She is a graduate of the University of Wisconsin at Milwaukee and works in the editorial department of Trade Press Publishing in Milwaukee.

FRANCIS M. NEVINS, JR., is an Associate Professor of Law at St. Louis University and author of mystery fiction and comment on mystery fiction. His short stories have appeared in Ellery Queen's Mystery Magazine, Alfred Hitchcock's Mystery Magazine and hardcover anthologies including Ellery Queen's Crookbook (Random House, 1974) and Best Detective Stories of the Year (Dutton, 1975). His first mystery novel, Publish and Perish, was published by Putnam's in 1975. His critical study Royal Bloodline: Ellery Queen, Author and Detective (Bowling Green University Popular Press, 1974) received a special Edgar award from the Mystery Writers of America. He was a regular contributor to Views & Reviews Magazine; an earlier version of this career study appeared in Films in Review.

439

DAVID L. PARKER is technical officer of the Motion Picture
Section at the Library of Congress, Prints and Photographs
Division. He has worked closely with archivists at the
American Film Institute and elsewhere. A contributor to
many cinema publications, for five years he contributed a
regular column to Views & Reviews Magazine. His Guide to
Dance Films, which he recently compiled, will be published
by the Gale Research Company in 1976.

HARRY SANFORD is the author of fourteen books. Two of
his novels were made into motion pictures, WACO (Paramount, 1966) and APACHE UPRISING (Paramount, 1966).
He worked in publicity for four and a half years at Twentieth Century-Fox, a year at Universal, and ten years at
Desilu-Paramount. For three years he was in the Foreign
Service for the Department of State. An earlier version of
his career study of Joseph Kane appeared in Views & Reviews
Magazine.

BURTON J. SHAPIRO is a graduate of the Cinema Studies
program at New York University and a former staff member
of the American Film Institute compiling the National Film
Catalogue.

JON TUSKA, for six years executive editor of Views & Reviews Magazine and now general editor of the Close-Up on
the Cinema series, is the author of The Films of Mae West
(Citadel, 1973), The Filming of the West (Doubleday, 1976),
and The Detective in Hollywood (Doubleday, 1978). In 1969,
he produced THEY WENT THATAWAY for the Public Broadcasting Service, a ten-part program on the history of the
Western seen over 223 affiliate stations. He has just completed a new fifteen-part series titled THE FILMING OF THE
WEST which, after first television run, will be available for
cable television and non-theatrically through United Films of
Tulsa, Oklahoma. He is presently at work on Close-Up:
The Hollywood Director, the next entry in this series,
and Hollywood Filmmakers, to be published by Doubleday
and Company. His articles and essays have appeared in
several magazines and have been anthologized in a number
of general cinema surveys.

INDEX